Kyrgyzstan

the Bradt Travel Guide

Laurence Mitchell

edition
I

www.bradtguides.com

Bradt Travel Guides Ltd, UK
The Globe Pequot Press Inc, USA

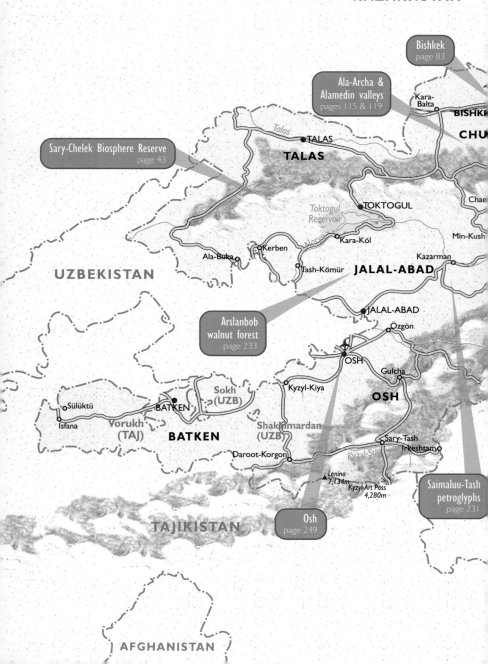

KAZAKHSTAN

Bishkek
page 83

Ala-Archa &
Alamedin valleys
pages 115 & 119

Kara-
Balta

BISHKE

CHU

Talas

● TALAS

TALAS

Sary-Chelek Biosphere Reserve
page 43

Toktogul
Reservoir

● TOKTOGUL

Chae

Min-Kush

○ Kerben

Naryn

● Kara-Köl

Ala-Buka ○

● Tash-Kömür

Kazarman

JALAL-ABAD

UZBEKISTAN

Arslanbob
walnut forest
page 233

● JALAL-ABAD

Özgön

OSH

Gulcha

Sokh
(UZB)

● Kyzyl-Kiya

OSH

○ Sülüktü

BATKEN ○

Shakimardan
(UZB)

Sary-Tash

Irkeshtam

Isfana

Vorukh
(TAJ)

BATKEN

Daroot-Korgon

Kyzyl-Suu

▲ Lenina
7,134m
Kyzyl-Art Pass
4,280m

Saimaluu-Tash
petroglyphs
page 231

TAJIKISTAN

Osh
page 249

AFGHANISTAN

Laurence Mitchell is a travel writer and photographer with an interest in forgotten places, border zones and territories in transition. After taking a degree in environmental science and pursuing a varied career that has included teaching English in rural Sudan, clerical work and surveying historic farm buildings, he retrained as a geography teacher, which he pursued for a dozen years before giving it up for the uncertainties of full-time travel writing and photography. Born on the edge of the Black Country in the English West Midlands, his taste is more for hills and mountains than for the coast. He has lived in Norwich for many years, which he thinks would be perfect if it could trade locations with somewhere like Chesterfield. This is his third title for Bradt. His photographic website may be viewed at www.laurencemitchell.com.

AUTHOR STORY

My first experience of Kyrgyz culture was not in Kyrgyzstan itself but across the border in Xinjiang Province in China, where I stayed in a yurt whilst on the way to Pakistan via the Karakoram Highway. What I discovered when I finally visited the republic a few years later was a newly independent country that was far more than just the sum of its parts. If Russia, as Churchill famously claimed, is a riddle wrapped in a mystery inside an enigma, then Kyrgyzstan is a central Asian *matryoshka* doll of interwoven Turkic, Mongol and Slavic cultures that have been coloured by successive shamanistic, Islamic and communist traditions.

Getting around the country to do research was not always easy. One fateful shared taxi ride from Talas to Jalal-Abad took around 16 hours, rather than the seven I had been promised. This was partly due to the driver's insistence on frequent stops for tea and *shashlyk* but mostly because of the poor quality, water-diluted petrol that he had filled the car with. At first, the taxi would stall when going up the steeper hills; later on, it could hardly manage on the flat – in a country where 90% of the terrain is mountainous this is not a good thing. I have vivid memories of pushing the taxi at two in the morning along a coal-black road just north of Jalal-Abad while overloaded trucks whistled past in the dark. My pushing accomplice was a customs officer from Batken Province who kept laughing maniacally into the night and repeatedly shouting *'Ekstrim turizm, da? Ha! Ha!'* at me. Happy days! Such occasional unpredictability is all part of the experience but, on the whole, things tend to work out and most travel in Kyrgyzstan is as adventurous as you would like it to be.

PUBLISHER'S FOREWORD

The first Bradt travel guide was written in 1974 by George and Hilary Bradt on a river barge floating down a tributary of the Amazon. In the 1980s and '90s the focus shifted away from hiking to broader-based guides covering new destinations – usually the first to be published about these places. In the 21st century Bradt continues to publish such ground-breaking guides, as well as others to established holiday destinations, incorporating in-depth information on culture and natural history with the nuts and bolts of where to stay and what to see.

Bradt authors support responsible travel, and provide advice not only on minimum impact but also on how to give something back through local charities. In this way a true synergy is achieved between the traveller and local communities.

* * *

I settled down to read this book in happy anticipation. Laurence Mitchell has already shown what a good guidebook writer he is with *Serbia*, and this is all that I hoped for: carefully researched, well written, and full of interest and surprises. Most importantly, it makes you want to go to Kyrgyzstan.

First edition January 2008
Bradt Travel Guides Ltd
23 High Street, Chalfont St Peter, Bucks SL9 9QE, England; www.bradtguides.com
Published in the USA by The Globe Pequot Press Inc, 246 Goose Lane,
PO Box 480, Guilford, Connecticut 06437-0480

Text copyright © 2008 Laurence Mitchell
Maps copyright © 2008 Bradt Travel Guides Ltd
Illustrations copyright © 2008 individual photographers and artists
For Bradt: Editorial Project Manager Anna Moores
Edited and designed by D & N Publishing, Hungerford, Berkshire

British Library Cataloguing in Publication Data
A catalogue record for this book is available from the British Library
ISBN-10: 1 84162 221 4
ISBN-13: 978 1 84162 221 7

Photographs Heather Angel/Natural Visions (HA), Nigel Blake (NB), Christopher Herwig (CH), Laurence Mitchell (LM), Eduard Opperman/Central Asia Birding (EO)
Front cover Boy on horseback, Kochkor (CH)
Title page Yurt framework (CH), Shepherds on horseback (CH), Yurts at Sarala-Saz *jailoo* (LM)
Back cover Old man (CH), Lake Sary-Chelek (LM)
Illustrations Carole Vincer
Maps Dave Priestley

Printed and bound in Italy by Legoprint SpA, Trento

Acknowledgements

First and foremost, my thanks go to all of the Bradt team. I am grateful in particular to former commissioning editor Tricia Hayne, who first showed an interest in the idea back in 2004, and her successor, Adrian Phillips, who provided a firm commission in late 2005; also thanks to Anna Moores, editorial project manager and Helen Anjomshoaa, publishing services manager.

I have many to thank in Kyrgyzstan itself. In Bishkek, my gratitude goes to the staff of the Kyrgyz Community Based Tourism Association, especially to executive director Anar Orozobaeva and to reservation manager Asylbek Rajiev. Ian Claytor was also a great source of invaluable advice about the country and freely gave of his time, while Ernist Djumagulov and his family provided hospitality and helpful support. In the preliminary stages, David Berghof contacted me by email with excellent advice on the region, particularly on the logistics of travelling the Pamir Highway to Tajikistan. Caroline Juter also provided some useful contacts in the country, as did Paul Brummell, fellow Bradt author and non-resident British ambassador to Kyrgyzstan. I would also like to thank Alex McHaines for his assistance with flights.

I am very grateful to the following who went out of their way to help me whilst travelling through the country: Ruhsora Abdullaeva in Jalal-Abad, Natalya Ovcharova in Karakol, Myrzabek Ozubekov in Kochkor, Kubat Abdyldaev in Naryn, Dinara Abdyrakhmanova in Osh and Lachin Sader in Arslanbob. In Arslanbob, I would also like to thank Tamta Shabutishvili for sharing her knowledge of the region and for her assistance in translating local folk tales, as well as the Mamajanova family for providing an exceptionally pleasant base in the village. My gratitude also goes to Ilyatbue and Mirgul Saratova for their welcome in Toktogul, to Bazarkul Jooshbaev for the ride to Arkyt, and to mountain guides Ainura and the two Sergeis for their cheerful company whilst trekking in the Karakol and Altyn Arashan valleys.

Whilst moving around Kyrgyzstan, I met and occasionally joined up with a number of individual travellers and I am grateful to all of them for their companionship as well as for their help and encouragement with the guide. In particular, I would like to thank Nick Brown, Nana Canter, Jerome Hayez, Leah Kehr, Rabih and Susanne Khoury, Gait Leferink, Volker Pabst, Oren Peled, Louise Wells and René Zimmerli.

As always, my profound gratitude goes to my wife, Jackie, for putting up with my long absences, both away in central Asia and also while upstairs in the attic poised over a computer.

Contents

Introduction

Kyrgyzstan is a name that does not spring readily to most people's lips. The majority have never heard of it and those who think they have tend to become confused by the 'stan' part at the end. Even those who do know a little of the country are usually hard pushed to locate it on a map. So why is it so little known? Part of the reason is because less than two decades ago the country did not exist at all and was merely a far-flung autonomous region of the vast, crumbling USSR. Then, in 1991, just like its immediate neighbours, it found itself suddenly independent and, as no such country had ever existed in the pre-Soviet period, having to invent itself for the first time. The present country's boundaries were drawn up in the 1920s by Stalin whose aim was to divide and rule in Soviet central Asia. The notion was for an autonomous Kyrgyz republic within the USSR but what resulted was only an approximation and, although ethnic Kyrgyz currently make up around two-thirds of the population, the country is a mosaic of ethnicities that includes Russians, Uzbeks, Dungans, Uyghurs, Tajiks and Tatars.

Kyrgyzstan is an outdoors sort of place; that is, if you wish to spend most of your time looking at beautiful buildings and drinking espresso in chic cafés then this may not be your ideal destination. If you enjoy trekking, horseriding, birdwatching, camping and visiting remote prehistoric sites, then it most certainly is. The Kyrgyz landscape is magnificent and hugely varied and Swiss, Scots, Canadians, Italians and even Israelis can all be heard to exclaim that in places the scenery reminds them of their homeland. This is no exaggeration as the country has it all – alpine lakes, fast-flowing rivers, arid steppe, snow-capped peaks, conifer forest, agricultural plains, rolling meadows and vast walnut forests. But, if there is one physical characteristic that stands out above all else, it is mountains: 90% of Kyrgyzstan lies above 1,500m and the country's topography is dominated by various ranges of the Tien Shan system.

The beauty of Kyrgyzstan for visitors is that it has something of everything: nomadic traditions, central Asian mystique, Soviet-era trappings, a few spectacular prehistoric and Silk Road sites and, above all else, a culture that can best be described as a palimpsest that over the centuries has absorbed the influence of shamanism, Zoroastrianism, Sufism and communism to become something entirely unique.

A visit to Kyrgyzstan is as adventurous as you would like it to be, which can mean everything from lazing on a beach at Lake Issyk-Kul to glacier walking in the Central Tien Shan. The low prices, hospitable people and gorgeous scenery are simply a bonus. For all those who come and see, *Ak-Jol!*

A BRIEF NOTE ON TRANSLITERATION

There are many variations on the standard Latin spelling of Kyrgyz words and place names, depending on whether this has been done entirely phonetically or by transliteration from either Russian or Kyrgyz Cyrillic spellings. I have done my best to be consistent, either by adopting the commonest written form in normal use or by making a direct transliteration of the standard Kyrgyz Cyrillic form, hence Jalal-Abad rather than Dzhalal-Abad and Özgön rather than Uzgen.

I have used the word **Kyrgyz** in a very broad sense, not just to relate to that which is ethnically Kyrgyz but also to describe things that pertain to the modern Kyrgyz Republic, ie: a Kyrgyz travel agency (which may well be staffed by ethnic Russians and Dungans) rather than a *Kyrgyzstani* travel agency, which although strictly correct simply does not sound right. I have also done the same with my use of the words Uzbek and Tajik.

FEEDBACK REQUEST

Kyrgyzstan is a country that is relatively new to tourism and, although I have endeavoured to make this book as up to date as possible, some things will inevitably change over time. Please help to revise future editions of this book by sending in any information you may have about changes and developments, or simply your own travel experiences in the country, good and bad. Such first-hand feedback is invaluable and all comments will be gratefully received.

Please write or email via the publishers at: Bradt Travel Guides, 23 High Street, Chalfont St Peter, Bucks SL9 9QE; e info@bradtguides.com.

Siberian marmot

Part One

GENERAL INFORMATION

Official name Kyrgyz Republic

Location Landlocked in central Asia, bordered by Kazakhstan to the north, China to the east and southeast, Uzbekistan to the west and Tajikistan to the southwest

Size/Area 198,500km^2 (about the same as England, Wales and Scotland combined or Nebraska, USA)

Climate Dry continental to polar (Tien Shan); subtropical in the southwest (Fergana Valley); temperate in northern foothill zone

Status Republic headed by president, government headed by prime minister

Head of state President Kurmanbek Bakiev

Head of government Prime Minister Almazbek Atambaev

Independence Declared from Soviet Union on 31 August 1991

Population Approximately 5,284,000 (2007 estimate); Kyrgyz 69.5%, Uzbeks 14.5%, Russians 9%, others 7%

Life expectancy Male 64.8 years, female 73.0 years

Capital Bishkek, estimated population about 1 million

Other main towns Osh, Naryn, Jalal-Abad, Karakol, Talas

Economy Livestock, agriculture, mining, hydroelectric energy, recycled metal, tourism

GDP US$2,822million, equivalent to US$542 per capita per annum

Languages Official languages are Kyrgyz and Russian; also Uzbek, Uyghur, Dungan and others

Adult literacy rate Claimed to be 98.7% (1999 Census)

Religion Sunni Islam, Orthodox Christian, animistic beliefs

Ethnic diversity Kyrgyz dominate in the north with Russians, other Slavs and Dungans forming sizeable minorities; many Uzbeks in the south, forming the majority in some regions

Currency Kyrgyz som; US$1 = 35som, 1 euro = 51som, £1 = 73som (November 2007)

International telephone code 996

Time GMT+5

Electrical voltage 220V, 50Hz, standard two-pin round-prong plug

Flag Red with a yellow *tunduk* (yurt roof piece) in centre surrounded by a 40-rayed sun

Coat of arms Rising sun over mountain and lake within the wings of a spread eagle

Public holidays See page 72–3

Background Information

GEOGRAPHY

Kyrgyzstan is located at the heart of central Asia; it is a landlocked country that is surrounded by the former USSR territories of Kazakhstan, Uzbekistan and Tajikistan to the north, west and southwest respectively, with China lying to the east. At just under 200,000km² the republic is a little smaller in area than the United Kingdom minus Northern Ireland, or the state of Nebraska in the United States. Kyrgyzstan's territory extends roughly 900km from east to west and 410km from north to south.

MOUNTAINS The country is extremely mountainous with 90% of the land area above 1,500m in elevation above sea level and 71% above 2,000m. The country's average elevation is 2,750m. This mountainous character has led Kyrgyzstan to be known as the 'Switzerland of central Asia' on occasion, although the comparison does not extend much beyond physical geography.

The majority of Kyrgyzstan's mountain ranges belong to the Tien Shan system, the legendary Celestial Mountains of Chinese folklore. This mountain chain stretches west to east well beyond the political borders of Kyrgyzstan, from just to the east of Tashkent in Uzbekistan almost as far as Urumchi in China's Xinjiang Province. The eastern end of the range, made of mostly crystalline and sedimentary rock, is the oldest part of the range, created during the Palaeozoic era 540–250 million years ago; the western end is of softer and younger metamorphic rock. Within Kyrgyzstan itself the Tien Shan system is divided into several subsidiary ranges that include the Kungey and Terskey Ala-Too ranges that frame Lake Issyk-Kul north and south, the Kyrgyz Ala-Too south of Bishkek, the Fergana range in the southwest that hems in the Fergana Valley, and the Chatkal range in the far west that extends into Uzbekistan.

Many of the mountain peaks are perennially covered with snow and ice in the form of glaciers, the largest being the 62km-long Inylchek Glacier in the Central Tien Shan in the far east of the country near the borders with Kazakhstan and China, which is one of the world's longest. Altogether there are estimated to be 6,500 distinct glaciers in the country that together hold a store of 650km³ of water and cover a total of 4% of the land area: a quantity such that, if it were to melt, would cover the entire surface area of Kyrgyzstan with water to a depth of 3m.

The highest mountain peaks lie in the Central Tien Shan range too: Jengish Chokusu, formerly known as Peak Pobeda, is both Kyrgyzstan's and the Tien Shan's highest peak, standing at 7,439m on the border with China. Nearby, the slightly lower peak of Khan Tengri on the border with Kazakhstan reaches 7,010m and is considered by geologists to be the world's most northerly 7,000m summit. Kyrgyzstan's other major mountain ranges are the Pamir range in the far south, which it shares with Tajikistan and China's Xinjiang Province, and the Pamir Alay range, which separates the Pamir and Tien Shan ranges. In comparison, the Pamirs are older, more rounded mountains that lack the rugged peaks of the Tien Shan range, but only the most northerly range of the Pamir system – The Zaalaysky Ridge – is within Kyrgyzstan; the rest lie firmly in Tajikistan and China. Here there are high passes through to China and Tajikistan, with Peak Lenin at 7,134m, the second highest peak in the Pamir range, marking the frontier with Tajikistan. The southwest sector of the country that extends an arm beneath the Fergana Valley is dominated by the Pamir Alay range, a high range of 5,000m peaks that extends into the Turkestan ridge and has the aptly named 5,509m Piramida Chokusu (Pyramid Peak) marking the border with Tajikistan.

VALLEYS Enclosed in a pincer grip between the Pamir Alay and the Fergana range of the Tien Shan is the low-lying Fergana Valley, a farming region of which Kyrgyzstan has a share along with Uzbekistan and Tajikistan. This has the country's lowest point at 401m, in Kulundy village in Batken Province in the southwest. The Fergana Valley, along with the relatively flat Chui and Talas valleys in the north, comprise the only really suitable terrain for large-scale agriculture in the entire country.

WATERWAYS AND LAKES Kyrgyzstan has no navigable waterways and the majority of rivers are small, rapid run-off streams and tributaries of the Syr Darya system that flow into Uzbekistan and have their source in the Tien Shan near the Chinese border, the exception to this being the Chui River of northern Kyrgyzstan, which arises in northern Kazakhstan. The River Naryn is Kyrgyzstan's longest river at 535km in length; other major rivers include the Talas in the west, the Chui in the north, Sary-Jaz in the east and the Chatkal River in the extreme west, which flows into Uzbekistan.

None of these rivers flow into the country's principal lake, Lake Issyk-Kul ('warm lake') in Kyrgyzstan's northeast, which is the third largest body of water in central Asia after Lake Balkash and the rapidly shrinking Aral Sea and, standing at an altitude of 1,606m above sea level, qualifies as the second largest alpine lake in the world after Lake Titicaca in Peru/Bolivia. As well as covering a large area, being approximately 180km long and 60km wide, Lake Issyk-Kul is also very deep – up to 700m in places. The country's second and third largest lakes are higher still, but far smaller in both size and volume: Song-Köl at 3,016m in central Kyrgyzstan and Chatyr-Köl at 3,530m near the Torugart Pass into China, both of which belong to the Naryn river basin.

At around the same elevation as Chatyr-Köl Lake is Lake Merzbacher at the Inylchek Glacier in the Central Tien Shan: a rare geographical phenomenon that appears and disappears over a short period of time each summer. In contrast, the small jewel-like Sary-Chelek Lake at the modest altitude of just 1,873m in the southwest is considered by many to be one of Kyrgyzstan's most beautiful. A manmade lake, the Toktogul Reservoir lies in the valley between the Ala-Too and Fergana ranges in the west of the country and is an important source of both drinking water and hydro-electrical power.

CLIMATE

Kyrgyzstan's climate is partly influenced by its mountains and partly by its continental location far from any ocean. For the most part it is continental, with cold winters and warm summers. In the lowlands, the temperature ranges between –4°C and –6°C in January and between 16°C and 24°C in July. The coldest temperatures are in the mountain valleys where –30°C is not uncommon and a record of –53.6°C has been measured, although –14°C to –20°C is more usual. In summer in the Fergana Valley, the average temperature in July is around 27°C, although temperatures frequently reach the low 40s. Even in summer, temperatures may drop as low as −10°C at night on the mountain peaks. Of the major urban centres, Naryn has by far the most extreme climate with an average minimum temperature in January of −19°C and an average maximum July temperature of 25°C. Both Bishkek and Osh have much milder winter temperatures but warmer summers. Generally temperatures are far less extreme in the region of Lake Issyk-Kul where the presence of a large body of non-freezing, slightly saline water has a moderating influence on the local climate.

Rainfall is generally fairly low throughout the country – as little as 100mm per annum on the southwest shore of Lake Issyk-Kul to around 2,000mm in the mountains above the Fergana Valley. The national average is 380mm, with March to May and October and November usually the wetter months. There are sometimes heavy snowfalls in winter. Clear skies are common and Kyrgyzstan averages over 300 sunny days per year. Recent years have brought a number of unusual climatic events that are possibly linked with worldwide climate change and glaciers receding: droughts in the Fergana Valley and elsewhere, low winter snowfall, unusually heavy rains in spring and an increase in the water level of Lake Issyk-Kul, despite a preceding trend in which water level was dropping.

HISTORY

PREHISTORY The history of the tract of land that is now the Kyrgyz Republic stretches back to long before the territory was occupied by nomadic Kyrgyz, crop-growing Uzbeks or colonising Russians, the republic's present-day occupants. The earliest evidence of settlement comes from Tosor at the south shore of Lake Issyk-Kul, where evidence of human occupation has been found that dates back to the Palaeolithic period of 40,000 or more years ago. Most other archaeological evidence is of a much later date. Prehistoric petroglyphs have been found at various sites around the country, most famously at Saimaluu-Tash and Cholpon-Ata, which point to a continuous and widespread occupation of the territory in the period between the Bronze Age of about 2000BC to around AD500. Excavations around Lake Issyk-Kul have revealed evidence of sunken cities around the lake that date from this time and a number of artefacts from various periods have been found, including a Greek amphora that dates from the time of Alexander the Great 2,500 years ago.

ARRIVAL OF THE SAKA TRIBES During the 1st millennium BC it has been documented that Sogdian, Bactrian and Khorezm peoples were present in the region and it is known that the city of Osh in the Fergana Valley in the south was founded in this period, some time around 1000BC. However it is the Saka, a warrior clan normally considered to be a branch of the Scythians, who were the first notable residents to have been recorded in the region and who lived here from about the 6th century BC to the 5th century AD. Pushed eastwards by other Iranian tribes to the west, the Saka would have occupied much of central Asia by the 1st millennium BC, and what is now Kyrgyzstan would have been at the southeast of their territory. The Saka practised both settled agriculture and herding and were known for their creative skills with metal, particularly gold. They are responsible for the large number of burial mounds (*kurgani*) seen in the north of the country.

Although Alexander the Great conquered great tracts of central Asia with his Macedonian armies he did not succeed in conquering the Saka. They were eventually absorbed into the Kushan Empire, a state that stretched from the Fergana Valley south to central India, the Kushan being an Indo-European people that came from western China and practised Zoroastrianism and later Buddhism.

The Kushan Empire collapsed when the region came under the attack of marauding Huns who came to the area in the 4th century. As the Hun Empire eventually collapsed under the strain of its own ambition (they had marched west and almost conquered Rome) the power vacuum was filled by Tocharians who, in turn, were replaced by Turkic tribes.

THE WESTERN TURKIC KHANATE From the 6th century onwards the region came under the control of various Turkic alliances and at this time there was a sizeable population living on the shores of Lake Issyk-Kul, and settlements such as Balasagun (near Tokmok in the Chui valley) and Barskoon (on the southern shore of Lake Issyk-Kul) thrived on trade from the Silk Road. The Turkic Khanate was split into two factions at this time; the western Turkic Khanate was most probably based at Suyub in the Chui valley, where it was able to prosper from its pivotal position on the Silk Road, while the eastern khanate controlled Mongolia until it was defeated by the Chinese in around AD630. The western khanate established political and commercial links with the Sogdians of Persian origin who had settled in the region to farm and trade, and a number of prosperous towns developed and flourished in the Chui valley region. One such town was Navekat (now Krasnaya Rechka) where Buddhists, Zoroastrians and Nestorian Christians peacefully co-existed under the protection of the western Turkic Khanate.

THE ARRIVAL OF ISLAM Islam first came to the central Asian region in AD651 when Arab armies captured Merv in present-day Turkmenistan. The proselytising Arab invasion advanced east to the city states of Bokhara, Samarkand and Fergana in the early 8th century, where they were resisted and successfully repelled by the Sogdian and Turkic inhabitants. Taking advantage of the disruption caused by the aftermath of the Arab invasion the Chinese chose to invade the territories of the Turkic Khanate in the Fergana Valley. Rather than be defeated and be forced to succumb to Chinese expansion, the Sogdians and Turks made a strategic turnaround that was probably based more on pragmatism than ideology and joined forces with the same Arab armies that they had just repelled. In AD751, a decisive battle was fought near the modern-day city of Taraz in Kazakhstan, just over the present-day Kyrgyzstan border on the banks of the Talas River. The combined might of the Turkic Khanate and their newfound Arab allies proved too much for the invaders and the Tang Chinese army was driven from central Asia for good. Chinese expansionism in the region had been halted and Islam had arrived to become the major religious voice.

THE KARAKHANIDS The Arabs did not remain in the region for long and by the middle of the 8th century had been ousted by a new Persian Dynasty founded by a Zoroastrian noble who had converted to Islam – that of the Samanids – and whose spiritual and political base was in Bokhara.

The Samanids themselves were dislodged from power in the 10th century, this time by the Karakhanids, a Turkic people related to the Uyghurs of Chinese Turkestan. The Karakhanids were a cultured people who had firmly embraced Islam at the outset and would prove to be the ones who would ensure that the religion had a foothold in the region for good. They took over Bokhara from the Samanid Dynasty and maintained the city as a centre for Islamic study while developing three Silk Road cities to serve as their power base in the region: Balasagun in the Chui valley, Özgön on the edge of the Fergana Valley and Kashgar in Chinese Turkestan (Xinjiang).

In the mid 11th century, another Turkic group from the lower reaches of the Syr Darya, the Seljuks, conquered the entire central Asian region and established their capital in Merv in what is now Turkmenistan. The Karakhanids, whose strength had been reduced by now by constant internecine warfare, were reduced to the role of vassals, while the Seljuks would expand westwards to conquer Anatolia, until they too would fall into decline at the beginning of the 13th century.

ENTER THE KYRGYZ... AND THE MONGOLS While various Turkic and Persian peoples had been struggling to hold on to power in central Asia, the early Kyrgyz tribes had been living a nomadic life to the north in the upper Yenisey valley of southern Siberia, between Lake Baikal and the Altai mountains. According to Tang Dynasty (AD618–907) Chinese sources, these Kyrgyz tribes were described as fair-skinned, green-eyed and red-haired people ('black hair', the chronicler explains, was considered an evil omen among them) with a mixture of European and Mongol features – not generally the physical characteristics associated with the Kyrgyz of today, but perhaps an accurate description of their appearance before they started to widely intermingle with other Turkic and Mongol peoples in the region.

The Kyrgyz tribes had originally inhabited the region that is now northwest Mongolia. During the 4th and 3rd centuries BC Kyrgyz bands were actively raiding Chinese territory and became part of the 'barbarian' impetus that led to the Great Wall of China being constructed as a defensive measure. The Kyrgyz warriors achieved a fierce reputation and became well known in the region as both great fighters and traders.

In the centuries that followed some Kyrgyz tribes moved northwards to inhabit the Yenisey valley of southern Siberia. The first Kyrgyz state, the Kyrgyz Khanate, which existed between the 6th and the 13th centuries, went on the offensive in AD840 and swept through central Mongolia to destroy the Uyghur Khanate that was based in the region. They were routed a century later by the Khitan Khanate and this precipitated a drift southwards towards the Tien Shan and their present-day territories. There is little agreement as to exactly when the Kyrgyz first started to arrive in the Tien Shan region in any appreciable number: some sources suggest that it may have been as early as the 10th century while others put the date much later. In all probability it was most likely a gradual migration that became accelerated in the 13th century by the emergence of the Mongol Empire under the leadership of the warlord Genghis Khan. The Kyrgyz that remained in the Yenisey valley in the north are believed to have largely complied with the demands of the invading Mongols, whereas those that had migrated to the Tien Shan fought the Mongol invaders fiercely in order to maintain their identity.

Genghis Khan's Mongolian Empire had emerged in the early years of the 13th century. From his Mongolian stronghold, Genghis Khan and his mounted warriors staged a succession of ferocious attacks on central Asia in 1219, and within the space of just two years all of central Asia's cities of culture and learning – Samarkand, Bokhara, Khiva and Merv – had been overpowered and razed to the ground. The Kyrgyz tribes that had initially offered resistance to the attacks suffered devastating defeats at the hands of the Mongols and so chose instead to offer allegiance in order to survive. Their territory in the Yenisey region was occupied by Genghis Khan's oldest son Jochi without any further opposition. Following Genghis Khan's death in 1227 his conquered lands were divided up, and the younger of his two sons, Chaghatai, inherited the territory that is now Kyrgyzstan. The Kyrgyz would continue to remain vassals of the Mongols and the Golden Horde until the end of the 14th century.

TAMERLANE AND OYRATS By the 15–16th century Kyrgyz had settled in large numbers in their new home that is present-day Kyrgyzstan. The domination of the Kyrgyz by the Golden Horde ended in 1510, but their freedom was lost again in

1685 when Mongol Buddhist Oyrats of the Zhungarian Empire (sometimes referred to as Kalmyks – those Oyrats who later migrated west from central Asia) forced many Kyrgyz to escape south into what is now Tajikistan. In 1758 the Oyrats were defeated by the Manchu Qing Dynasty, which had seized the opportunity to invade during an internal dispute over Oyrat succession.

As a result, the Kyrgyz automatically became nominal subjects of the Chinese. The Manchus by and large allowed the Kyrgyz to follow their nomadic ways in peace, but in the early 19th century those living in the southern territory of the present-day Kyrgyz Republic suddenly found themselves as feudal subjects of the far more demanding Uzbek Kokand Khanate. By the 1820s the Kokand Khanate's power reached into most of what is today's Kyrgyzstan and the khanate built a chain of fortresses to protect its Silk Road trade interests, including one at Pishpek in the Chui valley. Reeling under the impact of high taxation, enforced military conscription and harsh penalties imposed by Kokand, Kyrgyz protests against the khanate were frequent and fervent; so too, were the cruel punishments and violent repression meted out by their Uzbek masters.

RUSSIAN TSARIST RULE Russians first arrived in the area as Tsarist empire-builders in the early part of the 19th century and soon made their influence felt. To stamp their presence in the region they built their own fortress at the tiny settlement of Pishpek in the Chui valley, where the Kokand Khanate had already established a base, and which would later expand and develop to become Bishkek, the Kyrgyz capital. The Russians eventually defeated the forces of the Kokand Khanate at Tashkent in 1865, and then went on to conquer their capital Kokand, transforming the once powerful khanate into a Russian vassal state.

Most Kyrgyz in the region were pragmatic in their attitude towards accepting Russian protection, which they saw as the lesser of two evils when compared to the corrupt and cruel rule they had been subjected to under the Kokand Khanate. The Russians went on to annex the entire territory for the Tsar and the Russian Empire in 1876. The Kyrgyz peoples for the first time had been brought under Russian control.

In the latter years of the 19th century, Russians and other Slavic peoples such as Ukrainians started to arrive in the area in large numbers. The first settlers, mostly Cossacks, started arriving in the region in the 1860s, encouraged by the Tsarist wish to populate the region with its own people in order to establish a Russian presence along the Chinese frontier. The new settlers inevitably took the best and most fertile land for themselves, appropriating land that had previously belonged to the nomadic Kyrgyz population as seasonal grazing. As a result, the local Kyrgyz soon became resentful of the new Russian influx even if, in general terms, life under Tsarist control was vaguely preferable to the cruelties of Kokand rule. For the Russians settling in the region it was quite a different matter: this was the equivalent of the Promised Land, as many of the new settlers were landless peasants that had recently been released from serfdom in European Russia or Siberia. The offer of free land and building materials in exchange for populating this frontier zone in the name of the Tsar was too good to turn down.

In 1877–78, the population of the territory was swelled further when Chinese Hui Muslim refugees started to arrive in large numbers from across the Tien Shan, following uprisings in the Chinese provinces of Xinjiang, Gansu and Shaanxi, in which the Han Chinese authorities had meted out brutal repression on the local Hui Muslim population following the insurrection of the Dungan revolt. Another wave of Hui and Uyghur migration followed in the early 1880s when Hui and Uyghur people of the Chinese Turkestan border region were allowed to move into Russian territories following the withdrawal of Russian troops in the zone.

In 1916, in the dying throes of an empire that had been caught up in World War I, a widespread rebellion took place in the region against the Russian authorities. The rebellion had been triggered by the imposition of a military draft for non-Russian central Asians that required them to assist the war effort in Europe by building roads and producing food. By August of that year, the rebellion reached the Kyrgyzstan region. The insurrection, which had arbitrarily killed many Russian civilians as well as bona fide military targets, was brutally suppressed by the authorities and in October 1916 a mass exodus of Kyrgyz left for China over the high passes of the Tien Shan. Between 25 June 1916 and October 1917 it is estimated that one and a half million central Asians died in total. It is thought that 41% of the Kyrgyz population in the north of the country were killed and that another 120,000 fled to China, a large proportion of which died along the way as the victims of winter cold or banditry.

THE EARLY SOVIET PERIOD The October Revolution that took place in Moscow and St Petersburg in 1917 (which was actually in November by today's Western calendar) was slow to make an immediate impact in this far-flung corner of the former Russian Empire. However, on New Year's Day in 1918, Bolsheviks seized power in Pishpek, the provisional government was overthrown and Soviet power was established in the region, with local revolutionary firebrand Aleksei Ivanitsyn at the helm. This triggered a counter revolution in the territory, initiated in the small town of Belovdsk just to the west of Bishkek, at the end of the same year, but this was easily defeated within a few days by summoning troops from nearby Vyernyi (Almaty) in what is now Kazakhstan.

In 1922 the territory of Kirgizia, as it was then known, became part of the Turkestan Autonomous Soviet Socialist Republic (Turkestan ASSR) within the Russian Soviet Federated Socialist Republic (RSFSR). The Kara-Kyrgyz Autonomous Oblast was established within the RSFSR in October 1924, to be renamed as the Kyrgyz Autonomous Oblast in the following year (up until that time, Kara-Kyrgyz ('black Kyrgyz') had been a term that had been used to distinguish the Kyrgyz (the Kara-Kyrgyz) from the Kazakhs (then also confusingly referred to as Kyrgyz), a division that was as much about geographical location – mountain- or steppe-dwelling – as it was about ethnicity).

The creation of the Kyrgyz Autonomous Oblast involved the drawing up of some rather eccentric political boundaries, particularly in the Fergana Valley, as part of Stalin's divide-and-rule approach. Stalin himself may well have had direct involvement in the drawing up of the boundaries as he was chairman of the Minorities Committee that had instigated this spurious nation-building. These jigsaw-like ethnic and political demarcations continue to have repercussions to this day and have proved disastrous for trade and the free movement of people in the post-independence period (see *Enclaves and Exclaves: A Political Jigsaw*, page 267).

The Soviet partitioning of central Asia that took place at this time had been inspired by a wish to create 'nations' largely based on linguistic differences. The fear in the region for the authorities was the double-edged sword of Islam, which was practised by all five central Asian nationalities, and pan-Turkic revolt, as four of the five nations were peopled by inhabitants of Turkic stock. The introduction of these slightly bogus national divisions was intended to weaken the bonds of Islam and pan-Turkism in the region and dilute the threat posed to the larger Soviet state.

Widespread land reforms started to take place around this time. In many cases this worked to the advantage of Kyrgyz as some of the land originally taken by Russian settlers was redistributed back into Kyrgyz hands – an astute move by the authorities and a clever way of assuaging the understandable anti-Russian sentiment that had previously been prevalent in the country. Rapid economic and social development took place; free, universal education was introduced and levels of literacy started to increase dramatically, albeit from a very low base. To encourage the educational advancement of the Kyrgyz people, it was important that literacy in the Kyrgyz language be encouraged. An Arabic-based script for the Kyrgyz language was introduced in 1924 but this was replaced by a Latin script just four years later, which remained until 1941, when the modified Cyrillic alphabet still in use today was adopted.

In the Soviet mould, of course, education meant far more than a simple matter of raising literacy levels. It was necessary to introduce the creed of Marxism-Leninism as a suitable ideological replacement for the rather syncretic version of Islam that the Kyrgyz had adopted. It was essential to repackage national culture as socialism with a Kyrgyz twist – to inaugurate a new hierarchy of identity in which Marxism-Leninism and the Soviet state were positioned above any form of religious or tribal identity. This transition required the use of propaganda in a myriad of forms. One such vehicle for propaganda was the Society of the Godless (later known as The Union of Belligerent Atheists), a movement consisting of workers, peasants, students and intelligentsia which was dedicated to eradicating religious beliefs that were not conducive to the Soviet ideal.

At the same time the propagandising of socialist 'good practice' was also encouraged, and one particular group of young, idealistic volunteers travelled across the territories of the USSR to Soviet Kyrgyzstan to work and spread the socialist message. In 1925 the first **Interhelpo** volunteers started to arrive in Bishkek – volunteers from Eastern Europe that formed workers' collectives dedicated to building socialism in Soviet Kyrgyzstan and improving the country's infrastructure. Interhelpo involved themselves in projects such as setting up factories to produce textiles and furniture, building power stations, constructing Bishkek's *Dom Druzhby* (Friendship House), the first seat of the republic's government, and building Bishkek's first housing estate, which became known as Workers Town (*Rabochiy Gorodok*). The first group of volunteers to arrive were from Czechoslovakia and included the family of Alexander Dubček, who would go on to become Czechoslovakian president during the Prague Spring of 1968.

As determined volunteers they were highly successful and by 1934 Interhelpo were producing 20% of the Kyrgyz ASSR's total industrial output. Interhelpo brigades continued coming to the Kyrgyz ASSR to work as doctors, teachers and builders and perform revolutionary good works until the onset of the Great Patriotic War (World War II) in 1941 introduced far more urgent priorities. The co-operative was finally liquidated in 1943, after many of its members had been persecuted in the purges of the 1930s and declared enemies of the state by Stalin.

The year 1926 brought yet another change of name and the republic became known as the Autonomous Socialist Soviet Republic of Kyrgyzstan. This, in turn, would be changed to the Kyrgyz Soviet Socialist Republic (Kyrgyz SSR) in 1936, when it would become established as a full union republic within the USSR. In the same year, 1926, the capital Pishpek was also renamed Frunze in honour of the Bolshevik general, Mikhail Frunze, who had been born in the city and who had died the year before.

THE BASMACHI MOVEMENT In the early years of the Soviet period an Islamic guerrilla movement known as the Basmachi Movement started to gain sway in the region. It had begun in 1916 as a protest against the Russian Empire, when the Tsarist government ceased exempting Muslims from compulsory military service. This revolt had led to brutal massacres and the forced exodus of many Kyrgyz from the region.

Following the October Revolution of 1917, anti-Russian rebellion continued to foment in the Fergana Valley, an ethnic Uzbek region that was traditionally a bastion of conservative Islam, and which today belongs mostly to Uzbekistan but partly to the Kyrgyz Republic and Tajikistan. In the period 1918–19 the Basmachi seized the southern Uzbek-dominated strongholds of Osh and Jalal-Abad, and the movement was even supported by Russian settlers from the region for a short period. (The same settlers deserted the cause later on when Mikhail Frunze, head of Lenin's newly appointed Tashkent Commission, negotiated with them and offered food supplies in exchange for defection.)

Over the next few years, Basmachi revolt spread throughout the Uzbek and Tajik territories from its Fergana source, with some groups receiving support from both British and Turkish intelligence services. Advances were made for the cause when the movement was joined by the charismatic leader Enver Pasha in May 1922, but support started to flounder when he was killed in August of the same year. Lacking firm leadership, the movement had mostly died out by the time the Kyrgyz ASSR was established in 1926, but activity continued intermittently throughout the region until 1934, when the last seats of Basmachi power, in this case within the Kyrgyz ASSR itself, were destroyed.

POLITICAL REPRESSION AND SOCIAL CHANGE As well as dissent that came from a religious background, politically different points of view were badly tolerated too. This was a one-party state, with the Kyrgyz Communist Party as the only legal representation, and the unwavering imposition of Stalin's hard-line policies meant that the new regime would brook no dissent. As a consequence, as elsewhere in the USSR during this dark period, many questioning intellectuals 'disappeared' overnight or were summarily executed; many more were arrested and imprisoned in the barbaric conditions of prison camps that almost guaranteed an early grave.

The repression and purges in the Kyrgyz ASSR/SSR, as elsewhere in the Soviet Union, reached their zenith during the mid 1930s. One such incident in the Kyrgyz SSR, which was not revealed until many years later, was the 1937 massacre at Chong-Tash near Bishkek, in which almost 140 prominent political figures were assassinated in secret. This included almost all of the Kyrgyz SSR's regional government and the father of Kyrgyz novelist Chingiz Aitmatov (see box, *The Chong-Tash Massacre*, page 118).

Meanwhile, the land reform programme, which had begun immediately after the creation of the Kyrgyz ASSR and which had pleased many Kyrgyz with their regaining previously confiscated territory, went a stage further in the years 1928–32 when mass collectivisation was introduced. This decreed that all farm land – both arable and pasture – be taken under state control to be worked as collective farms supervised by an autonomous local committee. The nomadic or semi-nomadic practices of the Kyrgyz pastoralists no longer had a role to play and the herders had to learn to adapt to a settled way of life. This proved traumatic in the extreme for many Kyrgyz, to whom the freedom of a nomadic existence meant everything. Not only were they forcibly settled, many also became disenfranchised by the process as the collective farms were more often than not headed by ethnic Russians. This enforced transition to a collectivised – and perhaps more importantly, settled – way of life that was alien to the nomadic Kyrgyz spirit inspired some to escape over the mountains into China. Others, rendered powerless by the hand of the state machine, merely slaughtered their herds in defiance.

THE GREAT PATRIOTIC WAR 1941–45 Many Kyrgyz, along with other indigenous central Asians, were enrolled to fight in the campaign against the Nazis. Some of these, sensing little difference between Nazi and Stalinist repression, or perhaps out of mere pragmatism, defected at the front to the German side; but many more joined the ranks of the German army's Muslim Turkic division, the **Turkestan Legion**, as captured prisoners of war, having little choice in the matter. Many of those who survived would inevitably be branded as 'traitors of the motherland' on their return and end up in Soviet prison camps.

During the war much of the Soviet Union's armament-producing industry shifted base to new factories in central Asia, and specifically Kyrgyzstan, well away from the theatre of war and German bombs in European Russia.

It was not only the factories of the Soviet war machine that were moved eastwards in this period. During the war years all of the major film studios from Moscow, Leningrad and Kiev, as well as filmmakers like Sergei Eisenstein, were evacuated to central Asia, where they could help the war effort (by way of propaganda) in safety. Large numbers of Axis prisoners of war ended up in camps in central Asia where they were used as enforced labour to build roads and railways, or to work in farming, forestry and mining. Others were enlisted for construction projects in the Kyrgyz capital – Bishkek's railway station was built by German POWs in 1946.

THE LATE SOVIET PERIOD Following the movement of much of the Soviet Union's war machine to the region during World War II, Kyrgyzstan was set, along with its other central Asian neighbours, for further industrialisation in the period that followed. More Russians moved to the region as managers, engineers and technicians, continuing the earlier tradition in which Europeans took the best, and more highly qualified, positions.

Kyrgyzstan's isolated geographical position well away from the prying eyes of the West encouraged the Soviet Union to locate some of its most militarily sensitive and politically secretive activities in the republic. Lake Issyk-Kul, well off the permitted circuit for even those lucky enough to get tourist visas, was used as a secret base for the testing of naval weapons, while the mining of uranium for use in nuclear weapons was carried out at Mailuu-Suu near the Fergana Valley, leaving a horrendous environmental legacy for subsequent generations to have to deal with.

There were serious riots in the capital in 1967, following an incident in which widespread resentment against the police made itself known. The incident, which was precipitated by a drunken soldier being beaten up by a group of policemen, ended in widespread street rioting, a mass march on the KGB headquarters, and police officers being dragged from their cars to be beaten up by protestors. It was quelled with the support of the army and KGB units and the blame attributed to Chinese agitators.

The period of the 1970s and 1980s that followed were considered by many to be Soviet Kyrgyzstan's 'golden period'. After decades of Stalinist repression followed by economic hardships, there were now goods in the shops and full employment. Hunger had finally been banished and a number of grandiose building projects were taking place in Frunze (Bishkek) that exuded confidence and pride in Kyrgyzstan's modest but valued place within the Soviet Union.

It was during this period that the White House, the Philharmonic building, the National Library and Ala-Too Square were constructed in the capital, despite an increasing lack of decent workers' housing in the city. By 1988, the housing shortage had become so acute that the mere rumour that homeless victims of an Armenian earthquake were to be allocated housing in the capital prompted mass demonstrations that called for the government to resign.

The spirit of *glasnost* that took hold further west in the USSR during the late 1980s had very little influence on provincial Kyrgyz political life, and in 1990 the

Kyrgyz Communist Party leadership firmly opposed changes to the Soviet constitution that allowed non-Communists to participate in politics. However, there were more immediate concerns at that time that were ethnically rather than politically based. Ethnic tensions were surfacing in the south, where Uzbeks formed the majority group. A state of emergency and curfew was announced in June when violent inter-ethnic conflict between Uzbeks and Kyrgyz took place in and around Osh and Özgön. The clashes, which were not pacified until August, had been sparked by disputes over the perennial problem of land access and housing issues. The conflict left up to one thousand victims dead in a horrifying bloodbath that shocked everybody with both its spontaneity and its ferocity.

INDEPENDENCE In October of 1990, the same year as the Uzbek-Kyrgyz inter-ethnic strife in the south, Askar Akaev, a physicist academic in favour of reform, was elected by the legislature to the newly created post of president.

Akaev had been elected as a compromise candidate in a role that was designed to be wholly symbolic and without any serious political clout but, responding to the zeitgeist of *glasnost* and *perestroika* that was taking place in Moscow, he immediately introduced new government structures and appointed a new government of fellow reform-minded members. In December of the same year, the republic was renamed Kyrgyzstan (it had been known as Kirgizia in Soviet times and would be re-titled the Kyrgyz Republic in 1993). Wishing to extend this new Kyrgyz identity a stage further, the capital Frunze was renamed Bishkek in February 1991.

Just as the August putsch was taking place, unsuccessfully, in Moscow, a coup attempted to remove Akaev from power on 19 August 1991. This failed, and the following week both Akaev and his vice president German Kuznetsov announced that they would be resigning from the Communist Party of the Soviet Union; the entire politburo and secretariat immediately followed suit. The Supreme Soviet declared independence from the USSR on 31 August. Akaev announced that Kyrgyz would become the new official language of state and dissolved the Communist Party, seizing its assets and declaring it, temporarily at least, illegal.

In October 1991, Akaev was voted in for another presidential term, with 95% of the vote in an election in which he ran unopposed. On 21 December 1991 Kyrgyzstan acceded to the newly formed Commonwealth of Independent States (CIS) and the following year Kyrgyzstan became a member of both the United Nations and the OSCE.

Shortly after the initial period of independence Akaev started to come under scrutiny because of allegations of corruption against some of his close associates. This required him to dismiss his first government in 1993 and call upon a former communist prime minister, Apas Djumagulov, to form a new one. Several referenda followed over the next couple of years that made changes to the constitution.

In December 1995, Akaev was re-elected for a further five-year term in elections that were considered fair overall. However, the parliamentary elections that took place in early 2000, and the presidential one that occurred later that same year, were seen as badly flawed and declared invalid by international observers.

THE BATKEN INSURGENCIES 1999–2000 The Batken region in Kyrgyzstan's remote southwestern arm was, and still remains, the part of the country most distant from Bishkek in both geographical and political terms. It is a region that is surrounded on three sides by the neighbouring states of Uzbekistan and Tajikistan and is also the home of half-a-dozen Uzbek and Tajik territorial enclaves that lie politically landlocked within Kyrgyz territory (see *Enclaves and Exclaves: A Political Jigsaw*, page 267).

For a number of reasons, mainly a sense of neglect by central government but also because of ethnic differences and its precarious geographical position, Batken was the region where political unrest was most likely to emerge in the new republic. This came to fruition in 1999 when incursions into the Batken region were made by fighters of the IMU (Islamic Movement of Uzbekistan), who were waging a low-scale war against the might of Islam Karimov's Uzbek forces in the Fergana Valley. (The IMU, in some ways similar to the Basmachi rebels of the 1920s and 1930s, were mostly young Muslim Uzbeks who were fighting to establish an Islamic state in Uzbekistan's Fergana Valley, where the majority of them had originally come from. They had trained and fought in Afghanistan, where they had possibly been supported by the Taliban and other Islamic rebel groups. Having left their Afghanistan and Tajikistan bases, their route back home led across Kyrgyzstan's south-western Batken region.)

The first so-called 'incident' took place in 1999, when a group of IMU fighters kidnapped a group of Japanese geologists who were working in the mountains of the southwest. Some sporadic fighting took place before negotiations were initiated and the hostages were eventually released and the IMU rebels withdrew to their bases in Tajikistan.

In response to these incursions, President Akaev created a new regional administration for Batken (the region had previously been part of Osh Oblast) in addition to tightening up border controls. The Uzbek government's reaction in Tashkent was altogether more hard-line, launching air attacks on suspected bases within Kyrgyzstan, and laying minefields along the border, which killed a number of innocent civilians going about their daily lives.

The insurgents returned the following year and a number of skirmishes took place between the IMU and Kyrgyz government forces. This time, it was groups of climbers in the region that were captured. One group of four young American climbers managed to escape from their captors, while the others were eventually released. In total, 49 Kyrgyz soldiers died in combat during the incidents of 1999 and 2000. Since then there have been no more armed incursions recorded in the region, apart from an incident in May 2006, when a Tajik border post was attacked, killing two people, although the evidence suggests that this was more likely connected with a drug running operation than with Islamic militants.

THE AKSU INCIDENT In January 2002 Azimbek Beknazarov, a deputy in the Jogorku Kenesh parliament, was arrested on charges of corruption and abuse of power. His supporters claimed that the arrest had been politically motivated and engineered by President Akaev as a means of removing an opponent who had been critical of his ceding Kyrgyz territory in the high Tien Shan to China. Following his conviction a large group of Beknazarov's supporters gathered to march to the court where he was going to be sentenced in order to protest against the decision. The road to the court was blocked by the police and a confrontation ensued in which six protesters were killed by gunfire and even more injured. The authorities made the claim that the initial gunfire had come from the crowd, whereas the protesters observed that the police had fired indiscriminately into the crowd in panic. The government opened an investigation into the incident but while the elected commission was making enquiries more protests started up around the country demanding Beknazarov's release. A month later, the commission released their report that found that the police and local authorities were at fault for the incident. Some local officials were arrested and jailed but were later released under an amnesty.

Weakened by the controversy created by the incident, the government fell and a new prime minister, Nikolai Tanaev, was appointed, although Askar Akaev still remained in place as president. Protests continued but somehow the new government managed to survive, despite the tensions that were building up throughout the country.

THE TULIP REVOLUTION The parliamentary elections of 2005 were seen as an improvement on those held in 2000 but they still fell short of the mark. The opposition, which had won just a few seats, clamed that they were rigged and as a result, sporadic protests against the perceived fraud of Akaev and his associates erupted around the country. These escalated into more widespread protests, particularly in the south, that called for the government to stand down. Government buildings in Osh and Jalal-Abad were seized by angry protesters and the whole of the south went over to the opposition and beyond government control.

Following this, on 24 March 2005, a demonstration of 15,000 pro-opposition protesters took to the streets of the capital to call for President Akaev's resignation. The main government building was occupied and Akaev fled, first to Kazakhstan, then Moscow, claiming that he had decided to leave in order to prevent civil war breaking out in the country. He resigned his office on 4 April and this was ratified by the Kyrgyz parliament on 11 April.

The Kyrgyz parliament appointed the former prime minister, Kurmanbek Bakiev, as acting president at the head of an interim government. On 1 September 2005 Feliks Kulov was appointed as prime minister, a role he kept for just over a year until he resigned with his government on 19 December 2006 in a move to accelerate the holding of parliamentary elections and push through reforms.

Azimbek Beknazarov, who had long been a sworn enemy of Akaev and had been at the heart of the Aksu incident in 2002, was appointed Prosecutor General of the Kyrgyz Republic and immediately waged a campaign against Akaev and his family, seeking a return of the fortune amassed by the former president's family. He resigned from this position a few months later when his reputation came under scrutiny following allegations of corruption.

Following the collapse of Akaev's rule, the immediate aftermath was a brief period of rioting and looting, in which foreign-owned concerns such as big department stores were targeted, partly out of resentment and partly because the goods they contained were normally beyond the means of the vast majority of Kyrgyzstan's citizens. The looting soon abated and ceased completely after the second night, hindered as much by bad weather as it was by active policing.

The 'Tulip Revolution' was so named because of the tulips that many of the demonstrators carried on the protests to signify their peaceful intent; many others carried daffodils and so Daffodil Revolution might well have been an equally appropriate soubriquet.

KYRGYZSTAN POST-TULIP REVOLUTION Even after the revolution, political stability in Kyrgyzstan seemed to remain elusive, with various factions, some allegedly linked to organised crime, jostling for a share of power. Of the 75 members of the new government that was elected in March 2005, three were assassinated shortly afterwards, with another being killed in May 2006, shortly after winning his brother's seat in a by-election. All four victims were said to have links with disreputable business interests. 2006 saw further political crisis as thousands demonstrated in a series of protests in Bishkek. Bakiev was accused of reneging on his promised constitutional reforms to limit presidential power as well as failing to eradicate crime and corruption. A new prime minister, Azim Isabekov, was approved by parliament on 29 January 2007 to replace Feliks Kulov who had resigned the month before but he, too, was forced to resign after just three months, having dismissed a number of ministers in an attempt to incorporate new people in the government. Spring 2007 saw another brief period of rioting in the capital with mass demonstrations calling for President Bakiev's resignation.

GOVERNMENT AND POLITICS

The Kyrgyz Republic is technically a semi-presidential representative democracy in which the president is the head of state and the prime minister the head of government. In this system, the government exercises executive power while legislative power lies in the hands of both government and parliament.

Following independence from the USSR in 1991, Kyrgyzstan's first president, Askar Akaev, announced his full commitment to the process of political reform and as a result received enthusiastic backing from the IMF and other Western donors who were keen to see the new republic's transition from centrally-planned communist colony to free-market economy.

A scandal emerged in 1993 when close associates of Akaev, including the prime minister, Tursunbek Chyngyshev, were accused of corruption. Chyngyshev was dismissed along with the government, and Akaev called upon Apas Djumagulov, who had been the last communist premier, to form a new government. A referendum was held in January 1994 to ask for a renewed mandate for Akaev to complete his term of office and he achieved this with 96.2% of the vote.

In May 1993, a new constitution was passed by parliament, but in 1994 parliament failed to achieve a quorum for its last scheduled session before the expiration of its term and Akaev was accused of having manipulated a boycott. The president announced another referendum for October 1994 that proposed two changes to the constitution: one that would permit amendment of the constitution by referendum; a second that created a parliament with two legislative chambers called the Jogorku Kenesh. Elections took place in February 1995 for the new parliament, which were championed as being free and fair by international observers despite a few polling-day irregularities. On 24 December 1995, Akaev was re-elected for another five-year term and in February 1996 a referendum amended the constitution to award the president more power, including the power to dissolve parliament. A referendum in October 1998 made further reforming constitutional changes.

Parliamentary elections were held in early 2000 but on this occasion international observers were less impressed by the even-handedness of the proceedings and declared them invalid, as they also did with the presidential election that took place later that same year. Akaev continued in power until spring 2005, when the so-called Tulip Revolution ousted him from power and Kurmanbek Bakiev was appointed as acting president at the head of an interim government. Bakiev subsequently won a presidential election in July of that year with a landslide victory.

'Revolution' or not, the honeymoon period of the new administration did not last for long. In the brief period post-Revolution there have been shootings of politicians (particularly those with alleged links to the criminal underworld), prison riots and further mass demonstrations. This has lead to a renewed political crisis, with large-scale demonstrations in Bishkek in April and November 2006 calling for the president's resignation. The main accusation levelled at the president was of failing to live up to his election promises of reform of the country's constitution, and reneging on his promise to share power with parliament.

In April 2006, Bakiev signed amendments to reduce his own powers, but this was insufficient for many protestors who demanded his full resignation. As before in the Akaev period, there were wider criticisms of corruption and cronyism, along with what was perceived as increasing criminality in the country and a failure to alleviate poverty (a view fuelled by the frustrations of people who had seen no improvement in their lives since the new regime took over).

Bakiev's fragile hold on power had not been helped by a rapid succession of incumbents in the role of prime minister. In the immediate period that followed the Tulip Revolution Feliks Kulov, a former mayor of Bishkek who had been imprisoned in the period 2001–05 on trumped-up corruption charges, was appointed as prime minister in September 2005, but was forced to resign just over a year later in December 2006 because of the worsening relations between the executive and legislative branches of government. Bakiev attempted to re-nominate him in January 2007 but this move was opposed by parliament. The president then nominated Azim Isabekov, a close associate, as prime minister but he, too, was forced to resign in March 2007 when his move to dismiss a large number of ministers was rejected by Bakiev. To replace Isabekov, Almazbek Atambaev, the former chairman of the opposition's Social Democratic Party, was appointed as acting prime minister. In April 2007, Atambaev attempted to address one of the mass demonstrations in Bishkek to demand President Bakiev's resignation but this was met with boos from the crowd.

Ex-prime minister Feliks Kulov went on to join the opposition in February 2007, an allegiance that further weakened Bakiev's authority. This split also served to highlight the traditional north–south rivalry that exists in Kyrgyzstan's clan-based politics, in which Bakiev with his many Jalal-Abad connections represent the south of the country and Kulov, along with many other opposition leaders, serve the interests of the north.

ECONOMY

A 2006 IMF survey estimates the GDP of Kyrgyzstan to be US$2,822 million, which makes its position 144th in a world ranking of 181, just above Tajikistan and Mongolia but below Fiji and Guinea. As a per capita figure this comes out at US$542 per capita per year, at 152nd place out of 182 – a similar figure to Haiti and even lower than African countries like Kenya. Considering that Kyrgyzstan used to be an integral part of one the biggest economies in the world – the Soviet Union's – this is a very lowly position in economic terms.

As is the case with the other central Asian republics, Kyrgyzstan was very badly affected by the collapse of the Soviet Union and its guaranteed trading market. In 1990, before independence, virtually all of the Kyrgyz SSR's exports went to Russia or other parts of the Soviet Union, but with the collapse of the USSR these markets diminished, as did the subsidies that came from Moscow. In the early 1990s, immediately after independence, the weakness of Kyrgyzstan's economic performance was only surpassed by those former ex-Soviet nations, like Tajikistan, Armenia and Azerbaijan, that were embroiled in war at the time.

To overcome the initial economic difficulties brought about by the collapse of its markets, the new republic introduced major reforms, reducing expenditure, ending price subsidies and introducing VAT, which caused great economic hardships for its nationals but which were seen as necessary measures in order to successfully make the transformation to a market economy and encourage long-term growth. These reforms were not echoed by Kyrgyzstan's immediate neighbours like Kazakhstan and Uzbekistan, which were on the whole better resourced, and even small-scale regional trade deteriorated as a result.

Such acts of economic reform ensured that, for a brief period at least, the newly independent republic became a darling of the World Bank and the IMF, and was lauded as a model of post-communist economic transformation. The downside was high unemployment due to privatisation, soaring food prices, fuel shortages and low wages. Fuel and energy shortages also meant that industrial production decreased significantly, a trend that was exacerbated by an exodus of skilled Russians from the new republic.

A slow recovery came about from about 1996 onwards, and since accession to the World Trade Organisation in 1998 the economy has picked up to some extent. Nevertheless, many difficulties remain and these are felt most acutely by the poorest sector of society – the rural unskilled, the old and those who are dependent on pensions or state support.

Currently, nearly 40% of Kyrgyzstan's GDP is earned by agricultural production, 23% by industry and the rest by the service sector. Agriculture is by far the biggest employer, with the main crops being cotton, tobacco, hemp and vegetables, along with meat, wool and leather from livestock. Kyrgyzstan is rich in mineral wealth, with appreciable deposits of coal, uranium and gold, although it lacks oil and natural gas in any useful quantity and needs to import these – a major expense. There is seen to be much potential in developing Kyrgyzstan's mining base but the problem with this, even putting environmental considerations to one side, is the inaccessibility of most of its mineral resources. However, considerable investment has been made in extracting and processing gold with the establishment of joint ventures with Western companies, notably the Kumtor gold mine in the Barskoon valley near Lake Issyk-Kul.

With a convoluted physical landscape that is 90% mountainous and an adequate water supply, mostly in the form of ice-melt, Kyrgyzstan has plentiful water resources and hydro-electrical power is one commodity that the country is able to successfully export to its immediate neighbours, although currently this is only exploited at a fraction of its true potential.

Apart from this, Kyrgyzstan's main exports are non-ferrous metals and minerals like antimony, mercury and rare-earth metals, which by and large are exported to other CIS countries, while animal hides, fleeces and scrap metal are taken by lorry over the Tien Shan for sale in China. Goods like fuel, grain, medicine, machinery and agricultural equipment are all imported.

Beyond the major concerns about markets, investment and accessibility, one of the major stumbling blocks facing Kyrgyzstan's economic development is that of widespread corruption, which is widely acknowledged as being present at every level of bureaucracy from the top down.

On a domestic level, Kyrgyzstan may be seen as having a 'kiosk economy' in which most local economic transactions take place at small local markets or at village kiosks. As a result, much local trade is unregulated. Many everyday consumer goods are unavailable outside the cities and this, coupled with low expectations that hark back to Soviet-era rationing and periodic shortages, has encouraged self-sufficiency in food products like meat, dairy goods and fruit preserves.

PEOPLE

KYRGYZ It is easy enough to assume that, given its name, Kyrgyzstan is a country that is composed entirely of people of Kyrgyz ethnicity. This is only partly true: while Kyrgyz form the majority in many parts of the republic there are some areas of Kyrgyzstan where they constitute a minority or have hardly any presence at all. Overall, Kyrgyz form about 70% of the total population and are generally the most numerous ethnic group in northern and central Kyrgyzstan, especially away from the towns.

Although their precise origins are unclear, the Kyrgyz are a Turkic nomadic people that migrated to central Asia from the upper Yenisey valley of Siberia from the 10th century onwards. Recent genetic studies have demonstrated that they are closely related to the present day indigenous population of the central Siberian region. Over the centuries, and in the course of numerous migrations, they have mixed and intermarried with local populations so that, in genetic terms, they are less

Traditional Kyrgyz society can be broken down into a hierarchy, of which the smallest component is the family unit that is called a *tutun* ('smoke'). Above this is the *uluu* (literally 'sons'), a group of families who are able to trace a common ancestor, then *uruk* or 'clan', which is comprised of several *uluu*. These clans of blood relatives, in turn, combine with other clans to form a tribe or *uruu*. Clan membership demands loyalty and any wrongs that are inflicted between clans need to be avenged or at least compensated for. To most Kyrgyz, clan ties are just as important as family ties and two Kyrgyz strangers meeting for the first time will be quick to establish their corresponding lineages.

According to the standard translation of their name, the Kyrgyz are a people made up of 40 separate tribes, although this number should not be taken too literally as the number 40 occurs frequently in Kyrgyz folklore and may have been chosen for its mystical quality rather than any precise anthropological meaning. Because the terms tribe and clan are rather vague it is hard to be exact, but one current source suggests that there may be a total of 38 tribes in Kyrgyz society.

Kyrgyz tribes may be roughly broken down into two separate groups: those of the north – the *Tagai* – where there are a small number of large tribes, and the southern group of tribes known as the *Ichkilik*, which has a large number of smaller tribes. The northern *Tagai* tribes, which belong geographically to the region north of the Naryn River, include the Bugun, the largest clan, the Solto, who are predominant in the Bishkek area, and the Sary-Bagysh, who prevail in the Karkara valley and are the clan of former president Askar Akaev. In the south, the Adygene are the main clan found in the region around Osh, but other smaller clans include Boston, Kesek, Kydyrsha, Kypchak and others.

On the whole, given their greater degree of exposure to Russian culture, the northern clans tend to be more Russified than those of the south, which tend to observe a slightly more orthodox version of Islam than their northern neighbours as a result of living for centuries side by side with the more conservative Uzbeks and Tajik of the region. Those tribes that live in the central part of the country in the mountains and valleys between Naryn, Lake Song-Köl, Suusamyr and Kazarman are probably the ones that are least affected by outside influences and hence have the 'purest' culture. One such clan from this region is the Sayak. The term Kara-Kyrgyz, which use to be used in early Soviet times to distinguish the mountain-living Kyrgyz from the steppe-living Kazakhs, is now sometimes used to refer to those clans that inhabit the border zones with China and Tajikistan.

Tribal conflicts were often the cause of bloodshed in the past and even today there are considerable rivalries between groups. Historically there has always been a struggle between northern Kyrgyz and the tribes of the south. At the time just before the initial Russian migration into the region there was a bloody civil war taking place between the Bugun and the Sary-Bagysh for supremacy in the region, and while most northern Kyrgyz tribes were keen to enlist the aid of the Russian Empire to help rid themselves of the Kokand Khanate, many southern tribes, who had sometimes assisted the khanate in the past, were far less enthusiastic (see page 8).

Such divisions still exist today. In modern Kyrgyz politics, rather than straightforward clan loyalty, the struggle for influence is generally between the two tribal power blocks that represent the geographical regions of north and south. This polarised division carries far more weight than party or political ideology and goes some way to explaining why it is hard to completely eradicate bias and cronyism from Kyrgyzstan's political milieu, where the notion of democracy is a relatively new concept in comparison to tribal loyalties that have been firmly entrenched for centuries.

Background Information **PEOPLE**

homogenous than they were in the past. According to historic Chinese sources, the Kyrgyz had green eyes, fair skin and red hair, but on the whole, having mixed with Mongolian and other Turkic groups over the centuries, most contemporary Kyrgyz no longer exhibit these characteristics. Although they are of quite varied physical appearance, in general they are fairly short and dark skinned, with wide faces and almond eyes.

The name Kyrgyz comes from two Turkic words that either mean 'forty tribes' (*kyrk* – forty; *uz* – tribes) or, alternatively, 'forty girls' (*kyrk* – forty; *kyz* – girls). Both of these meanings correspond to the Manas epic; the first relates to the 40 small tribes that are said to have united against Chinese and Muslim expansion to the west, the second, to 40 servant girls who swam in a mountain lake and became pregnant, giving birth to the first Kyrgyz people. It is also represented on the national flag, which has 40 rays emanating from a central sun.

Another possible etymology is *kyrgys*, which means 'imperishable', 'inextinguishable' or 'undying' – a popular derivation that echoes the Kyrgyz propensity towards chivalry and bravery. Today the world's four million or so Kyrgyz are spread throughout the central Asian region, with the greatest population in the country that bears their name (around 3.35 million), alongside sizeable populations in northwest China (145,000), Tajikistan (81,000), Uzbekistan (225,000) and Kazakhstan (11,000). Many Kyrgyz also live in Russia as migrant workers, along with a permanent population there of around 32,000.

Kyrgyz are for the most part Sunni Muslims, although they practise it fairly superficially – usually little more than a veneer over an underlying core of shamanistic beliefs and practices. Some Kyrgyz in China – and a very small number in Kyrgyzstan – practise Tibetan Buddhism.

UZBEKS Uzbeks are Kyrgyzstan's second most numerous group with around 711,000 living in the country – about 14.5% of the total population – principally in the south in Osh, Jala-Abad and Batken *oblasts*. With a population of around 20 million in neighbouring Uzbekistan, they are by far the most numerous ethnic group in central Asia as a whole.

Like the Kyrgyz, the Uzbek forefathers originally hailed from Siberia, although they settled down centuries earlier to become farmers, a practice which they keep until this day. The modern Uzbek population is composed of a heritage of Turkic, Mongol and Iranian peoples and is generally considered to be descended from the tribes that arrived in the central Asian region with the Khan Shaybani in the 16th century.

In contrast with the Kyrgyz population, Uzbeks are generally settled farmers who practise a more rigid form of Islam than their nomadic neighbours. They have a culture quite distinct from that of the nomadic Kyrgyz and are usually instantly recognisable by their dress: the older men in black, square skull caps that are called *doppi*; the women in brilliantly coloured long dresses with the *ikat* pattern that first became popular in Bokhara and Samarkand in the 19th century. Uzbek families usually live in houses surrounded by high walls, inside which is a private courtyard with individual rooms facing out onto it. They dine at low tables with raised seating platforms at which they sit cross-legged; restaurants with this seating arrangement can be found throughout southern Kyrgyzstan.

RUSSIANS Russians, and to a lesser extent other Slavic groups like Ukrainians, maintain a prominent but decreasing population in Kyrgyzstan. Many have left since independence, but currently they make up around 9% of Kyrgyzstan's population, with around 600,000 remaining in the country, mostly in the north in Bishkek, the Chui valley and the north coast of Lake Issyk-Kul. Many Russians came as Cossacks and freed serfs to farm and trade in the region in the second half of the 19th century, lured by the offer of fertile land, tax breaks and other incentives that were offered by the Russian government in its desire to populate the Chinese border regions. Later, during the communist period and particularly at the height of Stalinist repression within the Soviet Union, other communities from further west, like some Ukrainians and Volga Germans, were moved here wholesale.

In the Soviet era Russians tended to have the better paid and more skilled jobs in industry and collectivised agriculture, working more as technicians and managers than labourers. Since independence they have seen a considerable turn-around in their fortunes, particularly as there has been some resentment and prejudice against them by ethnic Kyrgyz because of the more favourable positions they previously held. As a result many, especially the young, have left for Russia, while those that remain on the whole tend to be the older and more vulnerable sector of the community.

DUNGANS Dungans are Muslims of Chinese origin who make up just over 1% of the population and who mostly live in villages of the Chui valley, in Karakol, and to a lesser extent along the north shore of Lake Issyk-Kul. They arrived in central Asia in three separate waves of migration following persecution in central China, in the wake of the Hui Minorities War in the second half of the 19th century. Despite a shared religion and country of origin, they are not to be confused with Uyghurs, who are also Muslims from China but who are of Turkic descent. Dungans are ethnically Chinese and within China and within their own communities they refer to themselves as Hui. They speak a language that is closely related to the Shaanxi dialect of Mandarin Chinese with loan words from Arabic, Turkish and Persian, which is written in Cyrillic script. They work mostly as farmers and are well-known for their industriousness.

UYGHURS Like the Dungans, many of the Uyghur people found in the north of Kyrgyzstan arrived as refuges from oppression in China, where the vast majority of their kinsmen still live in the northwestern province of Xinjiang (East Turkestan). Uyghurs are Turkic Muslims who are closely related to Uzbeks in both culture and language, and who practise the same pursuits of farming and trading. Unlike those who live in the north, those Uyghurs who are settled in the south of the country, in the vicinity of Osh and Özgön, have been settled in the area for centuries. Altogether, Uyghurs make up around 1% of Kyrgyzstan's population.

TATARS Tatars – often spelled 'Tartars' in English – are a Muslim Turkic people descended from Volga Bulgars and the Mongol Golden Horde who originally came from the Volga region of Russia and the Ukrainian Crimea. Some Tatars arrived in Kyrgyzstan along with the early waves of Slavic settlers at the end of the 19th century, while others groups, mostly from the Crimea, arrived during World War II as a consequence of expulsions by Stalin. In 1999 there were reported to have been around 45,000 Tatars living in Kyrgyzstan, but the number is undoubtedly lower now as many of those whose families arrived in the 1940s have since returned to the lands of their forefathers.

KAZAKHS Kazakhs are quite similar to the Kyrgyz in both linguistic and cultural terms and during the early Soviet period were confusingly described as Kyrgyz in contrast to the Kara-Kyrgyz ('black Kyrgyz') appellation that was given to the true Kyrgyz at the time. With a clan-based social structure and a traditionally nomadic lifestyle, Kazakhs are effectively a lowland or steppe counterpart of their highland cousins, the Kyrgyz. With about 45,000 Kazakhs living in Kyrgyzstan, mostly along

Kyrgyzstan's northern border in the Chui valley, the Karkara valley and the Talas region of the northwest, they make up about 0.7% of the total population.

KOREANS Kyrgyzstan has a small population of Koreans who arrived here during World War II as a result of mass deportation from the Vladivostok region in the Russian Far East by Stalin, who feared they might co-operate with the Japanese who had occupied Manchuria and Korea at the time. Like the Dungans, they tend to work mostly as farmers and market gardeners, and, despite some Russification of their culture, manage to maintain a highly distinctive cuisine.

GERMANS Some of Kyrgyzstan's tiny ethnic German community arrived in the region during World War II as part of a mass deportation from the Volga region of southwest Russia where, from 1924–41, they had their own Soviet territory – the Volga German ASSR. Others were already long established in Kyrgyzstan: Lutheran Mennonites who had joined the late 19th- and early 20th-century migrations of Russian colonists to the area. Many Germans have left for Germany since independence and the 2005 estimate of the number remaining is around 12,000 (see *A Long Way From Home: Germans in Kyrgyzstan*, page 122).

TAJIKS Tajiks are an Indo-European people with Mediterranean features who are related to present-day Iranians and speak a Persian language. They are found in small numbers in the south, often close to the border with Tajikistan (although many more also live in Uzbekistan). There are also a couple of enclaves belonging to Tajikistan within Batken Oblast, as well as a Tajik majority in the large Uzbekistan exclave of Sokh in the same province (see *Exclaves and Enclaves: A Political Jigsaw*, page 267).

LANGUAGE

Kyrgyz is a Turkic language that has the usual characteristics of that language group, most notably vowel harmony, which is strictly adhered to (with the exception of Slavic and Persian loan words). As part of the Kyrgyz-Altay group of Turkic languages it is most closely related to the Altay language and fairly similar to Kazakh.

Modern Kyrgyz did not have a standard written form until 1923, when an alphabet using Arabic characters, like Ottoman Turkish, was introduced (this is still used by the Kyrgyz population of Xinjiang, China). This was changed to a Latin-based alphabet in 1928, which in turn was replaced in 1940 by the modified Cyrillic alphabet that is still in use today. Following independence, there have been some suggestions of reverting back to the Latin alphabet, as has been the case in Uzbekistan, but this has not been followed through, probably because the Cyrillic suits the language well.

Modern day Kyrgyz may be divided into two distinct groups of different dialects. Standard Kyrgyz was defined during the Soviet period as the northern variation of the language that has a large number of loan words from Mongolian languages, whereas the southern dialects contain far more words from the Uzbek, Persian and Tajik languages. Modern Kyrgyz naturally also has a large number of words of Russian derivation in its vocabulary.

When Kyrgyzstan was an autonomous republic within the Soviet Union, **Russian** was the official language of state, but immediately following independence in 1991, Kyrgyz was promoted as the official language, and in 1992 a law was passed that called for all public business to be converted fully to Kyrgyz by 1997. Kyrgyzstan's Russian-only speakers were strongly against this move and public opinion was so critical that it even caused an ethnic Russian member of President Akaev's staff to threaten resignation as a protest against what he saw as the 'Kyrgyzification' of the new republic's non-Kyrgyz population.

In response to this and other, more widespread, protests, a resolution was passed in 1996 to make Russian an official language of state alongside Kyrgyz. This move, which reversed the earlier commitment and bucked the trend of other central Asian states that had demoted Russian as the language of state, was meant to encourage ethnic Russians to remain in the new republic and not take their skills elsewhere, although by this stage many had left anyway.

It was a pragmatic reversal in many respects, considering that other minorities such as Uzbeks spoke their own tongue, not Kyrgyz, in addition to Russian, and that for many northern, urban Kyrgyz, Russian was both their mother tongue and the preferred language of business and politics. Nevertheless, since independence use of the Kyrgyz language has been encouraged to the extent that it is now the main language of parliament. The current constitution states that it is necessary for the president to be a fluent speaker of the language. For a guide to pronunciation, the Kyrgyz alphabet and a brief vocabulary see *Appendix I: Language* (page 270).

Apart from Russian, of which almost all Kyrgyz citizens have some knowledge and in which many are fluent, the other widely spoken language in the country, though commonest in the south, is **Uzbek**, spoken by Kyrgyzstan's sizeable Uzbek minority. Like Kyrgyz, Uzbek is a Turkic language but, unlike Kyrgyz, it belongs to the Qarluq family of Turkic languages and is closely related to Uyghur. On the whole, Islam has had a greater effect on the Uzbek language than it has on Kyrgyz, and as a result Uzbek has a greater proportion of Persian and Arabic loan words. While in neighbouring Uzbekistan the language is now written using an adapted Latin script, in Kyrgyzstan a Cyrillic alphabet is still in use.

RELIGION

ISLAM After the 70-year long interregnum of atheism under Soviet rule – at least officially – Kyrgyzstan has emerged from the post-Soviet meltdown as a secular, but predominantly Muslim, country in a region where Islam has held great sway for almost a millennium.

The relaxed version of Islam observed by most Kyrgyz, however, is in sharp contrast to that practised in more conservative parts of the region and is best understood as a syncretic combination of Islam and earlier shamanistic practices. There is a saying that when the region was conquered by Muslim invaders the Kyrgyz took just enough Islam with them to suit their nomadic lifestyle, and there is some value in this as, on the whole, Islam forms a cultural background rather than a strict framework for religious devotion.

Technically, most Kyrgyz are Sunnis of the Hanafi school, but in practice they tend to mix and match their religion with animistic elements of pre-Islamic shamanism, along with other cultural practices that reflect Buddhist and even Zoroastrian influence. Most Kyrgyz today, if asked, would say they were Muslims but few regularly attend Friday prayers at the mosque and many see no conflict in visiting a shaman healer or drinking vodka. In general terms, Kyrgyz tend not to attend mosque or pray unless led by a mullah. Ramadan also has little impact.

Compared with much of the region, Islam came quite late to the Kyrgyz. Islam was first introduced to Kyrgyz tribes between the 9th and 12th centuries but it was not until the 17th century that it really took hold, when they were driven from the Tien Shan into the firmly Islamic Fergana Valley by invading Oyrat tribes of the Zhungarian Khanate. Later, when their territory came under the control of the Kokand Khanate in the 18th century, the Kyrgyz slowly converted to, or rather adopted, Islam, and by the end of the 19th century Islam was widely recognised as their chosen faith, even if on a rather superficial level.

In contrast to the nomadic Kyrgyz's light-hearted interpretation of Islam, Kyrgyzstan's long-settled Uzbek community tend to be stricter practitioners. They converted as early as the 8th century, when Arab armies invaded the region and defeated the Chinese at the Battle of Talas. Uzbeks are far more likely to attend mosque than their Kyrgyz counterparts and Ramadan is observed more consistently in predominantly Uzbek parts of the south, with cafés failing to open during daylight hours, and sometimes closing down for business completely, during the month of Ramadan.

Islam was tolerated by the Orthodox Church during the years of Russian colonisation that preceded the October Revolution, but during the Soviet period most religious practices were outlawed and virtually all mosques and religious schools were closed down. Such intolerance was one of the factors that prompted the Basmachi Rebellion in the conservative Fergana Valley. Limited concessions were made later but only in cases where religious practice could be strictly controlled. Since independence there has been a resurgence of interest in some quarters, particularly in the Uzbek southern part of the country. One noticeable sign of this is the new mosques that are appearing throughout the country. Some of these are large and impressive, like those at Osh, Naryn and the capital itself, and these have been paid for by funding from Saudi Arabia or Turkey; elsewhere, even in small villages, modest brick mosques with stainless steel roofs are being erected, sometimes paid for by foreign beneficiaries, sometimes by local funding. In the south, there has been an even more enthusiastic revival with the Uzbek population, but as a people they have been practising Muslims for far longer than the Kyrgyz.

Unlike in neighbouring Uzbekistan, where President Islam Karimov's government heavily represses Islamic practice for fear of fundamentalism, Uzbeks in Kyrgyzstan's Fergana fringes are free to observe their religion. The Kyrgyz government, however, is keen to discourage radical Islamic and what it terms 'Wahhabi' elements, as these are seen to be a destabilising influence. Armed incursions into the mountains of Batken Oblast from Tajikistan in 1999 and 2000 by Islamic militants of the IMU did little to assuage these fears, although there have been no more significant incidents since then.

CHRISTIANITY Christianity first came to the central Asian region with Nestorians travelling the Silk Road in the 7th and 8th centuries and traces of Nestorian churches have been found in the Chui valley. It is thought that early Armenian Christian communities may have existed on the shores of Lake Issyk-Kul and there is even a popular and partly substantiated belief that St Matthew may have died at Svetly Mys on the lake's eastern shore (see *Did St Matthew Die in Kyrgyzstan?*, page 151).

The Russian Orthodox Church came to the region with Slavic colonists that moved here in the mid to late 19th century. By 1914, Bishkek had two Orthodox churches, one of which still exists today, and Karakol had its wooden church that was erected without the use of nails by the town's Orthodox community. As was the case with the region's Muslims, religious practice was discouraged during the Soviet period and churches were closed or, as in the case of Karakol's Holy Trinity Cathedral, which found a new function as a ballroom, put to more profane use.

Since independence there has been a renewed church attendance by the country's dwindling Slavic community. In addition there have been a number of missionary and evangelical projects at work in the country, which includes Baptists, Seventh Day Adventists (who have six churches in Bishkek), Korean Presbyterians and Jehovah's Witnesses, who have had some success in converting small numbers of nominally Muslim Kyrgyz to their cause.

Bishkek has a small Catholic diocese that was officially registered in 1969, and a small church, which is attended mostly by ethnic Poles and Germans. Most of

Kyrgyzstan's remaining ethnic Germans are, however, Lutheran Protestants and have their own modest churches in the villages in the Chui valley. A further example of the sort of religious syncretism that is unabashedly practised in Kyrgyzstan is an ethnic Kyrgyz Baptist community in Naryn Oblast where Christian worship takes place using adapted Muslim modes of prayer.

SHAMANISM An earlier shamanistic practice of the Kyrgyz tribes had been a belief in totemism, in which they recognised a spiritual kinship with an animal like a bear or a snake, or a celestial body like the sun or moon. Traces of this survive in Kyrgyz religious practice today, a phenomenon that links to both their nomadic lifestyle and their Siberian origins. Traces of earlier shamanistic practices can also be seen in Kyrgyz cultural items like *shyrdaks* (Kyrgyz rugs), which bear many of the same designs seen on petroglyphs throughout the country.

Many shamanistic beliefs and practices have faded as a result of both Islamic influence and Sovietisation, but others persist as part of the everyday cultural backdrop of Kyrgyz daily life. One such practice is the hanging of an animal carcass or part of an animal (such as a tail) from a tree to render the place – a tree, stream or rock – of special spiritual significance. Another common practice, which extends right across the central Asian world as far west as the Caucasus, is the tradition of tying votive rags to chosen trees, usually close to a stream or a waterfall, or en route to a traditionally holy site like the tomb of a Muslim saint. This common practice, which probably has little more significance to modern practitioners than mere good luck, is undoubtedly an echo of an ancient animistic tradition that worshipped the spirit of the earth rather than a single supreme deity. Also common is the burning of fragrant juniper branches – *archa* – to rid a house or a yurt of bad spirits.

Shamans still exist in Kyrgyz society and there are both men and women – usually referred to as *bakshi* – who practise healing using herbs and chanted incantations. Even today, many Kyrgyz would consider using the services of a *bakshi* if they were ill, perhaps in tandem with Western medicine just to be on the safe side.

BUDDHISM There is a substantial amount of archaeological evidence to confirm that Buddhism was once quite widespread in the territory that is now Kyrgyzstan. The village of Tamga on the southern shore of Lake Issyk-Kul has a carved stone in a valley nearby that has the legend *Om Mani Padme Hum* inscribed in it in Tibetan script. There are more Tibetan inscriptions at Issyk-Ata near Bishkek (which also became the home of a well-known Uzbek female shaman in the 1950s and a place of pilgrimage) and remains of a Buddhist temple at Ak-Beshim near Tokmok. Buddhist practices have little bearing on contemporary Kyrgyzstan but there are small numbers of Kyrgyz in China and the Central Tien Shan region of Kyrgyzstan that continue to observe a form of Tibetan Buddhism rather than Islam.

RELIGIOUS HOLIDAYS The Kyrgyzstan government recognises a number of religious events in its annual calendar. The Muslim feasts of Orozo Ait and Kurban Ait are celebrated at the beginning and end of Ramadan and Orthodox Christmas on January 6 is also recognised. More important than both of these is Nooruz, which corresponds to the spring equinox and which is a very important cultural event that is celebrated throughout central Asia, even Iran, and which dates back to Zoroastrian times.

EDUCATION

Before the Russians came to the region almost all Kyrgyz were illiterate and the only educational facilities that existed were a few Koranic schools, attended by boys only, scattered throughout the territory. With the arrival of Russian colonists at the end of the 19th century, a few 'native' schools were opened for the children of the indigenous population, which taught Russian language and culture to mixed classes of Kyrgyz, Uzbeks, Tatars and Dungans.

After the revolution of 1917, a decree was passed that established the Commission on Enlightenment in the Turkestan Republic, which aimed to extend the educational system in the central Asian region. More schools opened and girls, for the first time, were also eligible to attend. The Soviet system was highly successful and raised education levels dramatically, so that a high degree of literacy was soon attained with levels as high as 97–100%, with 84% of the population completing a secondary level of education.

Despite problems of funding since independence, education continues to be a high government priority, with most 5–17-year-olds attending school. The school year always begins with 'First Bell' (*Pyervi Zvonok*) on 1 September, regardless of whether or not this is a weekday. On this day, when children dress in their very best clothes and bring flowers to school, the streets of even the most isolated of villages are thronged with groups of excited girls with bows in their hair and boys smartly dressed in black suits and ties. The tradition of starting the school year on this day began during the Soviet era, when the first day of term was named the 'Day of Peace'. By convention, all lessons on this day were dedicated to the theme of peace, and this tradition has continued since independence. The school year officially ends on 25 May, a day known as *Posledniye Zvonok* ('Last Bell') in Russian, and summer examinations are taken after this.

As Kyrgyz has become an increasingly important language since independence there have inevitably been shortfalls with provision of adequately trained staff and textbooks for teaching the new language of state. Lack of funding has also meant that many schools are currently in poor physical condition and an overall shortage of suitable buildings means that 37% of students attend schools that operate a shift system. In recent years there has been a decline in educational achievement due to these shortfalls in funding and some schools are pressing for subscriptions from parents to assist with costs. Part of the problem is down to a shortage of teachers, as an estimated 8,000 teachers quit their posts in the immediate post-independence period because of poor salaries and the demands of being expected to work double shifts. Since then, more have emigrated to work abroad, mostly in Russia, but the situation is beginning to stabilise now.

Higher education is a growing sector and there has been a considerable increase in student numbers since independence. On the whole, higher education tends to be more accessible for the urban, wealthier segments of the population. As well as Bishkek, there are universities scattered throughout the country to provide locally based higher education – in Osh, Talas, Jalal-Abad, Batken, Karakol and Naryn. The capital itself has the Bishkek Humanities University, the Turkish-Kyrgyz-Manas University, the Kyrgyz Russian Slavonic University and the American University of Central Asia, amongst others.

CULTURE

TRADITIONAL KYRGYZ CULTURE Kyrgyz nomadic society is traditionally organised into various **clans** and **tribes** (see box, *The Kyrgyz Clan System*, page 19), with clan leadership coming from a *bai* (or *manap*), a chief who makes decisions following consultation with a council of *aksakals* that represent each village (or *ail* – collection of yurts) within the clan. An *aksakal*, quite literally, means a 'white beard', ie: an aged and presumably wise, village elder. The *bai* is not elected but usually earns his position by being the most senior of the *aksakals*, a role in which respect has to be earned for the *bai*'s decisions to carry any weight. Sometimes the position is hereditary but the son would always be required to earn the respect of the clan members, lest his position be usurped by a rival. Any petty tyranny by the *bai* would be to the chief's detriment as the various *ails* that constitute the clan are always free, as nomads not tied to a particular location, to join another tribal group with a less autocratic leader.

Although in traditional Kyrgyz society **women** have rarely held positions of power, there have been exceptions. The most notable of these was Kurmanjan Datka, who took on the leadership of the southern Kyrgyz tribes when her husband, Alymbek Datka, died – there is a statue of her in the centre of Osh. Kurmanjan Datka's place in Kyrgyz history is perhaps the exception that proves the rule, as women in patriarchal Kyrgyz society generally have little influence on decision making other than within the home, and only 4% of the members of Kyrgyzstan's parliament are women.

In the pre-Soviet period, women had a subordinate status that depended exclusively on their fathers, until the time came for a potential husband to offer a **dowry** or *kalym* for them to become a wife. In some cases, the ritual of bride kidnapping took place and there are well-documented accounts that these incidents continue to occur quite frequently even in recent times (see box, *Bride Kidnapping in Kyrgyz Society*, page 29). The *kalym* was, and still is, usually paid in livestock and is viewed as promoting both financial and social ties between the would-be groom and the family of his prospective wife. On some occasions, in order to raise the necessary capital for the *kalym*, a young man will work for his prospective father-in-law for a specified period of time, thus cementing the social bond between the two families even further.

In standard *jailoo* life, everyday tasks are shared between men and women while domestic duties like cooking, cleaning and milking are always performed by women. However, given the liberating nature of the nomadic Kyrgyz lifestyle, women are usually equal partners in practice, even if they are not in status in the eyes of Kyrgyz society.

The long period of Soviet rule brought about far more equality for Kyrgyz women, raising educational levels and life expectations enormously. While many women still have access to higher education and achieve important positions in society, economic pressures and a reversion in some quarters to pre-revolutionary chauvinistic values have meant that there has been a slight reversal of this trend since independence.

The average age for **marriage** between Kyrgyz is around 25 for men and 22 for women. Providing that he is not planning to commit *ala kachuu* (see box, *Bride Kidnapping in Kyrgyz Society*, page 29), when a man decides to marry he goes with his family to visit the home of his prospective bride, where his intention is made known and negotiations begin regarding the *kalym* (bride price) required to marry the girl.

Traditionally, once the *kalym* has been agreed between the groom and the bride's family, the groom gives a present of golden earrings to his future bride and they are considered to be engaged. The wedding takes place as soon as possible afterwards, although it is normally traditional for older brothers to marry before their younger siblings, and a younger brother may have to wait for his older brothers to marry before he can get wed himself.

On the day of the wedding, the bride's female relatives erect a white yurt from which the bride is collected by the groom's party. A ritual called *arkan tosuu* is frequently performed before the ceremony takes place, in which a rope is strung across the road and a ransom demanded for the bride, accompanied by wailing from the bride's female relatives and friends. The ceremony itself usually takes place at a registry office or a wedding palace – a secular inheritance of Soviet times – after which the couple may go to the mosque for a blessing, although sometimes a mullah is invited to the wedding itself in order to bless the union. The ceremony is normally followed by a group promenade in which frequent stops are made for photographs at scenic or historically important spots like war memorials or sculpture parks. The party then proceeds to the reception where everyone present takes turns in expressing their good wishes to the newly wed couple.

After the ceremonial proceedings are completed the groom's family bless the bride by placing a scarf over her head. The bride customarily spends three days with her new family, a period in which she receives visits from well-wishers. Following this, the married couple move to their own home, apart from occasions where it is a youngest son who has married, in which case they will stay with his parents because, as the most junior male offspring, it is his responsibility to care for his parents in old age. The bride herself is not permitted to visit her own parents on her own until a preliminary visit has been made, in which she is accompanied by her new in-laws who offer a present to the bride's mother as recompense for the trouble she went to raising the daughter. After marriage, a daughter-in-law is expected to be subservient to her new family and serve her new parents as dutifully as her husband.

YURT LIFE Before the Soviet period and the collectivisation of a nomadic lifestyle, the yurt – the round, felt-covered tent that has been the traditional dwelling throughout central Asia for centuries – was the centrepiece of Kyrgyz life. Since independence there has been a move back to a nomadic way of life or, as in many cases, a compromise lifestyle in which several months a year are spent grazing livestock at an alpine *jailoo* and the rest settled in a village in the valleys. These days, Russian-made tractors and battered Zhigulis may have replaced the beasts of burden of earlier times, and some yurts may have the dubious benefit of battery-operated television sets, but what is without doubt is that to observe the gentle rhythm of the daily routine at a summer *jailoo* is to witness a way of life that has remained basically unchanged for millennia.

The daily routine starts early at a *jailoo*. Women start cooking breakfast at dawn and, once their menfolk have set off to lead their herds to pasture, they see to their other daily tasks such as cleaning, making *kumys*, fermented mare's milk, and *kajmak* (cream). Rarely do they move far from the yurt, unlike the men who often spend the whole day on horseback with their herds, only returning to the warmth and comfort of the yurt as dusk falls.

The yurt is a unique type of movable dwelling that can be found from Mongolia in the northeast to Turkish Anatolia in the southwest, but they are most numerable in the lands of the Kyrgyz, Kazakhs and Mongols. Yurts have been around for thousands of years; they were described by Marco Polo on his travels in central Asia, who was astonished to see nomads travelling the land with their homes disassembled in carts.

The structure of a yurt is simple but highly effective: a criss-cross framework of wooden laths, rather like a wall-trellis for climbing garden plants; a thick felt covering to keep the elements out; and a heavy wooden *tunduk* that is the centrepiece for the wooden struts that hold the roof in place and that surround the smoke-hole. The basis behind the yurt's design is that of strength, warmth and portability; their design is such that they may be taken down and reassembled within a matter of hours, and that the materials, although bulky and heavy, can be carried on the backs of a few horses, or more likely on a trailer tugged along by a Russian car.

Erecting a yurt Yurts, which in Kyrgyzstan are usually referred to as *bozoy* ('grey house') because of the grey sheep's wool that was used to make the poorer quality

The tradition of bride theft in Kyrgyzstan is not as common as it was in pre-Soviet times but it has by no means died out. The practice, known as *ala kachuu* ('to take and flee'), dates back to times when the Kyrgyz were fully nomadic, and similar customs are also found in other nomadic societies, like that of the Kazakhs. Today bride kidnapping is technically illegal – it was outlawed in Soviet times – and even in the past the tradition was usually frowned upon and often dealt with harshly by tribal councils. Notwithstanding this, the practice was relatively common in Kyrgyzstan's more isolated communities in the past and, with few victim families willing to bring charges against the kidnappers, the tradition of *ala kachuu* persists in the more remote regions of the country.

The kidnapping process is simplicity itself: a would-be Kyrgyz groom simply summons some accomplices to help him capture his chosen bride. He then carries her across the threshold of his family home, where the groom's female relatives attempt to persuade the kidnapped girl to accept the groom by tying on a bride's headscarf – a ritualised way of proclaiming the pair to be married.

In practice, the execution of the tradition can range from a purely ritualistic display in which a consenting couple put on an act simply for tradition's sake, to an almost caveman-like act of violent abduction. If the act is consensual between both families, it can hardly be considered a true kidnapping, even if the woman is supposed to put up some symbolic resistance, but on the other occasions, when the act is accompanied by physical violence, or even rape, the kidnapping is a terrifying ordeal for the victim.

The motivation behind the practice encompasses a spectrum of explanations that range from the mere observation of a time-honoured tradition to avoidance of, or inability to pay, bride price, to evading the wishes of the bride's family who may not approve of the match. Kidnapping may even occur in circumstances in which the groom's first choice of bride has already been kidnapped by another party. In the worst case scenario of an unfortunate woman being taken unwillingly by force, the victim may well find herself in the invidious position of being unable to return to her own family because of the disgrace her unplanned kidnapping has brought upon them. In such cases, she has little choice but to accept her fate. Similarly, would-be brides who do manage to return to their own families after abduction often have to bare the brunt of malicious rumours spread by the family of the failed kidnapper who, equally, are incensed and shamed by an abduction that has been unsuccessful.

The number of such forced marriages appear to have increased in recent years, with some estimates suggesting that as many as one-third of Kyrgyz women become married as a result of non-consensual abduction by their husbands. The same statistics point to the practice being most common in the north and centre of the country and in almost two-thirds of kidnapping cases the stolen brides were unwilling victims rather than consensual parties. Drunkenness on the part of the groom and his cohorts appears to play a significant part too – hardly ideal conditions for the setting up of a successful marriage. Unsurprisingly, many such marriages end up in divorce; far more than in the case of those traditional marriages that have a negotiated *kalym* agreed between two families.

A documentary film on this practice, *Bride Kidnapping in Kyrgyzstan*, was made in 2005 by film maker Petr Lom. The documentary met with a considerable degree of controversy, mainly because of ethical concerns about the filming of actual kidnappings. For more information on this topic see *Bride Kidnapping, Benign Custom or Savage Tradition?* at http://faculty.philau.edu/kleinbachr/freedom.htm.

Background Information CULTURE

felt of the past, are constructed entirely without the use of nails – instead, all of the wooden members are lashed together with leather straps. The setting-up procedure begins with the door frame (the *bosogo*), which is oriented to the southeast to catch the morning light. The round trellis wall (*kerege*) is attached to this, supported at intervals by long wooden poles, usually of birch or poplar, called *kanat*. Once the circular wall of *kerege* and *kanat* has been erected, the wooden struts that support the cupola are inserted into place and the *tunduk* raised and set in place. The *tunduk* is central to the entire structure and without doubt the most valuable and least-easily replaced part of the yurt framework.

With all of the skeletal structure in place, the outer coverings of felt matting can be draped over the framework – successive layers that are called *chiy, kiyiz, tuurduk* and *jabuu*. The final layer is folded back from the *tunduk* in daytime, unless it is raining, to allow air to flow through the structure; in cold and inclement weather it is kept tightly shut. A final touch, if the yurt is new, is to toss a sheep's head through the *tunduk* as a gesture of good luck.

Yurt interior geography The yurt interior is laid out according to an age-old pattern. The fireplace goes directly below the *tunduk*, although many modern yurts have a flap at the side for the chimney of a stove that is set to the side. Behind the fireplace, opposite the entrance, is the stack of blankets, quilts and pillows known as the *juk*, which is piled high on top of chests and serves as an indicator of wealth. In front of the *juk* is the most prestigious position in the yurt, the *tyor*, which is reserved for the head of the family or guests of honour such as *aksakals* and, inevitably, curious Western visitors. The less favourable, draughtier area close to the entrance is the space designated for the women of the household. Right of the entrance is the female half of the yurt, the *eptchi zhak*, where tasks such as needlework and dishwashing take place, and where knitting, embroidery and decorative bric-a-brac are kept. The opposite side, the *er-shak*, is the reserve of men and is the area where manly possessions like whips, knives and harnesses are kept.

KYGYZ TRADITIONAL DRESS The most visible feature of traditional Kyrgyz clothing as worn by men is the distinctive white felt hat, the *kalpak*, which tells, without any shadow of doubt, that the wearer is a Kyrgyz. This felt trilby worn by many Kyrgyz men, young and old (but generally older) is made up of four panels of white felt with a tassel dangling from the top. Traditional patterns in black are stitched to the panels in decoration, which are highly stylised and echo the sort of ancient designs that are seen in *shyrdaks* (traditional Kyrgyz rugs – see page 31).

In normal use, the brim is turned up all the way round, but there are great variations in the way that *kalpaks* may be worn, which range from the rakish to the comical. Despite its awkward shape, Kyrgyz men who sport *kalpaks* tend to keep their headgear on without trouble even in challenging circumstances, such as climbing into a small car or galloping at speed on a horse.

The traditional four-panel *kalpak*, which is said to resemble the shape of Khan Tengri peak in the Central Tien Shan, is by far the most widespread, but in recent years variations on the *kalpak* theme have emerged in which the same traditional designs have been adopted for brimless skullcaps (the traditional shape is quite hopeless for performing standard Muslim prayer rituals) and even baseball caps.

The traditional Kyrgyz headgear is certainly practical – it provides shade in hot weather and warmth in cold – and is such an icon of Kyrgyz culture that a number of traditions concerning the wearing of them have permeated Kyrgyz folklore. In fact, the hats are so iconic that in Kyrgyzstan even bus shelters are sometimes constructed in the shape of a *kalpak*. It is said that you should never kill a man who is wearing a *kalpak* – certainly sound advice – and that, like bread, they should never be placed on the ground. At night they should be removed for sleep and placed beside the head, never next to the feet.

The traditional coat worn by the Kyrgyz – the *chapan* – is no longer as commonly worn as it used to be, having been replaced in the main by leather jackets and Russian-style sports gear for many younger Kyrgyz. It is, however, quite commonly worn by older men in rural areas. The *chapan*, designed for warmth and comfort whilst on horseback, is a type of three-quarter length coat that is padded like a dressing gown. In some cases a felt cloak is worn over the top of it, while underneath an open, cotton shirt called a *jegde* is worn, with baggy trousers that are sometimes fur-lined in winter (during which season the customary *kalpak* is replaced by a fur hat called a *tebetey* or a *telpek*). Light leather boots are worn on the feet, over which rubber slip-on over-boots are pulled on, to be removed whenever a dwelling is entered.

Women's dress tends to consist of long dresses in rich dark colours such as maroon, although the colour of preference varies from tribe to tribe. Most married women wear headscarves, which in summer at least is tied at the back of the head to expose the neck. The traditional Kyrgyz woman's costume of a tall headdress and white veil that surrounds the face and neck is now only usually worn on special occasions, such as horse sports and folklore events staged for tourists, and sometimes at weddings.

KYRGYZ CRAFTS Kyrgyzstan has a thriving craft tradition that mostly utilises raw materials that are produced by the livestock central to the Kyrgyz nomadic way of life – wool and leather. The handicrafts they produce reflect the ancient traditions of their nomadic way of life in both their design and the function that they serve. As a consequence, Kyrgyz handicrafts are essentially portable items that are produced without the need for complex tools or machinery. The most well-known of these handicrafts is undoubtedly the appliqué felt object that is known as a *shyrdak*.

Shyrdaks The *shyrdak* is the Kyrgyz equivalent of a rug or a carpet – a thick, patterned piece of felt that is usually rectangular in shape. They serve a wide range of purposes from floor coverings and wall hangings to seat and table covers, and more than any other domestic object, it is *shyrdaks* that characterise a typical Kyrgyz home, whether it is an isolated yurt on a lonely *jailoo* or a two-bedroom Soviet apartment in town.

Shyrdaks are made up of different pieces of coloured felt, which are arranged into patterns using a variety of traditional shapes that represent stylised themes from nature. Many of the traditional motifs used – birds' claws, flying birds, mountain peaks, *kumys* containers – would formerly have had a symbolic meaning (ie: ram's horns would represent masculine power and wealth), but most of these are largely forgotten now.

Most modern *shyrdaks* are brightly coloured affairs made with chemical dyes, but this was not the case up until the 1960s when most *shyrdaks* were produced in just two colours. To appeal to that sector of the tourist market that prefers 'natural', organically produced handicrafts, there has been a revival of the older, monochromatic tradition in recent years but, in catering for all tastes, these are produced alongside gaudily-coloured pieces that would rarely have had a place in a traditional Kyrgyz home in the past. Kyrgyzstan produces a range of different patterns and styles of *shyrdak* according to geographical region but, as a rule, those made in the Naryn area are widely considered to be among the finest.

The making of a *shyrdak* is extremely labour intensive – a slow, tiring process that requires both co-operation and considerable patience. Customarily, a group of women will work together to create a *shyrdak*, the production being a focused, but sociable, occasion that strengthens friendships and family bonds within the village or *ail*. First, the felt itself must be prepared. The wool is cleaned by laboriously beating it over a mesh. Once this has been done, the wool is spread out on a special mat made of reed (*chiy*) and hot water poured over it. The wool is then rolled up tightly inside the mat and this is rolled and trodden for several hours to ensure that the wool strands have fused into a single layer. The mat is unrolled, more boiling water is poured onto the wool, and the whole process repeated with the mat being rolled even more tightly, this time by the line of kneeling women working it. Once this is complete the felt is unrolled and allowed to dry in the sun.

When the felt is dry the *shyrdak* is created by loosely stitching two square pieces of coloured felt together; an outline of a pattern is then made with chalk and this is pressed into the second piece of felt and outlined as a mirror reflection of the first. The process is repeated by further stitching and folding to replicate the design and create a symmetrical pattern. When the pattern is complete, the outline is cut out with a sharp knife and the pieces sewn together; larger *shyrdaks* are made by joining several smaller pieces together. Finally, a border is added – often of black and white triangles – and another piece of felt is added as a backing to give extra thickness.

Ala-kiyiz Ala-kiyiz are felt carpets that are produced in a similar way to *shyrdaks* but without the use of stitching. Instead of sewing appliqué motifs to a backing, *ala-kiyiz* are created by pressing different coloured wools together on a felt background and then wetting and rolling on a reed mat in the same way that the felt for *shyrdaks* is made. The wool that is used is not spun into threads but kept loose. One colour is chosen as the background and this is spread on a background of felt on a *chiy* mat. Clumps of other colours are then laid down to create a pattern. This is covered with a cloth and sprayed with hot water before being rolled inside the mat as in the making of a *shyrdak*. Repetition of this process ensures that the wool fibres become firmly melded together and the multi-coloured felt created remains whole after it is dried in the sun.

As no stitching is used to hold these carpets together the end result tends not to be quite as strong as a *shyrdak,* but the advantage is that they can be manufactured more quickly. Also, because of the inevitable imprecision of their design, *ala-kiyiz* tend on the whole to be more individualistic than most *shyrdaks*. Some contemporary *ala-kiyiz* designs, instead of having a symmetrical pattern, use the differing colours to create an image – typically a landscape scene – that can serve as a wall hanging.

Tush kiyiz Tush kiyiz are wall hangings made from embroidered cloth in which chain stitching is used to create a montage of stylised natural shapes. Traditionally, *tush kiyiz* are sewn by grandmothers for young married couples and they often have the names of the couple sewn into the design. Tush kiyiz can sometimes be large enough to cover a wall, while most are smaller and are often used to decorate the headboard of a bed.

Kurak Another typical Kyrgyz embroidered handicraft is *kurak* or patchwork. This utilises scraps and oddments of material to create objects such as head coverings and other items of clothing, babies' blankets, crib covers and saddle bags. The patchworks follow two basic styles: either an assemblage of squares and triangles or one made up of a selection of long strips of material.

In Kyrgyzstan, *kurak* is associated with magical powers and patchwork pieces are thought to bring luck and guard against evil. Sometimes special rituals are connected with patchwork pieces, such as the gown that newborn babies traditionally wear after 40 days, which is created from 40 pieces of material collected by the mother from the yurts of the *ail* – a sort of collective village blessing in the form of a garment. Dowries, too, usually contain items of *kurak*, which are made from scraps of material collected from the family and community and are intended to pass on good fortune to the newly wedded couple.

Other crafts In the past, **weaving** was an important Kyrgyz craft, but with the ready availability of inexpensive factory-made goods the tradition is far less common these days. Weaving used to be a summer, fair weather activity that took place outdoors and involved only women. The wool was collected, cleaned and sorted before being spun into yarn. Natural dyes were used to colour the yarn before it was woven on a horizontal loom to produce a long, narrow strip of fabric. Sometimes, woven strips were sewn together to make rugs and coverings.

Carpet-making takes place mostly in the south of the country, in the Osh region. It usually uses woollen yarn (often from a camel), but sometimes cotton – in plentiful supply in the Fergana Valley – is used to weave the piles.

Leatherwork was a well-developed craft in the past and superb examples may be seen in some of Kyrgyzstan's cultural museums. The leather used would come either from the skins of nomads' livestock – cattle, goats, sheep, horses – or from animals that had been caught on hunting expeditions, like ibex and gazelle. Because of the Kyrgyz nomadic lifestyle most of the objects produced would have a practical use, like harnesses, whips, footwear and clothing. In addition, everyday objects such as *kumys* containers, with their distinctive anchor form that has two upturned compartments at the base, would also be produced from leather. Unlike the majority of craft activities, leatherworking was carried out by men and women alike.

Woodcarving was also important in the past, particularly in relation to *jailoo* life, in which the yurt would require a number of wooden chests for the storage of clothes and linen, as well as a *pishpek* (churn) for making *kumys*, fermented mare's milk, and wooden implements for cooking. Kyrgyz musical instruments such as *komuz* also require woodcarving skills in their manufacture.

KYRGYZ CUISINE The Kyrgyz are a nomadic people involved with raising livestock, mostly sheep, and so it is inevitable that they have evolved a cuisine in which animal produce features heavily, and cultivated vegetables have little part to play.

Although there has been some influence from the cuisine of the settled people of the region – Uzbeks and Russians – and from cooking traditions that have been brought through the region by Turks, Persians, Chinese and Arabs on the old trade routes, on the whole Kyrgyz food tends to be robust and fat-laden and similar to that of the other upland parts of the central Asian region.

More than anything else, most Kyrgyz greatly enjoy animal fat, particularly that of fat-tailed sheep, and from the Kyrgyz perspective the more animal fat a dish contains, the better. Such a high-fat diet suits a tough, physical lifestyle in a region where winters are long, cold and harsh, although the same diet may not be at all appropriate for those of a more temperate or Mediterranean climate. Certainly, low-cholesterol cuisine is not a characteristic of Kyrgyz cooking. A typical Kyrgyz cook book, if such a thing existed, would probably begin most recipes with 'First kill your sheep…'.

In Kyrgyz culture there are a number of special dishes that are associated with special events and religious holidays and this, coupled with a tradition of hospitality, means that some dishes are produced with great ceremony given the occasion. Kyrgyz hospitality sets great store in providing food for honoured guests. Meals are traditionally laid out on a large cloth on the ground called a *dostorkon*.

Food is handled with the right hand only, in typical Muslim fashion, and legs and feet are tucked away from the food, as to have feet pointing at the food is considered the height of rudeness. The end of the meal is signalled by the *omin* – a very characteristic gesture that is used throughout Muslim central Asia in which the hands are drawn down the face as if washing and the word *omin* ('Amen!') is spoken.

Beshbarmak is perhaps the quintessential Kyrgyz dish. Its name means 'five fingers', an indication that it is meant to be eaten with the fingers rather than with cutlery. A sheep is killed, butchered and boiled in a pot. The bones and meat are then presented to the guests. The best pieces are presented to the most honoured guests, with the head – and eyes – going to the lucky guest of honour. Traditionally, the *aksakals* are given pieces of the thigh bone, while female elders get the tail fat – the highly prized ***kuirik*** that delights all Kyrgyz but terrifies most Westerners. Leg and shoulder pieces go to the younger adults, while some of the remaining meat is separated from the bone and mixed with broth and a special sort of flat boiled noodles. *Beshbarmak* is very much a home-produced, special-occasion food, but sometimes the dish is offered in Kyrgyz restaurants, in which case it usually just means meat and noodles rather than a whole boiled sheep.

Other mutton dishes that are essentially Kyrgyz, with little Russian or outside influence, are ***samsa*** – meat dumplings that are baked in an oven; ***manti*** – steamed or fried dough parcels filled with meat; and ***kuirik boor*** – fried sheep's tail fat and liver.

As well as mutton, **horse meat** is also highly prized, although it tends to be reserved for more special occasions. One popular dish is ***chuchuk***, horse-meat sausages, which are considered to be the ideal accompaniment for vodka drinking sessions. Other meats such as chicken and beef are less popular and are rarely eaten by Kyrgyz (although they are easily found in restaurants). At animal markets, horses for horse meat are sold separately from those intended for riding, as different criteria are at play here. Pork products are not eaten, although these can be found in Russian, Chinese and Korean restaurants.

Meat aside, it is with some of its **dairy products** that the Kyrgyz diet really achieves its individuality, as there seems to be a strong preference for a sour, curdled milk flavour that is anathema to the average Western palate. ***Korut*** are one such example: small balls of sheep's milk cheese that taste rather like solidified – and very sour – yoghurt. *Korut* are extremely popular and are definitely the travel snack of preference for most Kyrgyz. Another sour milk product that is highly esteemed is the infamous ***kumys***, a lightly alcoholic drink that is brewed from fermented horse milk and that has an inordinate number of health-promoting and life-affirming properties associated with it (see box, *Kumys – Horse Milk For Your Health*, page 35). Other typical Kyrgyz drinks include *bozo*, another mildly alcoholic drink made from boiled fermented millet, and *maksym*, a wheat-based drink that is often referred to as *shoro* after the brand name of its commercially manufactured form.

Bread is central to Kyrgyz culture and is always afforded great respect. It should never be thrown away or tossed on the floor, and when it is offered to a guest it is imperative that they should at least take a small piece rather than refuse outright. At meals bread is usually torn into pieces by the host once it is brought to the table (to indicate that it is to share). Bread should never be placed face down on the table, ie: with the un-patterned side face up.

Homemade bread, *nan*, is invariably unleavened: the flat, round loaves that are found everywhere are often generically described by their Russian name – *lepyoshka*. Of these, *kalama* is the commonest, while another type of bread, *kattama*, is richer and made up of layers of rolled dough separated by butter. *Boorsok* are deep fried pieces of dough that are often provided in large numbers at feasts and special occasions. For a full account of food in Kyrgyzstan, see *Food and Drink*, page 71.

It may not seem the most obvious of alcoholic beverages but fermented mare's milk is a Kyrgyz speciality and a much-loved tipple throughout the country. *Kumys* is made by storing mare's milk in a specially made and smoke-cleaned container, a *chinach*, for a day or two, before it is mixed with fresh milk and allowed to ferment in a warm spot. This is then churned in a special cylindrical wooden vessel called a *pishpek* to produce a mildly alcoholic drink with a high lactic acid content. The finished product is traditionally stored in anchor-shaped leather bottles called *kookor*, although in reality it often gets no further than a bucket from which it is decanted for use. *Kumys* keeps for just a few days before it goes off completely and so its manufacture only takes place at those times of year when mares are actively lactating.

As a by-product of horse rearing, *kumys* is very much a product of the Kyrgyz *jailoo* and in season it is widely sold from yurts at road sides to willing customers who rate the drink far higher than modern upstarts such as imported Russian beer or Coca-Cola.

The health promoting properties of *kumys* have long been established, both in Kyrgyz folklore and by 19th-century Russian scientists who firmly believed in the drink's restorative properties and used it to treat a variety of diseases. Both Maxim Gorky and Lev Tolstoy took *kumys* rest cures at Russian sanatoria in the late 19th century and Anton Chekov, who had long suffered from tuberculosis, attended a *kumys* cure resort for a period in 1901, although in his case he was not cured. News of the miracle cure spread far beyond Russia's shores, and in 1877 a treatise was published in the USA that extolled the health-giving virtues of the drink (*The Great Russian Remedy for Wasting, Debilitating and Nervous Diseases*), which dubbed the product 'Milk Champagne'.

Despite what some Kyrgyz might claim, *kumys* is found not only in Kyrgyzstan but also throughout the upland areas of the central Asian region. It has also been popular in Mongolia since time immemorial, where it no doubt accompanied the horseback armies of Genghis Khan on their plundering attacks throughout the region.

Indeed, it would appear that the drinking of *kumys* has been around for as long as man has had an association with horses. Hippocrates is said to have declared it to be a drink 'of longevity, joy and mental agility' and Herodotus in his 5th-century BC chronicle, *Histories*, describes the Scythian processing of mare's milk. The Flemish Franciscan monk William of Rubruck, who travelled through the central Asian region in the 13th century, described the affect of *kumys* thus: 'it makes the inner man most joyful and also intoxicates weak heads, and greatly provokes urine'. In actual fact, *kumys* is not particularly intoxicating, having an average alcohol content of just 2%. Nevertheless, it is an acquired taste for most Westerners and drinking *kumys* can sometimes have a deleterious effect on the unprepared, making those unused to it become suddenly nauseous.

Background Information CULTURE

THE MANAS LEGEND Of all their legends and folk tales, nothing sums up the story-telling culture of the Kyrgyz people better than the thousand-year-old Manas epic, which in fact predates the Kyrgyz as a unified people and offers a historical-mythological background to their genesis.

Manas is a 10th-century legendary hero of the Kyrgyz, and the Manas epic is a long, complex cycle of legends associated with the exploits of a heroic khan or *batyr* who is deemed to have possessed all the valiant qualities associated with the Kyrgyz character. The complete cycle is estimated to be 20 times longer than Homer's *Odyssey* and *Iliad* combined, and about twice as long as the *Mahabharata*. Rather than being read as a text, the Manas legends are traditionally recited and embellished from memory by narrators called *manaschi* who are highly revered as story-tellers (*akyns*) in Kyrgyz society. The *Epic of Manas* is made up of three parts that concern the legendary hero's life and legacy: that of Manas himself, his son Semetey and his grandson, Seitek. As an oral tradition the legend has survived for centuries without being written down and *manaschi* have always been valued as much for their improvisational skill as they have been for their powers of recall. Fragments of the legend were finally written down for the first time in Russian in 1858 but the epic was not recorded in its entirety until the 1920s.

Historically, Manas was a Kyrgyz chieftain, or *khan*, who came from the Talas region, where his mausoleum or *gumbez* still stands. The epic's narrative tells of his various heroic feats in fighting off Uyghur invaders and defending his homeland, as well as his marriage to Kanykey, the daughter of a Samarkand khan, and the birth of their son, Semetey, and his subsequent exploits.

To sum up the 1,000-year-old-epic in one paragraph: Manas is said to have had tens of thousands of horsemen at his disposal and a personal guard of 40 warriors that represented the best of the various Kyrgyz tribes, and who would later become his personal friends and close companions. Manas was eventually killed by Kongurbai, a Chinese leader, and following his death the Kyrgyz tribes were led by his younger brothers, Abyke and Kobosh. The brothers wanted to marry Manas's widow Kanykey but she escaped with her son Semetey to Bokhara, where her father ruled as khan. When Semetey grew to become a man he returned to the land of his birth to avenge his father's death. Semetey managed to defeat his uncles in battle, but those of his father's original 40 companions that had survived would not serve him after being captured and so he had them beheaded.

The narrators of the legend – ***manaschi*** – are said to be born into their profession rather than made, chosen in dreams by visitations from Manas's spirit. As *akyns* (story tellers) dedicated to recounting the legends in time-honoured fashion, they have a vitally important role in keeping Kyrgyz culture alive. It is a calling that requires a great deal of devotion and responsibility as, apart from having to learn the world's longest epic by heart, they have a duty to pass it on to others and cannot refuse if asked to recount it.

The role of *manaschi* also calls for considerable dramatic, linguistic and people-handling skills in order to keep an audience fully engaged and stimulated. Expert *manaschi* are often revered by their audience as having considerable power, and a skilled practitioner is said to be able to make the story come alive for his audience, even for foreigners who cannot understand the language.

Some 20th-century *manaschi* who have become nationally famous include Sagymbay Orozbakov (1876–1930) who began reciting the Manas epic when he was 15 years old and was said to be able recount the classic version of nearly 200,000 lines; Seydene Moldoke-kyzy (born 1922), a rare female *manaschi*; and Toktogul Satilganov (1861–1933), Togoluk Moldo (1860–1942) and Sayakbay Karalaev (1894–1971, dubbed 'the Homer of the 20th century') who all appear on current Kyrgyzstan banknotes and often have streets named after them.

The *manaschi* tradition almost died out in the Soviet period, as much as a result of vastly improved literacy as it was of state disapproval. Since independence there has been a renewed interest in the tradition, partly prompted by the considerable government expenditure that accompanied the Manas epic's 1,000th anniversary celebrations.

In recent years, the Manas tradition had been brought up to date with surprising ease, with books, films and even television serials making an appearance. Some contemporary *manaschi* have toured abroad and, although the tradition is no longer passed on orally as it was in former times, there are now *manaschi* schools and competitions in which young bards can compete for approval by a panel of experienced *manaschi*.

Despite uncertainties concerning the legend's true age, 1995 was declared the **1,000th anniversary of the Manas epic** by UNESCO and internationally recognised celebrations were held throughout Kyrgyzstan in that year. An architectural complex to commemorate the occasion was built in the Kyrgyz capital and a new museum dedicated to the Manas legend was opened next to the mausoleum reported to have built for Manas by his wife Kanykey near the northwestern town of Talas.

For a translated selection of tales from the Manas epic look at: www.silkroad foundation.org/toc/index.html.

MODERN KYRGYZ LITERATURE   The most celebrated Kyrgyz writer without a doubt is **Chingiz Aitmatov,** who was born in Sheker near Talas in December 1928. Aitmatov's parents were both civil servants and his father was arrested and charged with 'bourgeois nationalism' in 1937 and secretly executed as part of the Chong-Tash massacre of that year.

While working as a journalist for the Moscow newspaper *Pravda* he began writing fiction. His first work in the Kyrgyz language was *White Rain* in 1954, followed by the better known novella *Djamila* in 1958, a love story, which won him the Lenin Prize a few years later in 1963, the same year that he published his collection of short stories, *Tales of the Mountains and Steppes*. These works were succeeded with further short novels – *Farewell, Gulsary* in 1966, for which he was awarded the State Prize for Literature in 1968, and *The White Steamship* in 1970 – and a play, *The Ascent of Mount Fuji*, in 1973. But it was not until 1980 that his best known work, *The Day Lasts More Than a Hundred Years*, was published, having first been serialised in the controversial Russian literary magazine *Novy Mir*.

The book's action takes place over the course of a single day and involves a railwayman living at a remote station on the edge of the Kazakh desert who is obliged to deal with the death of a colleague and bury him in the traditional Islamic fashion. The novel has an off-kilter science fiction subplot that involves two cosmonauts on a space station, an American and a Soviet, who make contact with intelligent life on another planet. The link between the two plots is the location of a Soviet space launch site close to the lonely railway station of the protagonist. The book is also peppered with strands of Turkic and central Asian mythology running through it, in particular the phenomenon of a *mankurt*, the dreadful fate that befalls a man – or a people – if they forget their language, culture and history.

Another full-length novel, *The Place of the Skull*, was published in 1988, and tells the tale of a she-wolf and her cubs and their interrelationship with human lives along with a subplot that involves drug trafficking. The theme of animal–human interactions is a common one in Aitmatov's work: a deranged camel is a central theme in *The Day Lasts More Than a Hundred Years* and *Farewell, Gulsary* has a stallion as one of the two central characters.

Chingiz Aitmatov is currently the Kyrgyz ambassador to the European Union, NATO, UNESCO and the Benelux countries.

KYRGYZ CINEMA   Although Soviet film-makers produced films in other parts of central Asia as far back as the 1920s, the first feature film to come out of Kyrgyzstan itself was in 1955, when Vasily Pronin directed *Saltanat*, although this was essentially a Russian production featuring a local subject.

The first home-grown Kyrgyz film to appear was *My Mistake*, which appeared two years later in 1957. Larissa Shepitko and Andrei Konchalovsky adapted a work by Chingiz Aitmatov, *Shepitko Heat*, in 1963 and this and *The First Teacher* by Andrei

Konchalovsky (1965) paved the way for later Kyrgyzstan cinema by turning poor production values and a documentary tradition to aesthetic advantage.

Another film maker to emerge during this period was Tolomush Okeyev who, like the Kyrgyz writer Chingiz Aitmatov, told his stories through the landscapes they were set in, producing minimalist works with eco-political themes like *The Fierce One* (1973), scripted by Andrei Konachalovsky, *There Are Horses* (1965), a beautiful, ten-minute documentary that captures the life-cycle of horses, and *The Snow Leopard's Descendant* (1984).

Since independence, the best known film to come out of Kyrgyzstan up until now is Aktan Abdykalykov's 1998 *Beshkempir* (Five Grandmothers), titled *The Adopted Son* in Anglophone countries, which concerns the life of a foundling adopted by five old women in a Kyrgyz village. It won the Silver Leopard Prize at the Locarno Film Festival of that year. The film was shot in black and white with occasional short colour sequences, and documents several Kyrgyz customs such as funerals and engagement ceremonies.

Another contemporary Kyrgyz director is Marat Saralu, whose 2001 debut, *My Brother Silk Road*, is an evocative modern-day journey through Kyrgyzstan that has two young boys and a girl boarding a train to cross the territory of the old Silk Road: a slow, bittersweet journey that is tinged with nostalgia and longing as it examines both the future and past of the country of their birth.

KYRGYZ MUSIC Kyrgyz traditional music is mostly played on a three-stringed, guitar-like instrument called a *komuz*. The instrument, usually made of apricot or juniper wood, is strummed rhythmically and is either played alone or used as accompaniment to singing or the narration of an *akyn*. An instrument that is often used in conjunction with the *komuz* is the *temir komuz*, a mouth harp that produces an evocative metallic drone. The *temir komuz* ('iron komuz') – or *ooz komuz* ('mouth' komuz') – is usually played by women.

Another typical Kyrgyz instrument is the *kyl kyyak*, a two-string fiddle made from apricot wood. The bow is made from horsehair and the strings are not pressed to the fingerboard but touched delicately to produce a muted tone. Both the *komuz* and the *kyl kyyak* are pictured on the reverse of the Kyrgyzstan 1som banknote. Various flutes and drums are also occasionally used in traditional music, especially in larger ensembles. The *sybyzgy* is a side-blown flute and the *surnai* is a reed instrument closely related to the *shenai* of the Middle East and Indian subcontinent, which is a little like a rudimentary clarinet. The *kerney* is a brass instrument, occasionally made out of goat's horns, that is a distant relative of the trumpet. Percussion instruments tend to be associated with the shamanistic practices of *bakshis* rather than story telling *akyns*. The *dobulba* is a frame drum played with the hands, while the *asa-tayak* is a baton-shaped piece of wood that has bells attached to it.

Kyrgyz traditional music can be divided into two basic categories: *kyy*, which is purely instrumental music and *yr*, vocal music. The playing of instrumental music sometimes features Jimi Hendrix-style trickery that includes playing the instrument over the shoulder or between the knees. *Komuz* players in particular often demonstrate a degree of dexterity and instrumental virtuosity that is at odds with the rudimentary nature of the instrument itself. Rarely having a sound-hole, the *komuz* is perhaps a little too quiet to do itself justice in most circumstances unless amplification is used.

The vocal tradition, *yr*, which covers poetry and story-telling as well as singing, is performed by singer-composers (*akyns*) who have the skill of being able to compose fairly spontaneously on any given topic, rather like calypso singers of the Caribbean region. Most *akyns* have a solid repertoire of well-known songs (as well as a supply of stories, folk tales and extracts from the Manas epic) but are able to extemporise as circumstances dictate.

Vocal performances in the Kyrgyz folk tradition are often characterised by the ability of the performer to hold a note for impressively long intervals. As elsewhere, unrequited love is a common theme; one much-loved standard is *Alymkan*, a ballad of the traditional repertoire that speaks of love for a village beauty who was married off to a village chief in the singer's absence.

KYRGYZ HORSE SPORTS Horses are central to the traditional Kyrgyz way of life and so it is natural that the most important sports activities in Kyrgyz culture all take place on horseback. Most of the activities mentioned below take place at tournaments held on special occasions throughout the year, particularly *Nooruz* on 21 March and Independence Day on the last day of August. Horse games also take place at the more informal *chabana* (cowboy) festivals that are not fixed events, but which take place at a pre-arranged location at a time that largely depends on the harvest and the pressures of work of the participants.

At chabysh This is a long-distance race that involves experienced riders and horses that are at least three years old. The race is generally held in connection with a public holiday or a festival, and the distant raced ranges between 4 and 50km, but is usually in the region of 20–30km. Although in the past participants included boys as young as ten, these days only those older than 13 are allowed to compete. The name *at chabysh* is now also given to an official annual cultural and sporting festival that is held in Bishkek and at Lake Issyk-Kul in autumn.

Dzorgosalysh These are horse races that are run at a gallop over a short distance in which speed is the essential ingredient, rather than endurance as in the case of *at chabysh*.

Jumby atmai This horseback sport involves shooting at a target whilst in motion, either with a bow and arrow or a rifle. Another variation that utilises similar equestrian skills is *tiyin enmei*, in which coins are picked up from the ground at a gallop.

Kyz-kumay *Kyz-kumay* ('kiss the girl') or bride-chasing has evolved from a practice that was once part of the traditional Kyrgyz wedding ritual. The object is for a male rider (the groom) to attempt to catch up with a young horsewoman who represents the bride so that he can kiss her. The groom is put at a disadvantage by being given the slower horse and, in addition, the bride is allowed to use a whip to defend herself from her pursuer.

Kyz-dzharysh These are horse races in which only women and girls are allowed to participate.

Oodarysh This is essentially a horseback wrestling competition in which two riders do their utmost to pull their opponent off their horse and throw him to the ground.

Ulak tartysh Otherwise known as *kok-boru* ('grey wolf'), this team game is the Kyrgyz version of the game of *buzkashi* that is played in other parts of central Asia, particularly northern Afghanistan. The name is said to have come from wolf attacks on herds of cattle that grazed in the mountain valleys of Kyrgyzstan. When they saw wolves attack their herds the *djigits* (horse riders) would chase them away then beat them with sticks when they fell. The game eventually evolved as *djigits* tried to snatch the wolf's body away from one another in good-natured competition.

The game is played with a goat or calf carcass and loosely resembles a cross between polo and rugby. The object of the game is to grab the carcass from players of the opposing team and then pitch it into a target circle marked on the ground. *Ulak tartysh* is a rough, highly competitive game with players using more or less any tricks at their disposal to thwart their opponents. Because of this, participants usually wear heavy clothing and protective headgear (ex-Soviet tank helmets are a popular accessory) to cushion themselves from the whips and boots of the opposing team.

There are two principal forms of the game – *Tudabarai* and *Qarajai*. In the former, the simplest version, the goal is to grab the carcass and merely clear it of other players; in the more complex *Qarajai* version it is necessary to carry the carcass around a marker before depositing it in the scoring circle. Otherwise, the rules of the game are few. Teams must be of equal size – in formal competitions they are usually of four riders. Players may not tie the carcass to their saddles; horses are not permitted to rear up and you are not allowed to grab the reins of your opponent. The playing field is roughly 300m long by 150m wide and competition games are divided into three periods of 20 minutes each.

NATURAL HISTORY AND CONSERVATION

With a wide variety of habitats, which range from temperate grassland to high mountain meadows, and conifer forest to cold steppe, Kyrgyzstan has an immense wealth of both flora and fauna. Overall, Kyrgyzstan has about 3% of the total animal species and 2% of the flora found in the world – an impressive figure for a small country that occupies just 0.13% of the world's land area. More importantly, with some highly specialised natural habitat, the country is also home to some of the world's scarcest species, particularly mammals.

FLORA Kyrgyzstan has at least 4,500 species of plant in total, of which 125 species are endemic and 300 are considered to be endangered. The country's extensive **forests** are particularly noteworthy, with large tracts of spruce, juniper (*archa*), pine, maple, poplar-willow, rowan and birch.

Jalal-Abad Oblast has the greatest percentage of forest cover (9.0%), which includes a large expanse of walnut forest in the region of Arslanbob; this is followed by Osh (5.1%), Talas (3.6%), Issyk-Kul (2.7%), Naryn (2.2%) and Chui (2.1%). Overall, 4.2% of the country (about 843,000ha) is estimated to be covered by woodland.

Kyrgyzstan's natural forests contain a total of 120 woody species. On the northern mountain ranges the most significant species are spruce (*Picea schrenkiana*), Tien Shan fir (*Pinus schrenkiana*), several junipers (*Juniperus* spp), rowan (*Sorbus tianschanica*) and birch (*Betula* spp), along with bushy scrub of barberry (*Berberis* spp), wild rose (*Rosa* spp) and buckthorn (*Hippophae rhamnoides*) among others. In the western Tien Shan range, in the more protected, drier areas, pistachio (*Pistacia vera*) is present in significant quantity, as is wild almond (*Prunus amugdalus communis*). In the wetter mountain areas, particularly on the southern slopes north of the Fergana Valley in Jalal-Abad Oblast, stand some of the world's most significant relic forests of walnut (*Juglans regia*), along with stands of wild fruit trees such as apple (*Malus* spp), cherry and plum (*Prunus* spp) and hardwoods such as maple (*Acer turkestanica*).

Unfortunately, some of Kyrgyzstan's forests, particularly its relic walnut forests in the south, are aging faster than they are regenerating and the over-mature forests are susceptible to damage from pests and diseases.

As well as its forests, Kyrgyzstan is also well known throughout central Asia for the variety of valuable medicinal herbs that are found in its meadows and valleys, a total of around 200 in all. These include plants such as plantain (*Plantago* spp), Jerusalem sage (*Phlomis* spp), wormwood (*Artemesia* spp) and *Ephedra* species. Some of the most spectacular flora is found at altitudes of 3,000m or higher, where, in high alpine meadows, edelweiss (*Leontpodium alpinum*) is common, as are crocuses, anemones, asters, wild onions (*Allium* spp), tulips that include Greig's tulip (*Tulipa greigii*) and Kaufmann's tulip (*Tulipa kaufmanniana*), and poppies (*Papaver* spp).

FAUNA Kyrgyzstan has well over 500 species of vertebrates and more than 3,000 types of insect, which include 60 dragonflies, 86 butterflies, 33 species of bee, 86 species of ant and 250 species of cicada. Reptiles are well represented too, with 28 species of tortoise, snake and lizard. Seventy-five different species of fish can be found in the various lakes, reservoirs and rivers of the country, with many of these being found in Kyrgyzstan's largest body of water, Lake Issyk-Kul, which has carp, trout, *osman*, bream, pike-perch and many other species (see *The Fortunes of Fishing at Lake Issyk-Kul*, page 140). Many of the species are endemic either to the central Asian region or to Kyrgyzstan in particular.

Birds Of the vertebrates, birds make up 368 of the species. Raptors and waterbirds are particularly well represented, with saker falcon (*Falco cherrug*), golden eagle (*Aquila chrysaetos*), lammergeier (*Gypaetus barbatus*) and white-tailed eagle (*Haliaeetus albicilla*) being among the former group, and geese (*Anser* spp), swans (*Cygnus* spp) and pelicans (*Pelecanus* spp) among the latter. Lake Issyk-Kul is good for many breeding birds such as Kentish plover (*Charadrius alexandrinus*), snipe (*Gallinago galinago*), little bittern (*Ixobrychus minutus*), ferruginous duck (*Aythya nyroca*) and paddy-field (*Acrocephalus agricola*) and Cetti's warblers (*Cettia cetti*).

As well as avifauna typical of mountains and lakes, birds that favour dry steppe habitat such as bustards and steppe eagle (*Aquila rapax*) may also be found in appropriate locations. Other rare raptors that may be seen include imperial eagle (*Aguilla heliaca*) and black vulture (*Aegypius monarchus*).

The mountains hold a mixture of Himalayan and western palaearctic passerines such as white-winged crossbill (*Loxia leucoptera*), black-throated (*Prunella atrogularis*) and Himalayan accentor (*Prunella himalayana*), and Güldenstädt's (*Phoenicurus erythrogaster*) and Eversmann's redstart (*Phoenicurus erythronotus*).

Migratory birds such as cranes (*Grus grus*) and ibisbill (*Ibidorhyncha struthersii*) are found at upland lake locations like Song-Köl and Chatyr-Köl, and many wildfowl winter on the non-freezing waters of Lake Issyk-Kul. In spring and autumn, a large number of migratory birds pass through Kyrgyzstan and at this time a wealth of migratory species such as larks, buntings, thrushes and raptors appear in farmland and even in city parks. Another migratory species is demoiselle crane (*Grus virgo*), which breeds in small numbers in Kyrgyzstan in the foothills near Lake Issyk-Kul, but which is present in large numbers on passage.

For more information on birding in Kyrgyzstan see www.centralasiabirding.com or www.fatbirder.com.

Mammals Altogether there are 83 species of mammals to be found, with the high spruce forests of mountain valleys like Suusamayr providing ideal habitat for brown bear (*Ursus arctos*) and Altai maral (*Cervus canadensis canadensis*). The bare mountain ridges and valleys are home to red fox (*Vulpes vulpes*), grey wolf (*Canus lupus*), weasels and stoats (*Mustela* spp), wild boar (*Sus scrofa*), Siberian roe deer (*Capreolus pygargus*), mountain hare (*Lepus timidus*), Siberian ibex (*Capra sibirica*), steppe polecat (*Mustela eversmannii*) and marmots (*Marmota* spp), which are common, while the dry, open steppe has goitred gazelle (*Gazella subgutturosa*) and corsac fox (*Vulpes carsac*). The rarest and most elusive mammal in the country is the snow leopard (*Uncia uncia*), which survives at altitude in small numbers in the Tien Shan, although it is notoriously difficult to see. The giant marmot, Menzbier's marmot (*Marmota menzbieri*), is also restricted to the Tien Shan region. Another rare, high altitude speciality is Marco Polo sheep (*Ovis ammon polii*), which like the snow leopard appears in Kyrgyzstan's Red Data Book (see below).

CONSERVATION ISSUES
Endangered species According to the Kyrgyzstan Red Data Book report of 1985, 15% of mammals and 10% of the plant species in the country are threatened to the point of extinction. Many consider this figure to be a serious underestimate. Altogether, 13 mammals, 32 birds, 71 plants, three reptiles, two fish and 19 species of insect are listed.

Threatened mammals include maral (*Cervus canadensis canadensis*), snow leopard (*Uncia uncia*), the Eurasian otter (*Lutra lutra*), Menzbier's marmot (*Marmota menzbieri*), Tien Shan brown bear (*Ursus arctos isabellinus*), Tien Shan mountain sheep (*Ovis ammon*) and Marco Polo sheep (*Ovis ammon polii*). Some of the Kyrgyzstan animals that appear in the International Red Data Book are snow leopard, Menzbier's marmot, dzheiran gazelle (*Gazella subgotturossa*) and grey monitor lizard (*Varanus griseus*).

Deforestation It is estimated that Kyrgyzstan's forest cover has been reduced by at least 50% over the past 30 years. Historically, it was undoubtedly much greater. Much timber was felled during World War II and centuries of uncontrolled grazing have taken their toll. Southern forests in particular are threatened by deforestation, either as felling for building and firewood or for conversion into arable land. Pests such as gypsy moth also wreak considerable damage. Attempts at reforestation have generally met with little success as young trees are highly vulnerable in Kyrgyzstan's unforgiving climates, and few survive transplanting.

Mining One of the most acute problems facing Kyrgyzstan's natural environment is **uranium exploration**, a legacy of the Soviet period. In 1999 there were 36 uranium tailings sites and 25 uranium mining sites in the country. Apart from the obvious problems concerned with dealing with such a hazardous substance, many of the mines are located in areas that are prone to earthquakes and landslides, and many are close to river basins that are important sources of drinking and irrigation water. The worst problems occur in the south of the country in the Mailuu-Suu region where, according to a report in 2004, two million cubic metres of radioactive waste were being stored in 23 dumps and 13 tailings in the area. Because of a lack of finance, local authorities are unable to secure the dumps properly and they remain highly vulnerable to floods or tectonic activity.

In addition to uranium mines, there are other mining operations at work in Kyrgyzstan that cause great environmental concern. Most notable among these is the Kumtor gold mine in the Barskoon valley of Issyk-Kul Oblast that has caused alarming spillages of toxic chemicals such as cyanide in the past (see *The Kumtor Gold Mine*, page 183). Including gold and uranium, Kyrgyzstan has more than 230 mining facilities that produce more than 600 million cubic metres of toxic waste annually.

National parks and conservation areas Kyrgyzstan has a network of 83 officially protected areas that include six state reserves (*zapovedniki*), eight national and 'natural' parks and 67 nature parks (*zakazniki*) – which are divided into 'forest', 'botanical', 'geological', 'multi-use' and 'hunting' – and two biosphere reserves that are recognised by UNESCO. Together, these cover a total area of 777,300ha or 3.9% of the total land area.

Unfortunately, many of these protected areas are too small to maintain viable populations of plants or wildlife within their boundaries and generally they are too widely dispersed and lack connecting wildlife corridors. Further problems are created by uncontrolled hunting and grazing. Despite considerable international interest in the area, there is a lack of funds to provide adequate management and control. The protected areas come under the jurisdiction of the Kyrgyzstan government's Department of Protected Areas but this is thought to have little real authority, as other objectives are frequently imposed, such as firewood collecting or livestock grazing, for the purpose of revenue generation.

State reserves (zapovedniki) State reserves were established for nature conservation and scientific research and allow only restricted public access. The six *zapovedniki* established in Kyrgyzstan are, in chronological order: Issyk-Kul (established 1948), Sary-Chelek (1959), Besh-Aral (1979), Naryn (1983), Karatal-Japyryk (1994) and Sarychat-Ertash (1995).

The **Issyk-Kul State Reserve**, occupying some 19,000ha, now forms part of the larger biosphere reserve. It was the first protected territory to be set up in Kyrgyzstan and was founded to preserve the habitat of wintering waterfowl in the Lake Issyk-Kul region. The **Issyk-Kul Biosphere Reserve** occupies 43,100km^2 or 22% of the total area of the republic, and has a large variety of ecosystems represented within its boundaries that range from near desert to alpine tundra. It is home to several species of flora and fauna that are seriously endangered, including Marco Polo sheep (*Ovis ammon polii*), Siberian ibex (*Capra sibirica*), Tien Shan brown bear (*Ursus arctos isabellinus*) and snow leopard (*Uncia uncia*). The reserve was registered under the Ramsar Convention on Wetlands of International Importance in 1976.

Sary-Chelek Biosphere Reserve is located in the west of Kyrgyzstan on the southern spurs of the Chatkal range. The reserve covers an area of 23,868ha and varies in altitude from 1,200m to over 4,000m above sea level. The reserve was originally established in 1959 to preserve the forests and mountain landscapes that surround Lake Sary-Chelek. It was declared a Biosphere Reserve in 1979. The reserve has over 1,000 species of plant present within its boundaries, which include many wild varieties of commercially important plants such as apples, cherries and plums. Roughly a third of the protected area is forest, but there are also meadows, lakes, steppe and rocky areas.

Besh-Aral State Reserve is in the southwest of the Jalal-Abad Oblast next to the border with Uzbekistan. It was established to preserve the forests of the Chatkal valley and to protect the habitat of the Menzbier's marmot and certain wild tulips – Greig's tulip (*Tulipa greigii*) and Kaufmann's tulip (*Tulipa kaufmanniana*).

Naryn State Reserve was founded to protect a range of coniferous forests and alpine meadows in Naryn Oblast.

Karatal-Japyryk Reserve consists of three separate areas within Naryn Oblast that constitute a total of 72,000ha: a forested area south of Song-Köl Lake, Song-Köl Lake itself and Chatyr-Köl Lake, south of Tash Rabat, close to the Chinese frontier.

Sarychat-Ertash Reserve lies in Issyk-Kul Oblast and has 72,000ha of high altitude mountain habitats.

National parks National parks were formed with the intent of preserving the natural environment whilst making it available for recreational use and so, in terms of protection for wildlife, are lower in the hierarchy than state reserves. So-called 'natural' parks also fulfil the same function. Together, they make up a protected area of 238,697ha.

Ala-Archa National Park was founded in 1974 to protect parts of the Ala-Archa river valley that lie close to the capital of Bishkek. The national park extends for 15km along the valley at an altitude that ranges from 1,500m to 2,240m.

Chong-Kemin National Park was founded in 1997 along the Chong-Kemin river valley. The park, which contains both hunting and botanical reserves and the mausoleum of Shabdan Batyr, was set up with the aim of preserving the diversity of fauna and flora within its environs.

Kyrgyzstan's Natural Parks include: **Karakol Natural Park**, which was founded in 1997 and has a total area of 38,256ha, 4,767ha of which are forest; **Kyrgyz Ata Natural Park** in Osh Oblast, founded in 1992, has 1,172ha of natural *archa* (juniper) forest; and **Kara-Shoro Natural Park** in Osh Oblast, which was established in 1996 and has 823ha of forest within 8,450ha of mostly pasture land.

Reserves (zakazniki) Reserves are the most numerous of the specially protected areas. In these reserves, which aim to preserve unique sites and habitat and provide recreational activities, only limited types of economic activities are permitted. There are 52 such protected reserves in the Kyrgyz republic, occupying 289,200ha in total and making up more than a half of the area of all the protected territories. Many of the reserves are relatively recent designations. They include: **Padasha Ata Reserve** in Jalal-Abad Oblast; **Saimaluu-Tash State Park**, established in 2001 in eastern Jalal-Abad Oblast along the Kurart valley in an area famous for its mountain-top petroglyphs and also important for biodiversity; and the 10,448ha **Salkyn-Tör State Park** in Naryn Oblast, also established in 2001, which is dedicated to re-establishing the Tien Shan maral, in addition to providing a recreational centre for the local population.

2

Practical Information

WHEN TO VISIT

With its tough, continental climate Kyrgyzstan is very much a seasonal destination. Unless travelling to the country for purposes of business most visitors tend to come between May and October. For those whose interest is primarily in outdoor pursuits, the peak trekking season is a little shorter, between early June and mid-September. The period from mid-July to late August is by far the busiest with overseas visitors, partly because of the climate and partly as a result of this being the main European summer holiday season.

Given complete freedom of choice in deciding when to come, it really depends on exactly what the visitor wishes to do and where they want to go. For trekking, the higher the altitude, the shorter the season, tends to be the general rule, and so those wishing to do high altitude treks in the Central Tien Shan are realistically limited to July and August. Lower-level treks are usually possible between June and September, although snow is always a possibility at passes above 3,000m at virtually any time of year.

The south of the country has a warmer climate in general and the low-lying Fergana Valley can be very hot during the summer months. Even Bishkek can be unpleasantly muggy in August. If these are the prime destinations to be visited it makes sense to time a visit for spring or autumn.

If no high altitude hiking is to be attempted, coming slightly out of season has its benefits. The northern shore of Lake Issyk-Kul, particularly Cholpon-Ata, can become very crowded in August, mostly with Kazakhs rather than European visitors; however, a visit in late September or early October is a wholly different matter, with few tourists, blue skies, turning leaves and a light dusting of snow on the mountains. It is too cold to swim at this time however. Early autumn is actually a very beautiful time to be in Kyrgyzstan, especially if visiting southern destinations of modest altitude, such as the Lake Sary-Chelek region and Arslanbob, which has its walnut harvest at this time of year. Nights may be quite cold but there are warm days with clear blue skies.

Spring is a little less certain, as it can take time for winter snow to thaw completely, and late snowfall can mean that many passes and even parts of the main Bishkek-Osh highway are under snow until mid-May. The months of April, May and June have the highest amount of rainfall, and this coupled with melting snow can sometimes pose risks of landslides and avalanches. Because of this, trekking conditions at the end of the season are usually a little more reliable than those at the beginning.

Holidays and festivals may also have some bearing on the timing of a visit. Nooruz, the ancient, Zoroastrian-influenced festival that is celebrated throughout central Asia on 21 March, is well worth witnessing, although this is rather too early to see the country at its best. Horse games tend to take place during high summer, especially around Independence Day at the end of August, and special festivals that involve horse sports, Kyrgyz crafts and music are staged at upland *jailoos* (meadows) during July and August for the benefit of visitors and locals alike.

HIGHLIGHTS

Kyrgyzstan has few real manmade 'sights' but plenty of delightful locations. The first two listed below are the exceptions that prove the rule.

TASH RABAT An extraordinary Silk Road caravanserai high in a hidden valley close to the Chinese frontier (see page 218).

SAIMALUU-TASH An enormous gallery of 5,000-year-old petroglyphs spread across the top of a mountain in a particularly hard-to-reach location (see page 231).

LAKE ISSYK-KUL The world's second largest alpine lake, which has bathing beaches thousands of miles from the nearest ocean and great hiking in the valleys near Karakol (see page 173).

LAKE SONG-KÖL Quintessentially central Asia: a picture-perfect place to ride horses and stay in a yurt (see page 206).

LAKE SARY-CHELEK A jewel-like mountain lake surrounded by lush forest (see page 244).

ARSLANBOB Observe a traditional Uzbek community in a breathtaking setting amidst the world's largest walnut forest (see page 233).

CENTRAL TIEN SHAN Serious hiking, enormous glaciers and disappearing lakes among 7,000m peaks (see page 175).

SUGGESTED ITINERARIES

Many visitors to Kyrgyzstan have just a couple of weeks to spare. Despite travel around the country being fairly slow, this allows a reasonable amount of the country, and a fairly wide variety of landscapes, to be visited.

Starting in Bishkek, a **fortnight** would be enough time to travel along the north coast of Lake Issyk-Kul, stopping overnight in Tamchy or Cholpon-Ata before reaching Karakol. From here, a short 2- or 3-day trek could be made into the valleys south of the town. Return west along the south shore of the lake, possibly spending a night in Tamga or Barskoon *en route* to Kochkor. At Kochkor, arrange transport to Song-Köl Lake the next day, spending a night or two there in a yurt, horseriding or walking around the lake in the daytime. From Kochkor head south to Naryn and meet up with pre-arranged transport over the Torugart Pass to Kashgar in China, stopping at Tash Rabat along the way and perhaps spending an extra day here to hike up to the ridge above Chatyr-Köl Lake. An **alternative** route from Kochkor that returns to the Bishkek starting point might be to hike north to the Suusamayr valley after visiting Song-Köl (or return to Kochkor to find transport here) and head west along the valley through the villages of Chaek and Kyzyl-Oi to loop around at the western end to reach the Chui valley and Bishkek.

Another circular route through Kyrgyzstan that requires a little more time, say **three weeks**, is to follow the above itinerary as far as Naryn and then to travel the rough road west to Kazarman, perhaps visiting Saimaluu-Tash (late July to early September only). From Kazarman, arrange transport south to Jalal-Abad and spend a night here before continuing to Osh. Then spend a night or two in Osh, visiting sights in the city and around, before flying back to Bishkek or continuing east over the Irkeshtam Pass to Kashgar and China.

A further possibility is to miss out Lake Issyk-Kul altogether and travel due south from Bishkek towards Osh, making a detour west of the main trunk road towards Lake Sary-Chelek and/or on to the east to visit the Arslanbob region, before continuing south to Jalal-Abad and Osh.

There will be other visitors, passing through Kyrgyzstan as part of a longer overland route, who have a little more time at their disposal and can probably afford to be more flexible. Traversing Kyrgyzstan between Kazakhstan or Uzbekistan and China to the east, or Tajikistan to the south, allows much to be seen with a carefully planned route.

A **month** in the country should allow time to visit most of the places mentioned above. The best approach is to work out where you most want to go and, given the time available, try and plan the most obvious route connecting them. Kyrgyzstan does not have a very comprehensive or well-maintained road network, nor does it have a flawless public transport system, but with a spirit of adventure and a bit of luck you should get there eventually. Much time can be saved on circular tours by **flying** one-way; flights between Osh and Bishkek are inexpensive, regular and reasonably reliable.

TOUR OPERATORS

UK

The Adventure Company Cross & Pillory Hse, Cross & Pillory Lane, Alton, Hants GU34 1HL; ↘ 0845 450 5316; f 0845 450 5317; e sales@adventurecompany.co.uk; www.adventurecompany.co.uk. As UK-based representatives of Shepherd's Way, The Adventure Company can organise a 14-day programme that includes a 7-day circular horse trek from Barskoon on Lake Issyk-Kul that takes in much of the Terskey range. Not suitable for novice riders.

Adventureworks The Foundry Studios, 45 Mowbray St, Sheffield S3 8EN; ↘ 0845 345 8850; www.adventureworks.co.uk. Organise 21- & 28-day trekking expeditions for schools & groups of young people starting in the Ala-Archa valley or the Ak-Sai canyon & ending at Lake Sary-Chelek. They can also arrange mountaineering programmes for the more adventurous.

Audley Travel New Mill, New Mill Lane, Witney, Oxfordshire OX29 9SX; ↘ 01993 838000 (for central Asia specialist, ↘ 01993 838200); www.audleytravel.com. Audley organise tailor-made trips to central Asia that take in Kyrgyzstan & its neighbours & provide a bespoke itinerary according to the client's personal interests. Also, escorted 21-day group tours through central Asia.

Cox & Kings Gordon Hse, 10 Greencoat Pl, London SW1P 1PH; ↘ 020 7873 5000; e cox.kings@coxandkings.co.uk; www.coxandkings.co.uk.

A company that offers luxury escorted group tours or bespoke itineraries for individuals to Kyrgyzstan & Uzbekistan.

Dragoman Overland Adventure Travel Camp Green, Debenham, Stowmarket, Suffolk IP14 6LA; ↘ 01728 861133; f 01728 861127; e info@dragoman.co.uk; www.dragoman.com. This overland company has various tours passing through central Asia that include Kyrgyzstan in the itinerary.

Equine Adventures Long Barn South, Sutton Manor Farm, Bishops Sutton, Hants SO24 0AA; ↘ 0845 130 6981; e sales@equineadventures.co.uk; www.equineadventures.co.uk. As the name suggests, a horse tour specialist that offers 14-day horse treks in Kyrgyzstan that ride from the Shamsy valley to the Song-Köl region.

Exodus Grange Mills, Weir Rd, London SW12 ONE; ↘ 0845 863 9600, ↘ 020 8675 5550, ↘ 020 8673 0859 for brochures & trip notes; e info@exodus.co.uk; www.exodus.co.uk. A well-known adventure travel company that offers a 21-day Silk Road tour that passes through Kyrgyzstan. Also, a high-altitude 15-day Central Tien Shan trek.

Explore Worldwide Nelson Hse, 55 Victoria Rd, Farnborough, Hants GU14 7PA; ↘ 0870 333 4002; e info@explore.co.uk; www.exlore.co.uk. Offer a variety of tours to Kyrgyzstan that include a Pamir jeep adventure passing through southern Kyrgyzstan,

2

& 21- 25- & 28-day overland tours from Uzbekistan to Kashgar or Beijing on the Silk Road.

Great Game Travel 112 High St, Holywood, Co Down BT18 9HW; ☎ 028 9099 8325; f 028 9099 8951; www.greatgametravel.co.uk. Great Game Travel mostly deal with Tajikistan & Afghanistan but they can also arrange tailor-made travel to other central Asian countries.

Guerba Wessex Hse, 40 Station Rd, Westbury, Wilts BA13 3JN; ☎ 01373 858956; e enquiry@intrepidguerba.co.uk; www.guerba.co.uk. Run a 14-day central Asia tour incorporating Uzbekistan & Kyrgyzstan, & a 28-day trans-Asia tour from Beijing to Moscow via Kyrgyzstan & Uzbekistan.

High and Wild Compass Hse, Rowden's Rd, Wells, Somerset BA5 1TU; ☎ 01749 671777; f 01749 670888; e adventures@highandwild.co.uk; www.highandwild.co.uk. Offer a 19-day 'Land of the Horse' itinerary that includes Talas, the Suusamyr valley, Song-Köl & Lake Issyk-Kul, before beginning a 7-day horse trek from the Barskoon valley.

Himalayan Kingdoms Old Crown Hse, 18 Market St, Wootton-under-Edge, Glos GL12 7AE; ☎ 01453 844400, ☎ 0845 330 8579 (local call charge, UK only); f 01453 844422; e info@himalayankingdoms.com; www.himalayankingdoms.com. Run a 19-day Kyrgyzstan & Kazakhstan trip that includes an 11-day trek in the Central Tien Shan with a helicopter transfer to South Inylchek basecamp. Treks are guaranteed to run with a minimum of 2 participants; late Jul & Aug only. Also, 19-day cultural tours of central Asia incorporating Uzbekistan, Kazakhstan & Kyrgyzstan.

KE Adventure Travel 32 Lake Rd, Keswick, Cumbria CA12 5DQ; ☎ 01768 771700; f 01768 774693; e info@keadventure.co.uk; www.keadventure.co.uk. Trekking & biking itineraries in the Central Tien Shan region of Kazakhstan & Kyrgyzstan.

Peregrine Adventures 8 Clerewater Pl, Lower Way, Thatcham, Berkshire RG19 3RF; ☎ 0844 736 0170; f 01635 872758; e sales@peregrineadventures.co.uk; www.peregrineadventures.co.uk. Have several tours on offer including a 14-day tour through Kyrgyzstan from Kashgar to Tashkent & longer central Asian itineraries.

Regent Holidays (UK) Ltd 15 St John St, Bristol BS1 2HR; ☎ 0845 277 3317; f 01179 254866; e regent@regent-holidays.co.uk; www.regent-holidays.co.uk. Regent have a 9-day tour of Kyrgyzstan, mostly in the Lake Issyk-Kul region, a combined Kazakhstan & Kyrgyzstan 13-day tour, & a 14-day Uzbekistan & Kyrgyzstan tour that takes in

Lake Issyk-Kul, Cholpon-Ata & the Altyn Arashan valley, with a day-trip to the Ala-Archa valley near Bishkek.

Ride Worldwide Staddon Farm, North Tawton, Devon EX20 2BK; ☎ 01837 82544; f 01837 82179; e info@rideworldwide.com; www.rideworldwide.com. Horseriding treks for experienced riders along parts of the Silk Route that include Kyrgyzstan. Private tours can be arranged for groups of 5 or more.

The Russia House Chapel Court, Borough High St, London SE1 1HH; ☎ 020 7403 9922; f 020 7403 9933; e russiahouse@btinternet.com; www.therussiahouse.co.uk. A long-established (1970) company that specialises in Russia & CIS countries & is able to book flights & secure visas for tourist & business visitors.

Scotts Tours 141 Whitfield St, London W1T 5EW; ☎ 020 7383 5353; f 020 7383 3709; www.scottstours.co.uk. Another company that specialises in Russia & the former states of the Soviet Union; they can organise flights, visas & accommodation for both business & leisure travellers.

Silk Road and Beyond 371 Kensington High St, London W14 8QZ; ☎ 020 7371 3131; f 020 7602 9715; e sales@silkroadandbeyond.co.uk; www.silkroadandbeyond.co.uk. Various tour itineraries for independent travellers that include a 9-day tour from Bishkek–Lake Song-Köl–Lake Issyk-Kul–Bishkek with optional white water rafting excursion, & a 16-day tour of Uzbekistan, Kyrgyzstan & Kazakhstan.

Steppes Travel 51 Castle St, Cirencester GL7 1QD; ☎ 01285 880980; f 01285 885888; e enquiry@steppestravel.co.uk; www.steppestravel.co.uk. Tailor-made or small group escorted itineraries that cover Kyrgyzstan, central Asia & China.

The Imaginative Traveller 1 Betts Av, Martlesham Heath, Suffolk IP5 3RH; ☎ 0800 316 2717; www.imaginative-traveller.com. Offer escorted small group tours along the Silk Road that incorporate Kyrgyzstan. This company offers a 35-day 'Heart of Asia' tour & also a 'Rhubarb Road' tour between Moscow & Beijing. Both take in Kyrgyzstan. Can also tailor-make tours for individuals.

Wild Frontiers Unit 6, Townmead Business Centre, William Morris Way, London SW6 2SZ; ☎ 020 7736 3968; f 020 7751 0710; www.wildfrontiers.co.uk. Adventure tours & horseriding in Kyrgyzstan & surrounding countries.

Wild and Exotic Nunnington, York YO62 5XF; ☎ 01439 748401; e info@wildand exotic.co.uk; www.wildandexotic.co.uk. Offer a 2-week horse-guided trek with author Alexandra Tolstoy that centres on the Sary-Chelek region. For experienced horseriders only.

USA

Boojum Expeditions 14543 Kelly Canyon Rd, Bozeman, MT 59715; ✆ +1 406 587 0125; f +1 760 454 7407; e info@boojum.com; www.boojum.com. Mongolia specialists who also organise a Kyrgyzstan horse trek & visits to a Kyrgyz horse festival using Barskoon's Shepherd's Way company.

Distant Horizons 350 Elm Av, Long Beach, CA 90802; ✆ +1 800 333 1240, ✆ 562 983 8828; f +1 562 983 8833; e info@distant-horizons.com; www.distant-horizons.com. Offer a Silk Road tour from Beijing to Samarkand across Kyrgyzstan.

East Site 40 Mara Court, Cherry Hill, NJ 08002; ✆ +1 877 800 6287; e travel@east-site.com; www.east-site.com. East Site have scheduled Silk Road tours of various durations that include Kyrgyzstan. They can also help with air tickets & visas.

KE Adventure Travel USA PO Box 8910, Avon, CO 81620; ✆ +1 800 497 9675; f +1 800 497 9675; e infousa@keadventure.com; www.keadventure.com. Run a biking trip in SE Kazakhstan that includes Kyrgyzstan; also trekking in the Central Tien Shan.

Geographic Expeditions PO Box 29902, 1008 General Kennedy Av, San Francisco, CA 94129-0902; ✆ +1 415 922 0448, ✆ 800 777 5535; e info@geoex.com; www.geoex.com. Run a Silk Road tour across the Torugart Pass to China & a 21-day tour including Turkestan, Uzbekistan & Kyrgyzstan.

MIR Corporation Suite 210, 85 South Washington St, Seattle, WA 98104; ✆ +1 206 624 7289, ✆ 800 424 7289; f +1 206 624 7360; e info@mircorp.com; www.mircorp.com. Offer various group tours along the Silk Road.

Overcross USA Suite 101, 3345 Bookman Av, Pittsburgh, PA 15227; ✆ +1 866 644 1357; e mail@overcross.com; www.overcross.com. A motorbike tour specialist that organises 3-week motorcycling tours of Kyrgyzstan & Kazakhstan.

Red Star Travel Suite 102, 123 Queen Anne Av N, Seattle, WA 98109; ✆ +1 206 522 5995, ✆ 800 215 4378; f +1 206 522 6295; e travel@travel2russia.com; www.travel2russia.com. Can arrange visas, flights, train tickets & tours to whole of the CIS region, including Kyrgyzstan.

Sokol Tours 27 Meetinghouse Lane, Bradfordwoods, PA 15015; ✆ +1 724 935 5373; e sokol@sokoltours.com; www.sokoltours.com. An American Russia & CIS specialist offering tours of Lake Issyk-Kul coupled with Kazakhstan, as well as a multiple-country Silk Route tour.

CANADA

Bestway Tours & Safaris Suite 206, 8678 Greenall Av, Burnaby, British Columbia V5J 3M6; ✆ +1 604 264 7378; f +1 604 264 7774; e bestway@bestway.com; www.bestway.com. Cultural tours to central Asia that include Kyrgyzstan.

AUSTRALIA

Gateway Travel 48 The Boulevard, Strathfield, NSW 2135; ✆ +61 2 9745 3333; f +61 2 9745 3237; e agent@russian-gateway.com.au; www.russian-gateway.com.au. Can assist with flights, accommodation & visas in Kyrgyzstan & throughout central Asia.

Intrepid Travel 84 Oxford St, Paddington, NSW 2021; ✆ 1300 364 512 (from outside Australia: ✆ +61 3 9473 2626; f +61 3 9419 4426); e info@intrepidtravel.com; www.intrepidtravel.com. Intrepid have 2 tours through central Asia that take in Kyrgyzstan.

Peregrine Adventures 380 Lonsdale St, Melbourne, VIC 3000; ✆ 1300 791 485 (within Australia), ✆ +61 3 8601 4444 (outside Australia); f +61 3 8601 4344; e websales@peregrineadventures.com; www.peregrineadventures.com. Several tours through Kyrgyzstan from Kashgar to Tashkent, as well as longer central Asian itineraries.

Sundowners Travel Suite 15, Lonsdale Court, 600 Lonsdale St, Melbourne 3000; ✆ +61 3 9672 5300; f +61 3 9672 5311; www.sundownerstravel.com. Offer several overland Silk Road & central Asia tours that include Kyrgyzstan.

TOUR OPERATORS IN KYRGYZSTAN The following are all based in Bishkek and between them offer a very wide range of tours and activities. To phone from abroad, add the country code, +996, plus the Bishkek code, 312, then the number below.

Advantour Kievskaya 131/2; ✆ 900 592; f 610 402; e bishkek@advantour.com; www.advantour.com. A travel agency with sister branches in Tashkent & Almaty, Advantour has a large number of Kyrgyzstan itineraries available of variable duration from 2 to 15 days. Advantour offers a Kyrgyz festivals tour, as well as rafting, horseriding, hiking & multiple activity treks. Also can arrange transport to Torugart from Naryn via Tash Rabat.

Adventure's Seller Chui 125/1; ✆ 295 374, ✆ 682 555; f 682 333; e saleman@intranet.kg; www.seller-travel.narod.ru. A small, relatively new company that offers tours in addition to services like visa support & reservations.

Ak-Sai Travel Baytik Baatyr (formerly Sovetskaya) 65; ✆ 544 277; f 544 219; e info@ak-sai.com; www.ak-sai.com. Ak-Sai offer a wide range of cultural & adventure tours in addition to treks to the Inylchek Glacier, heli-skiing in the Tien Shan, mountain biking, horseriding & mountaineering to various peaks in Kyrgyzstan.

Alltournative Kievskaya 107; ✆ 611 330; f 216 644; e alltournative@elcat.kg; www.alltournative.kg. This fairly new but well-organised company can organise day & w/end trips from Bishkek in addition to offering a range of adventure & Silk Road cultural trips that last from 3–14 days.

Asia Mountains Tugolbai Ata (formerly Lineinaja) 1a; ✆ 694 073, ✆ 694 075; f 694 074; e aljona@mail.elcat.kg, e asiamountains@mail.ru; www.asiamountains.co.uk (English), www.asiamountains.elcat.kg (Russian). Asia Mountains offer a full range of Silk Road tours, including travel to China via the Irkeshtam Pass; various trekking options that include Merzbacher Lake, mountaineering in the Pamir & Tien Shan ranges; & specialist programmes that investigate the botany & geology of Kyrgyzstan. They can also organise heli-skiing, rafting & canoeing packages. The same company runs the guesthouse of the same name in Bishkek.

Celestial Mountains Tour Company Kievskaya 131/2; ✆ 212 562; f 610 402; e celest@infotel.kg; www.celestial.com.kg. Celestial Mountains are a respected & reliable British-run company that can arrange more or less anything in the country, particularly transportation over the Torugart Pass to China & along the Karakoram Highway into Pakistan. Director Ian Claytor is very knowledgeable regarding the logistics of travel in Kyrgyzstan & is happy to give advice. The same company also has guesthouses in Bishkek & Naryn.

Central Asia Tourism (C.A.T.) Corporation Chui 124; ✆ 663 664, ✆ 663 665, ✆ 660 277; f 900 420; e cat@cat.kg, e info@centralasiatourism.com; www.cat.kg, www.centralasiatourism.com. This is the Bishkek office of a Kazakh company that deals with all aspects of travel & tourism, visa support & flights, as well as tours & hotel bookings.

Dostuck Trekking Igemberdiev 42/1; ✆ 545 455,

✆ 503 082, ✆ 540 327; f 545 455, f 559 090; e dostuck@saimanet.kg; www.dostuck.com.kg. Dostuck is a joint British–Kyrgyz venture founded in 1991 that organises trekking, climbing, heli-skiing, rafting & other adventure tours in Kyrgyzstan. Dostuck are partners of the MIR Corporation in the USA & Steppes Travel in the UK.

Ecotour 46-A, Donskoy pereulok; ✆ 502 802805, ✆ 555 913245; m 0502 802 805; e info@ecotour.kg; www.ecotour.kg. Ecotour organise yurt stays, cultural programmes & trekking, & cycling & horseriding tours throughout Kyrgyzstan. They have 6 yurt camps in the country.

Edelweiss 68/9 Usenbaev; ✆ 280 788, ✆ 284 254; f 680 038; e edelweiss@elcat.kg; www.edelweiss.elcat.kg. Edelweiss offer Silk Road tours between Almaty & the Torugart Pass, heli-skiing packages & a variety of trekking & horse tours. Also serious mountaineering to Khan Tengri or Pobeda peaks. They can tailor services according to individual requirements.

Flagman Travel Company Chui 4; ✆/f 533 999; m 0502 706 070; e flagman_kg@mail.ru, e info@flagman-kg.com; www.flagman-kg.com. Silk Road & historical tours; trekking, rafting & skiing.

Glavtour Toktogul 93; ✆ 663 232, ✆ 660 313; f 600 402, f 660 896; e glavtour@infotel.kg; www.glavtour.kg (also office at Kievskaya 95A; ✆/f 662 295). A Russian-Kyrgyz joint venture that offers day trips to Ala-Archa, Alamedin & Kashka-Suu gorges, 1- & 2-week hiking tours, winter skiing & rafting trips, as well as services like booking air tickets & hotel reservations.

International Mountaineering Camp (IMC) Pamir Apartment 30, Kievskaya 133; ✆ 660 464, ✆ 660 469; f 660 465; e imcpamir@imfico.bishkek.su; www.imcpamir.netfirms.com. Organise mountaineering expeditions to Peak Lenin, where they have a permanent basecamp, & to the peaks of Central Tien Shan.

ITMC Tien Shan Travel Molodaya Gvardya 1A; ✆ 651 404; f 650 747; e itmc@elcat.kg; www.itmc.centralasia.kg. ITMC have a wide range of programmes that include several Silk Road tours & trekking options in the Terskey Ala-Too & the Central Tien Shan ranges. Also offer horseback tours, heli-skiing, mountain biking, jeep safaris & mountaineering packages.

Kyrgyz Concept Chui 126; ✆ 666 006; f 661 011; e aero2@concept.kg; http://eng.concept.kg (also another office at Kievskaya 69; ✆/f 900 404; e aero3@concept.kg; & head office at Razzakova 100; ✆ 661 331; f 660 220; e aero1@concept.kg, e office@concept.kg). Kyrgyz Concept offer a range of services aimed at both business & leisure visitors that include visas, car hire, translation, flights & accommodation booking, in addition to a range of tours. **Kyrgyz Travel** Bakinskaya 237; ✆/f 679 975, ✆/f 670 764: e d-sasha@elcat.kg; www.kttc.elcat.kg. Silk Road tours, horseback trekking, bike tours, heli-skiing, rafting, fishing & mountaineering can all be arranged with this company who have their own guesthouse at Tamga on the south shore of Lake Issyk-Kul. **Muza Tours** Kievskaya 107; ✆ 210 752, ✆ 611 116; f 610 620; e info@gocentralasia.com; www.gocentralasia.com. Muza offer a range of adventure & cultural tours around Kyrgyzstan, as well as trekking, horseriding, yurt stays & Silk Road tours to China. They can also organise business services like reservations & translations. **Nomad's Land** Mederova 50; ✆ 936 479, ✆ 996 502, ✆ 446 666; e info@nomadsland.kg; www.nomadsland.kg. This is an ecotourism company that offers a variety of trekking, mountaineering, rafting & cycling tours in addition to services like camping equipment rental, bike hire & transportation.

NoviNomad Togolok Moldo 28; ✆ 622 381; f 622 380; e novinomad@elcat.kg; www.novinomad.com. NoviNomad have a wide range of cultural & Silk Road tours as well as treks, horseriding & mountain bike tours. They can also arrange visas, OVIR registration & organise the documentation for the authorisation of exporting goods. They also offer city tours & can arrange overland travel to China & Tajikistan. **Tien Shan Travel** Tsherbakov 127; ✆/f 270 576; e travel@tien-shan.com; www.tien-shan.com. This is a well-established company that specialises in mountaineering & high-altitude trekking. Tien Shan Travel has its own basecamps at Maida-Adyr, South Inylchek & North Inylchek in the Central Tien Shan & at Achyk-Tash & the Lenin Glacier in the Pamirs. **Top Asia** Toktogul 175; ✆/f 211 644; e topasia@mail.kg; www.topasia.kg. Top Asia offers a number of Silk Road tours, along with treks in the Central Tien Shan & Terskey Ala-Too, plus mountaineering trips to Lenin & Khan Tengri peaks, & horseback excursions. Also paragliding, kayaking & mountain bike tours.

TOUR OPERATORS ELSEWHERE IN CENTRAL ASIA

Stantours ✆ +49 12120 241 382; f +49 721 151 582 400; e info@stantours.com; http://stantours.com. Stantours is a pan-central Asian travel company run by German national David Berghof that has offices in Almaty & Ashgabat. As well as offering tours of the central Asian region, Stantours are excellent at sorting out red tape for groups or individual travellers. This is a good place to make enquiries if you plan travelling beyond Kyrgyzstan & require invitations or visa support for Uzbekistan or a Gorno-Badakhshan Autonomous Oblast (GBAO) permit for travel along the Pamir Highway into Tajikistan. Email enquiries are normally answered promptly. For matters relating to Kyrgyzstan travel, Stantours usually liaise with the Celestial Mountains Tour Company in Bishkek.

COMMUNITY BASED TOURISM Community based tourism in Kyrgyzstan started life in 2000 as an initiative to organise local groups offering accommodation and tourist services to visitors. In 2003, a national umbrella association, the KCBTA (Kyrgyz Community Based Tourism Association), was created to unite the CBT and Shepherd's Life groups around the country (*KCBTA Gorky 58, intersection with Matrosov, Bishkek;* ✆ *+996 312 540 069;* ✆/f *+996 312 443 331;* e *(reservation manager): cbttours@mail.ru,* e *asylbek75@yandex.ru;* e *(marketing): mambetalieva@yahoo.com; www.cbtkyrgyzstan.kg).*

This was done with the support of partner Helvetas (*www.helvetas.kg*), the Swiss Association for International Cooperation, which had helped inspire the first Shepherd's Life groups in 1997, and which has committed to a long-term alliance.

From a modest beginning the organisation has quickly gained momentum, enabling foreign visitors to stay with families and utilise local services for adventure travel at a very reasonable price. In addition to offering a range of homestay accommodation at each of the organisation's 17 regional centres, the local CBT co-ordinator can arrange private transport and yurt stays at *jailoos*, organise guides and horses, advise on trekking and stage special demonstrations of folk craft such as *shyrdak*-making and Kyrgyz traditions such as eagle-hunting and horse games. The accommodation and services offered by CBT and Naryn-based sister organisation,

2

Shepherd's Life, is of especial value to backpackers and individual travellers who may not be able to afford, or wish to participate in, a fully organised tour of the country. The national umbrella association KCBTA is able to advise and plan bespoke itineraries throughout Kyrgyzstan either by phone, email or a personal visit to their Bishkek office. They can pre-arrange services throughout the country, or you can simply turn up at regional CBT centres and arrange it there *ad hoc*. Some, but by no means all, local co-ordinators speak English, but communication is rarely much of a problem.

As well as the homes of local co-ordinators, CBT also have separate information offices in some towns throughout the country. At the time of writing these could found in Karakol, Bokonbaevo, Kochkor, Naryn, Osh, Jalal-Abad and Arslanbob. The organisation is continually expanding its range of operations and in 2007, a number of new CBT networks were set up in Batken in the far southwest and the villages of Gulcha and Sary-Mogol in the Alay valley south of Osh. Details of local CBT groups are given as appropriate in the text.

Overall, CBT is a splendid organisation that offers excellent services for very affordable prices and has been a great boon to budget travel in Kyrgyzstan over the past few years. It is low impact, economically and socially sustainable, and it goes without saying that most of the income generated goes directly into the local community. Some critics point out that it is usually possible to do things slightly cheaper than CBT fixed rates, particularly in terms of hiring private transport, but at least with CBT there is the knowledge that the driver is approved, trustworthy and used to dealing with tourists. The CBT website (*www.cbtkyrgyzstan.kg*) has a great deal of information including a full list of standard prices for services.

RED TAPE

Compared with most of its central Asian neighbours and Russia, Kyrgyzstan is a relatively straightforward place to visit with a minimum of paperwork.

VISAS Most, but not all, visitors to Kyrgyzstan require a visa, which can be obtained in advance at a Kyrgyzstan embassy or on arrival at Bishkek airport (not on land crossings) and on international flights from outside the CIS. A few nationalities – eg: Japanese – do not require a visa but are required to register with the Office of Visas & Regulations (OVIR), while others require a visa but do not have to register – most EU countries fall into this category. There are a few countries that need to both register and obtain visas such as India, Iran and Pakistan, and others, mostly CIS countries, that require neither visas nor registration. For most nationalities it is no longer necessary to receive an invitation to apply for a tourist visa. Visas are normally issued for 30 days.

Countries not requiring visas for entry Azerbaijan, Albania, Armenia, Belarus, Bulgaria, Bosnia and Herzegovina, China (for up to 1 month), Croatia, Cuba, the Czech Republic, Georgia, Japan, Kazakhstan, Macedonia, Malaysia (up to 3 months), Moldova, Mongolia (3 months), North Korea, Poland, Romania, Russian Federation, Serbia, Slovakia, Slovenia, Tajikistan, Turkey (up to 1 month), Ukraine and Vietnam.

Countries requiring a visa but not OVIR registration (invitation or visa support not required) Australia, Austria, Belgium, Canada, Cyprus, Denmark, Finland, France, Germany, Greece, Iceland, Ireland, Israel, Italy, Liechtenstein, Luxembourg, Malta, Monaco, the Netherlands, New Zealand, Norway, Portugal, South Korea, Spain, Sweden, Switzerland, the United Kingdom and the United States.

All other countries *not* listed above and nationals of countries listed above **intending to travel for a period of more than 30 days** are required to obtain a visa support letter from the Consular Department of the Ministry of Foreign Affairs if travelling for business purposes or, if travelling privately or for the purposes of tourism, an invitation letter issued by the Ministry of Internal Affairs. This additional paperwork can be issued, at a price and with some advance notice, by contacting one of the Bishkek travel agents listed in *Tour Operators in Kyrgyzstan*, page 49.

Applying for a visa The best advice is to try and obtain a visa in advance in your own country. Visa applications usually involve the following: a valid passport with at least one blank page, a completed application form, one passport-sized photo, the appropriate fee and a stamped, addressed envelope if applying by post. Additional charges are made for an express service.

Countries that do not have a Kyrgyz diplomatic representation may apply at a Kazakh embassy or consulate instead. These include the following: Canada, Croatia, the Czech Republic, Egypt, France, Greece, Hungary, Israel, Italy, Lithuania, Mongolia, the Netherlands, Poland, Romania, Saudi Arabia, South Korea, Spain, Thailand and the United Arab Emirates.

Arriving by air, it may be possible to get a visa at Bishkek Manas Airport (see *Visas on arrival*, below).

Visa fees At the Kyrgyz embassy in the **UK** in London, standard charges are £45 for a 1-month tourist visa and £60 for a 1-month multiple-entry visa. 'Ordinary' visas (ie: business and private visas that require a letter of introduction) cost £40 for 1 month; £60 for 1-month, multiple-entry; £60 for 2-months, single-entry; £110 for 6 months and £140 for 1 year. Applications normally take 5 working days.

In the **USA**, a 1-month, single-entry tourist visa costs US$70; a 1-month, double-entry tourist visa US$90; a 3-month, single-entry visa US$110; and a 3-month, double-entry visa US$130. Business visas cost from US$100–300, depending on the period of stay and number of entries. Allow 10 working days for processing.

Visas on arrival Tourist visas are issued on arrival of international flights at Manas Airport in Bishkek. The visa desk is opened for the arrival of international flights from *outside the CIS*. If planning to arrive by air from a European destination, or anywhere else outside the CIS, this can save a lot of hassle; it is generally cheaper too. Single-entry, 1-month visas cost just US$35; double-entry, 1 month visas are US$55. Be sure to have the exact fee in crisp new banknotes. Visas are issued and stuck into passports before immigration; the whole process takes only about 10 minutes once the issuing officer has turned up.

Visas in central Asia If possible, avoid collecting visas *en route* through central Asia as this can involve a lot of hanging around in capital cities and may ultimately represent a false economy in terms of both time and money. For example, the Kyrgyzstan embassy in Dushanbe, Tajikistan is only open to receive visa applications twice a week and then it takes at least a week to issue the visa. Similarly, the Uzbekistan embassy in Bishkek is infamously unhelpful and a bad place to apply for a visa to that country. This said, applying for a Kyrgyz visa in Kazakhstan and Uzbekistan is usually straightforward and fairly swift.

Entry and exit stamps In legal terms it is only possible to enter or leave Kyrgyzstan at an approved border post. The stamp on your visa proves that you have entered by such a post and any lack of one in your passport has the potential to cause problems with the authorities. The problem is that at some border posts, particularly those that are less frequently used, they may fail to stamp you in. This happens on leaving the country too (although it is less problematic), with officials claiming that they have no stamp, have run out of ink, or just cannot be bothered. Try and insist, but if they do not have stamp there is not much that you can do about it. If this is the case, make a note of the time and date that you crossed the border (and perhaps also get the officer's name and number) then go to the OVIR in the first big town that you reach and explain the situation where they will, hopefully, stamp your passport. Any dated documentation like a ticket or hotel receipt would also be good to have.

Visa extensions Tourist visas of 30 days may be extended relatively easily in Kyrgyzstan at the OVIR offices in Bishkek, Karakol, Naryn and Osh. OVIR is also where registration needs to be done, although this is now redundant for most nationalities. Extensions are normally for one week, although some claim to have received a month's extension without any trouble. Bring a copy of your main passport page and one or two passport photos. Having a Russian–speaking accomplice is helpful if you do not speak the language as the forms are in Russian only. The fee is in the order of 300som.

OVIR Bishkek Kievskaya 58 (near junction with Shopokova); ⏰ 09.30–12.30 & 14.00–17.00 Mon–Fri
OVIR Karakol Tumanova 146a, room 114; ⏰ 09.00–13.00 & 14.00–17.00 Tue–Fri

OVIR Naryn Togolok Moldo 11 (junction with Lenina)
OVIR Osh City Administration Building, Lenina 199 (junction with Sovetskaya)

Ⓔ KYRGYZ EMBASSIES ABROAD

Austria Naglergasse 25/5, 1010 Vienna; ☎ +431 5350 378, ☎ 5350 379; f +431 5350 313; e kyrbot@mail.austria.eu.net; kyrbot@kyrbotwien.or.at
Belgium 47 Rue de l'Abbaye, 1050 Brussels; ☎ +322 6401 868, ☎ 6403 883; f +322 6400 131; e aitmatov@photohall.skynet.be
Belarus Starovilenskaya 57, Minsk 220002; ☎ +375 17 2349 117; f +375 17 2341 602; e manas@nsys.minsk.by
China 241 Ta Yuan Diplomatic Office Bldg, Chaoyang District, Beijing 100600; ☎ +86 10 6532 6458; f +86 10 6532 6459; e kyrgyz@public3.bta.net.cn, kyrgyzch@95777.com. Consulate in Urumqi: Central Asia Hotel, North Hetan Rd 38 (near intersection of East Xihong Rd & Hetan Rd), Urumqi, Xinjiang.
Germany Otto-Suhr-Allee 146, 10585 Berlin; ☎ +49 30 3478 1338; f +49 30 3478 1362; e info@botschaft-kirgisien.de; www.botschaft-kirgisien.de. Consulate in Bonn: Ännchenstr 61, 53177 Bonn; ☎ +49 228 365 230; f +49 228 365 191. Consulate in Frankfurt: Brönnerstr 20, 60313 Franfurt am Main; ☎ +49 69 9540 3926; f +49 69 2165 8918
India C-93, Anand Niketan, New Delhi 110021; ☎ +91 11 2411 8008; f +91 11 2411 8009; e kyrgyzembassy@eandex.ru; www.kgzembind.com
Iran PO Code 1957935611, 5th Naranjestan Alley 12,

Pasdaran St, Tehran 195 793 5611; ☎ +98 21 2830 354; f +98 21 2281 720; e krembiri@rier.net
Japan 6-16 5-chome Shimomeguro, Meguro-ku, Tokyo 153-0064; ☎ +81 3 3179 0828; f +81 3 3719 0868; e saliev@kyrgyzemb.jp
Kazakhstan Luganskii, 3a Astana; ☎/f +7 3172 916 610; e ktr@mail.online.kz. Consulate in Almaty: Amangeldy 68a, Almaty; ☎ +7 3272 632 911, ☎ 636 525; f +7 3272 633 362; e alche@kyrgyz.almaty.kz
Malaysia 10-C Lorong Damai 9, 550 00 Kuala Lumpur; ☎ +60 3 2163 2012, ☎ 2164 9862; f +60 3 2163 2024; e kyrgyz@tm.net.my, e lira_sabyrova@yahoo.com
Pakistan 15/1 Main Khayaban-e-Ghazi, Phase V, Defence Officers, Housing Authority, Karachi; ☎ +92 21 5374 447; f +92 21 5374 448; e gckgirp.karachi@mail.ru
Russia Bolshaya Ordynka 64, Moscow 109017; ☎ +7 95 2374 601, ☎ 2374 882, ☎ 2374 481, ☎ 2374 571; f +7 95 2374 452, 2374 571; e 3235.g23@g23.relcom.ru. Consulate Ekaterinburg: Bolshakova 105; ☎ +7 3432 2511 559, ☎ 2572 461, ☎ 2577 614; f +7 3432 2577 614; e kyrgencon@mail.ru
Switzerland Chemin de la Voie-Creuse 16, Geneva 1202; ☎ +41 22 7340 900; f +41 22 7340 901;

e mission.kyrgyzstan @ ties.itu.int
Tajikistan 3 Proesd Chekova 41, Dushanbe; ℡ +992
372 272 008, ℡ 211 931, ℡ 215 468; f +992 372
210 843, ℡ 216 812; e kyremb @ tajnet.com
Turkey Boyabat Sokak, GOP 11, 06700 Ankara;
℡ +90 312 4468 411, ℡ 4468 408; f +90 312
4468 413; e kirgiz-o @ tr-net.net.tr. Consulate in
Istanbul: Lamartin caddesi 7, Taksim, Istanbul;
℡ +90 21 2356 767, ℡ 2930 919, ℡ 2353 737;
f +90 21 2359 293; e genkon @ anet.net.tr
Turkmenistan Kerogly 14, 744000 Ashkhabad;
℡ +993 12 355 506, ℡ 353 494; f +993 12 355
506; e kg @ online.tm
Ukraine Artema 51/50, Kiev 252901; ℡ +380 44
2468 889, ℡ 2468 897; f +380 44 2468 889;

e chukik @ public.ua.net
UK Ascot Hse, 119 Crawford St, London W1H 1AF;
℡ +44 207 9351 462; f +44 207 9357 449;
e email @ kyrgyz-embassy.org.uk,
kyrembuk @ aol.com; www.kyrgyz-embassy.org.uk
United States 2360 Massachusetts Av NW, Washington
DC 20008; ℡ +1 202 3385 141; f +1 202 386
7550; e consul @ kgembassy.org; www.kyrgyzstan.org.
Consulate in New York: Suite 514, 866 UN Plaza,
New York, NY 10017; ℡ +1 212 319 2836;
f +1 212 319 2837; www.kyrgyzembassy.org
Uzbekistan Samatovoi 30, 700000 Tashkent;
℡ +998 71 1374 794, ℡ 1374 292, ℡ 1398 613;
f +998 71 1374 791; e krembas @ globalnet.uz

REGISTRATION Thankfully, this is a thing of the past for most foreign visitors now, as compulsory OVIR registration was abandoned in 2002 for the United States, Canada, Israel, Australia, New Zealand and most EU countries. Those passport holders that still need to register can report to one of the OVIR offices listed above.

PERMITS Generally speaking, trekking permits are no longer required as these were abandoned, along with OVIR registration, in 2002. However, there is some uncertainty as to whether they are required in the Ak-Suu region of Batken Province. **Military border permits** are required for some areas, notably those zones within 50km of the Chinese border – the Central Tien Shan area around Khan Tengri peak, the Inylchek Glacier and Merzbacher Lake, and the Ak-Say valley east of the Torugart Pass. A border permit (*propusk*) is *not* required for the straightforward overland journey to China by either the Torugart or Irkeshtam passes as long as travellers are in possession of a Chinese visa and there is no deviation from the route in the border region itself. Tash Rabat caravanserai does not require a permit.

Border permits may be arranged by a travel agency or tour operator but should be applied for well in advance as they take at least a week to issue.

GETTING THERE AND AWAY

BY AIR Kyrgyzstan's main international airport is Bishkek's Manas Airport (airport code: FRU; ℡ *693 109;* e *info@airport.kg; www.airport.kg*) although a few flights from Russia also go direct to Osh. Manas Airport lies about 25km north of the capital, a 40-minute, 350som taxi drive away. For details of how to reach the airport from the city see page 88.

From the UK **British Airways** franchise partner, **BMED**, operate flights between London Heathrow and Bishkek. For further information or to book flights visit www.ba.com or call British Airways reservations in the UK on ℡ 0870 850 9850 or in the USA on ℡ 1-800-AIRWAYS.

This direct service runs three times a week on Sunday, Wednesday and Friday afternoons, arriving in Bishkek in the early morning. Flights back to London leave on Monday, Thursday and Saturday mornings from Bishkek. The flight time is approximately 9 hours, with a refuelling stop in Tbilisi, Georgia. The average price of a return flight is around £770.

Other less convenient options include flights with Aeroflot changing planes at Moscow's Sheremetyevo airport, which start at about £500, and with Turkish Airlines via Istanbul, at around £700 return.

From Europe Other than BMED flights from London, the only other direct flights from Europe are with **Turkish Airlines**, which fly four times a week from Istanbul, and regular flights from Moscow with **Aeroflot** and other carriers. Flights to Bishkek from Western European countries tend to connect with either Aeroflot in Moscow or Turkish Airlines in Istanbul. Lufthansa and KLM do not fly to Bishkek but do regularly fly to Almaty in Kazakhstan (see below).

From CIS countries Kyrgyzstan has regular direct flights from Moscow with Aeroflot, Itek Air and Kyrgyzstan Airlines, as well as three times a week from St Petersburg, twice a week from Krasnoyar, three times a week from Yekaterinburg and weekly from Novosibirsk and Chelyabinsk in Siberia. There are flights four times a week from Dushanbe in Tajikistan with both Kyrgyzstan and Tajikistan Airlines, as well as regular flights to Tashkent in Uzbekistan and flights three times a week from Almaty in Kazakhstan.

From elsewhere Xinjiang Airways and Kyrgyzstan Airlines fly to Bishkek several times a week from Urumqi in Xinjiang. There are three flights a week from Tehran in Iran and one flight weekly from Mashad. There are two flights each week from Seoul, South Korea and weekly flights from New Delhi, Sharjah and Dubai.

From the United States and Canada There are no direct flights. Flights from North America can either link with the direct BMED service from London to Bishkek or alternatively go via Moscow (Aeroflot) or Istanbul (Turkish Airlines).

From Australia and New Zealand Probably the easiest way to reach Kyrgyzstan from Australasia or southeast Asia is to fly to Tashkent via Bangkok and then either take a connecting flight or travel overland to Kyrgyzstan.

Flying to Almaty, Kazakhstan There are far more flights to Kazakhstan from Europe than flights to Bishkek. **British Airways**, **Lufthansa** and **KLM** all fly to Almaty from their respective hubs in the UK, Germany and the Netherlands. Return flights from London to Almaty with BA start at around £570 including taxes.

Almaty is only 3–4 hours by road from Bishkek and both KLM and Lufthansa provide their own shuttle service. The problem with this route is the need for a Kazakh transit visa and then for another if returning to Almaty for the flight home. Transit visas are now reported to be available at Almaty airport for holders of onward visas, ie: to Kyrgyzstan, but there has been some talk of the Kazakh authorities also requiring an onward *air* ticket to Bishkek in order to issue a visa. Check this with the nearest Kazakhstan consulate (and perhaps, airline) before flying, and if in any doubt be sure to obtain a Kazakh transit visa in advance.

BY TRAIN The great adventure of arriving in Bishkek by rail may not quite be as romantic as its sounds. It is a very long journey and there is an awful lot of dull Kazakh steppe to stare at before Kyrgyzstan is reached. In addition, many of the passengers travelling in *platskart* are smugglers, and many consider that it is not a safe journey for foreigners to take, at least in the lowest class.

In theory at least, it is possible to reach Bishkek by train from anywhere in Europe by way of Moscow and the service from there. Naturally, having to travel through both Russia and Kazakhstan *en route*, there are inevitably going to be plenty of visa considerations. A transit visa for Kazakhstan will be required as well as a Russian and Kyrgyz visa.

Train number 018, a Kyrgyz train, leaves Moscow's Kazan station three times a week at 23.16 on Thursday and Sunday to arrive 75 hours later in the early hours of the fourth day. This currently costs 2,754 roubles (about US$120) in *platskart* (3rd class open carriage) and 4,490 roubles (about US$180) in *kupe* (four-berth sleeper). Train number 28, a Russian train, leaves Moscow on Tuesday and Saturday evenings, costing 2,941 roubles in *platskart*, 4,926 roubles in *kupe* and 9,898 roubles in a first class, twin-berth compartment.

An alternative to these services is to take the Moscow–Almaty service, train number 8, that leaves every other day from Moscow to reach Almaty 77 hours later. Rather than going all of the way to Bishkek or Almaty it is possible to leave any of the trains at Taraz (Dzhambul) in Kazakhstan and then enter Kyrgyzstan's northwest Talas Province by minibus, saving 6–8 hours on the time to the final destination.

Real rail enthusiasts might also wish to reach Moscow by train from the UK by taking the Eurostar to Cologne and then on to Moscow, or by changing trains in Berlin or Warsaw for overnight services to the Russian capital. For details of rail travel to Russia from the United Kingdom see www.seat61.com.

The Russian Railways website (*www.rzd.ru*) has details of all Russian services. Online booking and payment is possible (*http://ticket.rzd.ru*) but it is Russian language only. Train tickets for travel in Russia and the CIS may be booked in advance using a Russian agency such as the following: Svezhy Veter (*www.svagency.udm.ru/sv/trains.htm*), G&R International (*www.hostels.ru*) and Way to Russia (*www.waytorussia.net*).

Trains run three times a week between Bishkek and Tashkent but they are very slow (18 hours) and require a Kazakh transit visa.

BY ROAD

From Kazakhstan There are frequent services between Almaty and Bishkek by bus, shared taxi and *marshroutka* taking about 4 hours. From Taraz (Dzhambul) there are regular minibuses that connect with Talas in Kyrgyzstan's northwest.

From Uzbekistan The northern route between Tashkent and Bishkek passes through Taraz in Kazakhstan, where there is usually a change of transport. A Kazakh transit visa is vital on this route. To reach Bishkek from Tashkent it may well be quicker and cheaper to go first to Osh via the Fergana Valley and then fly to Bishkek from there.

From Dostlyk near Andijan in Uzbekistan's Fergana Valley there are plenty of minibuses running to the Kyrgyz border close to Osh, from where another minibus may be taken into the city. Dostlyk may be reached either from Andijan or Tashkent by shared taxi. There is also another Fergana Valley crossing from Uzbekistan at Khanabad, just to the south of Jalal-Abad. Although there are further crossing points between the two countries in the Fergana Valley, some of these may not allow foreign travellers through as they may be designated for locals only.

From Tajikistan There is no regular transport along the Pamir Highway between Murgab and Osh, although private 4×4 vehicles may be hired for this route in either direction. Travelling this route requires a Gorno-Badakhshan Autonomous Oblast (GBAO) permit in addition to a Tajik visa. There are shared taxis between Isfara in the Tajik section of the Fergana Valley and Batken in southwest Kyrgyzstan, and also Khojand and Isfana, at Kyrgzstan's extreme southwestern corner. At the time of writing, the Kyrgyz-Tajik border between Garm and Daroot-Korgon was closed for foreign nationals, although this route may well reopen in the future.

From China There are two overland routes to and from China. The **Torugart Pass** in southern Naryn Province is technically closed to foreigners but permission to cross is granted if travellers have pre-arranged transport meeting them on the other side of the border and have documentation to prove this. The public bus that plies this route between Kashgar and Naryn cannot be used by foreign nationals. Further south, the **Irkeshtam border**, to the east of Sary-Tash in Osh Province, permits crossing in either direction without any special conditions or documentation. A public bus runs between Kashgar in China's Xinjiang Province and Osh twice a week in either direction, and is available for all to use. From Kashgar, the bus runs on Monday and Tuesday mornings and takes at least 18 hours overnight. For further details regarding these crossings see the appropriate chapters.

✚ HEALTH *with Dr Felicity Nicholson*

Kyrgyzstan is a healthy place on the whole and although they should be prepared for any eventuality, travellers should not expect to fall ill here, excepting the odd bout of traveller's diarrhoea. Nevertheless, all visitors to Kyrgyzstan should be in possession of adequate **health insurance** as state health care in Kyrgyzstan is rudimentary at best. Insurance is particularly important if such activities as trekking, horseriding or mountaineering are planned, and ideally should cover emergency medical repatriation.

A list of doctors, dentists and health clinics is provided in the Bishkek chapter. There are no compulsory requirements but the standard **immunisations** of

LONG-HAUL FLIGHTS, CLOTS AND DVT

Dr Jane Wilson-Howarth

Long-haul air travel increases the risk of deep vein thrombosis. Although recent research has suggested that many of us develop clots when immobilised, most resolve without us ever having been aware of them. In certain susceptible individuals, though, large clots form and these can break away and lodge in the lungs. This is dangerous but happens in a tiny minority of passengers.

Studies have shown that flights of over 5½ hours are significant, and that people who take lots of shorter flights over a short space of time form clots. People at highest risk are:

- Those who have had a clot before – unless they are now taking warfarin
- People over 80 years of age
- Anyone who has recently undergone a major operation or surgery for varicose veins
- Someone who has had a hip or knee replacement in the last 3 months
- Cancer sufferers
- Those who have ever had a stroke
- People with heart disease
- Those with a close blood relative who has had a clot

Those with a slightly increased risk:

- People over 40
- Women who are pregnant or have had a baby in the last couple of weeks
- People taking female hormones or other oestrogen therapy
- Heavy smokers
- Those who have very severe varicose veins

tetanus, diphtheria polio and hepatitis A are all advised. Vaccination against typhoid may be recommended for longer stays or in poorer areas. Tuberculosis is all too common in Kyrgyzstan but it is unlikely to pose a threat to short-term visitors.

Malaria has been steadily increasing since 2000 and is mostly due to *Plasmodium vivax*. The risk is more common from June to October, mainly in Batken and Osh provinces. Up-to-date advice on this situation and the need for prophylaxis should be sought from a doctor or travel clinic. At the time of writing, chloroquine would be recommended for those travelling to risk areas during the risk season. In rural areas, and especially if cycling, dogs may be a nuisance and present the potential threat of rabies, although it is extremely unlikely that you will be bitten.

Although it is chlorinated, tap **water** is not of very good quality throughout the country and bottled or boiled water should be taken in preference. Thankfully freshly boiled tea is plentiful, abundant even, and perfectly safe to drink. Care should be taken with raw fruit and vegetables, particularly in the warmer months, and the standard recommendation to always peel or wash fresh fruit and vegetables is sound advice. Cooked food such as meat stews that have cooled and have been standing around for a while may be more problematic, as might some of Kyrgyzstan's dairy specialities such as *kumys* and *kurut* (dried yoghurt balls), which are sometimes plucked out of a horseman's grubby pocket to be popped in the mouth of the appreciative visitor. *Kumys* – fermented mare's milk – is not at all harmful (indeed many make claims to its health benefits), but it can upset the

- The very obese
- People who are very tall (over 6ft/1.8m) or short (under 5ft/1.5m)

A deep vein thrombosis (DVT) is a blood clot that forms in the deep leg veins. This is very different from irritating but harmless superficial phlebitis. DVT causes swelling and redness of one leg, usually with heat and pain in one calf and sometimes the thigh. A DVT is only dangerous if a clot breaks away and travels to the lungs (pulmonary embolus). Symptoms of a pulmonary embolus (PE) include chest pain that is worse on breathing in deeply, shortness of breath, and sometimes coughing up small amounts of blood. The symptoms commonly start 3–10 days after a long flight. Anyone who thinks that they might have a DVT needs to see a doctor immediately who will arrange a scan. Warfarin tablets (to thin the blood) are then taken for at least 6 months.

PREVENTION OF DVT Several conditions make the problem more likely. Immobility is the key, and factors like reduced oxygen in cabin air and dehydration may also contribute. To reduce the risk of thrombosis on a long journey:

- Exercise before and after the flight
- Keep mobile before and during the flight; move around every couple of hours
- Drink plenty of water or juices during the flight
- Avoid taking sleeping pills and excessive tea, coffee and alcohol
- Perform exercises that mimic walking and tense the calf muscles
- Consider wearing flight socks or support stockings (see *www.legshealth.com*)
- Take a meal of oily fish (mackerel, trout, salmon, sardines, etc) in the 24 hours before departure to reduce the tendency of the blood to clot, and thus DVT risk

If you think you are at increased risk of a clot, ask your doctor if it is safe to travel.

stomachs of those not used to its sour milk acidity and cause nausea and vomiting in the hapless visitor.

In the summer months, and particularly at altitude, some form of **sun protection** is essential in the form of a hat and/or sunscreen. Without this sunburn is likely, which causes not only discomfort but also dehydration and skin damage. The mountains may also bring problems of cold weather too, and it is important to ensure that whilst trekking you have adequate food, clothing and warm sleeping bags.

Altitude sickness is an ever-present threat above an altitude of 2,500m or more. Usually a sudden increase in altitude just causes minor discomfort such as a shortness of breath, dizziness, a racing heartbeat, a mild headache and loss of appetite. These are normal symptoms that can be ameliorated to some extent by taking painkillers, drinking plenty of fluids and shunning alcohol and tobacco. If these symptoms persist beyond a day or two, or rapidly worsen, then the only solution is to descend to a lower altitude. Altitude sickness is fairly indiscriminate in terms of who it affects; youth and fitness are no guarantees of avoidance – in fact, perhaps even the opposite, as it is often those in a hurry that come down with it. The best way to avoid altitude sickness is to ascend as slowly as possible, and if trekking over high passes observe the time-honoured maxim: 'walk high, sleep low'.

TRAVEL CLINICS AND HEALTH INFORMATION A full list of current travel clinic websites worldwide is available from the International Society of Travel Medicine on www.istm.org. For other journey preparation information, consult www.tripprep.com. Information about various medications may be found on www.emedicine.com. For information on malaria prevention, see www.preventingmalaria.info.

UK

Berkeley Travel Clinic 32 Berkeley St, London W1J 8EL (near Green Park tube station); ☎ 020 7629 6233
Cambridge Travel Clinic 48a Mill Rd, Cambridge CB1 2AS; ☎ 01223 367362; e enquiries@travelcliniccambridge.co.uk; www.travelcliniccambridge.co.uk. ⊕ 12.00–19.00 Tue–Fri, 10.00–16.00 Sat
Edinburgh Travel Clinic Regional Infectious Diseases Unit, Ward 41 OPD, Western General Hospital, Crewe Rd South, Edinburgh EH4 2UX; ☎ 0131 537 2822; www.mvm.ed.ac.uk. Travel helpline (☎ 0906 589 0380) open weekdays 09.00–12.00. Provides inoculations & antimalarial prophylaxis, & advises on travel-related health risks.
Fleet Street Travel Clinic 29 Fleet St, London EC4Y 1AA; ☎ 020 7353 5678; www.fleetstreetclinic.com. Vaccinations, travel products & latest advice.
Hospital for Tropical Diseases Travel Clinic Mortimer Market Bldg, Capper St (off Tottenham Ct Rd), London WC1E 6AU; ☎ 020 7388 9600; www.thehtd.org. Offers consultations & advice, & is able to provide all necessary drugs & vaccines for travellers. Runs a healthline (☎ 0906 133 7733) for country-specific information & health hazards. Also stocks nets, water purification equipment & personal protection measures.

Interhealth Worldwide Partnership Hse, 157 Waterloo Rd, London SE1 8US; ☎ 020 7902 9000; www.interhealth.org.uk. Competitively priced, one-stop travel health service. All profits go to their affiliated company, InterHealth, which provides health care for overseas workers on Christian projects.
Liverpool School of Medicine Pembroke Pl, Liverpool L3 5QA; ☎ 0151 708 9393; f 0151 705 3370; www.liv.ac.uk/lstm
MASTA (Medical Advisory Service for Travellers Abroad) Moorfield Rd, Yeadon, Leeds, West Yorkshire LS19 7BN; ☎ 0113 238 7500; www.masta-travel-health.com. Provides travel health advice, anti-malarials & vaccinations. There are over 25 MASTA pre-travel clinics in Britain; call or check online for the nearest. Clinics also sell mosquito nets, medical kits, insect protection & travel hygiene products.
NHS travel website www.fitfortravel.scot.nhs.uk. Provides country-by-country advice on immunisation & malaria, plus details of recent developments, & a list of relevant health organisations.
Nomad Travel Store/Clinic 3–4 Wellington Terrace, Turnpike Lane, London N8 0PX; ☎ 020 8889 7014; travel-health line (office hours only) ☎ 0906 863 3414; e sales@nomadtravel.co.uk; www.nomadtravel.co.uk. Also at 40 Bernard St, London

WCIN ILJ; ℡ 020 7833 4114; 52 Grosvenor Gdns, London SW1W 0AG; ℡ 020 7823 5823; & 43 Queens Rd, Bristol BS8 1QH; ℡ 0117 922 6567. For health advice, equipment such as mosquito nets & other anti-bug devices, & an excellent range of adventure travel gear. Clinic also in Southhampton.

Trailfinders Travel Clinic 194 Kensington High St, London W8 7RG; ℡ 020 7938 3999; www.trailfinders.com/travelessentials/travelclinic.htm
Travelpharm The Travelpharm website, www.travelpharm.com, offers up-to-date guidance on travel-related health & has a range of medications available through their online mini-pharmacy.

Irish Republic
Tropical Medical Bureau Grafton St Medical Centre, Grafton Bldgs, 34 Grafton St, Dublin 2; ℡ 1 671 9200; www.tmb.ie. A useful website specific to tropical

destinations. Also check website for other bureaux locations throughout Ireland.

USA
Centers for Disease Control 1600 Clifton Rd, Atlanta, GA 30333; ℡ 800 311 3435; travellers' health hotline (fax service) f 888 232 3299; www.cdc.gov/travel. The central source of travel information in the USA. The invaluable *Health Information for International Travel*, published annually, is available from the Division of Quarantine at this address.
Connaught Laboratories Pasteur Merieux Connaught, Route 611, PO Box 187, Swiftwater, PA 18370; ℡ 800 822 2463. They will send a free list of

specialist tropical-medicine physicians in your state.
IAMAT (International Association for Medical Assistance to Travelers) 1623 Military Rd, 279, Niagara Falls, NY 14304-1745; ℡ 716 754 4883; e info@iamat.org; www.iamat.org. A non-profit organisation that provides lists of English-speaking doctors abroad.
International Medicine Center 915 Gessner Rd, Suite 525, Houston, TX 77024; ℡ 713 550 2000; www.traveldoc.com

Canada
IAMAT Suite 1, 1287 St Clair Av W, Toronto, Ontario M6E 1B8; ℡ 416 652 0137; www.iamat.org
TMVC Suite 314, 1030 W Georgia St, Vancouver BC

V6E 2Y3; ℡ 1 888 288 8682; www.tmvc.com. Private clinic with several outlets in Canada.

Australia, New Zealand, Singapore
IAMAT PO Box 5049, Christchurch 5, New Zealand; www.iamat.org
TMVC ℡ 1300 65 88 44; www.tmvc.com.au. Clinics in Australia, New Zealand & Singapore, including:
Auckland Canterbury Arcade, 170 Queen St, Auckland; ℡ 9 373 3531

Brisbane 75a, Astor Terrace, Spring Hill, QLD 4000; ℡ 7 3815 6900
Melbourne 393 Little Bourke St, 2nd floor, Melbourne, VIC 3000; ℡ 3 9602 5788
Sydney Dymocks Bldg, 7th floor, 428 George St, Sydney, NSW 2000; ℡ 2 9221 7133

South Africa and Namibia
SAA-Netcare Travel Clinics Sanlam Bldg, 19, Fredman Dr, Sandton, P Bag X34, Benmore, JHB, Gauteng, 2010; www.travelclinic.co.za. Clinics throughout South Africa.
TMVC NHC Health Centre, Crnr Beyers Naude & Waugh

Northcliff; PO Box 48499, Roosevelt Park, 2129 (postal address); ℡ 011 888 7488; www.tmvc.com.au. Consult website for details of other clinics in South Africa & Namibia.

Switzerland
IAMAT 57 Chemin des Voirets, 1212 Grand Lancy,

Geneva; www.iamat.org

FURTHER READING
Wilson-Howarth, Dr Jane, and Ellis, Dr Matthew *Your Child Abroad: A Travel Health Guide* Bradt Travel Guides, 2005
Wilson-Howarth, Dr Jane, *Bugs, Bites & Bowels* Cadogan, 2006

THEFT Taking a few simple precautions will ensure that a visit to Kyrgyzstan is a safe and happy one. The Kyrgyz countryside is mostly very safe in terms of human menace, although inebriated locals can sometimes be a nuisance. The larger towns, and especially Bishkek, are another matter and caution should be taken after dark (see *Safety*, page 90).

At night the streets of all Kyrgyz towns and villages are generally pitch black with little – or nothing – in the way of street lighting and, putting the very real threat of tripping up over something to one side, there is a risk of mugging by locals whose resentment and coveting of the foreigner's wealth is further fuelled by strong drink. It should never be forgotten that, compared with Europe and North America, Kyrgyzstan is a very poor country, and that most Western visitors walk around with more cash in their pockets than most Kyrgyz could possibly earn in a year.

Alcohol often has a part to play in both aggravating resentment and giving Dutch courage to would-be attackers. Bishkek is the most problematic in this regard and taxis should be used after dark as there have been some nasty violent attacks over the past few years. Karakol, Osh and Naryn have occasional incidents too, although far less commonly than in the capital.

As well as the slight threat of robbery with violence, opportunistic theft is always a possibility – not especially common, but enough to ensure that you should be on your guard. Bustling markets and crowded *marshrutkas* are ideal environments for thieves to operate in. Special care should also be taken at cash machines and when leaving exchange offices. It goes without saying that cash and credit cards should be kept well out of sight in a money belt and preferably split up into a number of separate caches.

ALCOHOL Alcohol undoubtedly poses a serious social problem throughout the central Asian region; a problem that first came with Russian colonial rule, was ignored and partly contained during the Soviet period and has been exacerbated by poverty and a general lack of hope since independence. Remarkably, vodka is available more or less everywhere at rock bottom prices, even where there is little in the way of food to buy.

Heartfelt Kyrgyz hospitality is a wonderful thing but in all-male company it can sometimes quickly turn into little more than a kamikaze drinking session. It is crucial that moderate imbibers realise that there is no such thing as 'a small one', 'a quick one', or 'just one for the road'. An invitation to drink can be effectively the laying down of a gauntlet. The guest will be expected to keep up with the other drinkers and will find it difficult to detach himself from proceedings once a session is underway. It is considered very bad form to turn down further drinks once engaged in a boozing session and refusal may be seen as a grave insult to the host.

The best policy for those lacking livers of steel is to politely refuse in the first place, perhaps making something up on health reasons to explain one's abstinence. This will not be popular but at least it sets the tone and will be respected. If you start drinking, then you will be expected to continue to the dregs of the bottle… and then maybe start another one.

SAFETY FOR WOMEN The outward face of women in the country – both Kyrgyz and Russian – is one of self-confidence, independence and even feistiness. Even if this is not really an accurate picture, women travellers face no particular dangers in Kyrgyzstan. Sexual harassment is thankfully rare but, even though Kyrgyzstan is far from being a strictly Islamic regime, it is still unwise to dress scantily and in a provocative manner, despite the many young Russian women in the cities who do just that.

ROAD SAFETY Probably the greatest danger facing visitors is the poor condition of the roads, which coupled with eccentric, macho driving techniques and badly-serviced vehicles, make road accidents sadly all too common. The best advice is to be a little circumspect in choosing a driver, checking that they are not drunk or intending to become so during the trip (but do not worry about the odd bottle of *kumys*, this is standard issue and it is not very strong). Selecting an older driver is often a good idea as they tend to be calmer than tearaway youths, and also because if they have survived a driving career into middle age then they must be doing something right. Often, of course, you will have no choice, being squeezed into a minibus at the last minute before departure.

Seat belts are almost never used and drivers will laugh if you try to use them, or even be offended that you do not trust their skills. Overall, the best advice is to avoid travel at night where possible and shun drunken drivers and obvious speed merchants.

POLICE Crooked police officers are not exactly a safety issue but they can occasionally create problems in their attempts to extract money by subterfuge or intimidation (see page 90 for more detail and for potential trouble spots). Happily, this sort of incident is much less of a problem than it is used to be. The golden rules are to be polite, friendly even, stand your ground and try not to become separated from those around you. Police identification should always be shown and a note should be made of their name and number. Just doing this is usually enough to put off most would-be extortionists. It is important to remember that police do have the right to ask for passports, which you must carry at all times, but they are not permitted to stop and search in normal circumstances, or to count your money themselves. A missing US$100 note following a police money count appears to be by far the most commonly reported type of incident. If, for some reason, a *shtraf* (fine) needs to be paid, insist on paying it at a bank and not directly to the policeman in question, and also insist on a receipt.

TERRORISM Within Kyrgyzstan, **the region west and south of Osh** used to be considered dangerous by the British Foreign and Commonwealth Office (FCO) because of drug trafficking and incursions by Islamist fighters who took foreign hostages in 1999 and 2000. At the time of writing the FCO had dropped its advice to completely avoid this region and was merely warning about potential border tensions and the need to beware of land mines along the Uzbek and Tajik frontiers.

For the latest government warnings before leaving for Kyrgyzstan check the advice of the FCO at www.fco.uk or phone them on 0845 850 2829. Alternatively, check the travel advice of other governments: the Australian Department of Foreign Affairs (*www.smarttraveller.gov.au*), the Canadian Department of Foreign Affairs (*www.voyage.gc.ca*), the New Zealand Ministry of Foreign Affairs and Trade (*www.safetravel.govt.nz*) or the US Department of State (*http://travel.state.gov/travel*).

EMERGENCY TELEPHONE NUMBERS
Fire ☎ 101
Police ☎ 102
Urgent emergency medical assistance ☎ 103
Commercial emergency medical assistance ☎ 110

DISABLED TRAVELLERS

Apart from a few concessions in the capital, Kyrgyzstan has almost nothing in the way of facilities for disabled travellers. Exploring even Bishkek in a wheelchair would prove to be a challenge given the lack of ramps and poor condition of the pavements. On a more positive note, the majority of restaurants are ground-floor based, which is a slight advantage, and Bishkek's top hotels at least have ramps and reliable lifts. However, outside of the capital it would be unwise to expect any facilities whatsoever. For those disabled travellers planning to visit Kyrgyzstan, hiring private transport and a guide through one of the agencies listed here is a virtual necessity.

TRAVELLING WITH A FAMILY

Like most people throughout the world, central Asians love children and travelling to Kyrgyzstan with a young family in tow will definitely win points in terms of popularity with the locals. Having said that, there may be some problems of hygiene with very young children, and the sometimes rather limited food available might prove problematic with those young travellers who are fussy about what they eat. The typical home cooking of homestays, with plentiful fruit, jams and baked goods, is likely to be more popular than standard restaurant fare.

Independent travel in Kyrgyzstan can be hard work at times, with long, uncomfortable journeys that have few rest breaks. This type of travel is probably too onerous for the average child; hiring a car with a driver would be a much better bet, allowing regular breaks and toilet stops (although probably not toilets) and the opportunity to stop whenever something of interest is seen. Most children will naturally love some aspects of the country like its horses, plentiful wildlife and colourful markets, and the beaches of Issyk-Kul are also likely to be popular with most young travellers. On the other hand, few children will patiently spend hours examining Silk Road monuments or archaeological sites, and even fewer will be willing to spend long hours energetically hiking in the hills.

WHAT TO TAKE

Many visitors come to Kyrgyzstan to enjoy outdoor pursuits like trekking and horseriding and they should ensure that they bring all the necessary clothing such as walking boots, thermal gear and waterproofs with them. These are available in Kyrgyzstan, mostly in Bishkek, but the choice is poor and the quality generally not of a high standard.

A tent is essential for independent trekkers; these may be hired along with sleeping bags and other camping equipment from some trekking agencies or CBT groups but, again, the standard is usually not very good. Cooking stoves, if brought, should be of the multi-fuel type such as MSR or Primus that run on liquid fuel like white gas, or the gas type that run on Kovea cartridges, as Camping Gas stoves and their canisters are virtually unknown. It goes without saying that any cooking stoves to be carried on airplanes should be packed carefully, completely drained of fuel and thoroughly dried out. Stove fuel of any sort is most definitely not allowed on flights and so must be bought after arrival.

Any prescription drugs should be brought along, as well as a spare pair of glasses for spectacle wearers, and their optical prescription. Sunglasses are essential, especially if walking at altitude, as is sun cream, which is not easy to obtain in Kyrgyzstan. A torch (flashlight) is vital for those midnight forays to the outhouse at village homestays and is extremely useful even in Bishkek, where street lights are few and far between.

Photographers will find slide film very hard to obtain and should bring an adequate supply; similarly, digital photographers should bring sufficient memory cards to keep them going and also make sure that they have the appropriate adaptor (standard two-pin European) for their camera battery charger.

Any specialist or unusually sized batteries should be brought along and, although standard AA or AAA batteries for electronic devices like MP3 layers are widely available, these tend to be cheap Chinese ones that last a very short time, so a supply of these is a good idea too.

Adequate reading matter is important for those who like to have their nose in a book at night (sometimes there may not be much else to do). Literature in languages other than Russian or Kyrgyz is very hard to come across, even in Bishkek. Bringing along something that you can swap with fellow travellers is always a good idea. A Russian dictionary and/or phrase book is invaluable.

As with any travel off the beaten track, a small collection of various-sized plastic bags can prove useful to keep equipment dust-free, store dirty clothes and prevent food items from merging with other luggage items.

Most important of all is to bring enough money along, more than you think you will need, as although Kyrgyzstan is an inexpensive country for visitors there may be incidental expenses that may not have been budgeted for – tours, car hire, souvenirs, visas and flights. As there are few ATM machines in the country outside Bishkek, and bank transfers of funds tend to be slow and problematic, an emergency fund of a few high denomination dollar or euro banknotes is a wise precaution.

ELECTRICITY The electricity supply is standard for all of Russia and the CIS with 220V, 50Hz and European two-prong plugs. Despite supplying hydro-electric power to most of the region, power cuts are not unknown. Bring a good torch and perhaps buy some candles and a lighter.

MAPS

Detailed Russian 1:200,000 topographical maps of Kyrgyzstan are available in Bishkek at the GeoID map shop (see page 103), as are a number of political and physical maps of the whole country. For planning purposes, and to give an overview of the whole central Asian region, it is also good idea to buy a regional map before travelling to central Asia.

Nelles 1:1,750,000 Central Asia map is reasonable and marks some of the historical sites of interest to travellers. Its only drawback is the eccentric Turkish phonetic spelling system used – ie: Biškek, Oš – which is unknown in Kyrgyzstan. The *Gizi Map 1:1,750,000 Central Asia* is a good alternative, as is the *Freytag & Berndt 1:1,750,000 Central Asia: Road Map*.

$ MONEY AND BANKING

CURRENCY Following independence from the Soviet Union in 1991, Kyrgyzstan was the first central Asian country to introduce its own currency, the **Kyrgyz som**, which replaced the Soviet rouble as legal tender on 10 May 1993. The Kyrgyz som, which is relatively stable and currently trades at a rate of around £1 sterling = 73som, US$1 = 35som, is further divided into 100 *tiyin,* but these are rarely used in transactions.

Kyrgyz banknotes come in denominations of 1, 5, 10, 20, 50, 100, 200, 500 and 1,000som. There are also 10 and 50 *tiyin* notes but these are rarely seen. There are no coins. All of the banknotes feature prominent Kyrgyz historical figures on the front and a variety of images depicting Kyrgyzstan's buildings, sights and folklore on the reverse.

EXCHANGING MONEY Kyrgyzstan remains primarily a **cash economy**, although credit cards and ATM machines are slowly starting to catch up. In Bishkek there are a number of **ATM machines** that will issue both Kyrgyz som or US dollars using a debit service like Cirrus (see page 104 for locations). Outside of Bishkek, there are very few others in the country, although this should change. At the time of writing there were ATMs in Osh and Jalal-Abad but not Naryn or Karakol.

Credit cards can rarely be used to pay for transactions, apart from in smart Bishkek hotels and restaurants or top-notch gift shops. It is possible to arrange cash advances against a credit card at some banks in Bishkek, Jalal-Abad and Osh. Cash transfers may also be organised through Western Union, which operates through several banks in Bishkek. MasterCard and VISA are the most widely accepted credit cards by both businesses and ATM machines.

A number of banks will change cash, but it is usually simpler and quicker to visit an **exchange booth** or *obmyen valyoot* (обмен валют), which most large towns usually have a handful of, often near the central bazaar. Take care in counting the notes given to you and also be sure to tuck the money away securely before leaving the booth or office. If there are no exchange booths, there will nearly always be someone who is willing to change money if enquiries are made, although, like the exchange booths, they will normally insist on pristine banknotes. Exchange booths do not charge commission but make their profit from the small difference between the buying and selling price (which is nothing like as extortionate as it is in travel agencies and banks on every high street in the UK). There is usually very little difference, if any, between the rates offered by individual offices and so it is hardly worth shopping around.

It goes without saying that it is sensible to take an adequate supply of Kyrgyz money when venturing into areas of the country that are off the beaten track, which could be almost everywhere. Outside of the major centres, large denomination notes like 500som and 1,000som can be hard to change, so try and have a stash of smaller bills. Generally speaking, US dollars are by far the most popular currency, but euros can also be exchanged, as can pounds sterling at a few places. The currency of surrounding countries – Kazakh tenge, Uzbek som, Russian roubles – may also be bought and sold at exchange booths. For Tajik som and Chinese yuan, the bazaar in Osh is probably the best place to get hold of these.

For the time being at least, it is best to bring along a mixture of cash and debit and credit cards. **Travellers' cheques** are another possibility, although outside the capital there are few banks that will exchange them. If bringing travellers' cheques it is essential that they are issued by a well known company like American Express or Thomas Cook and that they are in US dollars. A fairly hefty commission is normally charged to change travellers' cheques.

Changing cash, large denomination notes – US$50 or US$100 – are preferred and they must be in excellent, if not pristine, condition. Smaller denomination bills – US$20 or less – will attract a lower exchange rate, as will any banknotes in a less than perfect state. Tatty, torn or scribbled-on notes will be rejected out of hand. US dollar bills should be of the post-1995 series, as forgeries of earlier series have created suspicion of these. If buying US dollars from a bank or exchange office before travelling to Kyrgyzstan, be sure to insist on brand new, high-denomination bills, as a tatty US$10 note is virtually worthless. Unfortunately, the dollar bills issued by ATM machines in Kyrgyzstan sometimes fail to live up to the same high standards that the money exchange industry insists upon itself.

BUDGETING Travelling in Kyrgyzstan is inexpensive and it is an extremely good value destination. Costs are far lower than in Kazakhstan and considerably less than in neighbouring Uzbekistan and Tajikistan. In Bishkek, staying in a five-star hotel, going to nightclubs and eating in the city's best restaurants, it is possible to spend almost as much as one would do in a city in Europe; however, few come to Kyrgyzstan just to do this. Throughout much of Kyrgyzstan it is perfectly possible to get by on an equivalent of US$20 a day, as homestay accommodation with full board is usually no more than US$10–12 and public transport is cheap. Even prices in Bishkek are quite reasonable and a daily budget of US$15–30 should be sufficient once accommodation has been paid for, as long as you do not pursue the extravagant lifestyle of an oligarch.

What tends to dent modest budgets the most are incidental expenses like renting a car and driver, hiring a guide, paying for the services of a tour agency and obtaining visas and permits. Even including these into the equation, Kyrgyzstan is still a good value destination that offers adventurous travel at a budget price. By far the major expense will be getting to Kyrgyzstan in the first place. Having invested all that money in travelling there it seems churlish to scrimp and save mere pennies after arrival. Of course, if you are visiting Kyrgyzstan as part of a pre-paid organised tour you will just need a little pocket money and some cash to buy souvenirs.

GETTING AROUND

Getting around Kyrgyzstan is reasonably straightforward between the major centres – Bishkek, Karakol, Naryn, Jalal-Abad and Osh. Public transport tends to be a little erratic at times and some of the roads are in poor condition. Hiring a taxi for a couple or small group for long distances is a relatively cheap and fast way of getting about. Self-drive car hire is almost unknown, mainly because of the complex paperwork needed. Given Kyrgyzstan's pot-holed roads, its eccentric driving habits and a police force keen to extort fines from their motorised victims, it is something that is best avoided by foreign visitors anyway. Flying may be a viable option for some north–south travel as it is markedly quicker, and may be only a little more expensive than travelling by road.

BY BUS AND MINIBUS Battered old Russian buses run between Bishkek, Karakol and other destinations. They are slow, reasonably comfortable and cheap. A conductor collects the fares along the way and they tend to make frequent stops. Smaller snub-nosed buses run along other routes, mainly to village destinations.

Many long distance bus services have been largely superseded by minibuses (*marshrutki*) running the same routes, which are considerably quicker and charge about 1½ times the bus fare. Minibuses tend to congregate outside bus stations and leave when full, usually with about 12–18 passengers plus the driver. Some *marshrutki* that travel relatively short distances along fixed routes, such as those along the shores of Lake Issyk-Kul, operate rather like a local bus service and do not wait to fill up before leaving, as they constantly pick up and drop off all along their route.

Fares are fixed and are either collected before setting off or somewhere along the way. A common practice is to pass money forward to the driver who then passes the change back. Tickets are rarely issued and there are no formal timetables, but long distance services more commonly leave for their destination in the mornings and early afternoons and avoid travel at night. Minibuses tend to have almost no proper luggage storage space behind the rear seat, but baggage will always be squeezed in somewhere with the minimum of fuss. Typical minibus fares are Bishkek–Cholpon-Ata 250som, Bishkek–Karakol 300som and Bishkek–Naryn 300som.

BY TAXI Kyrgyzstan's taxis will go almost anywhere if you pay them: a road surface of little more than loose rocks and sheep holds little fear for the average

CYCLING IN KYRGYZSTAN

This is the transport of choice for an increasing number of visitors to Kyrgyzstan and for those with the appropriate spirit of adventure it is an excellent way to see the country. Roads are often in a poor condition so the bicycle needs to be of robust construction, preferably a mountain bike or tough touring bike. As well as pot-holed road surfaces, road signs are extremely rare and drivers are sometimes drunk and/or too fast. Nevertheless, the general attitude towards cyclists is said to be respectful and most reports of cycling tours in Kyrgyzstan are favourable.

Away from the built-up Bishkek–Balykchy section, and the north side of Lake Issyk-Kul, roads are mostly quiet with light traffic. Cycling at night is obviously a very bad idea. Opportunities abound for trailblazers willing to get off the beaten track but it is vital that full repair kit, spares, food, stove and tent are carried to be fully self-supporting.

Popular routes include cycling around Lake Issyk-Kul, especially along the quieter southern shore, and common circular itineraries include Bishkek–Kochkor–Chaek–Suusamyr–Bishkek; Bishkek–Talas–Jalal-Abad–Naryn–Bishkek; Bishkek–Karakol–Kochkor–Bishkek; and Bishkek–Talas–Tash-Kömür–Bishkek. These range from 650–1,600km in length and sections of them may be combined to offer more varied itineraries. Even more adventurous, off-road, possibilities exist along various routes that cross the Terskey Ala-Too range to reach the Kichi Naryn valley and Naryn town, or up along the Barskoon valley and east towards Ak-Shyrak, although this route probably requires a border permit and military permission.

Long distance buses such as Bishkek–Karakol or Osh–Kashgar will generally take bicycles, but *marshrutki* and taxis usually will not have room unless they have a roof-rack. The larger planes flying between Bishkek and Osh (ie: an Antonov AN-24, not a Yak-40) can also transport bicycles.

Nearly all of the spare parts found in Kyrgyzstan tend to be of Chinese manufacture but there is a specialist bike shop in Bishkek run by Oleg Yuganov: Bike Master (*Serova 14a*; ✆ *0312 670 974*).

The best maps of the country for cyclists and hikers are the 1:200,000 Russian maps that are available at the GeoID map shop at Kievskaya 107 (✆ *0312 212 296*) in Bishkek.

Kyrgyz Lada or Zhiguli driver. Fares are loosely negotiable, but are usually about twice the bus fare multiplied by four, the number of passenger seats. In many instances there is no bus or minibus service and so a taxi is sometimes the only option.

If there is a CBT network in the town or village they usually have their drivers who are familiar with the funny ways of the tourist and knowledgeable about the sort of places that they wish to go. Taxis may be hired for less than the CBT rate in the bazaar, although this is very dependent on the language and negotiation skills of the client as well as on just how desperate the driver is to find a fare.

More popular routes often have **shared taxis** running the same routes as the minibuses and buses. They are effectively the same as ordinary taxis except that they run the same route regularly and aim to fill the car with four passengers who all pay the same share. Like minibuses, they leave when full, but will leave earlier with less than a full complement of passengers if those present agree to pay for the empty seat(s) between them. Other than flying, shared taxis are the best way to travel between Osh and Jalal-Abad and Bishkek. They tend to cost less heading south than they do returning to Bishkek. Typical shared taxi fares are Bishkek–Osh, 600–800som; Osh–Bishkek, 1,500som.

BY TRAIN Kyrgyzstan's train system is very sparse and, apart from the possibility of arriving on the international service from Moscow via Kazakhstan, it is unlikely that you will see a train, let alone use one. The only passenger service to speak of is the sporadic Bishkek–Balykchy service that takes up to 7 hours to reach somewhere that most people do not wish to go. The equivalent bus or minibus takes just 2 hours.

BY AIR Bishkek has a regular service with Osh and there are usually several planes a day between the two cities. With promotional fares as low as 1,500som this can be a worthwhile alternative to a long, tiring shared taxi ride between the north and south of the country.

Other domestic services include a daily service to Jalal-Abad and flights two or three times a week to Kerben and Batken. The domestic baggage weight limit is 15 kilos per passenger; anything over this will cost an additional US$0.20 per kilo.

ACCOMMODATION

Hotels in Kyrgyzstan range from luxurious to basic *gostinitsas*, although overall the majority fall into the lower end of this range. As the capital and largest city, Bishkek has the largest number and the widest range, having the Hyatt Regency, the country's best and only five-star hotel, along with a handful of large, comfortable four-star hotels that have mostly been built with foreign funding. These cost more or less the same sort of prices as would be paid in a Western city.

A fair number of Soviet-era hotels from before independence have survived and these still tend to be run on much the same lines as they were during the heyday of the USSR, giving a taste of the Soviet period that is nostalgic for some. Most large towns have at least one example of this sort of place and, depending on the alternatives available, they are at least serviceable and can sometimes represent reasonable value for money. Typically, they cost anything between US$8–20 for a double room.

In a few places a dual- or even triple-pricing policy applies in which foreigners pay twice as much as CIS passport holders, who in turn pay double that of a Kyrgyz citizen. It goes without saying that such places usually represent poor value. Some of the older state-run hotels have since been taken into private ownership and renovated, although sometimes the subsequent increase in room prices is not matched by an appreciable improvement in quality.

As well as Soviet-era hotels there are also health resorts and **sanatoria** from the same period, particularly on the north shore of Lake Issyk-Kul, which offer residential packages that combine health treatments with full board and the option of a variety of vacation leisure pursuits. It is usually possible just to book a room and meals at these places but they are far more used to catering for the tastes of CIS clients than those of Westerners. A more basic version of these resorts are *turbaza*, simple vacation camps that house guests in basic wooden huts and that are usually found in mountain valleys such as Ala-Archa or resorts like Arslanbob.

In recent years a number of small, purpose-built **boutique-style hotels** have been built with foreign visitors in mind. These tend to be in the middle price range of between US$50–80 for a double room and are found mostly in Bishkek, although there are also examples of these in Karakol, Naryn, Osh and Jalal-Abad too.

Organised **yurt camps** are another recent innovation, which are usually tucked away at beautiful but reasonably accessible *jailoos* and run by Bishkek tour companies who house their tour clients there as part of a trek. These are highly popular as they offer visitors the opportunity to stay in a traditional nomadic shelter without compromising comfort too much, as the best yurt camps provide a number of distinctly non-traditional features like hot showers, indoor toilets and Western food. Full board at a yurt camp usually costs in the order of US$15–20 a day.

More authentically, it is usually possible to stay in genuine **yurts** just by turning up at a *jailoo* in the summer months; indeed, some families erect an extra yurt for the use of guests. These usually lack any proper washing facilities and normally just have a pit toilet. The meals provided are often very good although, understandably, they tend to involve a high proportion of dairy produce. The price is usually negotiable but is of the order of 400som (US$10) per person including meals.

The most revolutionary trend in Kyrgyz tourism in recent years, especially as far as independent travellers are concerned, has been the setting up of a comprehensive **homestay** network through the **Community Based Tourism (CBT)** initiative. There are also homestays in Kyrgyzstan that are not affiliated to CBT or its Naryn-based sister network of Shepherd's Life, but those that do belong are vetted by local and national representatives for quality and their suitability for Western tourists.

CBT homestays are found in many towns and villages throughout Kyrgyzstan, especially in those places of interest to tourists like Kochkor, Karakol and Arslanbob. The only place they do not exist is in Bishkek, where there are plenty of other alternatives. Homestays are extremely variable and can range from a rural homestead with wandering cows and clucking chickens to a Soviet-era city apartment. Similarly, toilet facilities may be anything from a plush bathroom to an outhouse at the bottom of the garden. Food is normally available and the host usually makes use of home-grown ingredients to create delicious meals.

THE KYRGYZ HOMESTAY EXPERIENCE

Lake Issyk-Kul in late summer: the crowds of holidaying Kazakhs at Cholpon-Ata on the north shore are starting to head back to Almaty; the Western travellers who have come to Karakol to trek in the valleys to the south are starting to thin out too. This is a time of abundance, when apricots bend branches as they ripen and fall to the floor in every garden orchard. It is the jam-making season and nowhere does the jam taste better than in Kyrgyzstan's family-run homestays, especially those close to the shores of Lake Issyk-Kul.

Arriving at the homestay for the first time, hospitality dictates that refreshment is provided as you get to know your hosts and they try their best to make something of you. Tea is brewed and a large pot is placed centre stage on the table. Then saucers of boiled sweets and bowls of fruit are brought – apples, grapes, plums, apricots, pomegranates – whatever the small orchard outside is able to produce. Then bread is produced, perhaps more than one sort: crisp, usually fresh, often homemade, always delicious. Finally the *coup de grâce*, the jam … or rather the jams: strawberry, apricot, plum and best of all, wild blackcurrant. The flavour is intense, dark and delicious; you have arrived in jam heaven.

Full of tea, bread, jam and fruit your landlady asks you what you would like to eat for dinner, and when. The afternoon tea has just been the hors d'oeuvres, a ritual act of hospitality to welcome the foreign guest. You are shown to your accommodation, inevitably a room full of cushions, hand-embroidered throws and spare bedding, with carpets on the walls and Russian literature and children's school books in the bookcase. The room is cosy, homely, and full of the dreams of the children who used to sleep in it. You lie down for a minute, close your eyes and, replete with fine bread and jam of an almost narcotic quality, nod off briefly and add your own reverie to the dream-pool.

Prices are very reasonable and are set according to CBT criteria, which award a property a one-, two- or three-edelweiss rating based on facilities and quality. Most homestays fall into the one-edelweiss category. The beauty of staying in these, apart from their homeliness and quality food, is the experience of seeing everyday Kyrgyz (or Russian, or Uzbek) family life, and the knowledge that your money is going directly to the family and local community (once the co-ordinator's 10% commission has been taken off) rather than to a faceless multinational hotel company that really does not need it. Having said that, it is easy to forget that even given the sometimes humble surroundings of a village homestay the family that you are staying with is relatively well-to-do, at least in local terms.

CBT HOMESTAY ACCOMMODATION CHARGES Accommodation and meal prices vary between provinces, with the Naryn region being the cheapest and Jalal-Abad the most expensive.

B&B 1 edelweiss 250–350som
B&B 2 edelweiss 300–450som
B&B 3 edelweiss 350–500som
B&B in a yurt 250–350som
Lunch or dinner in a homestay 90–140som

✖ FOOD AND DRINK

Food in Kyrgyzstan tends to fall into two main categories – Kyrgyz and Russian – although sometimes what is on offer is more of a hybrid of the two. Staying in homestays, the food prepared by the hostess is always plentiful and usually very tasty and generally there is little point in looking to eat elsewhere. Away from the larger urban centres, the dining out options are usually rather limited, although the Kyrgyz capital has a large choice of places to eat. Bishkek has a wide range of smart restaurants that sell Turkish, Italian, American, Chinese, Indian, Korean and Japanese food in addition to the standard fare. Outside of Bishkek, the larger towns have a few upmarket restaurants between them, but generally food is sold at simple cafés, traditional *chaikhanas* or Russian-style canteens, *stolovaya*.

Kyrgyz cooking is very meat-based and that meat is usually mutton, but sometimes beef is used, particularly for *shashlyk*. Chicken rarely finds its way into Kyrgyz cookery and when it does the quality is not usually very good. Horsemeat is highly thought of and horsemeat sausages, *chuchuk*, are a popular accompaniment to vodka sessions. As Muslims, Kyrgyz, Uzbeks and Dungans do not eat pork, but it can be found at some Chinese and Russian restaurants. Fish is uncommon, apart from the smoked fish that are sold by the roadside near Lake Issyk-Kul.

Kyrgyz dishes that can be found more or less everywhere are *shorpo*, a mutton stew that always comes with a big chunk of bone with fatty meat attached; *laghman*, noodles with mutton and a spicy sauce; and *manti*, steamed mutton dumplings. *Shashlyk*, the central Asian kebab of skewer-grilled mutton pieces, can be found almost anywhere; just look for the grill-man at the front of the café, as the cooking is always done outside. *Plov* is made from a simple mixture of rice, mutton, carrots and onions all cooked together in a big pot, which can be delicious when it is well-made. It is actually an Uzbek dish but it can be found throughout the country, especially in the south.

The Kyrgyz national dish of *beshbarmak* is more of a home-cooked festival food than a restaurant item but some restaurants offer it. The ultimate Kyrgyz snack food is *samsa*, which are rather like Indian samosas but instead of containing spicy vegetables they are filled with mutton, onions and gravy. *Samsi* are generally sold directly from small bakeries, especially in the mornings and at lunchtime, and they make a good takeaway snack or quick lunch. They can be very fatty and are at their best when hot and fresh. For more on traditional Kyrgyz food see *Kyrgyz cuisine*, page 33.

Popular **Russian dishes** include *pirogi*, fried ravioli-like pastry packets, and *pelmeni*, small ravioli served in a broth. *Blini* are pancakes, either sweet or savoury, that, if you are lucky, your homestay hostess might prepare for breakfast. Most Russian menus usually involve several different types of salad that utilise copious quantities of mayonnaise. One excellent and surprisingly delicious salad combination is grated beetroot and diced walnuts.

In addition to Kyrgyz and Russian food, **Dungan dishes** are also sometimes found in the north, especially in the Chui valley, the Dungan stronghold. Dungan food is rather like Chinese food but spicier. *Ganfan*, made of rice and meat, is probably the most popular Dungan dish and this is often sold at markets.

Vegetarians will have a little more luck in finding something to eat in Russian restaurants than in their meat-centred Kyrgyz counterparts, but overall it is fairly difficult to find much in the way of purely vegetarian dishes. Fortunately, local markets always have a good selection of fruit, vegetables, cheeses and tinned goods. Some homestay hosts are able to rustle up vegetarian dishes, given adequate warning.

Bread, the staple carbohydrate in the region, is usually in the form of *lepyoshka*, a Russian flat unleavened loaf, or otherwise *nan*, the Kyrgyz equivalent. Both are delicious when fresh and far superior to the sliced, white variety that is found in supermarkets.

By far the most popular hot drink is **tea**, either green, which is preferred by most Kyrgyz, or black, the Russian favourite. Placing an order for food in a restaurant, it will more or less be assumed that you wish to order tea as well, even if you have already ordered beers or soft drinks. Kyrgyz going out to eat think nothing of ordering beer, vodka and tea all at the same time. Tea is invariably cheap at about 5som for a pot, and drinking plenty of it is the best and safest way to ensure hydration where the water supply is questionable. Coffee, where it is found, is instant and quite horrible, the only exception being the top Bishkek restaurants that have espresso machines.

Beer is widely available and quite good, the commonest brand being Russian Baltika, which is numbered according to its strength – Baltika 0 is non-alcoholic (hard to find!), Baltika 3 is moderately low gravity, Baltika 5 is reasonably strong, Baltika 7 is very strong and Baltika 9 is like rocket fuel. Another Russian beer that is widely available is Sibirskaya Korona, and there are Kyrgyz brands like Akademiya that are served on draught. Kyrgyz beers tend to be cheaper than Russian brands, although also weaker and less reliable in flavour. The Steinbrau beers of Bishkek that are produced by an ethnic German brewery of the same name are excellent.

Other popular drinks are, of course, vodka (*arak*) and *kumys*, although the latter is not generally sold in cafés, as it is seen more as a homemade drink of the *jailoos*; it is, however, commonly sold at the roadside from yurts. *Bozo* is a slightly alcoholic drink that is made from fermented millet wheat and Shoro is a well-known proprietary brand of *maksym*, a drink made from wheat. Kyrgyz wine is best avoided.

PUBLIC HOLIDAYS AND FESTIVALS

FIXED HOLIDAYS

New Year's Day	1 January
Orthodox Christmas Day	7 January
Orthodox New Year	14 January
Army Day	23 February

International Women's Day	8 March
Nooruz	21 March
Labour Day	1 May
Constitution Day	5 May
Victory Day	9 May
Kyrgyz Independence Day	31 August
October Revolution Day	7 November

It is likely that October Revolution Day will be abandoned as an official public holiday in the near future. Other important days in the year that are not officially holidays are 1 September, **First Bell**, the first day of the new school year in which children dress up in their best clothes to go to school. **Teachers' Day** follows on the first Sunday in October.

Nooruz (Navrus), which takes place on 21 March, is probably the most important of the traditional holidays in Kyrgyzstan. The festival, which dates back to Zoroastrian times and is celebrated throughout central Asia, is a syncretic mix of Zoroastrian, Islamic and old shamanistic practices that celebrate the spring equinox. Although pagan in origin, Nooruz has been adopted by Islam in the region and is even celebrated with great enthusiasm in religiously conservative Iran. Since independence, Kyrgyzstan and the other central Asian republics have reclaimed Nooruz as a national celebration after it had been officially discouraged, and even banned for a short while, during the Soviet period.

At Nooruz, a special meal that symbolises spring is prepared that includes seven items that all begin with a 'sh' sound: *sharob, shir, sheker, sharbat, shirinkilar, sham* and *shona* (wine, milk, sugar, sherbet, sweets, a candle and a fresh bud). In addition to this, *sumalak*, a special dish made of sprouted wheat, is served to women only, while men have their own special dish, *halim*, a sort of meaty porridge. *Archa* (juniper) twigs are burned for good luck, friends are visited, debts are traditionally paid off and the whole region celebrates with music, dancing and traditional games.

MOVEABLE MUSLIM RELIGIOUS HOLIDAYS
Kurban Ait (Feast of the Sacrifice) (*8 Dec 2008, 27 Nov 2009, 16 Nov 2010*) Known as Eid ad-Ahda elsewhere, takes place 9 weeks after the end of Ramadan and is a signal for the beginning of the *hajj* season, the pilgrimage to Mecca (although few Kyrgyz actually do this). It is traditional to slaughter a sheep at this time if you can afford to.

Orozo Ait (End of Ramadan) (*2 Oct 2008, 21 Sep 2009, 10 Sep 2010*) Otherwise known as Eid al-Fitr in Arabic, is the celebration that follows the end of Ramadan in which a large meal is shared by families and friends, gifts of new clothes are given to family members and alms are given to the poor. Ramadan is not rigorously observed by the Kyrgyz but it is taken more seriously by Kyrgyzstan's more orthodox Uzbek population.

🛒 SHOPPING

Bishkek has markets, department stores, supermarkets, souvenir emporia and a range of specialist shops. These tend to follow office hours and are open between 09.00–18.00, often later, and some of them close for an hour for lunch between 13.00–14.00. Elsewhere in the country, particularly in the villages, there are few formal shops other than the odd village store; most goods are either bought at weekly or daily outdoor markets or at any number of small kiosks that sell sweets, cigarettes, stationery and alcohol. Many people, especially old women, supplement their meagre incomes by selling a few things from a pavement pitch: pens, cigarettes, soft drinks, sunflower seeds and so on.

The bazaar is always the best place to purchase food items like cheese, fruit and vegetables, as this is where the best produce will normally be found in terms of both price and freshness. Customers are often invited to taste the goods on offer and a little good-natured bartering is perfectly acceptable. Most town bazaars are open everyday, although there is usually one day in the week when they are at their busiest. Smaller villages may have just a weekly market, although there may be a few stalls that are open every day.

SOUVENIRS Bishkek has by far the widest range of places selling souvenirs, although traditional crafts like *shyrdaks* may also be bought in the provinces in places like Naryn, Kochkor, Tamchy and Bokonbaevo, where there may be both better quality and lower prices on offer because they are being sold direct from the manufacturer.

Shyrdaks are by far the most popular souvenirs bought by Western visitors, along with unstitched *ala-kiyiz*, but most souvenir shops usually have a range of other traditional goods on sale that include items like felt slippers, miniature yurts, ceramics, hand embroidery, *kurak* patchwork, wooden objects, leather items and musical instruments like *komuz* or *temir komuz* (see also *Shopping*, page 102).

The exportation of antiques (which here means over 30 years old) requires a special **export certificate** that can be time-consuming to obtain. Many of the Bishkek tour agencies are able to provide the necessary paperwork given reasonable notice. Some of the more upmarket souvenir showrooms will automatically provide the certificate and include the cost of it into the price.

TREKKING EQUIPMENT It is impossible to find Camping Gas canisters in Kyrgyzstan and you will not be allowed to bring them with you on the plane. Korean-made Kovea screw-type gas canisters are available for US$5–6 and cost about 50som to refill. These may be found at the **Red Fox outdoor shop** in Bishkek, which is on Sovetskaya near the junction with Kulatov, south of the railway station, on the second floor of the same building as Ak-Sai Travel. Red Fox also stocks reasonable quality mountain bikes, a range of outdoor clothing, and trekking and climbing equipment. A safer bet for stoves is probably to take a multi-fuel type that runs on 'white gas', which will work using the lighter fuel (*benzin dlia zazhigalok*) sold in general stores in 0.5litre plastic bottles.

 ARTS AND ENTERTAINMENT

Bishkek has its nightclubs, cinemas, theatres and bars but outside the capital there is little in the way of entertainment apart from in larger towns that have cinemas showing films that have been badly dubbed into Russian. Bishkek has at least one cinema that shows films in their original foreign language, although all theatrical performances are in either Russian or Kyrgyz. There are occasional classical music concerts and ballet performances in the city, especially in the winter months.

Throughout the more rural regions in summer, a number of traditional festivals are staged that celebrate typical Kyrgyz pursuits such as horse games, eagle-hunting, dancing and Manas recitation. Although these may have the slightly artificial feel that comes from having been staged for the benefit of tourists, they are well worth attending for a first hand experience of traditional games like *ulak tartysh* and *kyz-kumay*. The *chabana* 'cowboy' festivals held in late summer are an altogether more authentic experience if you manage to come across one, although they are harder to pin down in terms of time and place.

PHOTOGRAPHY

Kyrgyzstan is, as the cliché goes, a photographer's dream. With gorgeous scenery and striking-looking people there is plenty to photograph throughout the country. Most people do not mind having their photographs taken but it is polite to ask first. Be a little cautious about snapping anything that might be considered to be of military importance – railway stations, industrial plants, border posts and airports – but generally speaking there are very few restrictions.

As well as sufficient film, batteries and memory cards make sure that you have an adaptor for the battery charger, a cleaning brush and a plastic bag to put the camera in when conditions get dusty. Some internet cafés may be able to write digital files onto disk but it is best to ensure that you have sufficient flash cards or space on a portable memory device to cover your visit. Slide photographers should be aware that professional quality slide film is almost impossible to find, even in Bishkek. Bishkek has plenty of Kodak shops that will process print film, most even offering an hour's turn-around service. The quality is usually reasonable although this is purely a matter of personal risk.

MEDIA AND COMMUNICATIONS

MEDIA
Newspapers and magazines The main English-language newspaper in the country is the twice-weekly Bishkek-based *Times of Central Asia* (*www.times.kg*), which covers stories from all over the region and is available from newsstands in the capital. Another, more parochial, English-language weekly newspaper is the *Bishkek Observer*, which has both a local and international edition.

Discovery Kyrgyzstan (*www.silkpress.com*) is an English-language magazine that is published four times a year and features articles of interest to foreign visitors.

Foreign English-language newspapers like *The Times* and *The Washington Post* can sometimes be found at newsstands and upmarket hotels in Bishkek but they tend to be at least two days old.

National newspapers include *Vecherniy Bishkek*, a privately owned Russian-language daily, *Slovo Kyrgyzstana*, a government-owned Russian-language paper that is published three times a week, and *Respublika*, a privately owned Kyrgyz-language daily.

Television and radio The state-run Kyrgyz National TV and Radio Broadcasting Corporation has two networks in Kyrgyz and Russian. There are a few private channels like Piramida and NTS in Bishkek, Ecological Youth in the Issyk-Kul region and Osh TV in Osh. Bishkek has cable TV, which offers packages that feature a large number of foreign stations like BBC World, Fox, CBS and Al Jazeera.

INTERNET NEWS AND RESOURCES
Akipress news agency www.akipress.com
Eurasianet www.eurasianet.org
Internews www.internews.kg
Kabar news agency http://en.kabar.kg
News agency 24 www.24.kg
Institute for War and Peace Reporting www.iwpr.net
Registan News www.registan.net. News from across the central Asian region.
Times of Central Asia www.times.kg. The web version of the newspaper.

Ariadne Van Zandbergen

EQUIPMENT Although with some thought and an eye for composition you can take reasonable photos with a 'point-and-shoot' camera, you need an SLR camera if you are at all serious about photography. Modern SLRs tend to be very clever, with automatic programmes for almost every possible situation, but remember that these programmes are limited in the sense that the camera cannot think, but only make calculations. Every starting amateur photographer should read a photographic manual for beginners and get to grips with such basics as the relationship between aperture and shutter speed.

Always buy the best lens you can afford. The lens determines the quality of your photo more than the camera body. Fixed fast lenses are ideal, but very costly. A zoom lens makes it easier to change composition without changing lenses the whole time. If you carry only one lens, a 28–70mm (digital 17–55mm) or similar zoom should be ideal. For a second lens, a lightweight 80–200mm or 70–300mm (digital 55–200mm) or similar will be excellent for candid shots and varying your composition. Wildlife photography will be very frustrating if you don't have at least a 300mm lens. For a small loss of quality, tele-converters are a cheap and compact way to increase magnification: a 300mm lens with a 1.4x converter becomes 420mm, and with a 2x it becomes 600mm. Note, however, that 1.4x and 2x tele-converters reduce the speed of your lens by 1.4 and 2 stops respectively.

For photography from a vehicle, a solid beanbag, which you can make yourself very cheaply, will be necessary to avoid blurred images, and is more useful than a tripod. A clamp with a tripod head screwed on to it can be attached to the vehicle as well. Modern dedicated flash units are easy to use; aside from the obvious need to flash when you photograph at night, you can improve a lot of photos in difficult 'high contrast' or very dull light with some fill-in flash. It pays to have a proper flash unit as opposed to a built-in camera flash.

DIGITAL/FILM Digital photography is now the preference of most amateur and professional photographers, with the resolution of digital cameras improving the whole time. For ordinary prints a 6 megapixel camera is fine. For better results and the possibility of enlarging images and for professional reproduction, higher resolution is available up to 16 megapixels.

Memory space is important. The number of pictures you can fit on a memory card depends on the quality you choose. Calculate in advance how many pictures you can fit on a card and either take enough cards to last for your trip, or take a storage drive onto which you can download the content. A laptop gives the advantage that you can see your pictures properly at the end of each day and edit and delete rejects, but a storage device is lighter and less bulky. These drives come in different capacities up to 80GB.

C **TELEPHONES** To dial an international number the country code is preceded by 00; for an internal long-distance intercity call, 0 is dialled before the area code. Local calls from a private phone are effectively free; from a street phone they require either a *zheton* (token) or a phone card – both can be obtained from kiosks. Pre-paid phone cards come in denominations of 50, 100, 200 and 400 units, with the price clearly stated, although the seller will probably add a slight mark-up.

Long-distance calls are charged according to a tariff, the cheapest being domestic intercity calls that cost about 5som per minute up to international calls to Europe at around 25som per minute. Calls to CIS countries cost considerably less than this. International calls need to be made at Kyrgyz Telecom offices and the call pre-paid

Bear in mind that digital camera batteries, computers and other storage devices need charging, so make sure you have all the chargers, cables and converters with you. Most hotels have charging points, but do enquire about this in advance. When camping you might have to rely on charging from the car battery; a spare battery is invaluable.

If you are shooting film, 100 to 200 ISO print film and 50 to 100 ISO slide film are ideal. Low ISO film is slow but fine grained and gives the best colour saturation, but will need more light, so support in the form of a tripod or monopod is important. You can also bring a few 'fast' 400 ISO films for low-light situations where a tripod or flash is no option.

DUST AND HEAT Dust and heat are often a problem. Keep your equipment in a sealed bag, stow films in an airtight container (eg: a small cooler bag) and avoid exposing equipment and film to the sun. Digital cameras are prone to collecting dust particles on the sensor, which results in spots on the image. The dirt mostly enters the camera when changing lenses, so be careful when doing this. To some extent photos can be 'cleaned' up afterwards in Photoshop, but this is time-consuming. You can have your camera sensor professionally cleaned, or you can do this yourself with special brushes and swabs made for the purpose, but note that touching the sensor might cause damage and should only be done with the greatest care.

LIGHT The most striking outdoor photographs are often taken during the hour or two of 'golden light' after dawn and before sunset. Shooting in low light may enforce the use of very low shutter speeds, in which case a tripod will be required to avoid camera shake.

With careful handling, side lighting and back lighting can produce stunning effects, especially in soft light and at sunrise or sunset. Generally, however, it is best to shoot with the sun behind you. When photographing animals or people in the harsh midday sun, images taken in light but even shade are likely to be more effective than those taken in direct sunlight or patchy shade, since the latter conditions create too much contrast.

PROTOCOL In some countries, it is unacceptable to photograph local people without permission, and many people will refuse to pose or will ask for a donation. In such circumstances, don't try to sneak photographs as you might get yourself into trouble. Even the most willing subject will often pose stiffly when a camera is pointed at them; relax them by making a joke, and take a few shots in quick succession to improve the odds of capturing a natural pose.

Ariadne Van Zandbergen is a professional travel and wildlife photographer specialising in Africa. She runs The Africa Image Library. For photo requests, visit www.africaimagelibrary.co.za or contact her on ariadne@hixnet.co.za.

for at the counter before a booth is allocated. Change is given for time not used, or a complete refund if there is no answer. Some older exchanges require that you dial 3 when your call is answered in order to be able to talk.

IP international calls can be made from internet cafés in the larger towns using an internet connection. These are always much cheaper than using Kyrgyz Telecom, although there will inevitably be a slight time delay, which tends to be a little off-putting.

Mobile phones Kyrgyzstan's main providers are **BITEL** (↘ 0502) and **KATEL** (↘ 0517). With BITEL, which operates on the GSM system, it is possible to use a roaming service and one's own number. BITEL's coverage is mostly around

Bishkek and the north, while KATEL's coverage is wider, extending to Lake Issyk-Kul and the cities of the south. See *Communications*, page 106, for details on buying a local SIM card.

✉ **POSTAL SERVICES** The Kyrgyz postal service is slow but reasonably reliable. Postcards will usually get to their destination quicker if you post them once you have flown home. Letters and parcels home should have the destination country written at the top in Cyrillic *before* the rest of the address ie: АНГИЯ for the UK (*Anglia* = England = United Kingdom) or США for the USA. Parcels may be posted to international destinations from any main post office but will need to be left open to allow for customs inspection. For more certainty, and at correspondingly greater cost, important express mail may be sent from either Bishkek or Osh using the services of DHL or Federal Express.

INTERNET Most large towns have internet cafés where emails may be sent, the web surfed and IP telephone calls made. The quality of the service varies enormously from fast and efficient to painfully slow and erratic. Charges are usually around 30som per hour. Few internet cafés have facilities for writing CDs.

BUSINESS

In 2006, Kyrgyzstan ranked 90th in the World Bank's Ease of Doing Business index, just below Sri Lanka but above Turkey, China and Russia. This was an improvement of 14 places from the previous year.

The country undoubtedly abounds with investment potential but for those used to doing business in the West things are done rather differently here. Kyrgyzstan is probably no worse than the rest of the CIS, perhaps a little better, but succesful business ventures invariably involve a certain amount of palm-greasing that can range from the blatant to the virtually invisible. As elsewhere in the region where newly founded republics are making the difficult transition from communism to capitalism, low-level corruption is a fact of life. It goes without saying that a trustworthy local business contact or contacts is vital in order to help smooth the way through the troubled waters of the local business world.

Whatever the pitfalls, the Kyrgyz government is keen to attract investors and overseas partners to modernise its industry and bring in new technology, and it is especially interested in investment in mining, industry, petroleum, hydro-electricity and agriculture. To encourage this, it has introduced a number of recent laws to encourage and protect foreign investors, in addition to some significant tax breaks.

To be eligible to invest in Kyrgyzstan, foreigners have to be registered with the Ministry of Economy and Finance. Applications to set up in Kyrgyzstan should be sent first to the State Technical Committee on Foreign Investments and Economic Assistance.

State Technical Committee of the Kyrgyz Republic on Foreign Investments and Economic Development Room 210, Erkindik 58A, 720040 Bishkek; ☎ (312) 223 292. ⏰ 09.00–17.00 Mon–Fri, 09.00–13.00 Sat

Kyrgyz Chamber of Commerce and Industry, Foreign Affairs Department Kievskaya 107, 720001 Bishkek; ☎ (312) 210 565; www.ihk-kg.de

CULTURAL ETIQUETTE

Kyrgyz are for the most part cheerful, highly hospitable people with a genuine interest in foreigners. In the villages and *jailoos* the tradition of hospitality is so strong that unexpected guests are still honoured and seen as a gift from God. An increase in the number of tourists over the past few years has taken the edge off this a little, as locals, understandably, are starting to view tourism as a viable way of supplementing their income; even so, foreign visitors are still courteously welcomed and are rarely seen as being little more than cash cows.

Having said this, it should not be forgotten that economic collapse and severe poverty since independence has engendered an atmosphere of resentment in some quarters, especially in Bishkek, where some foreign nationals are seen to be so patently overpaid and culturally insensitive that their lavish lifestyle and occasional boorish behaviour give some Kyrgyz the impression that all foreigners are of the same stripe. To try and counter this unfortunate image it is important to avoid flashing money about and to not act in a way that might be considered ostentatious, superior or immodest.

Kyrgyz society is relatively conservative, although far from hard-line Islam. Dress should be reasonably modest, with nothing too revealing, especially for women, and skimpy tops, shorts, miniskirts and skin tight trousers should not be worn. Headscarves for foreign women are not necessary in purely cultural terms but they are useful on occasions and provide a useful barrier against sun and dust.

If invited to a Kyrgyz home or a yurt, a small gift is appreciated. This does not have to be anything extravagant, just a little fruit or some sort of snack, or something for the children of the family. Family life is all-important and small gifts that say something of your own home life will be highly valued, such as family photographs or postcards of your hometown.

As a foreign guest one is placed on a pedestal: honoured but under close scrutiny at the same time. Therefore, it is important to acquit oneself well. A little of the language goes a long way, especially a few greetings and pleasantries in Kyrgyz, as does adopting the charming Kyrgyz gestures of putting the right hand on the heart after shaking hands and the *omin* face-washing gesture at the end of a meal.

Handshakes always take place between men, not between men and women, and it is considered unlucky to shake hands across a threshold. Shoes should always be removed on entry to a house or a yurt.

At any meal, bread is treated respectfully; it is never put on the floor, placed upside down or casually thrown away. If offered to a guest, bread should never be refused, even if it is just a mater of taking a little to eat. As elsewhere in the Muslim world, food is eaten and passed around with the right hand only, although there does not seem to be anything wrong with using the left hand for a bit of stabilisation when tearing bread into pieces.

Drinks – tea, vodka or anything else – do not have to be drained to the bottom of the glass; to do so is to invite a refill. It is quite acceptable to take just a sip, although with vodka there is usually much encouragement to drink it all down. To moderate intake, consider just drinking a third or half; this will, of course, be replenished, but at the end of the night it means a better outcome than having knocked back a dozen full glasses. As mentioned under *Alcohol*, page 62, earlier on in this chapter, once drinking has got underway it is usually impossible to make a polite withdrawal, so make an early decision on whether to participate or abstain.

GIVING SOMETHING BACK

Kyrgyzstan is a poor country in transition with a range of serious economic problems that are not going to improve overnight, despite a large number of NGOs working in the country. Much of the poverty is quite visible, particularly in the case of elderly Russians whose grown-up children have left for Russia, leaving them more or less abandoned on impossibly small state pensions. Many of these proud old people are forced into begging, hawking tissues and cigarettes or selling their few remaining possessions to make ends meet. Giving them a few notes, or buying something from them, is a drop in the ocean but at least it helps a little.

The elderly are not the only ones who suffer: wages are low, unemployment is high, and more than half the population live below the poverty line. One charity that does a great deal to help at-risk youth is the **Alpine Fund**, which in its own words is a non-profit, non-governmental organisation providing education and mountain adventures to at-risk youth in Kyrgyzstan and Tajikistan. The Alpine Fund runs two youth programmes in Bishkek: Clouds at their Feet, which prepares at-risk 13–17-year-olds for independent living, and Alpine Interns, which provides real-life work experience for youths from children's homes who are now living independently.

Donations may be made online using PayPal or by sending a cheque payable to the Alpine Fund to their US office at PO Box 583 192, Minneapolis MN, 55458.

The Alpine Fund also welcomes **volunteers** who are willing to stay for two months or more outside the main summer season. Volunteers must pay for their own housing, transportation and living expenses. Potential volunteers should send an email with a covering letter explaining why they wish to volunteer, and a CV (resume) of past experience in working with youths.

The Alpine Fund can be contacted at Prospect Mira 74/16, Bishkek; ☎ +996 312 542 499; ℮ info@alpinefund.org; www.alpinefund.org.

EveryChild 4 Bath Place, Rivington St, London EC2A 3DR; ☎ +44 20 7749 2468; f +44 20 7729 8339; www.everychild.org.uk. EveryChild is a charity that works with vulnerable children in a number of countries including Kyrgyzstan where they are active in developing community-based support services for children & families.

Mercy Corps ☎ +44 131 558 8244; www.mercycorps.org.uk. Another NGO working in Kyrgyzstan, Mercy Corps is a Scottish-based charity that provides microloans & business advice for rural families to set up small businesses. Mercy Corps has worked in Kyrgyzstan since 1994 & was one of the first NGOs to work in the new republic.

Donations can be sent to Mercy Corps, Dept W, 17 Claremont Crescent, Edinburgh, UK EH7 4HX, or they can be made online at www.mercycorps.org.uk. **Helvetas** 43/1 Grazhdanskaya, Bishkek; ☎ +996 312 531 240, ☎ 531 113, ☎ 682 308, ☎ 682 312; f +996 312 531 449; ℮ kalybek_po@helvetas.kg; www.helvetas.kg. Helvetas is a Swiss NGO with long-established links in Kyrgyzstan, having supported agricultural & water resources programmes, the instigation of the CBT network & various co-operatives such as Altyn Kol. Donations may be made through their Swiss website at www.helvetas.ch. The contact details for information on their Kyrgyzstan projects are Helvetas Kyrgyzstan.

As well as supporting charities that work in Kyrgyzstan, an obvious way of 'giving something back' is to purchase hand-crafted souvenirs from a women's craft co-operative like Altyn Oymok (Golden Thimble) in Bokonbaevo or Altyn Kol (Golden Hands) in Kochkor, rather than from a souvenir shop. Similarly, using the services of Community Based Tourism guarantees that most of the money goes directly into the local economy.

Part Two

THE GUIDE

3

Bishkek

Telephone code: 0312
One story relates that Kyrgyzstan's capital, Bishkek (**БИШКЕК**), takes its name from the plunger of the wooden churn (*bishkek*) used to make *kumys*, the popular Kyrgyz tipple that is conjured from fermented mare's milk. This is far from certain, however, as there are several quite plausible alternatives. Another possible derivation might be from *besh kek*, which translates literally as 'five chiefs', or even *besh bik*, which is Kazakh for 'five peaks'. The name Bishkek may even have a more ancient etymology and derive from *pishagakh*, an ancient Sogdian term that translates as 'place beneath the mountains'.

Whatever the name's origin, all of these appellations are of central Asian derivation, a fact that is at odds with the reality that Bishkek is clearly a Soviet city with a Russian – or, at the very least, the ghost of a Russian – soul. Like a scaled-down version of its Kazakh rival, Almaty, Bishkek is a Russian city displaced several thousand kilometres to the east by the geography of empire: a purpose-built capital with buildings and monuments resonant of Europe west of the Urals.

Also like the Kazakh capital, Bishkek has a remarkable amount of green space, with swathes of parks and woodland dotted about the city to soften the traffic noise and freshen up the air (the city is said to have more trees per person than anywhere else in central Asia).

The streets – a textbook example of Soviet planning – are arranged on a grid system, and as in many provincial Russian or ex-Soviet cities the boulevards and avenues that criss-cross the city are a tad wider than they realistically need to be to contain the traffic.

This is no urban jungle; in many aspects the city is almost village-like, with local communities focused around small markets and convenience stores. This village effect is heightened by the constant reminder of the alpine landscape that lies just beyond the city limits as, from virtually anywhere in Bishkek, the near-5,000m, snow-clad ridge of the Ala-Too is visible rising beguilingly to the south.

It is from the Ala-Too that the Ala-Archa, one of the range's main rivers, delivers much of the water needed to irrigate the city's impressive stock of greenery, the mountain melt-water channelled and distributed by means of a series of *aryk* canals. From the city, the mountains seem to be within a hand's grasp and indeed, they almost are: to go hiking in any one of the valleys that sever the Ala-Too range is an easily manageable day trip from the capital.

North of Bishkek, the landscape is far less dramatic, with the gently undulating, fertile agricultural plain of the Chui valley stretching modestly into neighbouring Kazakhstan. In such a vast geographical fastness as central Asia it might seem improbable that two capital cities should lie so close together but they do: Almaty, the Kazakh capital, lies just a few hours away by road.

In a country that is mostly characterised by mountainous terrain, Bishkek's modest altitude is unremarkable, almost an exception to the rule. The city stands at

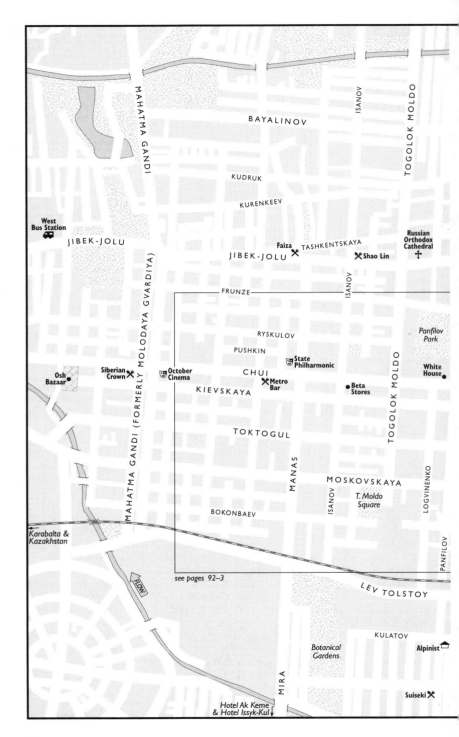

West
Bus Station

MAHATMA GANDI

JIBEK-JOLU

BAYALINOV

ISANOV

TOGOLOK MOLDO

KUDRUK

KURENKEEV

JIBEK-JOLU

Faiza ✗ TASHKENTSKAYA

✗ Shao Lin

Russian
Orthodox
Cathedral ✝

FRUNZE

ISANOV

Osh
Bazaar ✗

Siberian
Crown ✗

MAHATMA GANDI (FORMERLY MOLODAYA GVARDIYA)

October
Cinema

RYSKULOV

PUSHKIN

State
Philharmonic

CHUI

KIEVSKAYA

✗Metro
Bar

Panfilov
Park

White
House ●

Beta
Stores

TOGOLOK MOLDO

TOKTOGUL

MANAS

MOSKOVSKAYA

LOGVINENKO

ISANOV

T. Moldo
Square

BOKONBAEV

Karabalta &
Kazakhstan

FLOW

see pages 92–3

LEV TOLSTOY

PANFILOV

KULATOV

Botanical
Gardens

Alpinist ⌂

MIRA

Hotel Ak Keme
& Hotel Issyk-Kul ↓

Suiseki ✗

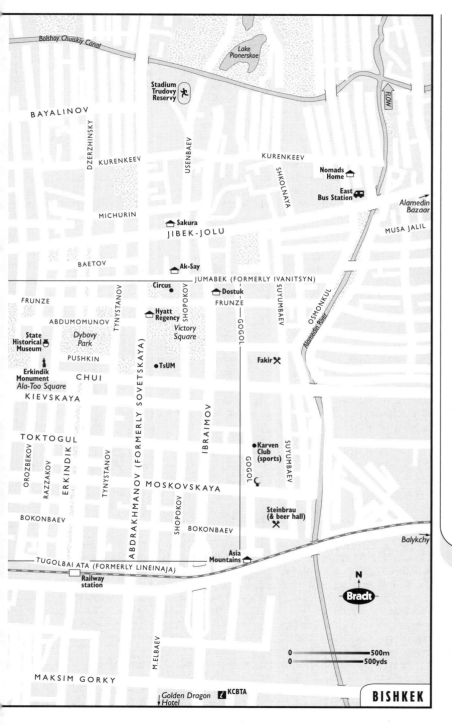

Bolshoy Chuiskiy Canal

Lake
Pionerskoe

Stadium
Trudovy
Reservy

FLOW

BAYALINOV

DZERZHINSKY

KURENKEEV

KURENKEEV

USENBAEV

SHKOLNAYA

Nomads
Home

East
Bus Station

Alamedin
Bazaar

MICHURIN

Sakura

JIBEK-JOLU

MUSA JALIL

BAETOV

Ak-Say

JUMABEK (FORMERLY IVANITSYN)

FRUNZE

Circus

TYNYSTANOV

SHOPOKOV

Dostuk

FRUNZE

SUYUMBAEV

OSMONKUL

ABDUMOMUNOV

Hyatt
Regency

State
Historical
Museum

Dybovy
Park

Victory
Square

Alamedin River

PUSHKIN

ABDRAKHMANOV (FORMERLY SOVETSKAYA)

Erkindik
Monument
Ala-Too Square

CHUI

TsUM

Fakir

KIEVSKAYA

TOKTOGUL

IBRAIMOV

GOGOL

Karven
Club
(sports)

SUYUMBAEV

OROZBEKOV

RAZZAKOV

ERKINDIK

TYNYSTANOV

MOSKOVSKAYA

SHOPOKOV

GOGOL

BOKONBAEV

BOKONBAEV

Steinbrau
(& beer hall)

Balykchy

Bishkek

3

Asia
Mountains

TUGOLBAI ATA (FORMERLY LINEINAJA)

Railway
station

N

Bradt

0   500m
0   500yds

M. ELBAEV

MAKSIM GORKY

Golden Dragon
Hotel

KCBTA

BISHKEK

between 700 and 900m above sea level, the land rising gently in the south to morph into the foothills of the Tien Shan. Bishkek lies on much the same degree of latitude as Chicago, Barcelona, Rome and Istanbul, although its extreme continental position ensures that it differs dramatically from these cities in climatic terms, with short, sometimes fiercely hot, summers and winters that are uncompromisingly sub-zero. Autumn is a brief blaze of cool nights, bright days and quickly turning leaves, while spring is generally the wettest time of year.

Bishkek's population has risen dramatically since independence, when it was around 700,000 and predominantly Russian. In the year 2000 it was reported to be over one million and by 2004 some claimed it to be over two million, although this seems doubtful.

The city's demography has also changed markedly since independence, when it was still largely a Russian city. Although it still bears a largely Slavic appearance, the majority population these days is ethnic Kyrgyz. Nevertheless, Bishkek is still host to sizeable communities of Russians, Dungan Chinese, Tartars, Uyghurs, Uzbeks and Ukrainians, some of which – elderly Russians in particular – are suffering quite visibly under the new economic order.

Bishkek is not the sort of city you would travel halfway across the world to see for its own sake; it is not Samarkand, or Bokhara, or even Almaty. On the other hand, as a necessary stopover in most Kyrgyz itineraries, and with a good range of places to stay, a fairly wide selection of restaurants and a few minor sights of its own, it is a pleasant enough place to relax and take stock whilst sorting out onward transport and visas.

HISTORY

Bishkek is the most recent appellation for a city that was known throughout much of the 20th century as Frunze, after the Bolshevik military campaigner and associate of Lenin who was born in the city. Before that it was known as Pishpek. Despite these two changes of name it is a relatively new city, barely a hundred years old but built on the site of a much older Sogdian settlement that was a staging post on one of the lesser branches of the Silk Road. Even before this, there is evidence of habitation in the area, and stone hand-tools that date back 7,000 years or so have been discovered close to the present-day city.

The Sogdian settlement, Jul, existed between the 6th and 12th centuries and, although many artefacts from this period have been found, all evidence on the ground has since been destroyed. Artefacts recovered from here suggest that it was a very mixed settlement, populated by a mix of Buddhists, Nestorians, Manicheans and Zoroastrians. However, like many other Silk Road towns, this was subsequently destroyed by Mongols under the fearsome leadership of Genghis Khan in the 13th century.

The Sogdian town was abandoned and languished in ruins for centuries until 1825, when the same site was fortified by the Khan of Khokand, who built mud-wall fortifications and settled it with Uzbek soldiers. This, too, was destroyed when Tsarist Russians annexed the region and, responding to the appeals of local chiefs desperate to rid themselves of Khokand domination, supported the Kyrgyz in their attack on the fortress in 1862. It fell after 10 days of fighting and its administration was taken over by the Russians, who established an important Cossack base here, together with a relay point for mail travelling between St Petersburg and the far-flung reaches of the Russian Empire.

After the Russian headquarters in the region at Tokmok were flooded and damaged in 1877, the Russians subsequently built a more substantial fortress here the following year and named it Pishpek, although the etymology of this choice of name is now uncertain.

A slow migration of land-hungry Russians, many of whom were freed serfs, had started to settle here by now, attracted by the fertile soil of the Chui valley as well as by tax breaks and a free supply of wood with which to build houses. By 1914 the city had grown to around 20,000, but these were almost entirely newly arrived Russians or Dungans who had migrated from China, as at this time the number of Kyrgyz settled here were very few.

Shortly after the 1917 October Revolution, a group of Bolsheviks attacked the garrison on New Year's Day 1918, and within a few months had gained control over the region. A counter-revolution broke out in December of the same year and anti-Bolsheviks based in the village of Belovodsk marched on the city. The counter-revolution failed, however, and was put down within a fortnight.

In response to Lenin's plea for international assistance, a group of Czech socialist volunteers arrived by train in 1925 and helped to rebuild and develop the city, constructing schools, hospitals and some of the civic buildings that remain to this day. The city became the capital of the Kyrgyz ASSR in 1926 and was renamed Frunze; a decade later, it continued as the capital of the Kyrgyz SSR.

Despite its isolation far off in the central Asian steppe, many thousands of kilometres east of Moscow, the city was never beyond the iron grip of Stalinist repression. One notorious incident in 1937 saw the whole of the republic's Supreme Soviet Central Committee, along with other important political figures, murdered by the KGB at the small village of Chong-Tash, just to the south of Bishkek – an event which did not come to light until 1991. One of the victims was the father of Kyrgyz author Chingiz Aitmatov (see *Modern Kyrgyz Literature*, page 37).

During World War II some of the Soviet war effort was moved here out of the reach of German attack, and it was at this time that much of the city's heavy industry became established. A number of clothing and pharmaceutical factories were established here too. A great deal of this industrial base closed down following independence, to leave a capital that was noticeably less-polluted but also undeniably poorer than before.

The city was renamed Bishkek on Kyrgyzstan's achieving independence in 1991: a new name for the new capital of a brand new country, and one that spoke more firmly of the country's Kyrgyz tradition than its previous appellation – a name taken from a European (Moldavian) hero of the communist revolution.

GETTING THERE

BY AIR Bishkek's Manas Airport (*airport code: FRU;* ☎ *693 109;* e *info@airport.kg; www.airport.kg*) lies at some distance from the city, about 25km to the north. The airport receives a number of daily flights from various destinations in Russia and Europe, many of which seem to arrive at an unsociable hour of the morning. There is a visa desk immediately to the left of passport control, which should be manned to await international flights, although you may have to wait a while for someone to turn up. Visas are available on arrival for most Europeans and North Americans (see *Red Tape*, page 52).

There are several domestic flights each day between Bishkek and Osh, twice-weekly services to Jalal-Abad, and weekly flights to Batken in the southwest. Discounted flights to Osh can cost as little as US$40, which offers fierce competition to the alternative of a 12–14-hour, and only marginally cheaper, shared-taxi journey.

Once inside the terminal building, there are a few facilities like banks, shops and an information counter, which may or may not be open depending on the time of day. There is an ATM in the basement.

To reach central Bishkek from the airport there are a number of options depending on the time of day. Cheapest is the **bus** service – number 153 – which runs at half-hourly intervals between 06.00–01.00 and which takes around 45 minutes. The buses drop off and pick up at the crossroads of Chui and Molodaya Gvardiya in central Bishkek and originate/terminate by the Pinara Hotel on Mira. **Minibuses** also run along the same route: they are slightly more expensive but quicker, taking only about half an hour to reach the city. Minibus number 325 also runs between the airport and Osh Bazaar.

Given the early hour at which many international flights arrive, a **taxi** may be the only option, although it is unwise to put yourself at the mercy of the taxi sharks that congregate in the car park outside and who will inevitably try to overcharge. A better option is to go into one of the taxi offices at arrivals and pre-pay the agreed fare for the trip into town. One recommended firm is Super Taxi (↘ *152*), who will charge around 350som (US$10) for the journey (500som for a round trip), give a receipt and take you to the hotel of your choice. Taxis can also be pre-booked in advance by some of the online hotel-booking services, and this is a good way of reducing the stress of an early morning – or late night – arrival after a tiring long-haul flight. You might, of course, do better than this on your own and find a driver who desperately wants to get back to the city centre and is willing to take you for 250som or less, but this is unlikely.

Some visitors to Kyrgyzstan take advantage of the more regular flights between Europe and Kazakhstan and fly into Almaty airport. From Almaty to Bishkek takes about 3 hours by car, or 5 by bus. Currently, there are three flights a week between the two cities (see *Getting there and away*, page 56).

BY TRAIN There is a direct train link with Moscow and an indirect one to Tashkent in Uzbekistan. The journey between Moscow and Bishkek takes around 72 hours (see *Getting There and away*, page 57). The only viable train link within Kyrgyzstan is between Bishkek and Balykchy on Lake Issyk-Kul, an unreliable 7-hour journey that is most definitely for hardcore rail enthusiasts only. Bishkek's railway station (Ж.-Д. Вокзал; ↘ *624 865*) lies south of the city centre at the junction of Erkindik Boulevard and Lineinaja.

BY BUS Buses rumble their way all over Kyrgyzstan from two main bus stations. Generally speaking, long-distance buses heading east to Issyk-Kul, south to Naryn, west to Talas and north to Almaty leave from the largest of the bus stations, the **West Bus Station** (Западный Автовокзал – '*Zapadniy Avtovakzal*'; ↘ *656 575 for information*), on Jibek-Jolu at the junction with Kulijeva. Buses leave hourly for Karakol, in the morning at least, taking anything between 6–8 hours and costing between 150–300som depending on how luxurious they are. To travel as far as Cholpan-Ata cost about two-thirds of the full fare.

Buses with destinations closer to home – Tokmok, Kant, Issyk-Ata, Kemin and Kegeti – tend to leave from the **East Bus Station** (Восточный Автовокзал – '*Vostochni Avtovakzal*'; ↘ *664 529 for information*), which, again, is located on Jibek-Jolu, but this time further east on the junction with Osmonkula.

BY MINIBUS Minibuses run from the main bus stations, although the matter of which bus station serves which destination is not quite as clear cut as it is in the case of buses.

Minibuses to Karakol and Issyk-Kul leave, when full, from in front of the West Bus Station and cost around 200som. Another alternative is the shared taxis that tend to fill more quickly and cost something in the order of 300–400som between Bishkek and Karakol.

19	Chui to and from Osh Bazaar
48	Follows a circular route along Moskovskaya and between the railway station and the East and West Bus Stations
110	From Osh bazaar along Moskovskaya then south
113, 114	Between West Bus Station and Alemedin bazaar along Jibek-Jolu
125, 126	Along Sovetskaya, then south along Mira to Pinara Hotel

Minibuses running south to Osh and Jalal-Abad depart from **Osh Bazaar** at the western end of Chui, as do shared taxis.

GETTING AROUND

The central part of Bishkek is relatively compact and one can get around here on foot quite well. The city is laid out in a grid pattern and, with the mountains usually visible to the south, it is hard to remain lost for long.

For longer journeys to the outskirts, or journeys across the centre at night, it is best to make use of a taxi or the city's public transport system. Bishkek has a complicated network of city **buses** that are both very crowded and very cheap, costing just 3som. There are also a few remaining trolleybuses on some routes (enter the trolleybus at the rear door and pay the driver at the front on leaving).

Marginally better, and certainly more convenient, is the system of privately owned minibuses – *marshrutki* (singular *marshrutka*) – that travel everywhere in the city for a flat fare of 5som (pay the driver when you get on). The main difficulty with these is to know exactly when to get off, as much of the city is fairly devoid of recognisable landmarks and the minibuses tend to get so full that it is sometimes a problem to see out of the window.

Whatever the time of day, *marshrutki* are invariably very crowded, with drivers that are under a lot of pressure to pick up the maximum number of fares from A to B, and who are not generally well-disposed to having a chat or offering advice to a befuddled tourist. *Marshrutka* etiquette dictates that those who are travelling some distance should move to the back and that young men and boys should give up their seats to the elderly.

In theory they will stop anywhere – just put your arm out – although they tend to have frequent fixed points where they pick up from; just look for groups of people waiting by the roadside scouring the numbers of the oncoming minibuses. *Marshrutki* generally display their destinations (in Cyrillic) on a board in the front window but have usually whizzed past by the time you've read it. Many signs say TsUM (ЦУМ) or Osh Bazaar (ОШ), which makes life a little easier. As a rule, it is best to know the number of the route you require (see box, *Useful Minibus Routes in Bishkek*, above), otherwise, ask a local for advice. When you have reached, or are passing, your destination, ask the driver to let you off saying, '*Astanavitsya pazhalsta.*'

Both buses and minibuses run from early in the morning – 05.30–06.00 – until around 21.00 in the evening. After this time, taxis come into their own.

Taxis are everywhere in the city and, generally, are a good deal and the quickest way of getting around. They can be easily flagged down at the roadside or phoned in advance. The latter are slightly more expensive but more reliable. Of course, as elsewhere in the country, the old adage remains from the former Soviet Union that 'every car is a taxi' and anything on four wheels may be flagged down to take you where you wish to go for an appropriate payment. However, in Bishkek there are so many official 'chequerboard' taxis plying the streets that it is best to stick to these as it is never a problem to find one.

Fares within the city centre tend to be around 50–70som per journey, a little more at night. For taxi trips to the outskirts reckon on something more like 100som per trip. Fares are negotiable of course and should always be agreed upon before getting into the vehicle. Generally speaking, Bishkek's taxi drivers are a cheerful lot and will conscientiously help you find your destination even if you are not too certain where it is.

Dial-up taxi services like Super Taxi are more reliable but cost a little more – about 75som per journey within the city centre, 100som at night. One problem for visitors is that, like the drivers, the operators tend to speak Russian only. If you are really unsure of where you are going, or uncertain as to how to pronounce it, then get a Russian speaker to write your destination on a piece of paper for you. Rather than knowing landmarks or details like the name of a restaurant, taxi drivers tend to base their knowledge on the city's grid of streets, so ask for a junction like Isa Akhunbaev and Sovetskaya rather than your precise destination, which they probably will not be familiar with.

Some recommended taxi firms are:

Ak Jol	➘ 182
City Taxi	➘ 559 111
Doka Taxi	➘ 695 555
EuroTaxi	➘ 150
Express Taxi	➘ 156
Super Taxi	➘ 152
Salam Taxi	➘ 188
Udacha Taxi	➘ 154

Super Taxi has a list of its tariffs online in English (*www.dos.kg/eng-152-tariffs-0-0.html*).

SAFETY

Leafy, calm Bishkek does not feel dangerous at all, but after dark certain precautions should be taken as accounts of violent attacks on foreigners are frequent enough to be noteworthy. The motivation for attack is usually robbery, prompted by the obvious relative wealth of the traveller, who may well be carrying more on his person than a local might earn in a whole year. Other factors that come into play are alcohol-fuelled resentment and dislike of Westerners (or Russians, for which Western visitors may be mistaken). Often it is a combination of these factors, coupled with the opportunity that a dark, quiet street offers to an impecunious drunk, or worse, a whole group of them. This is not to be alarmist, but forewarned is forearmed and late night movements around the city, especially in the region of bars and nightclubs, should be done by taxi and preferably in a group. The red-light area around the Circus is said to be especially risky at night.

Bishkek is an extremely dark city at night, with street lights few and far between. To add to the danger, the pavements are in quite a dreadful state in places and it is easy to go careering down a pot-hole or trip on broken paving – many locals walk in the road itself. A precaution is to carry a torch (flashlight) but then, of course, this will clearly identify you as a foreigner.

The best advice is to not take too much money with you when you go out at night, and hand it over without any heroics if you are unfortunate enough to be

Since independence many streets and avenues in Bishkek have been given new names. The problem for the visitor is that in many cases the old names are still in use and both old and new tend to be used interchangeably by locals. Those given below are some of the commoner changes that may cause confusion.

Old name	New name
16-th	Shoorukov K.
18-th	Igemberdiev
Airport	Azhybek Baatyr
Alma Atinskaya	Kurmanjan Datka/Shabdan Baatyr
Bakinskaya	Elebesov
Belinsky	Manas
Chapaev	Bakaev A.
Donetskaya	Suerkulov
Druzhby	Karasaev
Dushanbinskaya	Toktonaliev Aliarskaya
Dzerzhinsky	Erkindik
Engels	Chokmorov
Ivanitsyn	Jumabek
Kamskaya	Samanchin
Karasuiskaya	Kerimbekov Kulchoro
Karl Marx	Junusaliev B.
Karpinsky	Suyumbaev A.
Kosmicheskaya	Borombay Sultan
Kremlevskaya	Abai
Krupskaya	Tabyshaliev S.
Leningradskaya	Bayalinov Kasymaly
Lineinaja	Tugolbai Ata
Molodaya Gvardiya	Mahatma Gandi
Nekrasov	Asanliev Uzengazy
Ordzhonikidze	Junusaliev
Pravda	Ibraimov Sultan
Sovetskaya	Abdrakhmanov (N of Lev Tolstoy)/ Baytik Baatyr
Stroitelnaya	Maytyev E.
Sverdlov	Umetaliev Temirkul
Voroshilov	Kolbaev
Zhigulevskaya	Suvanberdiev T.

mugged. Obviously, avoid drunken groups, shortcuts through parks, dark streets, underpasses and alleyways, and also the police, whose relationship with crime is not always one of prevention.

The problem with police harassment of foreigners appears to have improved over the past few years but it is still problematic at times. The common ploy is to stop foreigners and ask for their passports – they have a legal right to do this – and say they are looking for drugs. They then go on to isolate the victim and ask to see his or her money and count it. The common outcome of this is for them (they invariably work in pairs) to sneak a bill or two by sleight of hand. You should be aware that they *do not* have the right to see your money or search you or your bags, so stand your ground, refuse to go off alone into a room with them, make a fuss and

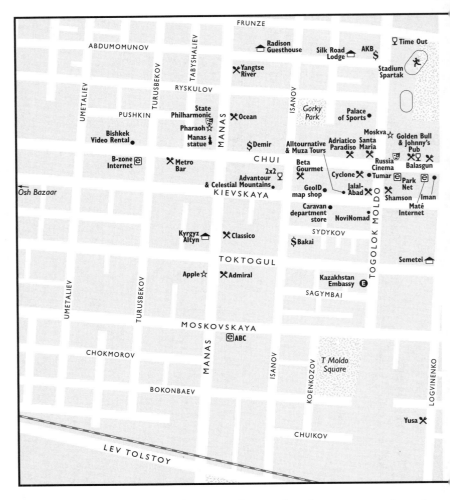

try and recruit the assistance and support of passers-by who are no great fans of crooked policemen either. Also be sure to ask for identification and note down their badge numbers before you show your passports, making it clear that you are doing this. Their modus operandi depends on the intimidation of individuals, so be confident and aware of your rights – not always easy of course. Despite the unpleasantness of the situation they cannot actually harm you in any way. The places where police shakedowns are most common are at Osh Bazaar and parts of the city centre close to TsUM but, as mentioned earlier, this scenario happens much less frequently these days and you are unlikely to be bothered.

Regarding the police, you are, by law, required to carry your passport with you at all times. This presents a dilemma for British and other nationals who do not have an embassy in Bishkek and for whom getting a replacement would prove a real hassle. If you are in Bishkek for some time you may consider getting a *pamyatka*, a foreigners' ID card, which can substitute for a passport in official dealings. The card can be obtained from the Centre for Legal Assistance for Foreign Citizens, Toktogul 64 (Toktogul/Ibraimov) and costs around 700som.

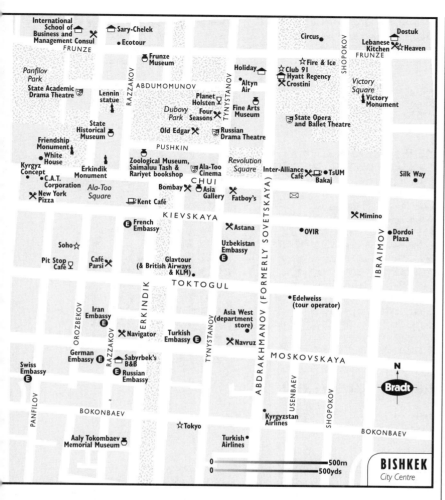

There is also a phone number that you can dial if there are problems with the police (☎ 285 978) that is said to have some English-speaking operatives at the other end who deal with matters of police harassment. If you have a mobile phone with a local SIM card it is a good idea to key this in, as well as the number of your hotel and your embassy/honorary consul.

TOURIST INFORMATION

There is no national tourist board as such, nor a dedicated city tourist office, but there are several organisations and agencies at hand to provide practical information. Bishkek is, of course, also the headquarters of the KCBTA (see page 51) and they can offer both regional and national advice from their Bishkek office.

Alpine Fund Prospect Mira 74/16; ☎ 542 499; e info@alpinefund.org; www.alpinefund.org. This non-profit organisation is dedicated to providing

educational & mountain experience to at-risk Kyrgyz youth. It welcomes volunteers & can offer advice on mountain expeditions to the Ala-Too range south of the city where it has a small mountain hut.

[i] Kyrgyz Community Based Tourism Association (KCBTA) Maksim Gorky 58; ☎ 443 331, ☎ 540 069; e reservation@cbtkyrgyzstan.kg;

www.cbtkyrgyzstan.kg. This is the head branch of the national community tourism organisation & the office can be found southeast of the city centre where Maksim Gorky intersects Matrosov.

Reputable Bishkek travel agencies such as C.A.T. Corporation, Celestial Mountains, Kyrgyz Concept and NoviNomad are all able to offer helpful travel information. The services offered by these and other Bishkek-based tour operators are detailed on pages 49–51.

AIRLINE OFFICES IN BISHKEK

✈ **Aeroflot** Chui 230; ☎ 651 422; f 651 452; e aflfruto@elcat.kg

✈ **Altyn Air** Abdumomunov 195; ☎ 225 446; f 666 687; e altynair@elcat.kg

✈ **Botir Airlines** Suyumbaev 14; ☎ 285 844; f 681 567; e baairlines@infotel.kg

✈ **British Airways** Toktogul 93; ☎ 660 092, ☎ 660 900 (also representative at airport, ☎ 603 629 f 664 220; e bmedfru@mail.kg). ⏰ 09.00–18.00 Mon–Fri, 10.00–14.00 Sat

✈ **China Xinjiang Airways** Chui 128/3; ☎ 664 668; e ebin999@sina.com

✈ **Enkor** Moskovskaya 86/1; ☎ 223 355; f 660 550; e 7777@imfiko.bishkek.su

✈ **Golden Rule Airlines** ☎ 512 498, ☎ 212 924; www.goldenruleairlines.org

✈ **Itek Air** Chui 128/10; ☎ 216 914, ☎ 664 698; f 664 057; e itek@infotel.kg; www.itekair.kg. ⏰ 09.00–19.00 daily

✈ **KLM** Toktogul 93; ☎ 661 500

✈ **Kyrgyz Air** Abdrakhmanov 129; ☎ 622 123

✈ **Kyrgyzstan Airlines** Baytik Baatyr 105; ☎ 545 815, ☎ 280 886; f 422 922, f 620 896 (also at airport, ☎ 603 410; f 681 002; e office@kyrgyzstanairlines.kg). ⏰ 08.00–19.00 daily

✈ **Lufthansa** (at Hyatt Regency hotel); ☎ 665 600; f 665 991; e Lufthansabishkek@dlh.de

✈ **Turkish Airlines** Abdrakhmanov 136; ☎ 660 008; f 621 580 (at airport, ☎ 660 008; e thymanas@airport.kg). ⏰ 09.00–19.00 Mon–Fri

✈ **Uzbekistan Airways** Kievskaya 107; ☎ 610 152; e uzb-air@elcat.kg

EMERGENCY TELEPHONE NUMBERS

Fire ☎ 101
Police ☎ 102
Ambulance ☎ 151

🏠 WHERE TO STAY

HOTELS Hotels can be pre-booked through a Bishkek agency such as Advantour (☎ 900 592; e bishkek@advantour.com; www.advantour.com), Bishkek Hotels online (☎ 210 752; www.bishkek-hotels.net) or Muza Tours (Kievskaya 107; ☎ 210 752, ☎ 610 620; f 610 620; www.gocentralasia.com). This may be a good idea if you are arriving late. The same agencies can also arrange airport transfers.

Top end $$$$$

🏠 **Ak Keme****** (156 rooms, 12 suites, 4 presidential suites) Mira 93; ☎ 540 143, ☎ 540 144, ☎ 540 145; f 542 365, f 542 408; e bishkek@akkemehotel.com; www.akkemehotel.com. Fully renovated to international standards as a joint Kyrgyz-Malaysian venture, this 17-storey business hotel was known formerly as the Pinara. The hotel is some distance to the south of central Bishkek at the bottom end of Mira, close to Pobedy Park. All rooms have AC, minibar, satellite TV & soundproof windows to keep traffic noise from Prospekt Mira to a minimum. Some rooms have views

over the mountains to the south. Health club, business centre, meeting rooms, casino, swimming pools & sports facilities, lobby bar, banquet hall in Italian style; also 'Star Sky' terrace restaurant on upper floor with view over Tien Shan mountains.

🏠 **Dostuk***** (174 rooms) Frunze 429b; ☎ 284 251, ☎ 284 291; f 284 466; e dostuk_hotel@netmail.kg. Soviet-style hotel built in 1983 & refurbished in 2001. Central location in the city centre, close to the Circus, in a slightly dodgy area known for its prostitutes. Most rooms have AC, satellite TV & refrigerator. Casino, disco, sauna, billiard parlour, gym, business centre & 'Arizona' restaurant. Three-tier pricing system.

🏠 **Hyatt Regency***** (180 rooms, 5 suites) Abdrakhmanov 191; ☎ 661 234; f 665 744; e bishkek@hyattintel.com; www.bishkek.regency.hyatt.com. In the city centre, close to the Museum of Fine Arts & State Opera & Ballet Theatre, this is the Kyrgyz capital's most prestigious hotel. With large, spacious rooms with cable TV, AC, internet access, separate work area & marble bath fittings, the Hyatt is clearly aimed at high-profile business visitors. Mediterranean-style Crostini restaurant & lobby bar; swimming pool, business centre & banqueting hall. *Buffet b/fast is extra.*

Mid-range $$$$

🏠 **Alpinist Guesthouse** (19 rooms) Panfilov 113; \/f 441 522; e alpinist@elcat.kg; www.alpinisthotel.centralasia.kg. Centrally located between Lev Tostoy & Gorky, this is a small comfortable place clearly aimed at climbing & trekking groups, hence the name. English & German spoken; all rooms with AC, cable TV & refrigerator. This is undoubtedly the only Bishkek hotel with its own climbing wall.

🏠 **Asia Mountains Guesthouse*** (12 rooms) Tugolbai Ata 1a; ☎ 694 075, ☎ 690 234, ☎ 690 235; f 694 074, f 690 236; e aljona@mail.elcat.kg; www.asiamountains.co.uk. This small, relatively new guesthouse, close to the railway station & central mosque belongs to the tour company of the same name & is often used by their clients at the beginning & end of expeditions. All rooms have en-suite facilities, cable TV & AC. The reception staff speak English &/or German. Small bar & restaurant; email facilities. A swimming pool & sauna are planned for the future. This place tends to fill quickly so it is best to book in advance. *Sgl* $$$, *dbl/suite* $$$$.

🏠 **Eldorado*** (12 rooms) Ordzhonikidze 184; ☎ 542 150, ☎ 545 866; f 541 021. Another hotel situated in the south of the city, close to the old airport. Facilities geared towards businessmen include a conference hall, a casino (24-hour) & a restaurant serving European, Chinese & national cuisine. All rooms come with cable TV & AC.

🏠 **Golden Dragon**** (36 rooms, 6 suites) M. Elebaev 60; ☎ 902 771; f 902 73; e GDHotel@saimanet.kg. All rooms with internet access, AC, minibar & satellite TV. Restaurant serving European, Indian, Chinese & Kyrgyz cuisine. Business centre, gym & sports facilities.

🏠 **Silk Road Lodge**** (10 suites, 18 rooms) Abdumomunov 229; ☎ 661 129; f 661 655; e silkroad@celestial.com.kg; www.silkroad.com.kg. The Silk Road Lodge is a modern, centrally situated hotel opened in 2000 under the same British ownership as the Celestial Mountains travel agency. All rooms have AC, bathroom with heated floor, tea/coffee making facilities & cable TV. The hotel has a business centre & shop, conference room, bar & restaurant (with vegetarian options), sauna, heated pool & outdoor summer garden, as well as a well-stocked library of English-language books. The hotel has friendly English-speaking staff, & the tariff includes a complimentary airport transfer. *Sgl* $$$–$$$$$, *dbl/suite* $$$$$.

🏠 **Holiday** (18 rooms) Abdrakhmanov 204a. A newly opened modern business hotel close to the city centre. All rooms with shower, satellite TV, minibar, AC & internet access. Conference room for 40. Free airport pickup offered. *Sgl* $$$$, *dbl* $$$$–$$$$$, *suite* $$$$$.

🏠 **Issyk-Kul*** (194 rooms) Mira 301; ☎ 550 746, ☎ 550 763; f 550 485, f 458 347; e Bosteriyeva@exnet.kg; www.issyk-kul.elcat.kg. A large, ex-Soviet business hotel on the southern side of the city close to the Flamingo Park & the American Embassy. The hotel was apparently constructed to represent the Soviet warship *Aurora* & it certainly does have something of the battleship in its design. Facilities include sauna, billiards hall, business centre, Korean restaurant & a conference hall for up to 200. *Sgl/dbl* $$$$, *suite* $$$$$. *Discounts are offered for longer stays & regular visitors.*

🏠 **Korund** (19 rooms) Bakaev 53a; ☎ 552 172, ☎ 552 173, ☎ 552 174. Centrally situated with swimming pool, billiards room, gymnasium & sauna. Restaurant & banquet hall. All rooms with AC, satellite TV & minibar.

🏠 **Ordo** (6 rooms) Kudruk 107; ☎ 611 760, ☎ 218 922; f 219 711; http://ordo.info-bishkek.biz. A small, modern b&b-style hotel, opened in 2003, within walking distance of the city centre. All rooms have minibar, satellite TV. 24hr internet access, billiards room, coffee bar & sauna. *Sgl/dbl* $$$$, *lux* $$$$$.

🏠 **Radison Guesthouse** (6 rooms) Abdumomunov 259; ☎ 663 785; m 0502 551 490; e rad_1983@mail.ru. On the same street as the Silk Road Lodge & close to the centre, this is a small, friendly place run by a charming Russian family. Comfortable, neat rooms face onto a courtyard & have AC, satellite TV & modern shower. There is no sign, but ring the bell at gate for admission. *Sgl* $$$, *dbl* $$$$.

🏠 **Shumkar Asia Guesthouse** (11 rooms) Osipenko 34; ☎ 272 105, ☎ 671 038; e shumkar-asia@inbox.ru. A small, modern hotel that has a sauna, swimming pool, conference room & bar. All rooms come with AC, refrigerator & TV.

Inexpensive $$$/$$

🏠 **Ak-Say** (16 rooms) Ivanitsyn 117; ☎ 261 465. This is a rather seedy, run-down hotel in a neighbourhood that is best avoided at night, so it really does not have a lot going for it. With shared bath & toilet facilities, & grotty rooms, the best you can say is that at least it's cheap. $$

🏠 **International School of Business and Management** (32 rooms) Panfilov 237; ☎ 623 120, ☎ 623 122; f 660 638. Just north of the centre, close to Panfilov Park, & otherwise known by its former name of 'Salima', this is a budget option that is popular with some. Access is by way of the Business School (sign only in Russian & Kyrgyz) at the top of the steps: turn right at the main entrance & enquire at reception immediately through the doors on the right. The rooms are upstairs. Rooms have no frills but are reasonable enough for the price. Unfortunately, solo travellers have to pay the full price of a dbl as there are no sgl rooms. B/fast is not included. Reception staff attitudes range from indifferent to quite helpful. $$$

🏠 **Kyrgyz Altyn**** (40 rooms) Manas 30; ☎ 664 412, ☎ 666 114; f 666 371. A smallish hotel with an extremely convenient location right in the city centre, on Manas between Kievskaya & Toktogul. Renovated in 2001, this would represent good value if there were no triple pricing system in which foreigners pay twice the price of a CIS citizen & 3–4 times the price of a Kyrgyz national. Mostly appeals to business travellers. Clean simple rooms. Reasonable café on ground floor; little English spoken. $$$

🏠 **Sary-Chelek** (24 rooms) Orozbekov 87; ☎ 662 627. Just around the corner from the Business School this is a cheaper, but less salubrious, option. Reports suggest that its rooms are reasonable enough if you can tolerate a few cockroaches. $$

🏠 **Semetei** (50 rooms) Toktogul 125; ☎ 218 324. This Soviet-style hotel has a good location close to the centre but is rather overpriced for what it offers & is not particularly welcoming. *Sgl* $$$, *dbl* $$$–$$$$.

HOMESTAYS

🏠 **Ernist Djumagulov** Asanbai 9/28, Asanabai Microdistrict; ☎ 440 956; m 0502 543 008; e ernistd@yahoo.com; www.bandb.net.kg. This is an apartment that has a room to rent in the southern outskirts of Bishkek, close to the Monte Carlo casino. Ernist is a university lecturer & his wife works in the hospitality industry; both can offer travel & sightseeing advice on the city. Use of kitchen & living room, with cable TV & washing machine; English, Turkish & Russian spoken. Only 1 room is available so pre-book. To reach it, take minibus 167 from Filarmonia. $$–$$$ *for sgl occupancy*, $$ *per person for dbl, including b/fast; other meals are available on demand.*

🏠 **Nomads Home** Drevesnaya 10; ☎ 299 155; m 0502 742 420 (Gulnara), ☎ 0502 805 146 (Raisa); e nomadshome@gmail.com, kyrgyzkyz@mail.ru; http://nomadshome.googlepages.com/home. Situated close to the Eastern Bus Station & run by Gulnara & Raisa, this is a recent addition to the list that first opened for business in 2007. Gulnara is Sabyrbek's niece (see below) & used to be one of the mainstays at his guesthouse. There is a dormitory & also sgl & dbl rooms, b/fast provided. Dinners can be provided for 100som with advance notice. You can also stay in a yurt in the garden or set up your own tent. English, Japanese & Russian are spoken. *Dormitory* $, *private rooms* $$.

🏠 **Sabyrbek's B&B** Razzazov 21; ☎ 621 398; e sabyrbek@mail.ru. Sabyrbek offers cheap beds to all-comers in his place, conveniently situated close to the city centre near the German Embassy. This place gets mixed reports; it can get quite crowded here when it's full & there is only 1 shower. Free use of kitchen for guests. *Dormitory* $.

🏠 **Sakura Guesthouse** Michurin 38; ☎ 666 326; m 0502 453 866; e kobuhei-hikita@hotmail.com. This small homestay was opened by a Japanese-Kyrgyz couple in the summer of 2006. Although fairly central, it is a little hard to find: it lies just to the north of Jibek-Jolu along Abdrakhamanov (Sovetskaya) & down a small alley to the right; the guesthouse is along here, down another alleyway to the right. The guesthouse has a small swimming pool, a common seating area & all the Japanese comics you could possibly desire. Naturally enough, Sakura is very popular with backpackers, particularly Japanese & Israeli. Japanese, English, Russian & Kyrgyz are all spoken. *Dormitory* $; *b/fast is included.*

Bishkek has a wide variety of food outlets to suit every taste and pocket. Within the city centre there is more or less everything available, from cheap takeaway *samsa* from a street stall to fancy international *haute cuisine* in a four-star restaurant.

Restaurants fall basically into two categories: simple *chaikhanas* that serve a fairly limited range of Kyrgyz and Russian dishes, and more elaborate, often foreign-owned, restaurants that serve international food at prices that are usually well beyond the budget of the most nationals. By Western standards, however, even these seem quite reasonably priced, although in many cases it is the décor and atmosphere that you are paying for rather than the food.

For less formal dining there are numerous options for fast food in the city. There are snack stalls all over the city serving up *samsi* and rather dangerous-looking *gamburgers* (hamburgers); one of the most popular spots for these is at the junction of Sovetskaya and Kievskaya near the university. There are stalls at the east side of Ala-Too Square that sell a variety of breads, snacks and, of course, *samsi*, and there is the shady area just inside Panfilov Park, where in summer a clutch of simple outdoor restaurants offer cheap and tasty staples like *manti*, *shashlyk* and *laghman*.

RESTAURANTS

✖ **Crostini** Hyatt Regency Bishkek, Abdrakhmanov 191; ✆ 661 234. ⏰ 06.30–24.00. Expensive but beautifully prepared Mediterranean cuisine & monthly international food promotions. **$$$$$**

✖ **Four Seasons** Tynystanov 116a; ✆ 621 548. ⏰ 11.00–24.00. On a leafy street next to Dubovy Park, this is one of the city's best known & most exclusive restaurants. There is outdoor dining on a cool terrace in summer & a warm, cosy interior for winter meals. A wide-ranging menu serving well-prepared European & Chinese dishes. **$$$$$**

✖ **Suiseki** Gorky 172 (junction with Panfilov); ✆ 548 510. A smart Japanese restaurant in a pagoda-style building to the south of the city centre where you dine at low tables in the Japanese style. **$$$$–$$$$$**

✖ **Adriatico Paradiso** Chui 219; ✆ 217 632. A smart Italian trattoria with crisply ironed tablecloths & a real Italian chef at work in the kitchen. A wide range of excellent pasta dishes that taste quite genuinely Italian rather than any Central Asian approximation & a good list imported Italian wines, along with regional beers & wines. Also good desserts & homemade ice cream. Elegant but not too formal an atmosphere & interesting Kyrgyz artwork on the walls. Live piano accompaniment some nights, otherwise piped 'Italian' music like Dean Martin. **$$$$**

✖ **Lebanese Kitchen** Frunze 429. Lots of Middle Eastern favourites & *mezze*. **$$$$**

✖ **Navigator** Moskovskaya 103 (on corner with Razzakov); ✆ 665 151, ✆ 664 545. ⏰ 10.00–24.00. A chic bar-restaurant on a quiet corner in the embassy district. Navigator is popular with well-to-do businessmen, embassy staff & the capital's expat community. The service can be rather haughty at times, but perhaps this reflects their clientele. Navigator serves well-prepared, attractively presented European food with plenty of vegetarian options, a rarity in the city. Good, if expensive, coffee. There is a play area for children outside near the outdoor terrace. Equally popular as a place for an evening drink, there is live music at night. **$$$$**

✖ **Ocean** Manas 61. A rare seafood restaurant (the ocean is a long way away!) close to the State Philharmonic building. **$$$$**

✖ **Bombay** Chui 110; ✆ 625 115, ✆ 665 683. A smart, upmarket restaurant that is a Kyrgyz-Indian joint venture, & which serves, as its name suggests, Bishkek's take on Indian cuisine. Live music most nights. **$$$–$$$$**

✖ **Consul** Frunze 477; ✆ 621 717. A large restaurant opposite Hotel Sary-Chelek that has European & Chinese cuisine. **$$$–$$$$**

✖ **Admiral** Manas 41a ✆ 218 235. A relatively new international restaurant with good service & live jazz most nights of the week. **$$$**

✖ **Alligator Green** Jukeeva-Pudovkina 75/1; ✆ 512 260; 📱 0502 540 909. Kyrgyz, Chinese, Korean & European cuisine. **$$$**

✖ **Aristokrat** Isa Akhunbaev 77; ✆ 470 603, ✆ 510 040; www.aristocrat.kg. Located above a delicatessen in a 19th-century building in the south of the city, on the junction with Matrosoba, the name says it all about this restaurant's aspirations: its website even claims that its waiters are 'pleasant to glance at: slim

& gallant fellows in dazzling white shirts'. Despite the hype, prices are not as outrageous as you might think; in fact, they are pretty reasonable unless you go for the French wine list. The menu is ambitious & incorporates a wide variety of European cooking styles — French, Spanish & Russian — with specialities like Sturgeon à la Novgorod. As well as the cosy main dining room, there are separate family & banquet rooms that may be reserved. $$$

✗ **Chili Steak House** Almatinskaya 169; ☎ 433 149. American-style food in a faux rustic setting. $$$

✗ **Dasmia** Gorky 2 (Alma Atinskaya); ☎ 432 625, ☎ 530 649. ⏰ 09.00–23.00. A large Kyrgyz restaurant that offers the opportunity to eat in a yurt, which you may want to take advantage of if you are not planning to head for the mountains. $$$

✗ **Doka Pizza** Akhunbaev 97a (junction with Abdrakhmanov); ☎ 510 359; www.doka.kg. A very popular pizza restaurant, with a live jazz combo playing here most nights. Doka serves more than just pizza, with a variety of other mains to choose from as well as sweets, salads & desserts. They even have their own taxi service (Doka-taxi; ☎ 695 555) to take you home should you require it. $$$

✗ **Golden Bull** Chui 209. Identified by a sign on the street that shows a Greek god-like figure (who bears an uncanny resemblance to Freddie Mercury) wrestling a bull. Good spicy steaks & a wider than usual selection of beers; Indian appetisers & some Indian-American fusion main courses. Johnny's Pub (see page 100) is attached to this Indian-run restaurant. Outdoor seating area, & live music 6 nights a week. $$$

✗ **Metro Bar** (also known as the 'American Pub') Chui 168 (junction with Turusbekova); ☎ 217 664, ☎ 217 665. ⏰ 10.00–24.00. If Fatboy's is the British expat hangout then this is the American equivalent. As well as a wide selection of drinks, the pub, in a converted puppet theatre, serves a variety of Mexican & American dishes like Tex-Mex burritos, nachos, hamburgers & pizzas. The Metro Bar attracts very few locals but is popular with Peace Corps volunteers, embassy officials & US airbase staff. Good draught beer; live music some nights. Special foreign (American) events like St Patrick's Day & Halloween are celebrated with some gusto here. The pub has a small bookshop area with English-language travel literature & regional guides & histories. $$$

✗ **Navruz** Moskovskaya 73; ☎ 625 524. ⏰ 10.00–15.00, 18.00–23.00. Turkish food & music some nights. $$$

✗ **New York Pizza** Kievskaya 89; ☎ 662 544, ☎ 909 909. As the name suggests, American-style pizza, also

24hr-delivery service. $$$

✗ **Old Edgar** (Stari Edgar) Panfilov 273 (besides Panfilov Park, between Chui & Firunze, next to Russian Drama Theatre); ☎ 624 408. ⏰ 12.00–24.00. The indoor dining room is rather like a Bavarian beer cellar, while the summer outdoor seating area has something of the Arabian Nights about it, with divans & plenty of cushions. There is an English menu & some English is spoken by the staff; good, friendly service; excellent lasagne & pizzas. Live music most nights. $$$

✗ **Café Parsi** Toktokul/Razzakov junction. Near the Pit Stop café & the Iranian Embassy, this is a restaurant with an Iranian flavour both in terms of food & décor. $$$

✗ **Santa Maria** Chui 217; ☎ 212 484, ☎ 610 532. An upmarket, central restaurant serving mostly Korean dishes. A picture menu of the dishes on offer makes life a little easier. There is also European food available. $$$

✗ **Shamson** Togolok Moldo 5; ☎ 621 543. Dungan food. $$$

✗ **Shao Lin** Jibek-Jolu/Isanova junction. Chinese restaurant with good soup. $$$

✗ **Siberian Crown (Sibirskaya korona)** Chui 186; ☎ 656 349. European food. $$$

✗ **Steinbrau** Gertzena 5; ☎ 293 881. Incongruously situated close to Bishkek's main mosque, Steinbrau is a Munich-style beer hall run by a Bishkek ethnic German family. The main hall is quite vast, with a high ceiling, enormous brass bar & large wooden tables. There is also an upstairs seating area & an outdoor courtyard. Busy waiting staff scurry about offering a choice of beers — pilsner, amber, dark — bar snacks & a good choice of mostly German & Austrian meat & fish dishes that you can select from a multi-lingual picture menu. The excellent home-brewed beer can be seen bubbling away though the windows by the entrance. A resident pianist & violinist provide musical accompaniment. Steinbrau has an easy going, convivial atmosphere & is popular with locals & visitors alike. $$$

✗ **Yusa** Logvinenko 14; ☎ 623 837. An old Bishkek favourite, renovated in summer 2005, Yusa is a Turkish restaurant with a range of medium-priced Turkish dishes & genuine Turkish coffee. With outdoor & indoor seating, it is popular with both expats & locals alike, especially at lunchtimes. $$$

☕ **Kent Café** Razzakov/Kievskaya junction. Just behind Ala-Too square, this 2-floor modern café-restaurant is a good choice for lunch, with a moderately priced international menu that, unusually for Kyrgyzstan, offers several vegetarian options as well as a good range of chicken, pork & fish dishes. Downstairs is a smart, modern café with window tables & a bar; upstairs is a little more formal. Menu in English & Russian. $$–$$$

✕ **Yangste River** Manas 91; ☎ 661 187. A brightly lit, modern Chinese restaurant between Chui & Jibek Jolu near the Filarmonia. $$–$$$

✕ **Astana** Kievskaya. An outdoor courtyard restaurant that offers a good range of Kyrgyz & Russian dishes, particularly *shashlyk*. Live music at night. $$

✕ **Balasgun** Chui 207; ☎ 625 670. Tucked away from the main road beside the Rossiya cinema & next door to the Golden Bull Café. Cheap Chinese food & also takeaway snacks like *samsi*. $$

✕ **Beta Gourmet** Chui 150; ☎ 213 296. This restaurant on the second floor of the Beta shopping centre on Chui is a little canteen-like & lacking in character but it does offer a wide range of Russian, Kyrgyz, Korean &, particularly, Turkish fast food that includes *pide* (Turkish pizza) & various kebabs. There is additional seating outside on a balcony overlooking Chui. A good place for b/fast (100som) or a quick lunch. $$

✕ **Classico** Manas 49; ☎ 664 394, ☎ 664 923. A straightforward, good-value place virtually opposite the Kyrgyz Altyn hotel. A reasonable choice of Russian & international dishes, with *shashlyk* available at night. Cocktails are also available & a 'KGB', a Kahlua & vodka-laced concoction, will set you back 250som. There is no outdoor seating area, which is a shame. $$

✕ **Cyclone** Chui 136 (junction with Togolok Moldo); ☎ 212 866. A centrally located restaurant serving decent Italian dishes that include pesto & pasta, good pizzas & desserts. Also genuine espresso coffee & a good bread basket. The small outdoor terrace here is often full but there is a small, smartly furnished dining area inside. The piped music can be a bit torturous at times, unless you are fond of endless ocarina solos. $$

✕ **Express Café** Moskovskaya/Abdrakhmanov. Recommended for its lunchtime *plov*. $$

✕ **Faiza** Jibek-Jolu 555 (junction with Manas); ☎ 663 747. A no-nonsense sort of place that is very popular with locals & family groups. It serves good-value Kyrgyz staples like *manti*, *laghman* & *lepyoshka*, &

what some consider to be the best *plov* in the city. Although it has a large dining area it can be hard to find a seat at lunchtimes. No alcohol is served. $$

✕ **Fakir** Suyumbaev 142; ☎ 290 608. Good-value restaurant, tucked behind a shopping mall on Suyumbaev, which is popular with locals for its fresh *laghman* & other traditional dishes. The restaurant has a glass-fronted kitchen where you can watch your food being prepared. $$

✕ **Fatboy's** Chui 104 (junction with Tynystanov); ☎ 287 327, ☎ 287 579. ⏰ 08.00–22.00. Probably the best-known place in town, this is a café-bar with pavement tables outside, & tables, a bar & a small no-smoking section inside. Very popular with Bishkek's expat community, particularly the British, Fatboy's has English magazines, a noticeboard & a small library of English-language reading matter. Good for beer or light meals, it is one of the few places in the city where you can get an American or British-style 'full monty' b/fast should you so desire. With more competition in the city these days, its reputation has suffered a little of late. $$

✕ **Inter-Alliance Café** Chui. Next door to TsUM, this is a good choice for a drink or meal after shopping or sightseeing. Tables are placed around a network of small pools, canals & a central fountain – a cooling influence on a hot day. Good draught beer & *shashlyk*, as well as ice cream & fruit salads. $$.

✕ **Mimino** Kievskaya 27; ☎ 661 375. Specialities include Georgian dishes. $$

✕ **Nayuz** Kievskaya. Right next door to the Astana & almost identical in terms of menu, ambience & prices. $$

✕ **Bakaj** A small café with tables under an awning that is a little cheaper than Inter-Alliance & has faster service. $–$$

✕ **Jalal-Abad** corner of Kievskaya/Togolok Moldo. ⏰ 08.00–24.00. This is a large sprawling Uzbek-style *chaikhana* with a vast, dimly lit dining hall inside & several separate dining pavilions on its terrace outside next to the road. The *shashlyk* grillers fan the flames in front of the entrance. There is a fairly limited menu (in Russian) but it is a good choice for grilled meats, *laghman* & salads. Very popular in summer at lunchtimes, when the outside tables are at a premium. No alcohol is served. $–$$

BARS Many of the places listed above double as places to enjoy a leisurely drink, in particular Fatboy's, Metro Pub, Navigator and Steinbrau. Below are some further options, some of which also serve food.

🍸**2x2** Isanov (between Chui & Kievskaya) close to Beta Stores; ☎ 212 497. Stylish Italian-run bar with a wide range of drinks & cocktails served from a circular bar. Light meals are also available. Good security.

♀ **Johnny's Pub** Chui 209; ☎ 212 465. Attached to the Altyn Oguz ('Golden Bull') steakhouse, this has good draught beer & beer snacks, & outdoor seating in summer. Live music on Thu–Sat (small cover charge).
♀ **Manchester Club** Kievskaya/Abdrakhmanov junction. English-style pub with TV screen showing sports events.
♀ **Metro Pub** Sovetskaya 22; ☎ 662 074. Not the same Metro Pub as the one at the west end of Chui. This one is at the intersection with Abdymomunov, in front of the Hyatt Regency hotel, & claims to be open '25 hours a day'.

♀ **Pit Stop Café** Toktogul 107 (Toktogul/Orozbekova junction); ☎ 665 065. ⊕ 10.00–24.00. Pit Stop is a café-bar that has a chequerboard racing theme for its décor & outdoor garden seating. Russian food served.
♀ **Planet Holsten** Tynystanov 122; ☎ 226 759. On the edge of Dubovy Park, a beer garden with a pleasant outdoor seating area.
♀ **Stars** Kievskaya, just east of Molodaya Gvardiya. High-class bar downstairs.
♀ **Time Out** Togolok Moldo 17; ☎ 661 139. European dishes served.

ENTERTAINMENT AND NIGHTLIFE

Bishkek's nightspots should be approached with some caution, as drunken violence and attacks on well-heeled foreigners are not uncommon. The cost of admission is generally around 300som for men and 200som for women. According to some reports people are routinely robbed in front of some of them – Heaven and Fire & Ice are mentioned in particular – as muggers wait outside bars and nightclubs for inebriated foreigners to emerge. Reduce the risk of this by not walking from nightclub to nightclub, but taking a taxi instead (100som at night) even for a short distance. Once inside avoid, if you can, any obviously dodgy Mafia-style characters and be careful whose drink you spill.

NIGHTCLUBS
☆ **Apple** Manas 28; ☎ 216 475, ☎ 219 752. ⊕ 21.30–04.00 Mon–Sun. A popular city disco with special events on Sun.
☆ **Arbat** Yunusaliev 91; ☎ 512 087, ☎ 512 094
☆ **City** Zhukeeva-Pudokin 85/1, Microdistrict 8; ☎ 510 581, ☎ 511 513. ⊕ 21.00–05.00. One of the city's biggest dance clubs with a DVD movie room & a café.
☆ **Club 91** Hyatt Regency Hotel. Live jazz Thu–Sun, no cover charge. Expensive, but happy hour with half-price drinks between 18.30–20.30.
☆ **Emporio** Akhunbaev 46a; ☎ 546 832. ⊕ 11.00–05.00 Tue–Sun. With dance floor, DVD room, swimming pool & café.
☆ **Fire & Ice** Frunze 338a; ☎ 681 700. Disco & live rock. ⊕ 21.00–05.00.
☆ **Heaven** Frunze 429b; ☎ 284 477
☆ **Iceberg** Isa Akhunbaev/Ordzhonikidze junction. Popular with the slightly older, 30–40s, age group. This has a wide range of drinks on offer & better-than-average security.

☆ **Moskva** Togolok Moldo7; ☎ 213 905. Latin & Russian pop.
Y **Pharaoh** Chui 253 (in the Philharmonia building); ☎ 219 647
☆ **Promzona** Cholpan-Atinskaya 16; ☎ 900 244, ☎ 900 245; www.promzona.kg. Live music with rock, jazz & blues acts playing most nights.
☆ **Soho** Orozbekov 62; ☎ 665 427. ⊕ 18.00–05.00. A top-end nightclub that has been going for years. Popular with locals & visitors alike. Rock, hip-hop & Latin music.
☆ **Tequila Blues** Turuzbekov/Engels junction. Located in a former bomb shelter & popular with Bishkek's Russian population. Local heavy metal bands perform on w/end nights.
☆ **Tokyo** Bokonbaev 104. DJ parties, chill-out & lounge.
☆ **Zepellin Bar** Chui 43; ☎ 283 492. ⊕ 14.00–02.00. A rock bar at the far eastern end of Chui with live music, a young local crowd & cheap beer.

GAY CLUBS
☆ **Club 69** (formerly 'Boys' Town') Togolok Moldo. A rare gay nightspot in Bishkek with a mixed clientele.

Drag shows & male strippers at w/ends.

THEATRES Most performances follow the Russian tradition of starting and finishing early, often beginning around 17.00. Tickets are relatively easy to come by at the box office and good seats are very inexpensive by Western standards. Posters outside the venues themselves advertise what is coming up; occasionally there are adverts in the local press. Tickets can usually be bought from the box office on the night of the performance.

🎭 **Conservatory** Jantoshev 115; ☎ 479 542. Occasional student concerts take place here.

🎭 **State Philharmonic** ('*Filarmonia*') Chui 210; ☎ 212 262, ☎ 212 235, ☎ 219 292 (box office ☎ 905 000, ☎ 666 624). On the junction with Manas, this Bishkek institution stages mostly Western classical concerts, with occasional dance, pop & Kyrgyz folklore events. Also home to the Pekin restaurant & Pharaoh nightclub.

🎭 **Russian Drama Theatre** Tynystanov 122; ☎ 228 630, ☎ 662 032, ☎ 621 571. Puts on Russian-language productions of national & international works.

🎭 **State Academic Drama Theatre** Panfilov 273; ☎ 665 802, ☎ 216 958. Located next to Panfilov Park, behind the White House, this theatre stages mostly works in the Kyrgyz language, sometimes Russian.

🎭 **State Opera & Ballet Theatre** Abdrakhmanov 167; ☎ 661 841, ☎ 661 548. This elegant Neo-Classical building opposite the State Museum for Fine Arts puts on both Kyrgyz & Western classical productions of ballet & opera. It has its own resident opera & ballet companies, although there are sometimes performances by visiting companies too.

There is also the **Circus** on Frunze that, although run-down, stages regular performances of local troupes and visiting performers from abroad (mostly CIS and China).

CINEMAS
🎭 **Ala-Too** Chui/Erkindik

🎭 **Dom Kino** ('House of Cinema') Logvinenko 13; ☎ 662 276. Sometimes hosts seasons of foreign films & shows foreign-language films in their original language as well as dubbed into Russian.

🎭 **Issyk-Kul** Jibek-Jolu

🎭 **Manas** Mira, to the south of Isa Akhunbaev

🎭 **October** Chui, near corner of Molodaya Gvardiya. This has been taken into private ownership in recent years & refurbished. Consequently, it is more expensive but more luxurious than most of the others.

🎭 **Russia** Chui/Togolo Moldo. With 3 screens, the biggest cinema in the city.

SPORTS

The city has a number of sports clubs and gymnasiums. Particularly popular are martial arts like Jujitsu and Taekwando.

Karven Club Gogol 77 (junction with Toktogul); ☎ 680 698. Tennis courts, fitness centre, sauna, solarium, badminton & swimming pool. Fairly expensive.

Sports Palace Togolok Moldo 40; ☎ 625 188. Gym, open-air swimming pool & sauna.

Sun Club Zhukeev-Pudovkin 2/1; ☎ 441 616; www.sun-club.kg

BOWLING
Bowling Centre Frunze 338a; ☎ 681 700

Florida Bowling Chui 219; ☎ 219 755

HORSERIDING
Equestrian School Bakinskaya 204a; ☎ 279 209

SWIMMING
Delphin Molodaya Gvardya 2; ☎ 254 607. Swimming pool & sauna.

Water World Gorky; ☎ 432 932

Silk Road Water Centre Jibek-Jolu 285; ☎ 284 142

TENNIS
Tai Break Chui 126 (tennis school, ☎ 216 941) &

Togolok Moldo 17 (tennis club, ☎ 217 842)

SHOPPING

Bishkek has a wide variety of shopping outlets where anything from stationery to souvenirs can be bought. As well as a handful of large, well-stocked department stores there are numerous street stalls, especially around the pedestrian underpasses on Chui and, of course, bona fide markets like Osh and Dordoi bazaars. There are also **kiosks** everywhere selling stationery, magazines, telephone cards, chocolate bars and soft and alcoholic drinks. Whatever else they might lack, you can always be sure that they will have a comprehensive selection of vodka and beer available.

DEPARTMENT STORES AND SHOPPING MALLS

Asia West Abdrakhmanov 152; ✆ 294 845
Beta Stores Chui 150a (corner of Isanov); ✆ 661 072. With a similar range of goods to TsUM, perhaps a little more upmarket, this Turkish-owned concern has an excellent, well-stocked food hall on the ground floor & the handy Beta Gourmet restaurant on the 1st. Some souvenirs on the 1st floor too, but these tend to be a little over-priced. ATM on the ground floor.
Caravan Kievskaya 128; ✆ 909 400
Dordoi Plaza Ibraimov 115a (corner of Kievskaya); ✆ 690 040. ⏰ 09.00–20.00 daily. A large, modern shopping complex that contains over 100 individual shops.
Europa Ibraimov 79 (corner of Toktogul). A good, well-stocked supermarket & a small department store.

Silk Way Chui 147/4; ✆ 621 313. ⏰ 10.00–20.00 daily. Clothes, sportswear, electronics, furniture, household goods. Also 24-hr KINO entertainment centre with cinema, bar, disco & billiards room.
TsUM Chui 155; ✆ 292 794. Bishkek's main department store, established in 1956 & at this location since 1976, has several floors that sell a wide range of electronic goods, photographic supplies, mobile phones, CDs & other necessities of modern life. Also furniture, household goods & local crafts, & souvenirs on the 4th floor. Probably the best place in the city for a cheap 'I've been to Kyrgyzstan' T-shirt. There is a Demir Bank ATM in one of the staircases & also several change places outside facing the east side of the building.

A good supermarket chain for everyday purchases is **Narodniy**, with several branches around the city – in the centre there is a branch behind Dordoi Plaza and another opposite the post office at Abdrakhmanov (Sovetskaya) 180.

SOUVENIRS

Altyn Style Chui/Ibraimov junction; S. Kyrgyz & Russian jewellery.
Antique Shop Manas 47; ✆/f 621 910; e alwian@elat.kg; http://alwian.host.net.kg. ⏰ 10.00–17.30 Mon–Fri (not Mon in summer); 10.00–15.30 Sat. A wide selection of coins, stamps, crafts & Kyrgyz & Russian collectables.
Asahi Chui 136 (next door to Tumar); ✆ 665 710; e info@asahikyrgyz.com. ⏰ 09.00–20.00, summer 09.00–21.00. Various handicraft items that are an individual & artistic (but expensive) take on the more standard craft traditions. *Shyrdaks*, embroidery, jewellery & leather goods.
Astral De Luxe Chui 140; ✆ 211 816. ⏰ 10.00–18.00, 10.00–19.00 in summer. Pottery, leather, embroidery & Kyrgyz handicrafts.
Bishfar Kievskaya 76; ✆ 664 916. Carpets from all over the Central Asian region.
Iman Chui 128; ✆ 212 405. ⏰ 10.00–19.00. Kyrgyz handicrafts.

Karema Manas 7. ⏰ 09.00–17.00. Kyrgyz handicrafts & costume.
Kiyal Chui 202 (at Osh Bazaar); ✆ 242 878, ✆ 651 442. ⏰ 09.00–17.00. Carpets & Kyrgyz handicrafts.
Kyrgyz Heritage Chui 120; ✆ 900 471; e kyr-heritage@mail.ru; www.kyr-heritage.com. Modern & traditional Kyrgyz handicrafts.
Kyrgyz Style Bokonbaev 133, apartment 12; ✆ 621 267; e kyrgyzstyle@infotel.kg; www.kyrgyzstyle.kg. Selling work by local artisans, this outlet began as an NGO in 1993 under the name 'Talent Support Fund' & helps organise & market craft produce from all over Kyrgyzstan – traditional clothes, hats, pillows, slippers, *shyrdaks* & felt toys.
Saimaluu-Tash Pushkin 78 (in Dom Druzhba, east of Ala-Too Sq); ✆ 620 413. ⏰ 10.00–18.00 Tue–Sat. Ceramics by Kyrgyz potter Dzumagol Tashibaev that incorporate intriguing copies of the Saimaluu-Tash petroglyphs into their design.

Tumar Togolok Moldo 36/2, corner of Chui; ☎ 212 653; e tumar@tumar.com; www.tumar.com. Good

range of high-quality Kyrgyz craft products: *shyrdaks*, pottery, felt goods & textiles.

ART

Al Hyatt Moskovskaya 49; ☎ 262 401. ⏰ 11.00–19.00 Tue–Sat.

Asia Gallery Union of Kyrgyz Artists, Chui 108; ☎ 624 505. ⏰ 10.00–17.00 Mon–Fri. This gallery on the 1st floor sells work by local artists.

BOOKS English-language reading material is hard to find in Bishkek, apart from English primers for language students. There is a small selection of English literature, local guides and history books on display inside the **Metro Bar** on Chui (see page 98) at more-or-less European prices. The Hyatt Regency hotel also has a small selection of books along with two-day-old American newspapers and magazines. Otherwise, the following may have the odd English-language title among their mostly Russian stock.

Bishkek Video Rental Chui 259; m 0503 928 016; www.bishkekvideo.com. ⏰ 10.00–21.00; 10.00–22.00 Fri & Sat. Close to the Metro Pub, this place has English-speaking staff, a large choice of videos to rent & a selection of used English language books that sell for 35–50% of the original purchase price.

Odyssey Manas 40, between Chui & Kievskaya. Also has a good selection of stationery & greetings cards.
Panorama/Akademkniga Moskovskaya 141. Secondhand books.
Raritet Pushkin 78 (inside Dom Druzhba), east of Ala-Too Sq; another branch at Chui 271, just before Mahatma Gandhi

MAPS

GeoID Kievskaya 107, room 4, 3rd floor; ☎ 212 202. ⏰ 08.00–17.00 Mon–Fri. This can be a little hard to find: take the entrance to the left of the DHL office, just to the right of another door in the same building that is signed БИТЕКС; walk past the woman at the corridor desk & take the stairs to the 3rd floor; the room is signposted. This is an excellent place to

buy both Cyrillic & Latin script maps of Bishkek as well as maps for the whole of Kyrgyzstan. They also have various themed maps such as the Silk Road in Kyrgyzstan & 1:200,000 topological maps that cover the whole country, which are helpful for trekking (although not sufficiently detailed or accurate to completely depend on).

MARKETS Bishkek has several markets, usually crowded and buzzing with customers and traders alike. Be very aware of your money and possessions amidst the bustle and jostle, as pickpockets systematically work all of these markets, especially Osh. Weekends are usually the busiest days, particularly Sundays for Dordoi.

Alamedin Bazaar Jibek-Jolu/Almatinskaya, just east of East Bus Station. The smallest of the four listed here but still pretty big. Most activity takes place within a covered main hall that sells mostly food produce. Money changers congregate opposite the main entrance.

Dordoi (also called Tolchok) Bazaar This enormous market is around 7km from the city centre to the north. Dordoi covers a large area filled with shipping containers double-stacked on top of each other, with narrow corridors for shoppers leading between them. At the edge of the site are outdoor stalls selling fruit and vegetables and cheap clothing. This is said by some to be the largest market in all central Asia (although also see *Kara-Suu* near Osh) and this is easy to believe with what is said to be around 15,000 traders and an annual turnover of US$100 million. The goods on sale here range from food and cheap clothing to household and electrical goods; a vast amount of it originates in China.

Kudai Bergen used car bazaar (Авторынок Кудайберген) This bazaar, 3km west of Osh Bazaar, is the place to pick up a bargain vehicle, with a huge range of second-hand cars, buses and minibuses on offer. A Lada that has seen better days may be had for US$700 or less, while a German minibus will cost in the region of US$2500. This is the obvious place to purchase that collectible 1970s Volga. The bazaar is open every day but is busiest at weekends.

Osh Bazaar (Ошский Базар) Kievskaya/Beishenalieva (south of the West Bus Station). Osh is the largest market within the city limits. This crowded market offers a genuine flavour (both literally and culturally) of the Kyrgyzstan countryside in the city. Selling mainly fruit and vegetables, but also meat, dairy and baked products, Osh Bazaar has both an open-air market and a covered area. It is liveliest at weekends but is always busy with traders: bakers wandering the aisles with *lepyoshka* piled high on trays; Kyrgyz, Russian, Korean and Dungan vendors shouting out in their different languages to compete for business; and gypsies with smoking dishes of herbs wafting smoke over produce for luck. Right next to Osh Bazaar are some old underground nuclear shelters that now serve as *shyrdak* showrooms, with probably the best prices in the city.

OTHER PRACTICALITIES

MEDICAL SERVICES Emergency health care is available free to foreign visitors. Although doctors are generally well trained, facilities and services will be well below normal European expectations and so a visit to a private clinic is advised. This is where comprehensive travel insurance comes into its own. In an emergency an ambulance may be summoned by dialling ☏ 151.

✚ **Chui Hospital** Saratovskaya 10; ☏ 280 794, ☏ 280 802. The hospital can help foreigners with medical consultations, treatment & surgery. Some English speakers available.
✚ **German-Kyrgyz Medical Centre** Akhunbaev 94/1 (junction with Jukeev-Pudovkin); ☏ 512 197; f 540 747; e balbakell@elcat.kg. A private clinic that offers modern, European-standard treatment & diagnosis & English-language consultation.
✚ **Medical Associates Clinic** Hyatt Regency, Sovetskaya 191, room 113; ☏ 680 262, ☏ 985 745
✚ **Trauma Clinic (Poliklinika stroitelei)** Manas 41 (junction with Toktogul). 24hr first aid for less serious accidents.
✚ **VIP Clinic** Kievskaya 110; ☏ 663 549, ☏ 661 901, ☏ 216 937 (for 24hr-duty or ambulance ☏ 660 356, ☏ 228 992)

Chiropractic Care
✚ **Dr Peter Dinch** ☏ 588 366. A US-certified doctor.

Dental clinics The following have English-speaking dentists:
✚ **Diplomat Dental Salon** ☏ 286 731
✚ **Hollywood Smile** Kievskaya 112; ☏ 666 522
✚ **VYTAS** Shopokov 89; ☏ 996 312, ☏ 284 659

Pharmacies
✚ **Central** Frunze 340; ☏ 681 005
✚ **Neman** All branches of the Neman Pharmacy network are open 24hrs: Akhunbaev 31, ☏ 545 413; Chui 94, ☏ 640 768; Chui 113, ☏ 531 423; Kievskaya 38, ☏ 292 981; Manas 8, ☏ 216 792; Moskovskaya 139, ☏ 622 937; **Prestige** Kievskaya 95a, ☏ 621 462

MONEY EXCHANGE It is easy to change **Cash** (US dollars, euros, Kazakh tenge, Uzbek som and to a much lesser extent pounds sterling) at one of many exchange booths, or *obmyen valyoot* (обмен валют), that are scattered around the city; many hotels, too, have an exchange desk. There are several on Toktogul, on Sovetskaya north of Bokonbaeva, inside (and beside) TsUM department store, and at the top end of Manas towards Chui. They do not charge commission but make their profit from the differential between the buying and selling rate; exchange rates, however, seem to vary very little from place to place as long as you present them with pristine notes. For more formal transactions, Bishkek is well provided with banks, although only few are of much use for the general needs of overseas travellers. **Travellers' cheques** may be exchanged, and **cash advances** organised with a little bit of paperwork, at the branches listed below.

$ **AKB Bank** Togolok Moldo 54. ⏲ 09.00–16.00 Mon–Fri. Commission of 3% is charged for changing most types of travellers' cheques; cash advances on Visa cards are also possible.
$ **Bakai Bank** Isanov 75; ☎ 660 610. ⏲ 08.30–12.00, 13.00–15.00 Mon–Fri. Will exchange

Thomas Cook, American Express & CitiCorp travellers' cheques for 3% commission; VISA cash advances.
$ **Demir Kyrgyz International Bank** Chui 245; ☎ 610 610. ⏲ 09.00–12.00, 13.00–16.00 Mon–Fri (closes 14.30 Fri). Will change Amex travellers' cheques for 3% commission & give advances on Visa & Maestro cards.

Unlike almost everywhere else in Kyrgyzstan, it is relatively easy to withdraw cash from **ATM machines** in Bishkek, although be aware that some will work for locally issued cards only.

Cash dispensers of **Kazkomerzbank** at TsUM department store, Dordoi Plaza at Ibraimov, and at Abdrakhmanov 136, will accept VISA, MasterCard, Maestro and Cirrus credit and debit cards, and will dispense both som and US dollars; a commission of 2% will be added to your bill, although this is not mentioned on the machine receipt. Further machines may be found in front of the C.A.T. Corporation office on Chui 124 (junction with Panfilova), at the airport, at the US Embassy at Mir 117, and at Fonex and inside the Caravan department store on Kievskaya. Demir Bank has recently installed cash machines in the city, which for now only accept local cards, but which should be able to deal with foreign-issued cards in the future.

Money transfers from abroad may also be made by way of **Western Union**, which operates through several Bishkek banks.

COMMUNICATIONS

Post Bishkek's **main post office** is at Chui 96, on the corner with Abdrakhmanov (☎ *626 045*, ☎ *662 561*; ⏲ *07.00–19.00 Mon–Sat, 08.00–19.00 Sun*). Large parcels may be posted here but leave them open to allow for customs inspection. There is a separate room that deals with EPS (Express Postal Service).

DHL at Kievskaya 107 (☎ *611 111*) and **Federal Express** at Moskovskaya 217 (☎ *650 012*) both provide courier services, while **American Resources International** (*ARI Cargo, Erkindik 35*; ☎ *660 077*; f *661 311*; e *bishkek@ aricargo.com; www.aricargo.com*) is able to ship larger items by air or overland.

Telephone The central **Kyrgyz Telecom** office is next door to the main post office (⏲ *07.00–23.30 daily*). The call-boxes outside can be used for local calls, but national and international calls should be made from the booths inside. Calls are pre-paid at the counter depending on the amount of time you want; change will be given after the call for any time not used, or a refund given if there is no answer. International dialling codes are preceded by 00 and you may need to dial 3 to talk when your call is picked up.

Calls to the UK tend to cost around US$2 for three minutes. Elsewhere in the city some phone booths take tokens (*zhetoni*) that can be bought from kiosks, although these may only be used for local calls (put in the token when the call is answered). Other phones called *taxophone* – perhaps the majority these days – use prepaid cards, which once again, can be bought from kiosks. They come in denominations of 50, 100, 200 and 400 units and the cost is clearly marked. Some kiosk vendors add a small mark-up to the indicated price. Card phones can be used for both local and long-distance calls. Local calls within the city are free if made from a private phone, but hotels usually make a small charge for these and invariably charge way over the odds for long-distance or international calls.

Cheap **IP international calls** may be made from internet cafés and other phone centres using an internet connection. They usually advertise their rates outside and these are generally much cheaper than Kyrgyz Telecom. There tends to be a slight time delay on these calls, so you need to speak one at a time and allow your correspondent to answer before butting in. The quality of these services is improving all the time and often they are better than an expensive satellite call.

Mobile phones The main providers are **BITEL** (↘ 0502), **KATEL** (↘ 0517) and **FONEX**, the most recent company to operate in Bishkek. BITEL operates on the GSM system, so you may be able to use a roaming service and your own number.

Local SIM cards may be bought relatively cheaply from many outlets in the city, especially the third floor of TsUM. Both BITEL and KATEL provide a service that does not entail setting up a local account. This works by purchasing a SIM card with a local number and a card with credits (Mobicard for BITEL, K-plus for KATEL). When your credit is exhausted you will need to buy another card and dial the service provider and enter a serial number, which will add the new credits to your account.

Important telephone numbers All of the three-figure numbers below are free from both private and street call phones.

Ambulance ↘ 103
Directory enquiries ↘ 109
Emergency medical service ↘ 151
Fire ↘ 101
Police ↘ 102

Police hotline ↘ 662 331, ↘ 284 305
Police helpline for foreign nationals ↘ 285 978. This is the number to ring if you have any problems with over-zealous, bribe-demanding *militsia*. They apparently have English-speaking staff working this service.

Internet There are a large number of internet cafés in Bishkek but, as everywhere else, new places open and close for business with great regularity. Charges are generally around 30som per hour; some are cheaper, charging around 20som per hour, but they may also charge for the actual amount of MB used, which can work out more expensive with a fast connection. A few of the seemingly more permanent institutions are listed below.

🖳 **ABC** Moskovskaya 162; ↘ 214 808
🖳 **B-zone Internet** Chui 170; ↘ 640 777
🖳 **Galaktika** Chui 257; ↘ 562 447. ⊕ 08.00–20.00. Internet & IP telephony.
🖳 **Maté Internet** Chui 128
🖳 **NeoPlanet** have several branches around the city centre at the following locations. All have reliable, fast connection for around 30som per hr, document copying, scanning & printing facilities; also IP telephone calls:
Togolok Moldo 3 (at junction with Kievskaya), ↘ 666 898; Abdrakhmanov 145 (behind Kara-Balta

store), ↘ 665 664; Manas 70, ↘ 548 496; Suyumbaev 14, ↘ 681 947; Chui 186, ↘ 656 214
🖳 **Park Net** Chui 134; ↘ 611 022. ⊕ 08.00–24.00. Internet, scanning, printing & IP telephony.
🖳 **Skyline Internet Club** Chui 125 (just west of Filarmonia); ↘ 211 919, ↘ 212 211. Also does IP phone calls.
🖳 **Valley Net** Kievskaya 159; ↘ 218 315, ↘ 665 592. ⊕ 08.00–23.00. Internet, scanning, printing, IP telephony & mobile phone rent.
🖳 **Vares** Toktogul, between Shopokov & Ibraimov. Also IP telephone calls.

VISA REGISTRATION AND EXTENSION

OVIR Office Kievskaya 58/2. ⏰ 09.30–12.30, 14.00–17.00 Mon–Fri. This is the place to register your visa should it be necessary, although many nationalities are no longer required to do this (see page 52, *Practical Information*). OVIR can also extend visas for a week or so without much fuss for around 300som.

Embassies Bishkek is not a bad place to while away time waiting for visas to be processed. Be aware though, that some are far more straightforward than others.

There is no **UK Embassy**, British interests are covered by the non-resident British ambassador in Kazakhstan (*Kosmonavtov 62, Renco Building 6th floor, Astana;* ☎ +7 3172 556 200; f +7 3172 556 211; e britishembassy@mailonline.kz; www.britishembassy.kz. The consular division is at Panfilova 158, Almaty; ☎ +7 3272 508 280; e AlmatyVisaGeneral@fco.gov.uk; www.britishembassy.kz). In Bishkek, British nationals should contact Honorary Consul Mike Atsoparthis at Kalik Akiyeva 11, apartment 24 (☎ 680 815; m 584 245; e gbhoncon@mail.kg).

Ⓔ Afghanistan Aini 4; ☎ 690 176; f 690 330; e afghanemb_bishkek@yahoo.com

Ⓔ Canada Moskovskaya 189; ☎ 650 506; ☎/f 650 101; e canada_honcon@infotel.kg. Honorary consul only; for consular matters refer to Canadian Embassy in Kazakhstan.

Ⓔ China Toktogul 196; ☎ 621 905, ☎ 222 423, ☎ 212 564; f 650 108, f 212 547. ⏰ 09.15–12.00 Mon, Wed & Fri. If you plan to cross into China overland the embassy will require an invitation from a Xinjiang travel agency in order to issue a visa. You can organise this with one of the tourist agencies like Celestial Mountains, but the visa will take at least a week to issue. It is definitely better to arrange Chinese visas before leaving home.

Ⓔ France Razzakov 49; ☎ 660 053, ☎ 660 364; f 660 441; e ag-consul@elcat.kg

Ⓔ Germany Razzakova 28; ☎ 224 803, ☎ 228 523, ☎ 666 624; f 666 207; e gerembi@elcat.kg

Ⓔ India Chui 164a/3; ☎ 212 823, ☎ 210 862, ☎ 210 863; f 660 708; e indembas@infotel.kg. ⏰ 09.00–13.00, 14.00–17.30 Mon–Fri

Ⓔ Iran Razzakov 36; ☎ 227 214, ☎ 624 929, ☎ 624 917; f 660 209. ⏰ 09.00–17.00 Mon–Fri. Individuals who apply here are usually told to apply for a letter of invitation (LOI) through www.iranjasminco.com, which will take a matter of weeks. Expect problems & unexplained delays even if you have the LOI.

Ⓔ Italy Chui 155, office 703 (honorary consul only); ☎ 292 794, ☎ 681 304, ☎ 681 229

Ⓔ Japan Frunze 503; ☎ 611 875, ☎ 611 880; f 611 882

Ⓔ Kazakhstan Togolok Moldo 10; ☎ 660 415, ☎ 660 164, ☎ 225 463; e kaz_emb@imfico.bishkek.su. ⏰ 10.00–12.00 Mon–Thu. 5-day Kazakh transit visas can usually be obtained reasonably quickly without an LOI if you have evidence of tickets out of the country & a 3rd country visa.

Ⓔ Netherlands Foundation Publishing Development Centre, Tynystanov 96, apartment 12 (honorary consul); ☎/f 690 565; e ben@berwers.nl. ⏰ 09.30–12.30 Mon–Fri

Ⓔ Pakistan Panfilov 308; ☎ 227 209, ☎ 226 479, ☎ 226 670; f 661 550; e parepbishkek@transfer.kg, pakemb@asianinfo.kg. ⏰ 09.00–11.00 Mon–Fri

Ⓔ Russia Razzakov 17; ☎ 624 736, ☎ 624 738, ☎ 624 739, ☎ 221 619; f 221 823; e rusemb@imfiko.bishkek.su (consular department for visas, ☎ 221 775, ☎ 217 700, ☎ 215 703; f 221 823, f 610 177; e ruscons@imfiko.bishkek.su). You will need an invitation (try Kyrgyz Concept, Celestial Mountains or C.A.T), which will take a week to arrive. To apply you will need the original invitation voucher (2 stamped documents on an A4 sheet), passport (make a copy), completed application form, photo & the exact payment in US$, which will probably be in the order of US$ 70–100.

Ⓔ Sweden (honorary consulate) c/o ABB Representation Office, Chui 114, room 407; ☎ 627 010, ☎ 627 008, ☎ 662 168; e abb@mail.kg

Ⓔ Switzerland (consulate) Panfilov 144; ☎ 666 480; f 666 489

Ⓔ Tajikistan Karadarinskaya 36, Kok-Jar Microdistrict; ☎/f 511 464; e tojsaforat@exnet.kg. Will issue visas for many nationalities without an LOI these days; takes 3–4 business days.

Ⓔ Turkey Moskovskaya 89; ☎ 226 021, ☎ 227 882, ☎ 620 378, ☎ 622 354; f 660 519. ⏰ 09.00–12.00 Mon–Fri.

Ⓔ USA Mira 171; ☎ 551 241, ☎ 551 242; f 551 264; http://kyrgyz.usembassy.gov. ⏰ 08.00–17.00 Mon–Fri.

Ⓔ Uzbekistan Tynystanov 213; ☎ 226 171, ☎ 662 065; f 664 403. ⏰ Closed Mon. Some reports suggest that Bishkek is not a particularly good place to obtain an Uzbek visa. The embassy may well require an LOI (it depends on your nationality & this keeps changing) & it sometimes insists that you produce an air ticket to/from Bishkek. You are also supposed to need to get a Russian speaker to telephone the embassy to make an appointment for you in advance if you do not speak Russian, although you can probably manage without. You will need a copy of your passport & a photo. Visas take 4–7 business days to issue.

WHAT TO SEE AND DO

Bishkek is a pleasant city but in terms of sightseeing there is little that might be described as a 'must see'. Nevertheless, there are a handful of worthwhile monuments, some pleasant parks and a few interesting museums and art galleries to seek out. All of the sights mentioned below are in the city centre, which might be defined as the area circumscribed by Jibek-Jolu to the north, Moskovskaya to the south, Molodaya Gvardiya to the west and Ibraimov to the east. Running east–west through this downtown area is the central avenue of Chui Prospect.

The heart of the city, such as it is, is centred upon **Ala-Too Square**, which was previously known as Lenin Square up until independence in 1991. This large, rather anonymous, concrete expanse facing Chui Prospect is where most official celebrations tend to take place. There is said to be an underground complex beneath the square that is connected to the White House by a secret passageway. The large subterranean assembly room here is purported to have portraits of the Soviet politburo still in place, but it has not seen much use since independence.

The square above used to have a statue of the eponymous Soviet leader as its centrepiece, but the monument was shifted in 2003 to a less prominent location just behind the State Historical Museum. Lenin has since been replaced by something that is more symbolic of the nation's newly minted Kyrgyz character, the **Erkindik (Freedom) Monument**. The statue, which was unveiled in 1999 to commemorate eight years of Kyrgyz independence, represents a woman holding a flame that is ringed by that most familiar of Kyrgyz symbols, the *tunduk*, the traditional wooden centrepiece of a yurt. The statue was moved here in 2003 when Lenin was shifted a block to the north. Just west of the monument stands the national flagpole, erected in 1998 and attended by an immaculately dressed guard of honour that changes every hour and devotedly packs away the flag for the night when dusk falls.

The newly located **Lenin statue**, which captures the man in 'pointing to the future' mode, dates from 1984 and stands around 10m tall, presiding over the paved square to the north of the State Historical Museum that was formerly home to the Monument to Labour Glory. This small square has since been designated as the replacement Lenin Square, although it is undeniably more low-key than its predecessor. In his former home, Lenin used to point south towards the Ala-Too peaks; now he has his back to the mountains and he gestures in the general direction of the American University, whether in righteous fury or in conciliation no-one can be certain. Perhaps it says much about Kyrgyzstan that Lenin was merely demoted to a less prominent location rather than destroyed outright, as was the case in less-forgiving neighbouring countries like Uzbekistan.

Facing south onto Chui Prospect just west of Ala-Too Square is the **White House**, a seven-storey neoclassical marble edifice built in 1985 that is the seat of Kyrgyzstan's government and houses the president's office. Just before this, between the State History Museum and the White House, is the **Friendship Monument**, a tall modernist study in concrete. The square here was inaugurated by Kosygin in 1974 to commemorate the centenary of the Kyrgyz peoples joining the Russian Empire. The trees around the monument were planted by key Soviet dignitaries such as Kosygin and Brezhnev.

Situated immediately behind the White House and its serious affairs of state is an altogether more fun-loving place – **Panfilov Park**, one of Bishkek's most popular green spaces. Naturally enough, Panfilov Park boasts a statue of its namesake, Ivan

Vasilyevich Panfilov, the Russian general and commander of the defenders of Moscow who died heroically in battle against the Nazis in 1941.

These days most Bishkek citizens visit the park less to admire the great-coated war hero than to avail themselves of the fairground rides, karaoke machines, ice cream stalls and *shashlyk* vendors that cluster near the eastern entrance. There is a Ferris wheel here too, and for a mere 15som you can get a crow's-eye view across the concrete squares and tree-lined avenues of central Bishkek to the mountains beyond. The park started out as a municipal garden planted by horticultural students in 1879; later on it became known as Red Star Park, as its walkways trace the shape of the five-pointed communist star. There appears to be no campaign as yet to rename it 'Freedom Park'.

East of Ala-Too Square is **Dom Druzhby** (Friendship house), which now serves as a community centre and zoological museum, but which in Soviet times was the headquarters of the Kyrgyz ASSR Central Committee. Behind this is another popular green space **Dubovy (Oak) Park**, which began as a grove of oak saplings in 1890. Like Panfilov Park, this is another good location for a quiet drink or a cool stroll among trees and away from the traffic.

The park hosts the **Memorial to the Red Guards**, a red granite obelisk erected in 1960 that marks the common grave of the Bolshevik casualties of the Belovodsk counter-revolutionary uprising of 6 December 1918. Oak Park also has a **monument to Marx and Engels**, who are depicted sitting next to each other on a bench deep in conversation. Their names have been removed from the plinth, which indicates some sort of compromise with the past in which out-of-favour ideologues may be depicted as long as they are not named – the same sort of logic that does not dethrone Lenin entirely but simply demotes him. The park also has a 2004 monument to Kurmanjan Datka, the Queen of the Alia, whose plinth formerly supported a statue of KGB-founder Felix Dzerzhinsky, and an outdoor sculpture garden with representations of cities from all over the former Soviet Union. The park is also home to the Russian Drama Theatre and two of the city's best restaurants – Stari Edgar and the Four Seasons (see pages 98–9).

Tree-lined **Erkendik (Freedom) Boulevard** stretches due south of Dubovy Park all the way to the railway station, its twin avenues bisected by a shady pedestrian zone that is dotted with benches and an assortment of statuary depicting Kyrgyz poets and war heroes. A shorter section extends north of Dubovy Park too, linking it with the frantic thoroughfare of Jibek-Jolu Prospect. The promenade dates back to 1883 when it was created by planting poplars along a filled-up streambed.

In summer there are always large numbers of people here taking advantage of the shade and welcome respite from the city traffic: cigarette vendors, office workers, students and exhausted Russian pensioners with carrier bags. The avenue has had several names before its present-day appellation was settled upon: originally it was simply 'the boulevard'; in post-Revolutionary times, it became Komsomolskaya; and then later, Prospect Dzerzhinsky, after the founder of the Cheka secret police, the forerunner of the KGB.

With independence from the Soviet Union and a political need for nation-building and a distancing from the past, 'freedom' must have seemed like an obvious choice for its new and, hopefully final, alias. Contrary to this new spirit of nationalism, and bolstering the city's former Russian identity, a monument to an existing Soviet hero has firmly remained in place. Right at the bottom of Erkendik, facing the railway station and constructed in 1938, stands an equestrian statue of the Bolshevik general Mikhail Frunze, who gave his name to the city in 1926 when it became the capital of the Kyrgyz ASSR.

A few blocks further east of Dubovy Park, continuing along Chui Prospect, stands **Revolution Square**, with the 1978 **Martyrs of the Revolution Monument** as its centrepiece; it's the work of local sculptor Tinibek Sadykov, for which he won the All Union Lenin Prize. The central figure here is Urkuya Saliyeva (1910–34), a young socialist organiser from southern Kyrgyzstan who was murdered by reactionary locals. She is surrounded by figures that represent the 'awakening proletariat'.

Just north of here along Abdrakhmanov (formerly Sovetskaya) stand two of the city's great cultural institutions almost face to face across the street. On the right is the elegant pink façade and classical columns of the **Abdylas Maldybaev Opera and Ballet Theatre** with its interesting friezes and hammer and sickle motifs on its pillars.

A little further east along Chui prospect and immediately north of the TsUM department store is the breezy plaza of **Pobeda (Victory) Square**, which until 1985 was the site of the city's central bazaar. More Kyrgyz symbolism takes pride of place here, with three massive curved arches that represent a section of yurt towering above a statue of a Kyrgyz woman waiting for her husband or son to return from the front (or, as some local wags say, for them to emerge from one of the nightclubs that surround the square).

The bulky monument was erected in 1985 to commemorate the 40th anniversary of the end of World War II. An eternal flame burns here, a focus around which an assortment of the city's drinkers and nefarious characters sometimes gather like wayward moths. At other times the square is besieged by wedding parties seeking a suitable backdrop for souvenir photographs and video takes.

If this concrete symbolism of traditional *jailoo* life is not enough, then there are clear reminders of the alpine terrain that lies beyond the city: the square is broad and uncluttered enough to afford clear views to the south of the perpetually snow-clad Ala-Too range. The view in the opposite direction is altogether less romantic: the bland bulk of Hotel Dostuk faces the square to the northeast, while to the northwest stands the unmistakeable lime green and pink form of the **Circus** building, shaped rather like a 1950s flying saucer. Beyond lie some of the less savoury quarters of the capital, and after dark the streets around here become the home-ground of prostitutes and their pimps.

Returning to Ala-Too Square and heading west along Chui Prospect past the White House, the 'Rossiya' cinema is on your right at the corner with Togolok Moldo, which leads north to Jibek-Jolu past **Spartak Stadium** on the right and the humdrum Palace of Sports on the left. The sports palace has a **statue of Kojumkol** outside, a semi-legendary giant of a man who is depicted here lifting a horse – certainly a twist on the usual equestrian statue theme. Kojumkol, who hailed from the Suusamyr valley and lived from 1899–1955, was reported to have been 2.3m tall and would lift enormous stones just for fun and, if the mood took him, even his own horse.

Continuing right down Frunze and then north down Logvinenko brings you to the thoroughfare of Jibek-Jolu and the nearby **Russian Orthodox Cathedral** with its sky blue domes. Back on Chui, two blocks further west is the intersection with Manas where the **State Philharmonic** concert hall stands set back from the road with a large area of paved walkways, fountains and flowerbeds in front of it. This is a popular meeting spot and a favoured location for street photographers to set up their equipment to tempt passers by. In front of the concert hall, surrounded by spurting fountains, is an **equestrian statue of Manas** on his horse Ak-Kula, with his wife, Kankei, and Bakai, his faithful friend and counsellor, represented at the base of the statue. Around the square itself are a scattering of smaller statues of well-known Kyrgyz *manaschi* (traditional story-tellers).

The next road junction west along Chui, with Turesbekova, has a smaller but still grand building that was the original State Philharmonic building, which later became a puppet theatre and now serves as an American-style pub for homesick expatriates – the Metro Bar. Continuing west leads past the National State Academy on the right and then, on the left, the 'October' cinema, one of the city's best-appointed film houses.

This brings you to Molodaya Gvardiya, a tree-lined boulevard, which is now officially referred to as Mahatma Gandhi. The former name translates as the **Avenue of the Young Guards** and the section that lies immediately off Chui is referred to as 'Heroes' Lane'. Originally this was the course of a tributary of the Ala-Archa River, but it was filled and planted with trees to create the present-day boulevard. The busts that line it are Soviet-era military heroes, and there is a large Komsomol (young communist league) statue of Soviet soldiers bearing the legend: 'We went to war for Communism'.

MUSEUMS Most museums have a small entrance fee of 100som or less. Many are closed on Mondays and some close for an hour's lunch break in the middle of the day.

Fine Arts Museum (Музей Изобразительных Искусств) (*Abdrakhmanov 196;* ✆ *661 623;* ✆ *09.00–17.00 Tue–Sun, 10.00–16.00 Fri; 100som*) This museum, opposite the Opera and Ballet Theatre and sometimes referred to as the Gapar Aytiev Museum of Applied Art, is dedicated to displaying temporary exhibitions along with a permanent collection of Kyrgyz folk and applied art, and Russian and Soviet fine art. The permanent collection was originally kept in St Nicholas's Russian Orthodox church in Dubovy Park (which now houses the Gallery of the Artist's Union) but the museum was built in 1974 to house the collection. The museum was renovated a few years ago.

Along with the obligatory yurt and a colourful display of *shyrdaks*, carpets and typical felt goods, there are several galleries of differing styles of Soviet-period art that include Soviet Realism and propaganda, and replicas of Egyptian, Roman and Greek statuary. Most captions are in Russian and Kyrgyz but some are in English. Sometimes Kyrgyz felt-ware craft markets are held in the courtyard facing the entrance.

Kyrgyz State Historical Museum (Музей Национальной Истории) (*formerly Lenin Museum, Ala-Too Square;* ✆ *626 097;* ✆ *09.00–18.00, Tue–Sun, but closed 13.00–14.00; 55som*) Despite its new name much of this museum – all of the second floor and part of the third – remains dedicated to the life and works of Lenin. In a post-Soviet climate, yesterday's propaganda becomes today's history lesson, and so this unapologetic shrine to the man provides a fascinating window on the recent past.

There is a highly impressive mural on the ceiling of the third floor that depicts a wedding party attended by representatives of every Soviet nationality – Kyrgyz, Uzbeks, Tartars, fair-haired Russians – all gathered in complete accord alongside the man making the speeches, Comrade Lenin himself; an idealised representation of the ethnic melting pot that was the Soviet Union (another superb mural shows reactionary religious types and Cossacks confronting revolutionary soldiers). In addition, there are various statues and paintings of Lenin addressing assembled revolutionary masses and doing a lot of pointing. Other Lenin memorabilia includes photos, texts and books associated with the leader. Unusually for this part of the world there are occasional labels in English, although the vast majority are in Russian and Kyrgyz.

Away from the Lenin exhibition are displays of Neolithic artefacts, including Saimaluu-Tash petroglyphs, which are well worth seeing if you're planning to go there, or even if you are not, and examples of Turkic stone culture and Talas burial stones. Also: coins, Bronze Age objects and musical instruments; golden artefacts from the Chui valley's Shushing tomb; beautiful blue pottery from the Talas valley; models of the buildings of the Karakhanid period like those at Özgön; and a large ethnographic collection of Kyrgyz nomadic paraphernalia that includes traditional costumes and equestrian fittings like saddles and harnesses. The old black and white photographs of pre-Soviet Kyrgyz life are particularly fascinating. The top floor has a large yurt in situ.

Mikhail Frunze Museum (Музей М В Фрунзе) (*Frunze 346;* ❧ *660 604;* ⊕ *09.00–17.00 Tue–Fri, 09.00–16.00 Sat–Sun*; *55som*) This museum is built around the house where Frunze, the Bolshevik leader who led the advance into central Asia, is said to have been born, although it is far more likely that this merely represents the *type* of house he was born in rather than his actual domicile. The displays outline his life and achievements and there is also an exhibition showing life in the city during the Soviet era.

Mineralogical Museum (Минералогический Музей) (*Chui 164;* ⊕ *09.00–15.30 Mon–Fri*) A mineral collection gathered from all over Kyrgyzstan. Guided tours in Russian only.

Open Air Sculpture Museum (*Frunze 346;* ⊕ *09.00–17.00 daily*) This was created in 1984 to commemorate the 60th anniversary of the Kyrgyz ASSR, and features work by sculptors from all over the Soviet Union on the theme of 'Peace and Labour'.

Ivan Panfilov Museum (*Toktogul, next to Hotel Semetei*) Reconstructed in 2004 (see page 109).

Tinibek Sadykov Museum (Музей Академии Художеств Т Садыков) (*Togolok Moldo;* ⊕ *09.00–12.00, 13.00–16.00 Mon–Fri*) This houses a collection of work by the Kyrgyz sculptor Tinibek Sadykov whose larger works include the Martyrs to the Revolution Monument as well as other works that stand in Victory Square and the grounds of the State Philharmonic.

Aaly Tokombaev Memorial Museum (Мемориальный Дом-Музей А Токомбаева) (*Chuikov 109;* ⊕ *09.00–17.00 Mon–Fri; 09.00–14.00 Sat; 55som*) This is the house museum of the Kyrgyz poet, *akyn* (bard) and composer who made significant contributions towards the standardisation of the written (Cyrillic) Kyrgyz language and who translated many international works of literature into Kyrgyz for the first time. There is a statue of him outside the Fine Arts Museum. A further exhibition details the 1916 exodus of many Kyrgyz to China following widespread Russian repression after the uprising of that year.

Toktogul Literary Museum (*Toktogul 109;* ⊕ *08.00–12.30, 13.30–17.30 Mon–Fri*)

Zoological Museum (Зоологический Музей) (*Pushkin 78, in Dom Druzhby, the 'Friendship House'*; ⊕ *10.00–17.00 Mon–Fri; 15som*) Renovated in 2004, this has a collection of stuffed animals and birds from all over the country, along with portraits of scientists eg: Przhevalsky who made a study of Kyrgyzstan's flora and fauna.

PARKS As already mentioned, Bishkek is a remarkably green city. As well as the central parks mentioned earlier, there are others, further away from the city centre, that may be worth visiting if you have time on your hands.

Ataturk Park South of the city on Akhunbaev between Mira and Baitik Baatyr (Sovetskaya), this park was formerly known as Druzhba (Friendship) Park but, post-independence, was renamed in honour of the founder of modern Turkey – Kemal Ataturk. The park is a popular place on summer weekends and attracts strollers and sellers and buyers of collectables such as stamps, coins and lapel badges. There is a statue of its eponymous Turkish founder near the entrance and a memorial to the fallen Soviet soldiers of the ill-fated Afghanistan campaign. In 2004, a memorial to the Batken heroes of 1999–2000 was erected in the park (see pages 13–14). Comprising three connected metal pylons 48m high, this is the tallest monument in the country and utilises a total of 60 tonnes of metal. The park also has a number of amusement rides and a large Ferris wheel, which some like to refer to as the 'Bishkek Eye'.

Botanical Garden and Arboretum Sandwiched between Gorky and Lev Tolstoy, this extensive park is managed by the Academy of Sciences.

Fuchika Park West of the city centre, close to Osh Bazaar, this park was created by Czech socialist volunteers who came to help construct the city in 1936 and was named after the Czech socialist leader of the time.

Gorky Park On the corner of Isanov and Ryskulov, just west of the Palace of Sports, this is tiny compared to its Moscow namesake. Sometimes used as the location for protests and demonstrations, at other times as an impromptu sports training ground.

Manas Village When UNESCO declared that 1995 would be the 1,000th anniversary of the Manas epic the country celebrated by staging a number of Kyrgyz cultural events, particularly in the Talas valley, where a new museum was opened. In Bishkek, a purpose-built village was created in the city's southern suburbs. Now it is fairly deserted but the complex of stages, podiums, yurts and towers may still be seen. The village's high tower affords a superb view of the Ala-Too range to the south and sunset is a good time to visit. The village stands near to a suburb occupied by Bishkek's nouveau riche, known to locals as *Tsarskoe Selo*, after the palace complex outside St Petersburg in Russia.

Karagachovaya Rosha (Elm Grove) This large park lies to the northeast of the city, north of Jibek-Jolu, with its southern boundary marked by the Bolshoy Chuisky ('Grand Chui') Canal and its northern by the Malyi Chuisky ('Little Chui') Canal. Originally swampland, there are two small lakes – Pionerskoe and Komsomolskoe – at its southern edge, and a road that bisects it north to south – Almykul Usenbaev. The northern part of the city around the park is a dusty Slavic suburb that has echoes of a rural Russia and Ukraine of yesteryear, with gingerbread houses, orchards and lovingly tended gardens – well worth a stroll in its own right.

Togolok Moldo Park A small, fairly central park south of Moskovskaya and just to the east of a 19th-century wooden house dating from the Tsarist period.

OTHER STATUES AND CURIOSITIES
Heroes of Batken This recent memorial on Kievskaya at the junction with Logvinenko has three Kyrgyz soldiers dressed in traditional costume. The monument commemorates those who fought against Islamist militants during the Batken incursions of 1999 and 2000. A much larger monument to the same cause stands in Ataturk Park.

MIG fighter On Kievskaya, in front of the headquarters of the National Guard, stands an old silver MIG jet fighter on a pedestal. In Soviet times, Kyrgyzstan was an important pilot-training centre and President Assad of Syria trained here during the 1960s.

Lenin (another one) This can be found outside the Kyrgyz technical university on Mira Prospect. A crack developed on the pedestal in 2004 and the statue had started to bend forwards,. To remedy this it has been repositioned and turned through 90° to face north.

Russian log house At Moskovskaya 145, this is a rare and well-preserved example of pre-Soviet architecture in the city.

Snow leopard

4

Chui Province

Chui (**Чуй**), the name given to the valley and its river, is also the name of this most northerly province that extends well beyond the flat land of the valley itself to cover an area of 18,684km². North to south, the province stretches from the Kazakhstan border to the mountain valleys south of Bishkek, over the ridge of the Kyrgyz Ala-Too mountain range to the Suusamyr valley beyond. Chui Province – or *oblast* (in Kyrgyz, **Чуй областы**; in Russian, **Чуйская область**) – is home to the capital and the towns of Kant, Tokmok and Kemin to the east of Bishkek and Kara-Balta to the west. Following a brief period (2003–06) when Tokmok was designated as provincial capital, Bishkek has returned to being Chui's administrative centre once more.

VALLEYS SOUTH OF BISHKEK

Seen from almost anywhere in the city, the snow-flecked peaks of the Kyrgyz Ala-Too range to the south loom close, a physical barrier between the flat Chui valley and the Kyrgyz hinterland. The Ala-Too range dominates the skyline with peaks that are not far short of 5,000m and stretches for almost 400km east to west. Close to the city, and easily visited on day trips, lie a number of valleys that give an authentic taste of upland Kyrgyzstan and which can serve as suitable locations for anything from gentle picnics to strenuous trekking. The best in terms of accessibility and alpine landscape are probably Ala-Archa and Alamedin. It is between these two valleys that the highest peak of the range – Semenov-Tianshansky (4,895m) – is found, its name given in memory of the 19th-century Russian explorer Pyotr Semyonov-Tyan-Shansky. The information given below refers to the main valleys to the south that lie reasonably close to Bishkek.

ALA-ARCHA CANYON This rugged, yet accessible, valley and gorge lies immediately south of the capital. Most of it belongs to the 120,000ha Ala-Archa National Park, created in 1976, and is nominally protected to some extent. The park has everything that you might expect of an alpine zone – snow capped peaks, fast-flowing streams, alpine meadows, pine forest and steep crags – and it can seem remarkable to find so much unadorned nature so close to a capital city. Having said this there are less pleasant reminders that the metropolis is nearby, mostly in the form of litter, but this is only around the trail heads. It is this very accessibility that is actually the park's greatest draw, especially to foreign expatriates and Bishkek's middle classes who come here to picnic. As well as a convenient spot for picnicking weekenders, the park is also a magnet for hikers, skiers and mountain climbers.

The scenery of Ala-Archa Canyon is wild mountain nature writ large, with over 50 mountain peaks, more than ten glaciers and 30 mountain passes. It is rich in both flora and fauna, with over 800 plant species, 170 types of bird that include many raptors, and roughly 170 other species of animal, with rarities like Marco Polo sheep as well as bears, marmots, deer, wolves, wild boar and even, it is said, the enigmatic snow

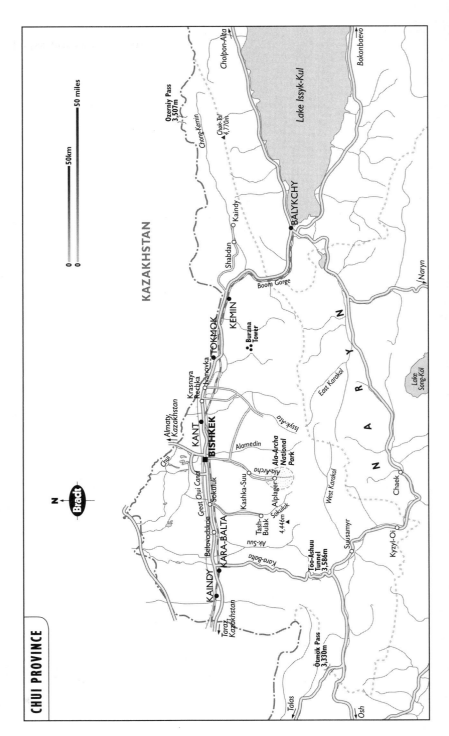

leopard at high elevations. Spruce, birch and juniper woodland dominate most of the steep slopes of the park and diminutive alpine flowers cover the meadows in drifts of colour in spring. The park's principal river is, of course, the Ala-Archa, but there are also two smaller rivers – the Adygene and Ak-Sai – that are fed by glacial melt-water. Both river and park both take their name from the *archa* tree, a brightly coloured juniper that is traditionally burned by Kyrgyz to chase away evil spirits.

The entrance to the park lies roughly 10km beyond the village of Kashka-Suu, around 20km south of the capital, at an elevation of about 1,500m. There is a road barrier and an entrance fee to pay here, both for visitors and their transport. Currently the levy is around US$2 per person and US$3 per car. Close to the park office by the barrier is a small nature museum filled with examples of the fauna found in the region. Beyond here, the road continues for another 12km or so, climbing gently up the valley beside the Ala-Archa River to reach the old Soviet mountaineering camp at 2,150m that is known as the Alplager. This has a weather station, a small, slightly run-down settlement of wooden houses and a recently constructed A-frame hotel that looks like a ski lodge. This is as far as the road goes for standard motor vehicles, although confident 4×4 drivers are able to continue another 18km beyond the hotel to reach the mountain ski base along a poorly maintained jeep track.

Certain restrictions apply to the park itself, although these are all obeyed and ignored to differing extents. Fishing, hunting, and flower, plant and fruit picking are all prohibited, as are dogs and the catching of butterflies. For motorists, a speed limit of 40km/h is applied and parking is only permitted at designated locations. Fires and barbecues are only allowed at specially designated areas and smokers are requested not to carelessly drop cigarette butts because of the danger of fire. Litter is supposed to be bagged and dropped in the bins provided.

Getting there Any of the Bishkek **tour agencies** will be pleased to organise an excursion into the park. Travelling independently, there is little in the way of public transport that goes all the way to the park. In summer, and particularly at weekends, there may be minibuses from the small bus station at the south end of Osh Bazaar running as far as the park gate (*vorota zapovdnika*) and possibly even occasional services that travel as far as the Alplager. The trouble is that the best chance of finding these services is at weekends, which is probably the worse time to visit if you want to experience peace and quiet rather than crowds from the city. It also means probably spending the best part of the day waiting for the minibus to fill up, before a slow drive and a long uphill walk of 12km to the Alplager.

Another, even less satisfactory, option is to take a *marshrutka* to Kashka-Suu and hitch or walk to the park from there (there may or may not be a taxi in the village). The best bet overall is to hire a **taxi**, which is really not prohibitively expensive if there is a group of you. You can either get the taxi to wait if you fancy a short hike or pay for just one-way and take your chances getting back to Bishkek. Ak-Jol Taxis (↘ *182*) charge 650som for a return trip with a free 1-hour wait and 50som per hour after this; Super Taxis (↘ *152*) charge 600som round-trip plus 140som per hour wait, or 450som one-way.

It is also possible to arrange for a taxi driver to pick up on another day, although it is best not to pay up front for this sort of arrangement. One way of saving money is to combine a taxi ride with a bus to the southern city limits. Take a number 11 or 26 bus from the city (catch it on Manas anywhere south of Moskovskaya) to the end of the line beyond the Alamedin Arch. From here, taxis will be much less expensive.

Where to stay If coming for longer than a day trip, camping is the way to go unless you wish to stay in the A-frame lodge at the road-head, where a double costs around US$50. There may also be basic rooms available at the Alplager itself, which also serves food when it decides to open. However, to fully enjoy what the park has to offer it is better to get away from the tawdry environs of the Alplager, and this requires being fully independent.

Hikes in Ala-Archa National Park The hiking potential here is enormous, although most visitors choose one of three main options. Be aware that altitude sickness is a distinct possibility if immediately climbing up high having just arrived from relatively low-lying Bishkek. A 1:50,000 topographical map of the park (*Prirodniy Park Ala-Archa*) can be obtained from GeoID in Bishkek.

A popular hike is to continue along the valley past the new hotel, following the dirt road all the way to **Upper Ala-Archa Mountain Ski Base**. Just a few kilometres along this track is a panoramic viewpoint with superb views of Ala-Archa peak and the Ak-Sai valley. In summer (July and August) a ski-lift operates from the base up to a high ridge where there is a ski chalet.

Another, altogether tougher, route is to head for the **Ak-Sai Canyon**, a hike that rewards the effort with excellent views of the Ak-Sai Glacier. Head up the dirt path beyond the hotel for about 30m then take the trail that veers to the left. This should be signposted. After 100m the trail climbs steeply to the left. There are several paths that can be taken but they should all lead to the same place: a large rock on top of a hill. The trail is gentler from here on and angles right across an alpine meadow. Beyond the meadow is a waterfall, which may just be a trickle in late summer, and where the trail meets the river is a copse of trees that makes a good picnic spot.

From here, the steep, rocky path leads up to a run-down stone hut called the Ratsek at 3,350m. This is a popular place to camp in summer although the hut itself has seen much better days. The hike from the Alplager takes around 4 hours to this point, so the stone hut is a good turn-round point for a strenuous day hike in the park.

Beyond this point, you really need mountain experience and the appropriate equipment. Just beyond the Ratsek is a large rock with memorial plates attached that commemorate perished climbers. A trail leads left from here towards Uchitel peak, a 3-hour climb, and there is another trail a little further on that angles left towards the rock wall of Bachichiki and the north wall of Korona. At the end of this trail is another small metal hut, reached after about 3 hours' walking from the Ratsek.

THE CHONG-TASH MASSACRE

Lying close to Kashka-Suu in the lower reaches of the Ala-Archa valley is the tiny ski-resort village of Chong-Tash, a place that gained a sinister reputation in 1991 following the televised excavation of a mass grave of the victims of one of Stalin's purges. Of the 138 skeletons found here it is thought that many belonged to the political elite of the time, and that the entire Supreme Soviet Central Committee for the Kyrgyz ASSR, along with other dignitaries, were murdered here by the KGB over two nights in 1937.

One of the probable victims was Torokul Aitmatov, father of the celebrated Kyrgyz author Chingiz Aitmatov (see page 37), who had gone missing in 1937. The crime finally came to light in the 1980s when a caretaker who had witnessed the slaughter, sworn to secrecy by the KGB and fearful of his life, told his daughter on his deathbed. When Kyrgyzstan became independent in 1991, the daughter felt able to inform the authorities of the deed. As a sign of respect for the victims and as a tribute to his own father, Chingiz Aitmatov financed the transfer of the victims' remains to the more hallowed ground of the Ata-Beyit Cemetery in the village.

Taking the trail past the rock with the plaques and then angling slightly right leads to the south side of Korona. The trail climbs steeply along the left side of the glacier before flattening out to reach a climbers' steel hut at 4,150m. From here, there are climbing routes to the peaks of Korona (4,692m) and Uchitel (4,572m).

For **climbers** there are numerous options in the valley, of varying degrees of difficulty, accessible from the Ratsek: the Bachichiki rock wall, Schwaba, Box, Tikitor, Free Korea and of course, Korona peak itself.

Another popular option, and ideal for a shorter excursion, is to head up the **Adygene valley** that leads southwest from just north of the Alplager. This is reached by heading north back down the road for around 300m then crossing the river by a rickety footbridge by a tree festooned with votive rags. Several paths lead up to both sides of the valley although they all eventually merge. The route on the right (north) side of the valley passes a cemetery for fallen climbers, which is hidden away in a larch grove. Most of the graves contain little more than fragments of clothing or scraps of climbing equipment, as the human remains of the victims were never found.

One mountaineer has a small monument positioned just outside the graveyard's boundary; this commemorates a climber who is reputed to have taken his own life, cutting himself free from his fellow climbers rather then dragging his comrades down with him. As such, this is regarded as an act of suicide and so he cannot be buried in consecrated ground. Elsewhere, a broken rotor blade commemorates helicopter pilots killed in the area.

The track from the climbers' cemetery continues for 7km or so through forest beneath the Adygene Glacier, ascending very gradually at first before becoming steeper as it approaches the magnificent glacial cirque of Stayanka Elektra. This route tends to be quieter than most and you are very likely to see birds of prey on the wing, particularly griffon vultures riding the thermals on the warm air radiated by bare rocky outcrops.

ALAMEDIN VALLEY Also south of Bishkek, running parallel to, and east of, the Ala-Archa valley, is the Alamedin valley, which follows the river of the same name, a tributary of the Chui River. Alamedin is reached by way of the village of Koy-Tash, which lies 30km south of Bishkek. Koy-Tash is a sprawling but pleasant enough place with many weekend *dachas* owned by wealthy Bishkek residents.

On the west side of the river, a road at the village's southern end climbs south over a ridge past the village of Tatyr and the Golubinyi (Pigeon) Falls, a well known local beauty spot, before meandering west to reach the Ala-Archa valley at Kashka-Suu.

South of Koy-Tash, the Alamedin valley narrows and the road continues for another 10km south to reach the Tyoplye Klyuchi (Hot Springs) sanatorium at an altitude of about 1,800m. The sanatorium is run by the government's Ministry of Power and there is cheap and cheerful accommodation in chalets available as well as simple meals. The sanatorium has a swimming pool and offers warm baths with a massage service. The spring water here contains traces of radioactive radon and so ten-minute sessions are the order of the day unless you wish to emerge with a radioactive glow. The spa waters are extremely popular with Bishkek residents and the place can become very busy on hot summer weekends. The sanatorium complex is undoubtedly more run-down than it was when it was first set up in 1984, but for those desiring a taste of Soviet-era spa tourism this might be a good choice.

Most Western visitors tend to prefer the hiking opportunities that the valley has to offer and the sanatorium serves as an excellent starting place for a day hike further up the valley. A trekking route continues south from the sanatorium over the mountains through gorgeous alpine scenery past waterfalls, meadows and birch, larch and juniper forest, to eventually skirt a glacier to reach the Alamedin Pass at

4,032m. Although this is certainly as beautiful a valley as Ala-Archa it has not been granted national park status. Consequently, there are no facilities whatsoever other than those at the sanatorium.

To get here make an arrangement with a taxi driver as for Ala-Archa – it should cost about the same as to the Alplager there. An alternative is to take a bus to Koy-Tash village from Alamedin Bazaar in Bishkek (near the East Bus Station) and hitch or try and find another taxi from there.

ISSYK-ATA VALLEY There is another spa complex in the valley east of the Alamedin valley, about 45km from Bishkek by way of Koy-Tash at the head of the Alamedin valley. Another, longer, road reaches the spa via the Chui valley towns of Kant and Ivanovka. The resort is nestled between meadows and orchards in the shadow of craggy mountains at an altitude of 1,775m.

There is a 10th-century Buddhist carving of the Curing Buddha on a large boulder near the entrance to the complex, where 19th-century visitors used to smear sheep grease in gratitude. Now, there is an eagle sculpture on top of the rock and, sadly, plenty of contemporary graffiti. Comfortable accommodation is available at the complex for around US$50 for a double. There is also a basic hostel with shared facilities.

Issyk-Ata (literally, 'Father Heat') has long been a place of pilgrimage for the healing properties of its waters. Both Turkic nomads and Russian colonists came here for the waters, and a female Uzbek shaman is said to have lived here as a hermit until the 1950s. Another legend tells of a local beauty who bathed every day in the river here and never grew old or wrinkled because of the magical power of the waters. Whether or not the river has such life-preserving properties is hard to ascertain but it certainly has plenty of trout and many come to fish here.

Trekking possibilities abound in the valley. The most ambitious route is to continue southwest to eventually reach the Issyk-Ata Pass at 3,929m. It would be possible here to either descend or to turn around and climb over the Alamedin Pass (4,032m) from the south and return along the Alamedin valley. Adventure Travel (*Moskovskaya 14, Bishkek;* ☎ *911 117;* e *info@atkg.com; www.atkg.com*) offer an itinerary that incorporates this route as part of an 8-day summer trek.

SOKULUK VALLEY This valley, southwest of Bishkek and to the west of Ala-Archa, is approached from the town of the same name that lies 30km west of Bishkek on the main M39 to Kara-Balta and Kazakhstan. The main village here is **Tash-Bulak** ('Stone Spring'), which is sometimes also referred to as Belogorka, its Soviet–era name.

The village is a sprawling settlement of attractively decorated wooden houses that cling to either side of the valley road. Formerly, when a large and successful collective farm operated from the village, the village had a mixed Kyrgyz, Ukrainian and Russian population, but these days Tash-Bulak is almost entirely Kyrgyz and far less prosperous than it used to be. In Soviet times there were vast numbers of sheep in the valley but now most of the villagers that remain squeeze a precarious living out of growing vegetables on private plots.

From Tash-Bulak, the road continues south up the valley for another 12km or so. With luck, you can arrange for a car in the village to bring you to the end of the road, from where a track leads through woodland to a waterfall, about an hour's walk away. You can continue from here further up the valley, following the river on your right. The valley narrows considerably after a couple of hours and a steep-sided valley with a waterfall veers off to the southwest.

In theory at least, it is possible to hike up this valley, crossing the river a few times, to reach the Suusamyr valley over the 3,775m Sokuluk Pass – a guide, or at least

top **Dordoi bazaar, Bishkek** (LM) page 103
above left **Özgön bazaar** (LM) page 260
above right **Jayma Bazaar, Osh** (CH) page 256

top	Cemetery decorated with Muslim and Soviet symbolism, Lake Issyk-Kul (CH) page 149
above left	Kyrgyz stone grave markers near Tokmok (LM) page 124
above right	Kyrgyz man travelling along the shore of Lake Issyk-Kul (CH) page 133
below	Kyrgyz Islamic cemetery, At-Bashy (LM) page 216

above **Russian Orthodox Holy Trinity Cathedral, Karakol** (LM) page 166

below left **Petroglyphs at Saimaluu-Tash** (LM) page 231

below right **At-Bashy town and At-Bashy range** (LM) page 216

top left   **Edelweiss flowers in the high alpine valleys** (CH)
page 41

top right   **Mountains south of Karakol, Altyn Arashan** (CH)
page 171

above left   **White-tailed eagle** (NB)
page 41

above right   **Maral deer, Iiri-Suu, Naryn province** (LM)
page 214

left   **White-browed tit warbler** (EO)
page 41

bottom left   **Snipe** (NB)
page 41

top left **Lesser grey shrike** (NB)
page 41

top right **Dipper** (NB)
page 41

right **Walnut forest, Arslanbob** (LM)
page 234

below **Snow leopard** (HA)
page 42

Lake Sary-Chelek (LM, page 240)

first-hand local advice, is highly recommended. The river disappears just short of the pass but reappears on the south side after about 800m of descent. Following the river downhill for about 18km or so brings you to a rough road that runs parallel to the Karakol River. From here, it is a further 16km west to reach the small village of Karakol. In Soviet times this route was used to drive sheep to land in the Suusamyr valley that was owned by the collective farm, but it has not been used as such for many years now. Because the snow now lies piled-up at the pass, undisturbed by livestock, any attempt at this route could only really be considered a viable option during high summer – July and August. Another possible trekking route leads from Tash-Bulak over the 3,900m Ozerniy Pass to the Ala-Archa valley to the east.

Practicalities There are limited **accommodation** options in Tash-Bulak village: Kenjibek Degembaev at Bulana 2 offers beds and meals and can be contacted at the municipal administration office in the village on Sovetskaya. He may also be able to arrange transport, horses and guides. If you are planning to do much trekking from Tash-Bulak bring supplies from Bishkek, as the village shop has a limited choice of goods on offer.

To reach Tash-Bulak from Bishkek, there are buses that leave at least once, and possibly more times, a day from Osh Bazaar. It is best to go there in the morning. Buses and minibuses that pass through Sokuluk on the main road are far more frequent and it should be possible to find a local bus or a shared taxi to the village from here. Taxis from Osh Bazaar are another possibility and should cost around 350som one-way.

AK-SUU VALLEY This valley lies to the west of Sokuluk and is reached by turning south after the village of Belovodskoe before reaching Kara-Balta. The road passes the small village of Kyzyl Dyikan, which has one of the earliest Russian Orthodox churches in central Asia.

CHUI VALLEY ЧУЙСКАЯ ДОЛИНА

This wide valley, the largest in Kyrgyzstan, is one of the few big expanses of flat land in the country. Although in many ways it is atypical of mountainous Kyrgyzstan, this largely agricultural valley contains a number of sites that are intrinsic to the history of the region. It is also one of the most densely populated and fertile regions, with an adequate water supply and fertile soils that produce sugar beet, potatoes, wheat, maize and fruit. Because of this, the Chui valley is today one of the country's more well-to-do regions, with prosperity levels higher than most other parts of the country. The population of the valley is generally more mixed than in other parts of Kyrgyzstan, with ethnic Russians, Ukrainians, Dungans, Germans and Koreans in addition to native Kyrgyz. The Dungan presence is particularly noticeable in places, with white Muslim caps above Chinese faces, and houses that have roofs topped by small pagoda-like forms. None of the towns of the valley are of special interest, but there are a few key sites located nearby that are well worth seeking out.

KANT This is the first town of importance heading east of Bishkek along the valley. Kant boasts a large cement factory, a Lenin statue and a war memorial – all pretty standard for a provincial Kyrgyz town. Many ethnic Germans used to live here and in the surrounding area (see box, *A long way from home: Germans in Kyrgyzstan*, page 122) and it might be assumed that the town takes its name from Immanuel Kant, the German moral philosopher. In fact, the name refers to the Kyrgyz for 'sugar cube', and there is a major sugar factory in the town that processes beet grown in the valley, a practice that dates back to Soviet times.

When, in 1941, many ethnic Germans from Russia's Volga region were forcibly relocated by Stalin to central Asia, some ended up in the Kant region of Kyrgyzstan's Chui valley, where there was already a sizeable German population established in the area. German settlers had started arriving in the area back in the late 19th and early 20th century as colonists of either the Russian Empire or the post-revolution Soviet Union. Most of these earlier settlers were Lutheran Mennonites who had been living in southern Russia and the Crimea, having emigrated from East Frisia 300 years earlier to avoid military service.

Some Chui valley villages like Luxembourg and Bergtal (which was known as Rotfront – or 'Red Front' – from the time of its establishment in 1927 until independence in 1991) still carry their German names and have German-speaking minorities. Although many have migrated to Germany following independence, Bergtal is still probably the only village in central Asia with a substantial German minority. At the time of Kyrgyzstan's independence there were around 900 Germans in the village, but now the figure is down to something like 200. Most of these continue to eschew alcohol, tobacco, television and dancing in strict Mennonite tradition. According to a 1999 census there were 21,471 ethnic Germans remaining in the country as a whole, but by 2005 the figure was estimated to be down to around 12,000.

The town came into the news in October 2003 when it was announced that its airport would be used as a base for the Collective Rapid Deployment Force of the Russian Air Force. With the decline of Russian bases in Cuba and Vietnam, this was to become Russian's only new base abroad since Soviet times. Although the premise was one of 'joint security', the selection of Kant as a Russian base was undoubtedly viewed as a counterweight to the American military presence at the Peter J Ganci air base at Manas Airport, which had been there to assist with Afghanistan operations since December 2001. As a result of this, Kyrgyzstan remains the only country in the world with both American and Russian bases. What is perhaps even more surprising is that the two bases are so close to each other: Manas is just five minutes' flying time away.

In 2005, Moscow proclaimed that it would double the number of personnel here and in 2006 it was announced that a ground force element would be added. This announcement came just before the statement that rent on the US Ganci airbase at Manas would be increased 100-fold if the Americans wished to continue their presence. President Bakiev later withdrew this threat but new terms for use of the base have yet to be resolved

KRASNAYA RECHKA The village of Krasnaya Rechka ('Red River') lies 8km east of Kant on the main road to Balykchy and Lake Issyk-Kul. The village also gives its name to a nearby ruined Silk Road settlement that was known as **Navekat** ('new town') in Sogdian times. Navekat was active between the 6th and 12th centuries and was the largest settlement in the valley at that time. The town was mentioned by the Chinese pilgrim Hsuan Tsang who visited the area in around AD620. The site was re-discovered in Soviet times when a tractor ploughing outside the village turned up a gold burial mask. Subsequent archaeological investigation has revealed a Buddhist temple containing the remains of an 8m-long reclining clay Buddha, originally painted red, and Bodhisattvas forms that were discovered in another corridor and outside the sanctuary gates. These are all now in the Hermitage Museum in St Petersburg.

The settlement was probably established in the 6th century although the temple itself dates from the 8th. As well as a Buddhist temple, Navekat also had a citadel, a large square, fortified walls and a Zoroastrian fire altar. There is also a necropolis that demonstrates burials in both the Buddhist and Nestorian Christian traditions. Other discoveries at the site have included fragments of wall paintings, a Chinese stela with inscriptions, and a birch-bark Brahmin manuscript in the Sanskrit language, along with deities of Sogdian and Indian origin.

The discovery of such a wide range of remains and artefacts demonstrates that Manicheans, Buddhists and Nestorians all co-existed here contemporaneously, and that Navekat was a true multi-confessional settlement. Indeed, the archaeological evidence of all of the Silk Road settlements in the Chui valley – Navekat (Krasnaya Rechka), Suyab (Ak-Beshim) and Balasagun (Burana) – reveals that they were all centres where Chinese, Turkic, Sogdian and Indian traditions met and prospered in a symbiotic melange of culture and religion: the typical, two-way exchange between East and West that characterised much of the Silk Road.

Although there is little to see on the ground here, the site is undoubtedly a significant one. It was excavated 20 years ago and many of the remains were then backfilled to prevent further erosion. However, much degradation has taken place in the interim and the site is under threat. A UNESCO/Japanese Trust Fund project has begun to document and protect the most important structures here.

Visiting Krasnaya Rechka To reach the site from Bishkek, take a Tokmok *marshrutka* that passes through Krasnaya Rechka village from the city's East bus station. This should cost 20som. Get off at the end of the village by the Ala-Too petrol station on the left. A dirt road on the left leads around fields towards the site, which lies a couple of kilometres away; you should be able to see the low artificial-looking hill of the citadel from the main road.

At the site there is little evidence that this was an important Silk Road settlement other than a sign that says, *NECROPOLIS VII–IX AD* and another, in Russian, that prohibits the passage of farm traffic through the site. The citadel is a low, grassy penumbra with the remains of some chambers sunken into it. The necropolis just north of this is a sunken pit that has obvious traces of human remains in the form of bones and skulls creepily exposed in the cliff face. Fragments of pottery litter the site.

Krasnaya Rechka is the sort of archaeological site that is rewarding if your imagination is powerful enough to make its own interpretation from mere bumps and lines in the ground. Good views of the surrounding countryside can be had from the modest 30m elevation that the citadel affords. The Kazakhstan frontier is very close, just a stone's throw north of the site. To return to Bishkek you could flag down a *marshrutka* heading west back at the garage, or you could continue eastwards towards Tokmok to visit Burana Tower. The two sites combined make a good half-day trip.

TOKMOK The provincial town of Tokmok ('hammer' in Kyrgyz and sometimes spelled *Tokmak*) lies another 25km or so further east, beyond the smaller town of Ivanovka. Tokmok is situated right on the Kazakhstan frontier, which is marked by the Chui River that flows just to the north. Tokmok was the Kyrgyz regional administrative centre until 1878, when floods destroyed much of the town, necessitating the move of its bureaucrats west to what was then Pishpek, today's Bishkek. Before this, Tokmok was an important strategic centre for the 18th-century Kokand Khanate, which had its forts strung along the Chui valley to protect their trade interests. Just outside the town to the south lie the ruins of another ruined Silk Road city, Ak-Beshim, but despite having unearthed a

4

Buddhist temple and a Nestorian Christian church here, there is little to see on the ground of this once-important settlement.

Tokmok became the administrative centre of Chui Oblast in 2003, but this role was returned to Bishkek in May 2006. The town's modern-day character is that of a quiet provincial town and farming centre. For those passing through, its most obvious feature is the MIG jet fighter that is mounted on a plinth in the middle of an intersection. Two roads pass by here from Bishkek: the new road that bypasses the town *en route* to Balykchy and an older road that reaches Tokmok via Kant and Krasnaya Rechka. The bus station lies on the main road near the entrance to the town, close to some large Soviet-era murals that stand unashamedly on display outside housing blocks of the same period. There is a small museum at Tryasina 146 that has examples of some of the archaeological finds in the Chui valley region – petroglyphs, clay vessels, oil lamps and prehistoric tools – but most visitors push straight on to the Burana Tower, 15km to the south.

BURANA TOWER Burana Tower is probably the best known monument in the north of Kyrgyzstan, although in a country where historic monuments are in short supply this is not so remarkable. Although the 'tower' cannot compare with any of the reconstructed architectural jewels that might be found elsewhere in the region, Burana is nonetheless worth a visit, both for its architectural merit and for the historical background of its location.

The tower is, in fact, a minaret: all that remains of the city of **Balasagun**, which was established by the Karakhanids at the end of the 10th century. Balasagun was the major Karakhanid settlement in the northern part of the territory that is today Kyrgyzstan, with southern counterparts at Mavarannahr, now Özgön, near Osh, and at Kashgar in Xinjiang, China. The city was extremely important in its day, but although it flourished for several centuries it eventually declined, and was virtually abandoned by the 15th century. The Uyghur poet, Yusuf (or Jusup) Balasagun, author of the epic poem *Katadgu Bilim* (*The Knowledge That Brings Happiness*) was born here in the early 11th century and gave the town its name. His image decorates the current Kyrgyz 1,000som banknote.

The minaret when first built would have been over 46m tall, but the present-day version stands at just over half its original height, at only 24m. What you see today is the result of both destruction and reconstruction. A succession of earthquakes reduced the original building almost to rubble – the last was in 1900 – when the upper part collapsed and its bricks were utilised by recent Russian settlers in the area. The current building is very much the product of 1970s restoration.

The tower is constructed of banded honey-coloured brickwork in a gently tapering round structure with an octagonal base. Lacking its original cupola, the top of the tower is now a viewing platform that offers views over the Chui valley north to Kazakhstan and to the mountains of the eastern Ala-Too range to the south. An external staircase has been bolted onto the tower's northern side, rather spoiling any sense of authenticity, and this leads inside to access a narrow, steep internal staircase that climbs to the viewing platform.

The name Burana is most probably a corruption of 'Monara', which means minaret. Originally the minaret and its accompanying mosque would have stood in the central part of the town. Major archaeological surveys in the 1920s, 1950s and 1970s discovered that the original town covered a total area of some 25–30km². There is a central fortress, dwellings, shops and baths, and a water main delivering water from a canyon nearby. The whole settlement was surrounded by two rings of walls.

Now very little else remains except for traces of three mausolea, a large mound that represents the remains of a palace or temple, and around 80 Turkic *balbals*, stone grave markers dating from between the 6th and 10th centuries that have been gathered here having been collected from all over the country. There is a small museum next to the tower that has a display of artefacts found at the site that include pottery and coins, as well as interesting black and white photographs that document the tower's reconstruction. The museum also has a small gift shop selling postcards and pamphlets.

Visiting the rather sterile reconstruction that is Burana Tower today, it is hard to get much sense of the grandeur that was Balasagun in its prime, especially if your visit coincides with noisy crocodiles of schoolchildren bussed-in from Bishkek. None the less, the Karakhanid city certainly impressed Genghis Khan sufficiently to persuade him to spare it, and even rename it 'Gobilik' ('good city'). Like the artefacts found at Krasnaya Rechka, there has been enough material evidence found here to indicate that Balasagun was an important Silk Road settlement where culture, language and religion mixed easily in the tolerant atmosphere of commerce – Chinese coins, Nestorian crosses, magical charms and Indian cowries all bear testament to this.

A Kyrgyz legend tells quite a different story about the history of the tower. It tells of a witch's warning to a powerful local king that his new-born daughter would die on her coming of age. Alarmed by this presentiment, the king built a tower to protect his daughter and no-one was allowed to enter apart from the servant who brought her food. Despite this precaution, a poisonous spider hid in her food and bit her and the girl died in the tower, aged just 18 years old. The tower, of course, was Burana, and the girl's name was Monara. This is just one version; in another, the tower was built to protect the king's beautiful daughter from the advances of young men. In this case it was a scorpion that bit and killed her. On hearing of his daughter's death the king is said to have sobbed so hard that he brought the top part of the tower down.

Practicalities To reach Burana Tower, take a *marshrutka* from Bishkek's East Bus Station to Tokmok (30som) and then get a taxi from there. Taxi drivers wait at Tokmok's bus station for independent visitors to Burana. A reasonable price for the return trip to and from the tower from Tokmok, including an hour or two's wait at the site, should be less than 300som. There are also occasional buses from Tokmok's bus station.

KEGETI VALLEY The village of Kegeti, 14km southwest of Burana, lies at the head of another valley that penetrates southwards into the Kyrgyz Ala-Too range. This is good hiking, mountain biking and horseriding terrain, and the valley is used by some Bishkek adventure travel companies for their activities. Trekking routes lead up a side valley to the east to Köl-Tor ('dead') Lake with numerous waterfalls. It is also possible to visit the **Bel-Saz** *jailoo* to the west, where a community tourism project can provide accommodation and horses for hire. From here, excursions can be made to the nearby Kushkonok forest and Sharkeratma waterfall. The road from Kegeti through to the Suusamyr–Kochkor road in the Karakol valley that is shown on the GeoID 1:200,000 topological map is generally not passable, even in summer. In Soviet times this was cleared regularly by snow-ploughs, but these days snow may lie until mid-August and this, coupled with frequent landslides, means that even horses have difficulty here.

Practicalities Kegeti can be reached by taxi from Ivanovka or Tokmok. Plenty of *marshruktki* pass through Ivanovka from Bishkek's East Bus Station and cost just 20som. Heading for the Bel-Saz *jailoo*, a local co-ordinator in Ivanovka, Gulnara Osmonova (m 03132 42252) at Furmanova 48, south of the main road, can organise a taxi to the Kegeti valley as far as the settlement of Leskhos (300som), from where a horse and guide can be arranged for the 1-hour ride to Bel-Saz. Another possibility is to go from Ivanovka by taxi to the village of Ak-Say, where a 4×4 may be hired to reach the *jailoo* by way of the German minority village of Rotfront (see page 122).

SHAMSY VALLEY This valley southeast of Tokmok is considered by some to be one of the most beautiful in the province and is well-known to archaeologists for its rich yield of Scythian treasure. A golden mask said to belong to a beautiful ruler, Queen Shamshy, was found in the valley and a former Shah of Iran chose the valley for the site for one of his hunting lodges.

As with all of the valleys of the Kyrgyz Ala-Too there are many hiking and horseriding opportunities to be had here. The **Shamshy** *jailoo* lies 36km south of Tokmok at an altitude of 1,800m. Here there is yurt accommodation available and horses for hire. Possible excursions from here include visits to alpine lakes or hikes up the Tuyuk valley to the southeast. A side valley leading off to the west has another *jailoo* – Tura Kain – where it is possible to stay in a farmhouse. From the main valley, it is also possible in summer to hike over the 3,570m Shamshy Pass to the village of Shamshy and Kochkor beyond.

Although there is no direct transport to the valley, it should be possible to arrange transport in Tokmok to reach both Shamshy and Tura Kain *jailoo*. The cost should be in the order of 300som.

CHONG-KEMIN VALLEY

The Chong (Big)-Kemin valley is the long panhandle of Chui Province extending eastwards from the Chui valley, which is circumscribed by the Kazakhstan frontier to the north and Issyk-Kul Province to the south. It starts at the town of Kemin, mid-way between Tokmok and Balykchy, and runs 80km west to east, parallel to the Kazakhstan frontier and sandwiched between the Kungey Ala-Too and Zailiysky mountain ranges.

Famously, the valley is the birthplace of erstwhile Kyrgyz president Askar Akaev, whose family hail from the village of Kyzyl Bairak. The Chong-Kemin valley is a spectacular combination of both wild and pastoral landscapes, with a pleasing mix of lofty mountains, verdant pastureland, coniferous woodland and alpine lakes. At its highest point, the valley reaches 2,800m in altitude and its upper reaches are shadowed by a number of peaks in excess of 4,000m – Kichi-Kemin (4,220m), Teke-Tor (4,190m), Alisher Novoi (4,170m) and Chok-Tal (4,770m), on the boundary with Issyk-Kul Oblast. Most of the people living in the valley are of Kyrgyz stock, as few Slavs, who commonly populate Lake Issyk-Kul's shores just to the south, have settled here.

The village of Kyzyl Bairak, still said to be the home of Askar Akaev's brother, has a mausoleum to Shabdan Batyr, who was a powerful chieftain of the Sary Bagysh tribe that ruled the valley in the 19th century and who remain the most populous clan here. The town of Kemin, formerly known as Bestrovka, at the head of the valley, also has an equestrian statue of the chieftain. Back in 1911, the town experienced one of the strongest earthquakes ever to be recorded in the region, measuring a massive 11 on the Richter scale.

In Soviet times, collective farms and mining in the town of Ak-Tyuz in the neighbouring Kichi-Kemin valley provided employment for the valley; these days, the local economy, such as it is, is mostly based on cattle-raising and growing potatoes. The defunct mine at Ak-Tyuz that used to mine lead and other heavy metals, and which suffered a serious spillage in 1964, has apparently been bought by an Israeli businessman, although what he intends to do with it is yet to be seen.

There is further uncertainty concerning the valley, as there is little doubt that Chong-Kemin's peaceful sanctity will be despoiled to some extent when (or perhaps if) the direct road between Almaty and Lake Issyk-Kul is completed in the future. Currently, many holidaying Kazakhs visit the lake in summer by way of the long, circuitous route via Bishkek. A direct route constructed through the Chong-Kemin valley would shorten the journey time considerably and encourage even more visitors to the lake; it would also shatter the valley's current isolation.

For the time being at least, the Chong-Kemin valley has abundant wildlife and a rich, varied flora. Its forests of Tien Shan Fir in particular are held in high regard throughout Kyrgyzstan for the bounty of their medicinal herbs, mushrooms and edible berries. There are a number of burial mounds in the valley, most notably near the villages of Shabdan and Tegirmenty, which date from the 3rd and 4th centuries, and a 6–11th-century settlement has been discovered in the mouth of the valley. The Chong-Kemin valley became a national park in 1997.

The valley offers several adventurous **trekking** possibilities. One very tough route starting from the village of Kaindy is to follow the Chong-Kemin River upstream before climbing up and over the Kungey range to the 4,061m Ak-Suu Pass, from where a descent is made along the Grigorievka valley to the village of the same name on Lake Issyk-Kul. Some knowledge of glacier walking is required here and this six-day route is only for the experienced, fit and determined.

There is a shorter (two or three-day) easier route to Lake Issyk-Kul that also starts in Kaindy. This follows the Chong-Kemin River east before climbing up to the 3,800m Kyzyl Bulak Pass and descending through arid mountains to the lakeside village of Toru Aygyr at the western end of Lake Issyk-Kul. A third route links the valley with the town of Balykchy at the lake's far western shore.

Rather than attempt to traverse high passes, another alternative would be to follow the valley eastwards towards picturesque Lake Jassyk-Kul, 50km east of Kaindy. This could be shortened considerably by arranging transport in the village to reach the point along the valley where the Kashka-Suu River joins the Chong-Kemin. The Chong-Kemin valley also serves as a start or end point for treks through to Kazakhstan (see box, *Trekking Routes to and from Kazakhstan*, page 154). Some travel companies also run white-water rafting expeditions in the valley, and kayaking is also a popular pursuit here.

Kaindy has several **accommodation** possibilities with local families, and the village makes an ideal base for trekking in the valley. There is also very comfortable accommodation available at the Ashu Travel Guesthouse in Kalmak Ashu village at Boruev 22 (✆ *03135 28108;* e *ashu@ktnet.kg*). Public **transport** runs as far as Kaindy village from Bishkek and two buses a day make the journey from Bishkek's East Bus Station. Alternatively, many *marshrutki* pass through Kemin at the head of the valley and you could take a taxi to Kaindy from here.

BOOM GORGE BOOMCKOE УЩЕЛЬЕ

This narrow, and slightly spooky, canyon ('Shoestring Gorge') lies at the eastern end of the Kyrgyz Ala-Too range, beginning about 20km south of Kemin. The gorge is the route by which the fast-flowing Chui River, the A365 main road and the railway all squeeze side by side to reach Balykchy and Lake Issyk-Kul. Before the coming of the road and the railway the canyon would have been one of the major trade routes of the northern Silk Road, linking China with the West via Lake Issyk-Kul and the Chui valley. The gorge is prone to fairly frequent landslides and so concrete barriers have been installed to protect the road and railway from falling rocks.

Just before entering the gorge is the Kyrgyz equivalent of a motorway service area, Holodnaya Voda ('Cold Water'), which takes its name from a local spring – a grand name for a motley collection of roadside buildings, kiosks and yurts. The yurts serve up the usual Kyrgyz staples – *manti, shashlyk* and *laghman*.

Close to the entrance of the gorge is a recently erected monument to the victims of the 1916 Urkun exodus, in which tens of thousands of Kyrgyz perished whilst fleeing over the mountains to China (see page 9). As the road climbs further into the gorge a number of other statues positioned above the roadside are passed. These date from the Soviet period but, rather than representing heroes of the Revolution, they are in the form of animals, a sample of Kyrgyzstan's natural bounty – eagles, snow leopards and deer.

Approximately halfway down the gorge there is a small bridge (Krasniy Most – 'Red bridge') crossing the river, and just beyond here to the west lies the rugged red sandstone terrain of the **Konorchok Canyon**, with its impressive wind-eroded rock formations. Konorchok is actually a network of canyons that include Korgon-Terek, immediately west of the bridge.

The canyons were formed between one-and-a-half and two million years ago and are generally much warmer than the surrounding region, with both rainfall and snow a rarity. Erosion by wind and rain has turned what was formerly a plateau into a forest of high stone pillars and curious landforms. As with many unusual geological formations, imagination has not been kept in check and the canyons that make up the network have been given names like Hiroshima, Bobsleigh, Sky Scraper, Fairy Tale and Aeolian Castle by those who have ventured here in the past. The whole canyon system is ripe for exploration. There is also an extinct volcano with lava flows and plentiful fossils on its surface.

Several Bishkek agencies organise treks and excursions here, or incorporate the Konorchok canyons into a longer Kyrgyzstan tour. With absolutely no habitation, and a location far away from any obvious cultural references, the area would serve as an ideal setting for a western or even a science fiction movie. Comparisons with Arizona's Grand Canyon are ambitious but not entirely fanciful.

Boom Gorge itself is a popular location for outdoor pursuits, particularly white-water rafting. The section of the river downstream from Krasniy Most to Kemin is said to offer some of the best rafting in the country. Alltournative in Bishkek (*Kievskaya 107;* ℡ *611 330;* f *216 644;* e *alltournative@elcat.kg; www. alltournative.kg*) run one-day rafting trips in the gorge.

KARA-BALTA КАРА-БАЛТА

Heading west from Bishkek the M38 highway continues straight as a die towards the Kazakh border. This is the most direct road to Tashkent from the capital, although the necessity of a transit visa for Kazakhstan for many nationalities does not always make it the most practicable route. The same road splits at the town of Kara-Balta (Black Axe) and heads south, skirting mountains and crossing passes on its way to Kyrgyzstan's second city of Osh and the southern part of the republic.

Kara-Balta is primarily a junction town and few visitors stop here on the way to more appealing mountain vistas further south. The town was founded in 1825 under the Kokand Khanate and developed to attain city status under the Soviet regime in 1975. Formerly, the main industry here was the processing of uranium ore from mines in Kyrgyzstan and Kazakhstan and because of this it was a closed city in Soviet times.

Following independence in 1991, the Kyrgyz mines closed down but Kara-Balta continued to process uranium imported from Kazakhstan. The uranium industry brought a certain amount of prosperity to the town and it is a reasonably attractive place, with leafy streets and Russian-style architecture. However, in environmental terms, the town has been left with an unenviable legacy in the form of unprocessed uranium tailings and toxic residues of gold and molybdenum. In February 2007, the Russian government purchased the Kyrgyz government's majority stake in the Kara-Balta uranium production facility. Despite this, most Kyrgyz associate the town with jollier things: Kara-Balta is also the name of a best-selling brand of Vodka.

SOUTH OF KARA-BALTA From Kara-Balta south, the road climbs steadily but steeply along the beautiful Kara-Balta gorge to traverse the ridge of the Kyrgyz Ala-Too. Eventually it reaches the **Töo-Ashuu tunnel** at 2,564m, which cuts through the mountain for 3km, 1km lower than the 3,568m pass itself, which the old road summits. The tunnel is said to have been built by the same Russian engineers who constructed the Moscow and Leningrad metro systems, although obviously they did not send in the same teams of artists to beautify it afterwards as they had done in the Russian metropolises.

The tunnel is a dank and stifling place; an exhaust-fume laden plunge into a dimly-lit underworld that is no place for the claustrophobic. Driving through it can seem to take much longer than it ought to and it is a tangible relief to emerge into daylight on the other side. The perceived horror is real enough: in 2001, several people died from fumes when a car broke down in the tunnel and halted traffic.

The road up to the pass is kept open in both directions throughout the year by snow ploughs and rock-clearing teams, but it is a cold, windswept spot, even in summer, where slanting rain is the norm and snow and ice might be expected at almost any time. The sorry wooden cubicle to the right of the road at the northern end of the tunnel ought to be eligible for a prize in any 'ten most miserable toilets' award, although that probably depends on whether or not it is sleeting outside. The views in either direction are, of course, spectacular. Leaving the pass, the road descends steeply before it divides to either continue west towards Ötmök, where a side road splits off to the west over the Ötmök Pass to Talas, or to double-back east along a lesser road that enters the Suusamyr valley.

SUUSAMYR VALLEY СУУСАМЫРСКАЯ ДОЛИНА

Less than an obvious valley, steppe plateau might a better description for the terrain of much of the Suusamyr region. Despite its position on the opposite side of the Kyrgyz Ala-Too from the Chui valley this, perhaps surprisingly, is still part of Chui Oblast: a far-flung outpost that has many of the characteristics of Kyrgyzstan's more central provinces. The valley lies at an average altitude of around 2,200m, and in spite of its relative proximity to the capital it remains a wild, bleak and generally little-visited part of the country.

Most of the population here are Kyrgyz who are still actively involved in herding and live a partially nomadic lifestyle. The population density is extremely low, a fact that is happily reflected in the zero casualty count that occurred when a spectacularly large earthquake, registering nine on the Richter scale, struck the valley in 1992.

In Soviet times the Suusamyr valley was an important centre for sheep grazing, and every year a large number were brought here from the collective farms of the Sokuluk valley over high mountain passes to graze. The land-use of the valley is a little more diverse these days, with potato and vegetable growing and honey-production supplementing more traditional sheep-raising. Adequate rainfall and not too-high an altitude guarantees lush and nutritious grassland that provides excellent grazing for horses as well as sheep, and the lack of artificial fertilisers ensures that the valley's meadows are a shock of colour with the drifts of herbs and wild flowers that flourish here in early summer. Tourism, great potential though it might have, is still in its infancy here.

This entry deals with the western Suusamyr valley as far east as Kyzyl-Oi, that lies within Chui Oblast. The eastern end of the valley, which extends towards Kochkor in Naryn Oblast, is generally a little more geared up to providing services to travellers and hikers and is covered in *Chapter 8: Naryn Province*. The GeoID 1:200,000 map *Suusamyrskaya dolina* covers the area around Suusamyr village and the western end of the valley.

SUUSAMYR VILLAGE AND SURROUNDINGS The turn-off to the valley lies some kilometres beyond the Töö-Ashuu Pass, where a minor road leads east off the main highway. Some 15km beyond the junction the small, eponymous village of **Suusamyr** appears – a series of single-storey houses strung nonchalantly along the roadside. There is an information point at the home of Kubanychbek and Norimira Amankulov (look for the sign), a charming elderly couple who provide bed and breakfast accommodation in their cottage for around 350som per person, including meals. Kubanychbek can also lay on transport to reach some of the nearby mountain *jailoos*, where further opportunities to stay exist.

Thirty kilometres east is the **Joo Jurak** *jailoo* where you can stay in a yurt belonging to the family of Negizbek Imankulov and rent horses for exploring the area. **Boirok** *jailoo* is a little nearer, 20km to the north of Suusamyr village, while closer still is **Sandyk** *jailoo*, just 13km southeast of Suusamyr. Both *jailoos* offer opportunities for a yurt stay. To return to Suusamyr after a *jailoo* visit, either make a prior arrangement with Kubanchybek for him to pick you up, or organise horses and a guide for the ride back to the village. A yurt camp is usually set up in the valley during the summer months.

A further possibility for basic accommodation close to Suusamyr village is at the village administration's *dacha* 8km beyond the village. The *dacha* is situated right by the West Karakol River, 1km beyond the point where the road splits left for the Karakol valley and continues straight on for Kyzyl-Oi and Chaek – take the left fork and after a few minutes follow the track down to the river and the *dacha*. Although accommodation here is supposed to be pre-booked, the caretaker lives on the premises and should be able to provide beds and simple fish meals on request.

The village of **Karakol**, 6km east of the *dacha* at the easternmost end of the West Karakol valley, is tiny and in no way resembles its Lake Issyk-Kul namesake. Trekking south across the Kyrgyz Ala-Too from the Sokuluk or Ala-Archa valley, this is the first village to be reached on the plateau. There is basic homestay accommodation available at a house in the middle of the village. Just ask around and someone should point you in the right direction.

Practicalities For accommodation, see above. Public transport to Suusamyr is scarce. There is just one bus a day from Bishkek's Osh bazaar that leaves in the afternoon and returns from Suusamyr very early in the morning. Another bus leaves for Suusamyr from Kara-Balta daily in the afternoon, continuing to Kojomkul. Taking a frequent bus to Kara-Balta from Bishkek and then hiring a taxi to Suusamyr (around 1,000som) is probably the most straightforward option.

KOJOMKUL Continuing south along the main road, the next village reached is Kojomkul, about 15km from Suusamyr. The village takes its name from a man who lived here between 1889–1955 and who was reputed to be 2.3m tall and 164 kilos in weight (see box, *Kojomkul – A Kyrgyz Giant*, page 131). This giant of a man lifted heavy rocks and even horses for fun (there is a statue to him in Bishkek, outside the Palace of Sports, performing this very act). A museum to his memory stands in the middle of the village with large stones outside its entrance.

Kojomkul was born in the Suusamyr valley in 1889 and died in 1955 at the age of 66. As an adult he stood 2.3m tall (7 feet 5 inches) and weighed 164kg (nearly 26 stone). Encouraged by his superhuman size and strength, he participated in many competitive bouts of strength in his youth. On one occasion, he took part in a wrestling competition in the Toktogul area where he beat many better-known wrestlers and won the prize of 50 sheep and several mares, which he is said to have distributed to the poor of his village. By the late 1920s there was no-one to rival him in Kyrgyzstan, and in the region as a whole the only challenge came from the Kazakh wrestler Cholok Balaban who he eventually fought and beat in the 23rd minute of an inter-republic wrestling contest.

Following the revolution and the region's inclusion in the USSR, Kojomkul adapted well to Soviet ways and served as chairman of the Suusamyr valley collective farm for over 20 years. However, during this time he was forced to spend 1 year in prison as a result of his unwillingness to write a damning testimony against the chairman of a neighbouring collective farm. His 'gentle giant' reputation grew further in prison where he became widely respected by prisoners and guards alike. Later, during World War II, he is reputed to have provided many poor villagers with food thanks to his skills at hunting.

His death in 1955 is surrounded by uncertainty although one version, with echoes of the David and Goliath legend, suggests that it was an insect that had crept into his food that caused him to fall ill and die. His memory is still revered in the village and it is widely believed that it was Kojomkul's spirit that protected the village in 1992 when the earthquake hit, badly damaging property throughout the valley but claiming no lives.

Photographs inside the museum reveal his truly impressive size, as do items from his wardrobe and examples of the objects that he was fond of moving about. His grave stands in a white mausoleum in the centre of the village next to a Soviet war memorial. On the road to Kyzyl-Oi stands another tribute to Kojomkul's strength in the form a massive stone that marks the grave of a local dignitary. The stone, which is said to weigh 700kg, is reputed to have been carried to the grave by Kojomkul himself, although there is undoubtedly some blurring of historical truth with legend here.

Accommodation in the village may be had at the comfortable home of Aybek and Gulnara Myrsahmatov. Aybek is a part-time geography teacher who can sometimes be found at the municipal office in Suusamyr. If he is not at home, his wife and daughters can help. The white-washed house is in the last (eastern) third of the village on the left. There are a couple of comfortable rooms available and meals can be provided on request. Aybek can also advise on walking in the area and help supply horses.

KYZYL-OI This village lies in the gorge of the Kökömeren River at an altitude of 1,800m, about 40km south of Suusamyr, at the Chui Province's most southerly limit. Here, the valley opens up to form a bowl surrounded by dry, red-coloured mountain slopes. In appearance, the village is more central Asian than most settlements in northern Kyrgyzstan, with a less obvious Russian influence than most. The village's name is faithful to its geographical setting, as *Kyzyl-Oi* means 'red bowl', and the colouration of the local rock is also apparent in the houses here, many of which are constructed from the red clay of the area. There is a Community Based Tourism project active in the village, which is supported by the

Chui Province **SUUSAMYR VALLEY**

4

British Department for International Development and, given this infrastructure, coupled with its gorgeous setting, the village serves as an excellent base for day hikes in the area or as a stopover point *en route* to Kochkor or Song-Köl. There are numerous options for **hikes and treks** from the village, either on horseback or on foot. These vary in difficulty and length. The Sary-Kamysh range to the south of the village has several peaks around 4,000m. Chychkan-Choku peak at 3,989m lies northwest of Kyzyl-Oi, and the best approach is along the Sandyk River on its northern slope. The highest peak in the area is Sary-Kamysh at 4,042m (also known as Ai-Soluu) and here the best approach is from the south by way of 3,701m Chukul-Tör Pass. Yr-Gailuu peak is lower at 2,664m and is situated to the east of the Kökömeren River.

The glacial lakes of Köl-Tör (Four Lakes) lie to the west of the village along the Char valley and over the Kum-Bel Pass, a 4- or 5-hour trip on horseback. One of the lakes contains plenty of fish. Easier options include a waterfall on the Burundu River to the north, 2km east of the Kökömeren River, or hikes to flower-strewn summer *jailoos* above the village, such as Chet-Tör. The Choin-Tash *jailoo*, a mere 40-minute horse ride from the village, lies on the way to a glacier that can be visited via the Munkur Pass. Some mountain biking groups pass through the village on tours between Bishkek and Kochkor, and a few Bishkek tour operators also offer late summer rafting expeditions along the Kökömeren River.

The 1:200,000 *Vnutrenniy Tien Shan* map from GeoID has Kyzyl-Oi village in its far northwest corner. Hikes that range far from the village will require the surrounding maps.

Practicalities A good local contact is Artyk Kulubaev, who owns the 'Askar' village shop and works as CBT co-ordinator in the village (m *0503 242 199*). There is a sign for tourist information just before the shop on the right-hand side coming from Suusamyr. Artyk can arrange accommodation, advise on trekking routes and organise transport.

Because Kyzyl-Oi does not receive many visitors, homestays tend to be allocated on a rotating basis. CBT homestays in the village include those of Tungutar Konushbaev at his house by the river, the last in the village on the road to Song-Köl, and Katya Kulmursaeva, who also has a riverside house and comes recommended. The family of Kanat Soltonkulov also accommodate visitors; Kanat's mother, Shamshe, is a *shyrdak* maker and usually has a range of felt goods for sale. Myrsabi Dubanaeva also has a comfortable homestay away from the main road – walk along the road opposite the shop, turn left, then right past an attractive house; the homestay is at the next junction on the right. Other households include those of Sveta Abylgasieva, Kuban Konushbaev and Moldobek Rysbaev, whose wife teaches in the village school and speaks German.

Naisa Shamshebekov, another CBT homestay owner, is a hunting inspector and experienced guide who can guide visitors to places where Marco Polo sheep and wolves may be seen. Other hunters in the village who can act as guides include Bailobot Rysbaev and Ydyrs Kerimkulov, who is familiar with the route up Sary-Kamysh. Horses can be easily hired at any of the CBT homestays or through the co-ordinator. Only Kyrgyz and Russian is spoken as a rule.

There is very limited **public transport** to and from Kyzyl-Oi, with buses running to Suusamyr less than daily. Cars with drivers can be rented through CBT at the standard rate to reach either Suusamyr or Chaek, from where occasional buses operate. A taxi to or from Kochkor will cost around 1,700som if booked through CBT; a taxi from Kara-Balta will be about 1,300som.

5

Lake Issyk-Kul
– North Shore

LAKE ISSYK-KUL ОЗЕРО ИССЫК-КУЛ

Lake Issyk-Kul, the second-largest alpine lake in the world (Lake Titicaca in Peru/Bolivia is the largest), gives its name to the *oblast* that surrounds the lake's shoreline and extends across the high Tien Shan range south to the Chinese border. Issyk-Kul Oblast, which in area makes up around 20% of Kyrgyzstan's territory, has a population of less than half a million, the vast majority of whom live around the lake's shores.

The lake's name, which is also spelled Ysyk Köl or Issyk-kol, means literally 'warm lake' in the Kyrgyz language, as does its Chinese equivalent, Ze-Hai. There is good reason for this: in a part of the world where winter temperatures can plummet to –25°C or worse, the shores of the lake have a microclimate that is relatively balmy and, even more aptly, its waters never freeze. This is all the more surprising considering that the lake stands at considerable altitude – 1,606m above sea level. Scientists have long debated the precise mechanics of this, and it would seem that it is down to a combination of deep water physics, slight salinity and underground thermal activity. Most locals are less questioning and are merely grateful for the respite the lake offers, assuming that it is because the water is warmed by heat wafting up from the earth's core.

GEOGRAPHY AND CLIMATE In geographical terms, the lake is one of two massive depressions that dent the Tien Shan range: in Issyk-Kul's case, the depression is ringed by mountains and filled with snow-melt to form a lake; the other depression, a lower and altogether hotter region, is the Fergana Valley.

Lake Issyk-Kul, 'the pearl of the Tien Shan', is in the shape of an eye, 182km long and up to 60km wide. The lake was created in the early Miocene period 20 million years ago, when tectonic activity created the depression that became filled with fresh water. During the Pliocene period it covered an area substantially larger than it does now. Today it covers an area of 6,236 km². Over one hundred rivers and streams flow into the lake, the largest being Jergalan and Tyup at its eastern end. The total distance around its shoreline is 688km. The lake's average depth is around 270m but it is as deep as 668m in places, making it the fifth deepest lake in the world. Most of the water in Issyk-Kul comes from snow-melt or is provided by springs, some of which are thermal. In hydrographical terms, Issyk-Kul is an endorheic basin like the Caspian Sea, in that there is no outlet for its water either by river or underground and water can only leave it by evaporation or seepage through the soil.

The lake's slightly saline water, which had been dropping in level by around 5cm a year since the beginning of the 20th century, has been rising in level since 1998, and in the past ten years has risen by 30cm, a remarkable increase for such a large body of water. Although this might be seen to be irrefutable evidence of the extent of global warming and increased ice-melt, the rise in water level may be, for the

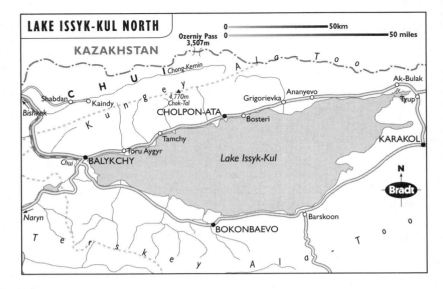

LAKE ISSYK-KUL NORTH

KAZAKHSTAN

Ozerniy Pass
3,507m

0 ———— 50km
0 ——————— 50 miles

Chong-Kemin

Ak-Bulak

Shabdan   Kaindy   4,770m   Grigorievka   Ananyevo   Tyup
Chok-Tal
Bishkek   CHOLPON-ATA
Bosteri

Tamchy   KARAKOL

Toru Aygyr   Lake Issyk-Kul
Chui   BALYKCHY   N

Bradt

Naryn   Barskoon
BOKONBAEVO

most part, a result of a changing local climate in the region in which there has been
far more rain and snowfall in recent years and which is not necessarily connected
with a global pattern. There are others who point the finger at industrial
development, in particular the Kumtor gold mine south of the lake, and suggest that
dust from the mine coats the glaciers to create a darker surface that absorbs more
heat and melts quicker. Geological evidence suggests that the lake's water level has
fluctuated considerably over millennia but the trend over the past 500 years has
mainly been one of decrease.

Rainfall is generally low but adequate, with an average of 248mm per annum in
Cholpon-Ata and 475mm in Karakol. The eastern end of the lake around Karakol
is considerably wetter than the western region close to Balykchy due to the presence
of air masses that collect moisture from the lake and release their payload as rain as
they rise into the mountains.

The vegetation type here is one of steppe and meadows, with elm trees and,
higher up, alpine meadows and forests of fir. The western part of the basin has rocky
deserts and more sparse vegetation: the coastal plain and mountains in the
southwest region between Bokonbaevo and Balykchy are particularly arid.

Temperatures, as already mentioned, are far milder than the Kyrgyzstan average
due to the moderating effect of the lake, with average summer temperatures rising
to around 25°C at Cholpon-Ata and winter temperatures dropping down to about
–5°C. The area receives around 2,900 hours of sunshine a year, which is relatively
high for the region.

Lake Issyk-Kul is flanked by two mountain ranges that run its full length from
east to west: to the north is the Kungey ('Sunny') Ala-Too range, beyond which lies
Kazakhstan; to the south is the Terskey ('Shady') Ala-Too. At the southeast end of
the lake, close to Karakol, are a number of narrow valleys that run south from the
Terskey range towards the lake – Altyn Arashan, Karakol and Jeti-Ögüz. Beyond the
Terskey range to the south are the even loftier peaks of the Central Tien Shan chain,
and the high glaciers that connect them. In the far southeast, nudged against the
Chinese and Kazakhstan borders in a frozen wonderland of rock and ice, are the
peaks of Khan Tengri (6,995m) and Pobedy, which, at 7,439m, is Kyrgyzstan's
highest point. The extensive Inylchek Glacier stretches out beneath these peaks.

This distant and inaccessible corner of the country is also home to the mysterious Merzbacher Lake, a geographical enigma par excellence (see page 177).

HISTORY Much evidence of some of modern-day Kyrgyzstan's earliest settlers, the warrior tribes of the Saka – or Scythians – has been found in the Issyk-Kul region, and a variety of rich bronze and gold artefacts have been recovered from their circular burial mounds. The Scythians occupied the region between about the 6th century BC and the 5th century AD. Before them, Neolithic settlers left their mark on the region, most notably at Cholpon-Ata, where a large number of petroglyphs and settlement remains from around 1000BC to the 6th century AD, and later, can still be seen.

Although the general trend until recently has been a drop of the lake's surface level, it would appear that Issyk-Kul was some 8m lower than its present level in medieval times, as remains of settlements have been found beneath its surface at this level. The Russian explorer Pyotr Semyonov Tyan-Shansky believed that a 'Kyrgyz Atlantis' might be discovered beneath the lake's waters. In 1857, some locals showed him some ruins in the water at Kara-Bulun cape, where the Tyup and Jergalan rivers divide and since then other underwater ruins have been found at various locations around the lake, The submerged city of Chigu in the Tyup gulf at the lake's eastern end has revealed artefacts that date back to the 2nd century BC. Chigu, referred to by the Chinese as 'the City of the Red Valley', was the capital of the state of Usun, and is presumed to have disappeared beneath the water in the 1st century AD.

Ancient legend points to St Matthew being buried close to the lake's shore at an Orthodox monastery, and some archaeologists believe that this would have been at the northwest shore of the lake, near to the settlement of Toru Aygyr, where the present-day tourist settlement of Ulan is located. A medieval bath complex was excavated here 50 years ago by a Kyrgyz archaeologist, along with many pieces of ceramics.

Later theories concerning this shifted their attention further east: Vladimir Ploskikh, a Kyrgyz archaeologist, believes that he has found remains of the monastery in which St Matthew was buried at Svetly Mys, on the northeast coast of the lake, although he admits that his hypothesis remains unproven (see *Did St Matthew die in Kyrgyzstan?* page 151).

Arabian chronicles make mention of many ancient settlements in the Issyk-Kul region, relating that the towns along the southern shore of the lake were celebrated for their riches and were populated by a large number of people. Of these towns, in the 8th century BC the major one was Barskhan, which roughly corresponds to present-day Barskoon, at the mouth of the river of the same name. This is mentioned in the works of the philosopher Biruni, who wrote that the residents of the town knew the secrets of iron alloys, which were only known to the Chinese at the time. All of these towns, it is believed, were later destroyed and inundated following an earthquake.

Because of its geographical position and obvious resources, Issyk-Kul became an important staging point along the more northern sections of the ancient **Silk Road**. Several routes use to ply its shores and one of the prime routes to the West led across the 4,284m Bedel Pass from China, before descending to the lake near present-day Barskoon. The lake was coveted by the Chinese for centuries, but they were never successful in conquering it and, despite its distance from St Petersburg, the Tsarist capital, it would be the Russians rather than the Chinese who would eventually colonise it.

Long before this, however, the lake's resources and mild climate were utilised by both Mongol and Turkic nomadic armies, who would often winter on its shores. Tamerlane is reputed to have banished captured Tartars to an island fortress that has long since vanished beneath the surface, probably as a result of earthquake activity.

Whether or is not this is true is uncertain, but whatever the precise history of the lake, washed-up fragments of pottery and brick bear witness to extensive periods of settlement here in the past.

Some historians believe that the lake was the point of origin for the **Black Death** that devastated Asia and Europe during the 14th century. These same historians believe that the plague began at a Nestorian Christian community at the northeast end of the lake in 1338 (while others say that it originated in the Gobi desert). Archaeological excavations have revealed extraordinarily high death rates for 1338 and 1339, and memorial stones attribute these deaths to plague, which has led some scholars to conclude that the 14th-century pandemic may well have originated here. From its origin at the lake, the plague spread westwards as merchants unwittingly transmitted the disease by transporting infested vermin along with their goods.

Following the decline of the Silk Road, the lake languished in obscurity for centuries and remained virtually unknown to the Western world until the 19th century, when Russian explorers like Pyotr Semyonov Tyan-Shansky ventured into the area to send back reports. At that time it was thought that the Chui River was the outflow of the lake, but Semyonov Tyan-Shansky proved that, although it would have had an outflow to the river at earlier times, this was no longer the case, despite it flowing within 4km of the western end of the lake. Another Russian explorer following in Tyan-Shansky's footprints, the scientist and geographer Nikolai Przhevalsky, died of typhoid in the town that then, as now, was known as Karakol but which, in the later Tsarist and Soviet era, was named after him.

Russian exploration arrived relatively late on the scene, but there had always been greater contact with the East: the Chinese traveller Jan Chan Tzan is reported to have reached the lake in around 128BC, while the first written account of the lake comes from another Chinese adventurer, Suan Zsan. The first written record of its name comes from an anonymous Tajik work *The Boundaries of the World from East to West* from AD982, which also accurately estimated the size of the lake.

During the Soviet period the eastern end of the lake was utilised as a base for testing submarine and torpedo technology for the Soviet navy. As the lake's waters were slightly salty and never froze, they were ideal for replicating the maritime conditions in which the Soviet fleet would normally be deployed. Even better was the lake's isolation, far from Europe and the prying eyes of the West. Throughout the late Soviet period Lake Issyk-Kul was strictly off-limits for non-Soviet citizens, although during this same period the lake was developed as a holiday destination for citizens of the USSR, and many sanatoria were opened up along the lake's shores, particularly in the north at resorts like Cholpon-Ata.

Because of its natural beauty, clean air and pleasant summer climate, the lake was considered to be one of the top leisure spots in the whole of the USSR. It was particularly popular with holidaying cosmonauts, and Yuri Gagarin journeyed here for well-earned rest and recuperation after his pioneering space mission in 1961 – there is a monument to him in the Barskoon valley. The lake's popularity even extended to Soviet leaders: Leonid Brezhnev himself had a *dacha* built here at the lake's north shore.

Following Kyrgyzstan's independence in 1991, the holiday industry swiftly plummeted into decline as Russians stopped visiting, and many of the lake's sanatoria were boarded up and abandoned. In recent times, there has been a turn-around of fortunes, with domestic tourists visiting the lake's shores in larger numbers, along with visitors from Kazakhstan, especially ethnic Russians, who make the trip over the mountains from Almaty to take advantage of the relative low prices and – for Kazakh citizens at least – a Kyrgyz visa-free regime.

As a result of this renewed interest some of the former sanatoria have been taken into private ownership and refurbished, and new hotels, especially small B&Bs, are being established. Since the late 1990s an increasing number of travellers from Western Europe and North America have been arriving in the region. On the whole, these come mostly to hike in the valleys southeast of the lake close to Karakol, or to visit the lake *en route* to the peaks of the Central Tien Shan. The administrative centre of Karakol has subsequently developed as the major centre for the outdoor pursuits and adventure tourism favoured by Western visitors, while Cholpon-Ata retains the crown for domestic tourism and the Kazakh beach set.

NATURAL HISTORY There are more than 20 types of fish in Lake Issyk-Kul, although human interference during the Soviet period has dramatically upset the lake's natural ecology (see box, *The Fortunes of Fishing at Lake Issyk-Kul*, page 140). The basic commercial fish used to be naked osman (*Dyptichus dybowslii*), Issyk-Kul chebak (*Leuciscus schmidti*), carp (*Cyprinus carpio*) and Issyk-Kul marinka (*Schizothorax pseudaksaiensis isskkuli*), but these have all diminished to a lesser or great extent following the introduction of non-native species like Sevan trout (*Salmo ischchan gegarkuni*).

Both eastern and western shores serve as wintering grounds for waterfowl – mostly pochard, mallards, bald coots and teal – with flocks that can be as big as 50,000. The lake was designated an official Ramsar Wetland Site in 2003. Altogether, there are around 200 species of bird that can be seen around the lake and the nearby mountains, with many birds of prey like saker falcon (*Falco cherrug*).

The mountains that surround the lake also provide a habitat for scarce and endemic mammal species that include lynx (*Flis unsia*), Marco Polo sheep (*Ovis ammon polii*), Siberian deer (*Servus eaphus*) and Siberian ibex (*Capra sibirica*). The highly elusive snow leopard (*Uncia uncial*) can also be found in small numbers.

In terms of vegetation, the foothill zone immediately next to the lake commonly has species like artemisia, acanthus, ephedra and sea buckthorn, while tree species like Turkestan juniper, and Tien Shan and Shrenk spruce, occur higher up, between 2,000–3,000m. Above this lie high meadows with specially adapted alpine flora.

Lake Issyk-Kul Biosphere Reserve This was established in 2001 with technical assistance from the German government. A draft plan was completed in 1998 and in September 2001, by decision of the co-ordinating committee of the UNESCO Man and Biosphere Programme (MAB), the Issyk-Kul Biosphere Reserve became No 411 on the list of the World Wide Network of Biosphere Reserves, with the two-fold goal of conserving its natural flora and fauna and supporting long-term economic and social development that is deemed to help restore natural resources.

The biosphere reserve is divided into four zones – core, buffer, transitional and rehabilitation – with each zone governed by rules about what sorts of activity are allowed or prohibited within it. Overall, the biosphere covers an area of 43,100km^2, which is about 22% of Kyrgyzstan's total area. It includes a number of previously protected territories of scientific value, like the Issyk-Kul State Preserve that was founded as the first protected territory of the Kyrgyz ASSR in 1948, to protect the lake's wintering waterfowl population.

The core area of the biosphere reserve incorporates a range of specially protected areas around the lake, the largest being the high-altitude, 72,000ha **Sarychat-Ertash National Preserve**, which lies deep in the Tien Shan mountains south of Karakol. Another important protected area is the **Karakol Natural Park**, founded in 1997, which has an area of 38,256ha and includes large stands of coniferous forest. In practical terms, one of the major challenges facing the integrity of the reserve is the activity of poachers and illegal loggers, along with the problems faced in containing polluting industrial development, especially the gold-mining operation at Kumtor, which is located just 20km from the Sarychat-Ertash preserve's western border.

One legend relates the tale of a king who had ears like an ass. The king's barbers were ordered to hide his ears and then each was killed in order to protect his dark secret. Understandably, the king soon exhausted the kingdom's supply of barbers and so was obliged to spare the last one, swearing him to life-long secrecy. The task proved too much for the barber, who fled to the mountains and asked a local hermit what he should do as he was tortured by the burden of his secret. The hermit suggested that he whispered the secret to a well, shutting the cover carefully after he did so. The barber did as he was told and announced his secret to a town well but he forgot to cover it afterwards. As a consequence of this, the water of the well rose up to flood the large-eared monarch's kingdom. Lake Issyk-Kul is said to be the result of this flood, its waters coming from the rising well of the legend.

Another story tells of a beautiful city that stood where the lake is today. One day, some young girls from the city went to the mountains to collect firewood. In their absence an enormous earthquake took place, flooding the city and killing all of its inhabitants. The girls came home to find a big lake where their city used to be. They were so grieved by the loss of their relatives and friends that they returned every day to the same place to mourn and weep. The salt of their tears slowly turned the lake's waters saline, which is why it does not freeze today.

A third tale tells of a cruel khan who once governed over a wonderful city. One day he saw a beautiful girl on a riverbank and immediately he wanted to marry her. The girl, however, was unimpressed and refused his proposal. Incensed by her refusal, the khan imprisoned the girl in a high tower until she changed her mind. Trapped in her prison tower she cried bitter tears and prayed to the heavens to take pity on her. Her prayers were soon answered and the river that flowed through the town burst its banks to inundate the whole town. Everyone perished in the flood – the khan, the girl, the townspeople – and since that day the lake formed by the flood has been salty and changeable: sometimes it is calm and quiet, like the dead girl; at other times, it is threatening and violent, like the tragedy that created the lake.

This final legend has similarities to the story of the ass-eared king. Many years ago there was a big city where Lake Issyk-Kul is located today. The ruler of the city was Khan Iskender, a cruel and violent man who lived with the terrible secret that he had a pair of horns on his head. To keep the secret he routinely executed everyone who came to cut his hair or to shave him. One day it was the turn of the son of a poor old widow to clip the khan, and his mother was fully aware of the risk her son was at. The widow cooked three round cakes made of her own milk and told her son to take them to the khan. On visiting the khan the son dropped the first two cakes as he had been told, but when he dropped the third cake the khan picked it up and tasted it, declaring it to be delicious. The khan asked what the cake was made of, and on being told he realised that he had inadvertently become a maternal brother of the son.

Because of this the son was spared, but made to promise to keep the khan's affliction secret. On the third day of visiting the khan the son was suffering from a stomach ache and an overwhelming desire to tell someone of the khan's secret. The khan ordered that a well in the middle of the town be opened up so that the boy could yell down it, 'Our Iskender Khan is two-horned!' On his third cry, water burst out of the well and flooded the city, thus creating Lake Issyk-Kul.

Balykchy (Kyrgyz for 'fisherman') is the largest settlement at the western end of Lake Issyk-Kul, and even a cursory glance tells that it is no longer the prosperous town that it once was. Originally named Kutmady, this town of around 40,000 was renamed Riybachye during the Soviet era, the Russian equivalent of its present-day name. The railway station still bears this name today, but it is not alone in echoing the name of a bygone age. Following independence in 1991, the town was known for a brief time as Issyk-Kul, but for obvious reasons this caused considerable confusion, and so a couple of years later the Kyrgyz equivalent of its earlier name was settled upon.

Fishing was one of the first industries to develop here in the late 19th century, when Russian colonists settled here and started working the lake on their doorstep. Unfortunately for Balykchy, fishing has not played much of a role in the town's fortunes since independence, and over the past two decades the town has steadily declined to the sorry state it finds itself today.

In Soviet times the town developed as an important transport and industrial centre, with shipping, fishing and shipbuilding all contributing to its economy; now, with the loss of the industrial base that the Soviet Union provided, all of these industries have virtually disappeared, and those who remain face unemployment and little promise for the future. Consequently, it is hardly surprising that depression, heavy vodka consumption and prostitution are pervasive in the town, given Balykchy's current unhappy lot.

The town's main function today is simply as the terminus of a railway line from Bishkek, and as a junction town on the road south to Naryn and China, and the roads to the east that skirt the north and south shores of the lake. For many locals, these roads are the best thing about the place, and many of those that are able to leave have done so, migrating to Russia, Ukraine and Germany. Those left behind – mostly the old – have to cope as best they can. As elsewhere in Kyrgyzstan, pensioners have been particularly vulnerable, as many are abandoned by their families in search of a better life elsewhere. Balykchy has more than its fair share of pensioners – perhaps 4,000 or more – all desperately trying to survive on the impossibly small pension of US$3 a month.

If you want a warts-and-all perspective of industrial decline in a post-Soviet transitional state, then Balykchy makes a good case study. Whatever your degree of interest, however, you probably do not want to stay here.

GETTING THERE There are infrequent **rail** connections with Bishkek but these are painfully slow, take more than 6 hours, and do not even deposit you in the town centre, as the passenger station lies someway out of town. It is better to get there by **minibus** from Bishkek's West Bus Station (100som), a 90-minute to 2-hour run. Balykchy's bus/minibus station is fairly conveniently situated, 10-minutes' walk west of the town centre on Frunze. There are plenty of minibuses to Cholpon-Ata from Balykchy (60som), some of which continue to Karakol. Minibuses along the southern shore are less plentiful.

Local buses run these same routes several times a day, too. Most direct buses to Karakol from Bishkek bypass Balykchy, as does transport running south to Naryn, which takes a shortcut via the west side of the Orto-Tokoy reservoir.

WHERE TO STAY AND EAT Should you wish to stay here there is a very basic *gostinitsa*, **Kyrgyz Altyn**, on the corner of Salima Orozbaeva and Issyk-Kul (✆ 22801; $) a few blocks north of the docks. Also, east of town on the way to Cholpan-Ata there is the **Ulan** *turbaza*, signposted just before you reach the village of Toru Aygyr. For food, there is the bazaar, or **Café Cholpan** (*Toktosunov 56*), and a few simple cafés along Frunze.

WHAT TO SEE AND DO Aficionados of Soviet-era statuary will find plenty to enthral them here: the town has at least three Lenin figures, along with a sad array of rusting communist totems. Also, on the outskirts of the town on the Bishkek side, set back from the road on a small hillock, stands a statue of Pyotr Semyonov Tyan-Shansky, in exploration mode leading a packhorse (see page 136).

THE FORTUNES OF FISHING AT LAKE ISSYK-KUL

Commercial fishing at Lake Issyk-Kul began in the 1890s, with the arrival of Russian colonists who took advantage of the 22 native species that the lake had to offer, many of which were good to eat. By the 1930s the populations of some of the more scarce species had declined, so commoner species like *chebachok* or Issyk-Kul dace (*Leuciscus bergi*) were targeted, a fish with a population that was considered to be virtually inexhaustible.

In an attempt to increase the value of the lake's fish stocks, more valuable fish like trout were introduced around this time. The Sevan trout (*Salmo ischchan*), a species endemic to Armenia, was first introduced to the lake in the 1930s, partly to boost fish stocks in the lake and partly to conserve a species that was becoming rare in its native Armenia. The trout grew to a large size in their new home – some older fisherman claim they would catch 17kg specimens on occasion – but the project was not an unqualified success as the alien trout ravaged many of Issyk-Kul's native species like *chebachok*, and within a few decades catches of this once plentiful fish had declined dramatically.

Later, in the 1950s, a few other non-native species were introduced – bream, pikeperch and carp – and, in the early 1970s, efforts to restock the lake took a different turn when a plan was devised to gradually reduce the number of *chebachok* to a minimum and to turn the lake into a reservoir for valuable fish like trout and whitefish. At this point, the Sevan whitefish (*Coregonus lavaretus*), another Armenian species, was introduced, along with *omul*, a fish from Lake Baikal in Siberia.

Like the Sevan trout, the introduction of whitefish turned out to be a misjudgement in ecological terms. Efforts were soon made to restrict their number but it was too late, as within a very short time the Sevan whitefish had established itself as the major component of the lake's fish stock. This has inevitably resulted in widespread changes in Lake Issyk-Kul's fish ecology. The number of most native species has diminished overall, while some species like the naked osman have virtually disappeared altogether. The lake now produces relatively low fish yields.

It should not be forgotten that Lake Issyk-Kul is an oligotrophic lake (low in nutrients), with a low productivity, and that it could never realistically be expected to produce large sustainable fish stocks. Nowadays, with an increased population living around the lake, together with a large number of annual visitors, the demand for fish far outweighs supply. Due to Lake Issyk-Kul's growing importance for recreation, one management solution might be to concentrate on sport and recreational fishing in order to satisfy the demands of visitors and bring in income. The trouble with this is that the two most voracious feeders on the lake's endemic species – the Sevan trout and pikeperch – are those very species which are most in demand by recreational fishermen.

Poaching is a widespread problem too, and has soared to massive levels in recent years. Bans on fishing during the spawning period have been introduced, but this being central Asia, corruption comes into play, and many inspectors are said to be either involved in poaching themselves, or are intimidated by the threat of violence from poachers who gang together in groups.

Although it is undeniable that few towns in Kyrgyzstan have rejected their Soviet past outright, you get the feeling that in Balykchy they mourn the past more than most, and perhaps one indication of this has been a reluctance to dispose of the monuments and ciphers that point to more prosperous times. There again, much of the town has an abandoned look to it, and what remains is more likely a matter of indifference than any conscious effort to conserve. The street names here are largely unchanged from the communist period and Cyrillic signs still point you along the cracked tarmac of thoroughfares with heroic names like Gagarin, Frunze, Komsomol and Pioneer.

A change of minibuses here gives the opportunity to wander awhile through the town, which at the very least offers a very different perspective on the lake from Cholpon-Ata or Karakol; an important contrast that is worth seeing, even if you are not tempted to linger.

Leaving the bus station and heading east along Frunze, you go past a building that has a metal framework Lenin on its roof. After 5 minutes, you will reach a small, and rather threadbare, bazaar area, with lots of men in tracksuits hanging around waiting for something to happen – although they know it won't – and stalls selling cheap clothes and vodka, which never seems to be in short supply.

The road south at the crossroads by the bazaar leads past an Orthodox church to the lake's shore. A freight railway skirts the shore east to an area of docks with rusting hulls and idle cranes. The largest of the dock buildings has a hammer and sickle motif attached to its roof, along with what looks like a brace of torpedoes.

There is nowhere in particular to go from here, just a meander back towards the bus station, which in a town like this seems to wield a strong gravitational pull. On the way back you might well pass another Lenin statue, this time in a weedy patch that fronts a closed-down cinema, which has had its windows blocked with breeze blocks to create a concrete cube rather like the space encapsulated by the artist Rachel Whitread's work, *House*. You will probably see a number of houses that have 'for sale' notices outside; they're often wooden and attractive but with peeling paint, which just reinforces the impression that this is a town whose fortune has deserted it. Close to the bus station, huddles of local woman at the roadside hold up smoked fish on strings and wave them at passing vehicles. You may see these for sale all around the lake's shore, although only in Balykchy do the vendors seem so desperate to make a transaction.

TORU AYGYR Leaving Balykchy along Lake Issyk-Kul's northern shore, this village is reached after about 20km. The remains of an ancient settlement have been found nearby, along with petroglyphs and stone statues. A medieval bath house was discovered here by archaeologists in the 1940s, that had ceramic pipes to channel the water, and glazed bricks on the floor. A potter's workshop has also been unearthed. Trekking routes over the Kungey Ala-Too from the village lead into the Chong-Kemin valley and Kazakhstan beyond. A 2-day, 45km-route goes as far as Kaindy in the valley although, given the climb, Toru Aygyr is probably better used as the destination rather than the starting point.

TAMCHY ТАМЧЫ *Telephone code: 03943*

Nestled on the northwest shore of Lake Issyk-Kul, this small village has become popular with domestic and Kazakh tourists in recent years as a quieter and less brash alternative to Cholpon-Ata. With a successfully established CBT project here too, it is also becoming increasingly favoured by overseas visitors, either as an overnight stop whilst travelling along Lake Issyk-Kul's north shore, or as a place to relax after a stint of strenuous trekking. As a village it is a pleasant but fairly unremarkable place, but it does have something that most others do not have: a location that is right by the water and a long lakeside beach. For visitors circumnavigating Lake Issyk-Kul, Tamchy makes a good choice for a first night's stay.

GETTING THERE Perhaps surprisingly, Tamchy lies close to the largest airfield around the lake. The nearby airport, 3km east at Chok-Tal, was renovated in 2003 and mainly provides summer charter flights for holidaying Kazakhs and Russians from Almaty. In 2006 Moscow announced that it would invest US$100 million dollars in the airport to upgrade it to international standards. This would involve lengthening the landing strip to make larger planes capable of landing there. There were also plans to build a hotel, casino and leisure complex, and to develop a large holiday resort in the area. Tamchy's current peacefulness may not last.

Frequent **minibuses** and **buses** pass by on the main road, heading west to Bishkek and east to Karakol. Both buses and minibuses leave from Bishkek's West Bus Station (*Zapadniy Avtovaksal*) and most will be bound for either Cholpon-Ata or Karakol; the minibus fare is around 200som, the bus, 100som – the same as to Cholpon-Ata – and the journey takes around 3 hours. Leaving Tamchy, there is a concrete bus shelter by the main road at the eastern end of the village where transport can be flagged down. Coming from Bishkek, look out for the unassuming sign that announces the village – it is quite easy to miss. The best place to get off is by the second road that leads down to the shore, just past the mosque and graveyard if coming from Bishkek. Occasional share taxis also ply the same routes, although returning to Bishkek most of these originate in larger towns like Cholpon-Ata, and are usually already full when they pass.

WHERE TO STAY AND EAT There is a well-run CBT set-up in the village. Tamchy's **CBT co-ordinator** is Baktygyl Asanlieva (*Manas 47;* ☎ *21 272;* m *0503 355 611*). The co-ordinator can also put you in touch with makers of good-quality *shyrdaks*, for which the village is well known. There are several good homestay choices in the village but the favourite for many if it is not fully booked is the so-called

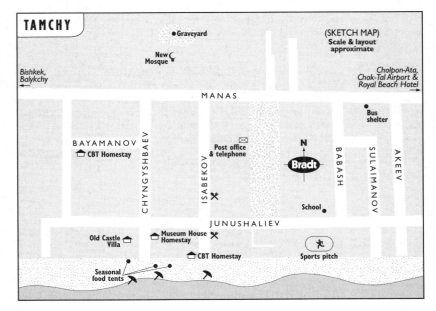

Museum House (✆ *211 24*) just around the corner at Chyngyshbaev 24, the street that runs parallel to Isabekov to the west.

The house, which also has a yurt in the garden that you can stay in, is indeed very much like a museum, with its central room packed with artefacts and costumes from all over the Turkic world. There is a dining platform in the garden, and toilet and shower facilities are outside too. This is a clean and restful place to stay, although your sleep might be disturbed by the karaoke singers who use the battery-operated street set-ups that are sometimes positioned immediately outside the gate. The host Dinara is both well-educated and well-travelled and speaks excellent English. She is a mine of information regarding Kyrgyz culture and history.

Meals are best taken at the homestay, but there are seasonal tents along the beach, which sell booze and snacks, and a couple of places along Isabekov close to the beach, which offer *shashlyk, manti* and *shorpo*. As Tamchy is popular with both Kyrgyz and Russian visitors, in summer there is absolutely no problem in finding beer and vodka on sale.

If you hanker for somewhere more exotic to stay there is the Villa Stariy Zamok **(Old Castle Villa)** hotel in the village, with its Mafioso connections, while out of town near the airport at Chok-Tal village is the **Royal Beach Hotel** (✆ *427 77*), a recently opened, comfortable hotel on the lakeshore that has both private rooms (US$50–90) and bungalows (US$70–200) with full three-meal pension. Prices are lower out of season. Besides the beach, entertainment includes tennis, volleyball and horseriding, and catamarans can be hired on the lake.

WHAT TO SEE AND DO Tamchy's prime attraction is its natural setting: a beachfront location with the backdrop of the mountains of the Kungey Ala-Too range. There are pleasant walks to be had along the beach in either direction. In summer there will be plenty of Russians and Kyrgyz swimming in the lake, and families picnicking on the beach or eating in the tents that have been set up along it. Umbrella and pedalo hire are both available at the beach.

Immediately behind the beach is a wet grassy area with the improbable sight of flocks of turkeys and the odd cow grazing upon it; beyond this is a poplar plantation where some people camp or park their vehicles. Away from the shore, on the main road, is a small modern mosque with a steel dome, and behind this, beyond an area of wasteland and just before open fields, is a cemetery that, oddly, has Orthodox and communist graves rather than Muslim ones.

Tamchy's most unmistakeable sight, however, is the Villa Stariy Zamok hotel near the beach, which as its name suggests looks like a castle, or rather the Disney version of one. This architectural conceit first appeared a few years ago, a blot on Tamchy's unspoiled and low-rise skyline. The hotel was the scene of internecine Kazakh mafia shootings a few years back and, although it is peaceful now, it is still said to be popular with *biznizmen* from Almaty.

FESTIVALS In late July 2006, the first **Oimo International Festival** took place at Tamchy over a period of 4 days. This cultural and craft festival was organised jointly by the Ministry of Culture of the Kyrgyz Republic and the Central Asia Crafts Support Association (CACSA). Following the success of the first event there were plans to make the festival annual. Events include craft master-classes, theatre shows, folk concerts and an ethnic fashion show.

ORGANISED TOURS FROM TAMCHY Between late June and late August CBT offer a 2–3 day 'Searching for Hidden Treasures Tour' that combines car travel with hiking and horseriding in the nearby mountains. The tour explores the area close to the village, visits petroglyphs and a Muslim *mazar* (tomb of a holy man), and continues to a high-altitude *jailoo* and a canyon, where legend says that treasure is buried. This is best booked in advance through KCBTA Bishkek.

CHOLPON-ATA ЧОЛПОН-АТА *Telephone code: 03943*

This town marks roughly the halfway point along Lake Issyk-Kul's north shore and is by far the lake's most developed resort in terms of domestic (and Kazakh) tourism. The town, with a permanent population of around 8,000, is well known for its beaches and sanatoria, which developed during the Soviet period then subsequently declined following independence. In recent years there has been something of a tourism renaissance here, with new private hotels being built, and some of the older, larger sanatoria being taken into private ownership for refurbishment.

The town stretches along the main road for some considerable distance, with new housing stretching north towards the mountains, while south of the main highway roads lead south to hotels, a holiday complex, sanatorium, yacht club and the town's beaches. For visitors, the town's epicentre is the area along the main road just east of the bus station, where many of its shops, restaurants, services and accommodation options are located. Further east, beyond a park, is another area of activity with the El Noor bazaar, a bus stop and more bars and restaurants.

The resort was always popular with visitors from the former USSR, particularly Russians, who came here for sun, sea and sanatoria. It used to be rather an elite sort of place, with intellectuals and writers coming from all over the Soviet Union to take the waters here, and athletes coming to train and take advantage of its gentle summer climate and modest altitude.

Cholpon-Ata remains popular in summer: the Kyrgyz president has a property here and during July and August the town is full of both domestic tourists and visitors from Kazakhstan, particularly ethnic Russians. The town still has a large permanent Russian population and it is noticeably less Kyrgyz than many other settlements of its size around the lake – there is even a statue of Boris Yeltsin, who took regular vacations here in the past.

Because of its popularity the town can get rather crowded at the height of summer and it can be difficult to find a room. Unless you especially want to lie on the beach then a visit at either end of the main season is probably a better choice. Early autumn is an especially appealing time, with turning leaves, blue skies and the mountains with a dusting of snow. The problem here is that, as the resort is mostly seasonal, many of the homestays may be closed, and once again it might be hard to find somewhere to stay.

Beaches aside, there are other good reasons to come here: Cholpon-Ata has a good local museum, there is an excellent petroglyph site just outside the town, and the town makes a good base for local walks or visits to other villages along the north shore that lack Cholpon-Ata's facilities.

GETTING THERE Regular **buses** run from Bishkek's West Bus Station and continue along the north coast to Karakol. However, during the summer months most buses arriving or leaving Cholpon-Ata's bus station seem to ply a route between the town and Almaty in Kazakhstan. Many of these travel overnight.

Minibuses also depart from Bishkek's West Bus Station and are generally faster and cost 150–200som. Minibuses from Balykchy are also regular and cost 60som. In Cholpon-Ata, minibuses and share taxis wait for passengers at the top end of the bus station by the road. Local minibuses to villages along the north shore are best caught at the bus shelter at the eastern end of the town near the bazaar, as are through buses heading east to Karakol.

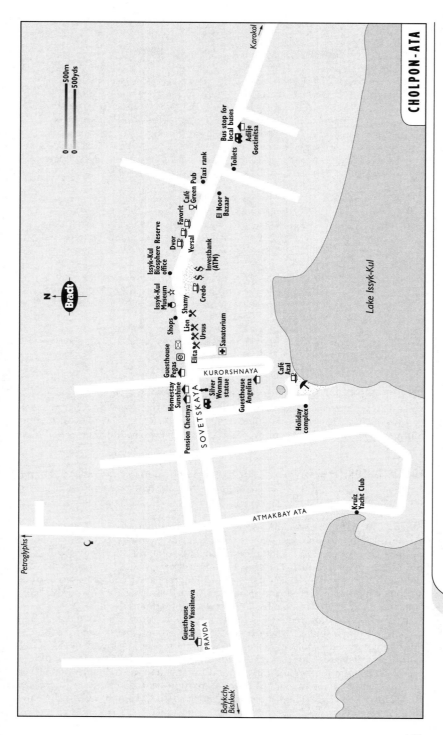

CHOLPON-ATA

Lake Issyk-Kul – North Shore CHOLPON-ATA

5

145

Long ago, when the Kyrgyz lived as one people in a single tribe near the mountains, there was a beautiful girl called Cholpon whose eyes were bluer than the sky and brighter than the stars. Two brave *djigits* (young warrior horsemen), Ulan and Santash, fell in love with her, but Cholpon could not decide which of them to choose, so the men fought savagely for her attention. They wounded each other, drawing blood, and the fighting became so intense that their relatives joined in on each side. Cholpon was faced with an impossible choice as she knew that she could not offend either of them with rejection, so she pulled out her own heart from her breast so that neither of them could possess it. The place where she fell dead on a hill facing the rising sun was named Cholpon-Ata in her honour.

The Kyrgyz people wept bitter tears for a long time over the loss of their beautiful daughter. Their tears flooded the valley between the mountains and formed a lake – Lake Issyk-Kul – and the Kyrgyz became divided into two tribes who settled on the north and the south shores of the lake – Kungey and Terskey. Ulan and Santash live on as the winds that blow from east and west, and whenever they meet they fight to exhaustion, causing the storms that ravage the lake from time to time.

Another legend tells a similar story, except in this case it is a cruel khan that yearned for Cholpon's favours. The girl, who loved another, refused his advances and in the end hurled herself from the high tower she was imprisoned in rather than submit to the khan.

It is said that if you stand at Cholpon-Ata's shore today you can see the face of Cholpon's father (*Cholpon-ata*) in the mountains opposite, his tears flowing down the mountainside to add salt water to the lake.

GETTING AROUND Cholpon-Ata is not a large town but it is quite spread-out and you might wish to take a taxi. Taxis congregate on the main road by the entrance to the bus station and there is another small taxi rank at the Noor bazaar. A short journey should cost 40–60 som. A local taxi firm that can be called up is **Kul Taxi** (↘ *177*).

TOURIST INFORMATION There is no CBT representation in Cholpon-Ata, but the Issyk-Kul Biosphere Reserve office opposite the park may be able to offer tourist information.

WHERE TO STAY There are lots of places in town that offer homestay accommodation; look for the signs that say *komnaty* (**КОМНАТЫ**) – rooms. Many of these are located close to the bus station, and sometimes landladies will go to meet buses to offer rooms. The strip along Sovetskaya, set just back from the road opposite the bus station, has several choices. There are also a couple west of the bus station along the main road, and also along Kurorshnaya, a narrow road that leads south after the small park that has a silver statue of Cholpon.

In summer, rooms tend to get full up and it can be quite hard to find accommodation in July and August; out of season, some places close for business. The homestays in Cholpon-Ata are not monitored or organised by the CBT network so standards vary, as do the facilities offered and the price. Most landladies tend to know one another and can probably point you in the right direction if they are full themselves. In an emergency there are rooms at the bus station (if you can find someone in charge) and at the basic *gostinitsa* **Adilje** behind the bus shelter at the eastern end of town.

Guesthouse Angelina Kurorshnaya 21; ℡ 429 04. Run by a friendly Russian couple, Yuri & Angelina, this is a comfortable place to stay in a quiet location (apart from Cholpon-Ata's canine chorus at night). Angelina cooks up enormous meals. The house opposite also has rooms. $$
Guesthouse Liubov Vassilevna Pravda 2; ℡ 421 02. 3 clean rooms with shared facilities. *Bed & 3 meals* $$.

Pension Chetnya Sovetskaya 87; ℡ 437 94. A comfortable place with a very central location. *Bed & 3 meals* $$.
Guesthouse Pegas Sovetskaya 81. A small place with just 2 rooms close to the post office. $–$$
Homestay Sunshine Sovetskaya 85; m 0502 122 364. Next door to Chetnya, more basic but cheaper. $

✗ WHERE TO EAT Most homestays offer full- or half-board but there a number of cafés, bars and restaurants for lunch, snacks or an evening out.

Near the bazaar at the eastern end of town is **Café Green Pub** with a variety of beers. Also close by are **Dvor**, **Favorit** and **Versal**, which has Steinbrau beer from Bishkek. The café **Credo** is on the south side of the central park, and in the centre of town, on Sovetskaya opposite the post office, there are several places like **Shamy**, **Elita**, **Lion** and **Ursus**, which is clean and tidy and a good choice for lunch ($$).

ENTERTAINMENT AND NIGHTLIFE The bars and cafés mentioned above are the obvious places that might lure you from tea and jam at your homestay. Otherwise, there is a **nightclub** that resembles a mock fortress next door to the museum.

OTHER PRACTICALITIES There is a central row of shops close to the post office that stock the usual range of goods. For fresh fruit and vegetables visit the **Noor bazaar** at the eastern end of town. For internet access there is an **internet café** with a fast connection and IP telephony just around the corner of the post office to the west. **Investbank** by the park has an ATM machine, but it would be unwise to depend upon this. The same bank should be able to give cash advances on Visa and MasterCard. Cash can be exchanged at the post office or at any of the exchange booths around town.

WHAT TO SEE AND DO The **Issyk-Kul Museum** (*Sovetskaya 69;* ℡ *421 48.* ⊕ *09.00–13.00, 14.00–18.00 Tue–Sun; 35som*) is well worth a visit, giving as it does an overview of the culture and archaeology of the region, as well as having artefacts from further afield. Unusually for this part of the world, a lot of care has been taken over layout and lighting. Unfortunately, captions are only in Kyrgyz and Russian, but it is easy enough to get a reasonable impression of what is on offer.

Much of the museum is given over to local archaeological finds that include items from Scythian burials, stones with Arabic inscriptions, pottery, underwater finds that include jars from Lake Issyk-Kul, and some remarkable leather-ware pots. Black and white photographs show the excavations themselves.

There is an interesting display showing photographs of some of the more notable petroglyphs from Saimaluu-Tash, including an aerial shot that gives a useful idea of the extent of the site, and some distinctly erotic petroglyphs that must be the closest thing to prehistoric porn. There are further petroglyphs from the Altai and Tuva regions of Russia that demonstrate many parallels to what has been discovered in Kyrgyzstan.

A room devoted to Kyrgyz history has photographs of everyday *jailoo* life that show women milking mares and sheep, singing and dancing, and erecting yurts. There are also some excellent *shyrdaks* and examples of weaving and embroidery.

Another room concentrates on the Manas legacy, with photographs of the 1,000-year celebrations and performances of local *manaschi* storytellers. Further displays are given over to the work of writer Chingiz Aitmatov, who often used to summer at Cholpon-Ata (see page 37), and also the artist Yuristanbev Shigaev whose work draws heavily on ritual and a Picasso influence.

Open-air petroglyph site This open site, sometimes referred to as the Stone Garden, covers an area of over 40ha just outside the town to the northwest. Although petroglyphs can be found at a number of locations in Kyrgyzstan – most spectacularly at Saimaluu-Tash – the ones on display here are certainly the most easily accessible in the country. Unfortunately, there have been well-intentioned attempts to preserve the petroglyphs in recent years that may turn out to be more damaging than if they had merely been left alone. Only time will tell if the chemicals used to preserve the carvings have had any long-term deleterious effect.

The site is covered with stones and boulders of varying size, some of which have carvings that date from the period between about 1500BC and the 1st-century AD. The majority date from the Saka–Scythian period (8th century BC to 1st century AD) and some from the Turkic period between the 5th and 10th century AD, but all pre-date the arrival of the Kyrgyz tribes in the region. It is thought that the site may have represented a large open-air temple where the heavenly bodies, in particular the sun, were venerated. In addition to the carvings there are some arrangements of rocks in circles that may have served an astronomical or ritual function.

Most of the carved stones, which range from 30cm to 3m in size, are oriented to face southwest or southeast, and this would indicate some form of sun worship. Most of the petroglyphs represent hunting scenes, or rather the hunted – ibex and deer with antlers like Christmas trees – although there are also hunters, other animals and sun symbols. Images of deer commonly feature in prehistoric carvings world-wide, although there may be a connection with deer worship that was widespread in the Altai and Siberian region in the same period. One of the largest of the Kyrgyz tribes, the Bugu ('red deer'), also venerated deer but would have migrated to the region many years after these petroglyphs had been fashioned.

Walking to the site takes around 30–40 minutes from the town centre. To reach it on foot, head west along the main road past the bus station. Turn right along Akmatbay Ata, opposite the turn-off for the boatyard and by a sign that points to the mosque (**МЕЧИТ**). Walk gently uphill past the mosque and a Muslim graveyard on your left until you come to a blue house that has a line of poplars on its north side, and where the road twists to the west. Continue north along the road, which by now has become a dirt track with a pipe crossing it. Soon you will reach some large new houses, and the site is just to the northwest behind these, in what used to be an enclosed area. The site is no longer fenced-off, at least not technically, because the fencing was (ingeniously) stolen, and now all that remains are the concrete posts that held it. Returning you can take a different route: head towards the concrete walled building then cross a field full of boulders to the south. This will lead to an electricity transformer and a small pond; continue south to reach a metalled road and then turn left, soon reaching the blue house on the corner and the road south to the mosque and town centre. Alternatively, if you have little time, take a taxi and get it to wait. One hour should be long enough.

The best time for a visit is in the late afternoon when the low sun hits the petroglyphs head on and makes them easier to see. It is also cooler and more atmospheric at this time of day, and the noise of water bubbling over rocks, which comes from the stream bisecting the site, can sound almost like distant thunder in the mountains. Many of the stones are numbered and some of the more interesting ones can be found at the top (northern) end of the site. There is an entrance fee to the site of 30som, although the caretaker who lives nearby may not always be present.

Beach and yacht club The **public beach** can be reached by heading down the dual-carriage road that leads south from the bus station. At the bottom on the right is a modern holiday complex with lurid-coloured roofs. A road leads to the left past a small tree-lined lake to reach the beach just beyond the Café Azal. The **Kruiz Yacht Club** is reached by heading west out of town and turning left along Akmatbay-Ata, opposite the road to the mosque and petroglyphs. The yacht club has sail- and motorboats that can be rented on an hourly basis. There is another small beach nearby.

BOSTERI   The resort village of Bosteri lies 10km east of Cholpon-Ata and is given over entirely to mass tourism. There are several sanatoria and large hotel complexes here that hark back to Soviet times, albeit at the more luxurious end of the market. A stay here certainly gives an insight into Russian and Kyrgyz domestic tourism if that is what interests you.

The prime sanatoria here are the **Kyrgyz Vzmorye** or 'Kyrgyz Seaside Resort' (➚ 356 48), with its extensive leafy grounds and beach access, which has been used for presidential conferences in the past, and the Kazakh-owned **Hotel Alma-Ata** (➚ 451 44) with its two swimming pools, tennis courts, discotheques and private beach. There are also smaller but equally upmarket hotels like **Pension Talisman-Village**, which has one- and two-room cottages (*all $$$$–$$$$$ for f/bd, depending on the class of room and the time of year*).

Leaving Bosteri towards Karakol there is an excellent **Kyrgyz graveyard** to the east of the village. After another 10km, in the village of Bulan Sogottu, formerly known as Komosomol, the most impressive of all the north shore sanatoria is reached: the **Issyk-Kul** (or **'Avrora') Resort** (*147 rooms, 7 luxury apartments;* ➚ 445 43; e *aurora@issyk-kyl.kg*). The Issyk-Kul Sanatorium is known as the Avrora for fairly obvious reasons: it resembles a beached ship, specifically the cruiser *Avrora* of revolutionary fame – the warship that fired the shot that prompted the storming of St Petersburg's winter palace in 1917. This battleship of a hotel complex has just about every facility you could wish for – swimming pool, tennis courts, exercise rooms, conference and banquet rooms and, of course, its own private beach. Its guests are not solely from Kyrgyzstan, but from all over the central Asian region and beyond, and at weekends in summer many come from Bishkek to live it up at the hotel's night club.

The sanatorium treats a wide range of conditions that include diseases of the blood system, digestive problems, bone and muscle illnesses and urological problems, amongst others. Treatments may include dousing with spring water from hosepipes, beating with birch twigs and time spent in the salt rooms (*sgl $$$$, dbl, suites, apts, $$$$$; winter prices about half summer tariff*).

Other hotel resorts near Cholpon-Ata

⌂ **Raduga** (58 cottages) Sary-Oy village (just before Cholpon-Ata, 243km from Bishkek); ➚/f 575 55 (or in Bishkek: ➚ 0312 627 194, ➚ 627 195); www.raduga.kg. Business centre, conference hall, swimming pools, tennis courts, disco. $$$$$ *with meals.*

⌂ **Rohat-NBU** (3 houses) Kara-Oy village. $$$$, *lux*

$$$$$; *also cheaper family rooms* $$$–$$$$
⌂ **Jamaica** (165 beds) Sary-Oy village. Games room, conference hall, water entertainments. $$$$ *with meals.*

⌂ **Ak-Bermet** (5 cottages, 4 houses) Kara-Oy village (just before Cholpon-Ata, 250km from Bishkek). Swimming pool. $$$ *with meals.*

GRIGORIEVKA   This pretty village 40km east of Cholpon-Ata is the starting point for treks up the Chon Ak-Suu canyon to a clutch of glacial lakes. The canyon is some 32km long, its slopes carpeted by dense stands of fir. From the lakes a trail leads onwards to the Chong-Kemin valley, as well as over the mountains to Kazakhstan (see *Trekking Routes to and from Kazakhstan*, page 154).

SEMYENOVKA   Just to the east of Grigorievka along the main road, this smaller village is the starting point for an asphalt road that leads into the mountains up the

5

Chon Ak-Suu valley, past a defunct *turbaza,* to reach a *jailoo* at 2,010m that has a yurt village in summer. A new ski base was constructed in the valley in 2002 and opened by the then president Askar Akaev. Just outside Semyenovka to the northeast are Scythian burial mounds that date from the 5th–3rd century BC. By the lakeshore close to the village is the *dacha* that was built in the 1960s for the use of Leonid Brezhnev. It was used just once by the former Soviet leader and now lies in a state of disrepair.

There is a good **homestay** ($) in the village at the house of Lilia and Slava (*Issyk-Kul 42;* ✆ *632 62*), which has its own sauna. Lilia offers excellent meals for 100som, and Slava will drive guests up into the mountains for a small charge, and is knowledgeable about the local area.

ANANYEVO This is the next sizeable village heading east, 52km from Cholpon-Ata. The village's name derives from that of a Soviet hero who was born in the village, Nikolai Ananyev, one of the 'Panfilov Heroes' who died defending the small village of Panfilov outside Moscow during World War II. There is a memorial to him in the village in a small park just off the main street (the next village east along the road, Zharkinbaevo, is similarly named after a local World War II hero).

Ananyevo was founded as a Cossack settlement in the 1890s and still retains much of this identity, with its quaint Orthodox church and plenty of Slavic faces and blond hair on the streets. Slavs – Russians and Ukrainians – still constitute more than half of the population here, with Kyrgyz and a few Dungans making up the rest.

The Orthodox church, with its blue and yellow spire, is just off to the left at the start of the village coming from Cholpon-Ata. There is also a newly built mosque with a pepper-pot minaret along this stretch of road. The village is typical of the region, but more attractive and better preserved than most, with low houses that have tidy gardens and blue window-frames. Heading east, there is a road (Lenina) that leads off to the right to a small bazaar and a threadbare *univermag* store. Taxis congregate on the corner here and *marshrutki* stop at the junction too – a regular service to Cholpon-Ata costs just 35som.

One of the monks, Irakily, survived the ransacking of the monastery at Svetly Mys and escaped here in 1916. After the revolution some Ananyevo villagers are said to have built a secret cell for him, in which he died in 1937. It was discovered 38 years later, in 1975, when another villager was being buried, that the monk's remains had not decayed at all. He was canonised by the Russian Orthodox Church in Moscow in 2000 and his body was exhumed and transferred to Bishkek's Orthodox cathedral.

SVETLY MYS This tiny hamlet is 48km from Karakol, just south of the village of Ak-Bulung (formerly Belovodsk), on the Zayachy peninsula at Lake Issyk-Kul's northeast corner. It is the site of up to eight monasteries that were founded here over a period of two thousand years and, more controversially, as the supposed burial place of the apostle Matthew. The macabre truth is that it is also perfectly possible that it was at this same Armenian monastery that the late 14th-century plague pandemic – the 'Black Death' – broke out before travelling west and east to devastate both China and Europe.

A Russian Orthodox monastery stood here in the late 19th- and early 20th-century, founded by the Tsar in 1888. It was attacked by rebels in 1916 who killed all but two of its 26 monks. The surviving pair escaped to Almaty and Ananyevo and both have since been canonised. Today the remains of the church, which was burnt down in the 1930s, has become a craft workshop, and the monks' storehouse is now a mill. The almshouse and refectory have been renovated under the directorship of Gulnara Degenbayeva, who uses the buildings as the Meerim Bulagy ('Spring Grace') children's home for their 60 or so children and 20 dedicated staff.

Svetly Mys certainly abounds in mystery. As well as the St Matthew claims, the monastery church was also once the home of an icon of the Virgin Mary that was said to cry blood, repel bullets and glow with an ethereal light when it came under

DID ST MATTHEW DIE IN KYRGYZSTAN?

Several sources hint that the remains of St Matthew are buried somewhere in the Lake Issyk-Kul area. It is thought that the apostle was on his way to India after having written the Gospel of St Matthew in Palestine, and left his homeland in AD42 to escape persecution. Other sources suggest that he may have travelled elsewhere, to Persia or even to Africa. Whatever the reality, it is perfectly possible that he made it into central Asia and Kyrgyzstan before dying here.

One Kyrgyz archaeologist, Vladimir Ploskikh, believes that he has found remains of the monastery in which St Matthew was buried. According to legend, St Matthew died while en route to India and established a number of Christian communities on his way there. A 14th-century map, which is kept in Venice and which is referred to as the 'Catalan map', mentions a place called 'Issicol' where it says there is a 'cloister of the Armenian Brothers where the body of the Apostle and Evangelist Saint Matthew is kept'. It marks a sign, shaped like a temple and decorated with a cross, on the lake's north-eastern bank with a note that says 'The Monastery of the Armenian brothers and the place where relics of St Matthew are kept'.

Aware perhaps of the risk of striking out prematurely into Dan Brown territory, Ploskikh insisted that further investigation was necessary before the theory could be proven. In September 2006, Ploskikh reported that he had discovered a medieval settlement with catacombs in the Zayachy peninsula on the northeast coast of the lake, although he admitted that the hypothesis about the discovery of the monastery 'still needed to be confirmed'. In a less cautious frame of mind, the claim to have found St Matthew's grave had already been announced four years earlier by Russian-born US photographer Sergei Melnikoff, a claim that was subsequently rejected by the Kyrgyz Academy of Sciences.

Whatever the truth of the matter it is indisputable that Svetly Mys has had religious institutions based here for almost two millennia, and has served as a place of pilgrimage throughout this period.

attack by the rebels in 1916. The icon can now be found in the Orthodox cathedral at Karakol.

A network of ancient catacombs and underground cells said to belong to a 4th- or 5th-century Armenian monastery have been discovered nearby on small lakeside peninsulas. Most of these are overgrown and filled with silt, but it is possible to explore some of them with a torch and little local expertise. **Turkestan Tours** based in Karakol are able to organise excursions to the catacombs of Svetly Mys.

In addition to the archaeological interest at Svetly Mys itself, nearby Ak-Bulung also has several unexcavated Scythian *kurgani* (tumuli), which can be seen just to the west of the village.

TYUP Tyup (or Tüp) lies at the far eastern end of the lake and is at the junction of the main road connecting Karakol with Bishkek, and another that follows the Tyup River east before stretching round the eastern limit of the Kungey Ala-Too mountains to enter Kazakhstan after Karkara. The town suffered a crushing defeat during the 1916 Kyrgyz uprising.

Today, there is little of interest in the town other than it serving as a gateway to the Karkara valley, but just to the west of the town archaeologists have discovered the ruins of what is believed to have been the 2nd-century BC settlement of Chigu

THE SUNKEN TOWNS OF ISSYK-KUL

There are around 20 locations around Lake Issyk-Kul where traces of old townships have been discovered. Some date back two millennia or so, while other settlements evolved during the peak years of the Silk Road trade from the 7th century AD onwards. Legends relate that four flooded cities lie beneath the present-day waters of the lake. In support of this, archaeological discoveries have been made that reveal dwellings and foundations beneath the lake's surface.

The sunken village of Chigu, which was the capital of the ancient Usun state in the 2nd century BC, has been discovered offshore near Sary-Bulan and the present-day town of Tyup at the eastern end of the lake. In 1956 divers exploring the underwater site discovered a range of artefacts that included fragments of pottery, a ceramic pipe, arrowheads, ironwork and human and animal remains. In addition, just offshore near the villages of Korumdy and Temirovka, and close to Grigorievka harbour, fragments of Bronze Age pots and various artefacts such as knife handles carved with figures of horses have been unearthed. Another major find was what was thought to be a square sacrificial table with legs like a woman's body, with slanted eyes, oval chin and wide nose. Another discovery has been a large round pot with twin handles whose purpose is believed to have been sacrificial. More than ten similar pots have been found in the Issyk-Kul region and they appear to date to the second half of the first millennium.

Various historic sources point towards the existence of sunken cities in the lake. Medieval Muslim recluses mention old fortresses being flooded and the existence of an island where Tamerlane is said to have imprisoned enemies in the late 14th century. A Russian merchant, Isaev, writing in the early 19th century, mentions underwater buildings being visible in the Tyup region, and around the same time the explorer Pyotr Semyonov Tyan-Shansky discovered bricks that had been carried ashore between the estuaries of the Tyup and Jergalan rivers.

Up until now, only a fraction of the underwater sites have been thoroughly investigated and the potential for future treasures to be discovered in the region is enormous.

('Red Valley') on a nearby lake peninsula. This would have been the capital of the Usun people, who were the prominent tribe in the Issyk-Kul basin at this time.

KARKARA VALLEY

This long, wide fertile valley at the far eastern end of northern Issyk-Kul has lush summer grazing that attracts herders from both sides of the Kyrgyz-Kazakh border. The valley extends west to east from the vicinity of Tyup to the Kazakh border and beyond, squeezed at its eastern end by the parallel ranges of the Kungey Ala-Too and the Central Tien Shan. Here, the Kazakhstan border is undefined, and not delimited by a physical barrier such as a mountain range or a river as elsewhere in northern Kyrgyzstan. As a consequence, herders from both sides of the border move along the valley with impunity, unhindered by artificial barriers such as political divides, and the yurts of both Kyrgyz and Kazakhs pepper the lush valley floor like odd clusters of mushrooms in summer.

The name Karkara translates as 'black crane' and comes from the delightful birds that visit the valley twice annually, touching down in June *en route* to their Siberian breeding grounds, and again in September when returning to their winter quarters in southern Africa. In early summer there is usually a well-attended **horse festival** held in the valley, attended by both Kyrgyz and Kazakh *chabana* (cowboys), in which a variety of horseback games and competitions take place, accompanied by much drinking, eating, singing and Manas-reciting. There is no fixed date for the event and it tends to be arranged fairly spontaneously by local word of mouth, so it is important to keep your ear to the ground if you wish to attend.

The village of **Ken-Suu**, halfway along the Kyrgyz section of the Karkara valley, has Saka burial mounds to the north and west of the village that date from between the 3rd century BC and the 3rd century AD; other mounds may be found close to the village of Chon-Tash further west along the valley.

It is widely believed that Tamerlane used the Karkara valley as an occasional summer base for his campaigns and at **San-Tash** ('counting stones') at the eastern end of the valley, just 20km short of the Kazakh frontier, there is a large, flat cairn of stones that is said to be composed of stones deposited by his troops. The stones were written about by the Russian explorer Pyotr Semyonov Tyan-Shansky during his 1857 expedition. The legend goes that in the late 15th century Tamerlane led a campaign into China's Ili Province from his base at Lake Issyk-Kul. The most convenient pass into Chinese territory was by way of an as yet unnamed pass to the northeast of the lake along the Karkara valley. Tamerlane ordered that each of his soldiers collect a stone from the shore of Lake Issyk-Kul and, close to the pass, they were required to deposit it on a pile before going off to battle in China. Returning to the lake later, after a long and successful campaign, the battle-weary soldiers were ordered to remove a stone from the heap, so that their leader was able to estimate overall troop losses. The fact that the pile contains such a large number of individual rocks would indicate that many of his troops must have perished in battle during the campaign. In their failure to return, the fallen had already contributed to building a monument to their own death. Although this is a highly appealing story, it is equally likely that the low cairn was created from stones that were piled up when a stone-lined burial chamber adjacent to the site was exposed.

To the south of San-Tash lies the Jergalansky canyon, with its dramatically layered rocks, and the Tyup State Zoological Reserve. Further east, just 3km short of the border at Basharin, are more burial mounds from between the 7th and 1st centuries BC, and the remains of a medieval castle that would have guarded this section of the Silk Road.

GETTING THERE Public transport in the valley is limited, most of it going only as far as Tyup, which has regular buses from Bishkek and Karakol. A couple of buses run to San-Tash daily from Karakol's bus station, via Tyup, and there are also services to the mining town of Jergalan to the south. No buses cross the border through to Kegen in Kazakhstan, so if you wish to enter Kazakhstan this way, you will need to arrange a taxi along the valley (best arranged in Karakol) from where public transport continues onwards to Almaty. A taxi organised in Karakol to take you as far as Kegen via San-Tash should cost in the region of US$50–80. If hiring a vehicle and driver it is probably best to approach San-Tash and the eastern Karkara valley by way of the minor road that goes via Novovoznesenovka rather than the longer route through Tyup, although the latter has better roads. Those taking a helicopter flight to access Khan Tengri, Peak Pobeda, or the Inylchek Glacier will need to visit the valley to reach the helipad.

WHERE TO STAY There are a few yurt camps set up in the Karkara valley where it is possible to stay. Get in touch with the Karakol Tourist Information Centre for contact details. Just over the border in Kazakhstan, **Kan Tengri**, an Almaty-based adventure travel company, have a basecamp with yurts, showers and most mod cons.

ORGANISED TOURS Several tour companies offer itineraries that encompass the Karkara valley, usually as part of a long-distance trek or bike trip to or from Kazakhstan.

Explore Worldwide www.exploreworldwide.com. Run treks through the Karkara valley from Kazakhstan, which end with a helicopter ride to the South Inylchek Glacier basecamp.
KE Adventure Travel www.keadventure.com. Offer 11-day mountain-biking excursions from Kazakhstan that include heli-biking excursions from their Karkara valley base, down-hilling from 3,500m, and culminating in a 4-day ride across the Mingtur (3,900m) and Chon Ashy

(3,820m) passes into the Kyrgyz part of the valley.
Wild Frontiers www.wildfrontiers.co.uk. Also run 15-day tours that trek through the valley before flying by helicopter to the Inylchek Glacier.
Turkestan Travel in Karakol itself (Toktogula 273, Karakol; \f 996 3922 598 96; e turkestan@karakol.kg; www.karakol.kg). Run cycling trips that begin in Karakol and incorporate the Karkara valley en route to Almaty in Kazakhstan.

TREKKING ROUTES TO AND FROM KAZAKHSTAN There are a number of possibilities in addition to following the straightforward and driveable route along the Karkara valley. These routes were popular with long-distance hikers in the Soviet era, but have become fairly neglected following independence. All require fitness, a reasonable amount of mountain experience and full camping equipment. Guides are highly recommended for the less experienced as the routes can be tricky in places, with glaciers and difficult passes to negotiate. The weather can turn suddenly and so it is essential to be fully prepared for this. It should be borne in mind that this is a border region where smuggling and banditry are not unknown: there have been many accounts of robbery along these trekking routes – another good reason to take a guide. Thankfully, theft is rare elsewhere in rural Kyrgyzstan.

One route that ends in **Grigorievka** begins at **Bolshoe Almatynskoe Lake** south of Almaty. It climbs south along the Ozerniy River to reach the Ozerniy Pass (3,507m) into Kyrgyzstan and descends to the Chong-Kemin valley. Here it briefly strikes east before climbing south past Jassyk-Kul Lake to the Ak-Suu Pass at 4,061m on the Kungey Ala-Too range, where there is a short stretch of glacier to traverse on the northern side. From here it follows the Chon Ak-Suu valley eastwards and then south to Grigorievka near Lake Issyk-Kul.

A longer and harder alternative route begins at **Medeu** outside Almaty and crosses the Bolshoe Talgarsky Pass (3,160m) before heading south along Levy Talgar River and west over the Turistov Pass (3,930m). It then continues along the valley of the Kyzylsai River to reach the Ozerniy Pass and Kyrgyzstan. The route generally takes between 4 and 6 days – add on another 2 or 3 days if the Turistov Pass alternative route is taken.

A more westerly route begins in the village of **Kokshoky** south of Almaty, and climbs up alongside the Prokhodnaya River to the 3,699m Prokhodnaya (or Almaty) Pass that marks the border with Kyrgyzstan. The route descends south past Primul Lake to the Chong-Kemin valley, from where it follows the Chong-Kemin west for a short distance before continuing south to climb up to the ridge of the Kungey Ala-Too to the Kok-Aryk Pass (3,890m). From here it descends along the Yuzhnaya Orto-Koy-Suu River to **Chong Sary-Oi** on Lake Issyk-Kul, 12km to the west of Cholpon-Ata. This route also takes around 6 days in total.

A 5–6 day route that combines elements of both of the above links **Grigorievka** with **Kokshoky** in Kazakhstan by following the Chong-Kemin valley to the Ak-Suu Pass and Jassyk-Kul Lake before climbing to the Ozerniy Pass at the frontier and down to the Bolshoe Almatynskoe Lake and Kokshoky.

A shorter, more easterly, route begins or ends in the village of **Sary-Bulak** (Balbay) at the northeast end of Lake Issyk-Kul. The route leads over the 3,274m Sary-Bulak Pass to Kazakhstan's three Kolsai lakes near the village of Saty, 110km east of Almaty. This relatively easy route can be done on horseback as well as on foot, in either direction.

Documentation One of the problems facing foreign visitors trekking across the mountains into Kyrgyzstan is that these routes are not officially designated crossing points and passports are not stamped on entry to the country, which can cause difficulties later on. Coming on an organised trek this will be taken care of, but for independent trekkers this presents a problem.

One solution for an individual or small group of trekkers is to pre-arrange for the Kyrgyz border police to stamp your visa at the end point of the trek. Coming from Kazakhstan, this can be arranged through Valentina Kayazhokov's guesthouse in Almaty (\ +7 327 2958 620; e ili@mail.ru), who will provide a guide for around US$50 a day, rent camping equipment, prepare meals for around US$10 per day, and arrange transfers at the beginning and end of the 5-day, Bolshoe Alamtynskoe Lake to Grigorievka trek. The entry stamp in your passport will be organised by the guesthouse in Karakol at the end of the trek, who will either transport the border guard to the finishing point of the trek in the Sary-Bulak gorge or simply state that you arrived that same day over the Sary-Bulak Pass and stamp it in Karakol. This service will cost between US$40–80. For further details of this service contact Marat Ainsanov (e ainsanov@yahoo.com).

Trekking companies

Bishkek A number of Bishkek travel companies can organise treks, with transfers to Almaty if necessary, although, generally you need a group of reasonable size to make it viable. One such company is **Adventure Travel** (*Mostovaya 34;* \f 911 117; e info@atkg.com).

Karakol The Karakol-based company **Turkestan** (*Toktogul 273, Karakol;* \f 996 3922 598 96; e turkestan@karakol.kg; www.karakol.kg) can arrange horses and guides for treks between Sary-Bulak and Kazakhstan's Kolsai lakes.

Russia The Russian, Omsk-based **K2 Adventures** (*http://extreme.k2.omsknet.ru*) run a 9-day expedition from Almaty to Lake Issyk-Kul between June and

September by way of the Ozerniy Pass, Jassyk-Kul Lake, Ak-Suu Pass and the Chon Ak-Suu river gorge down to Cholpon-Ata.

Kazakhstan Several Kazakhstan tour operators offer various trekking options from Almaty to Issyk-Kul, including **Tour Asia** (*Radostovtsa 359, 050060 Almaty;* ✆ *+7 3272 482 573;* f *+7 3272 497 936;* e *office@tourasia.kz*).

6

Lake Issyk-Kul South and the Central Tien Shan

KARAKOL КАРАКОЛ *Telephone code: 03922*

Of all the towns in Kyrgyzstan, Karakol tends to be the one in which the majority of foreign visitors spend the most time. This is down to the fact that as well as possessing a number of sights and monuments worth seeing, Karakol is also ideally situated for forays into the mountains to the south that beckon so tantalisingly from the town. Because of this, Karakol represents one of the focal points, perhaps *the* focal point, of Kyrgyzstan's fledgling tourist industry, and has, more than anywhere else in the country, including even Bishkek, a well-developed tourist infrastructure concerned with outdoor and adventure pursuits.

Having said that, Karakol remains low-key in the extreme; as yet, there are no brash hotels, fancy restaurants or lurid nightclubs. It is a delightfully serene sort of place, still resonant with the ghosts of 19th-century rural Russian life (along with the odd phantom from the Soviet period), and with an ambience that, paradoxically, feels both homely and comfortable *and* frontier-like.

Karakol can seem like a big village at times; apart from a park, a small bazaar, a cluster of shops and, of course, the ubiquitous Lenin statue, there is not really much of a centre. The town streets, set in a typical Russian grid plan, are long, straight and lined with poplars. Most of the houses are old, wooden 'gingerbread' houses, with neat florid gardens, picket fences and fruit-laden orchards – it might even be a Siberian village, or at least an idealised version of one.

The town has a pleasant climate, with warm summers and winters much milder than elsewhere in the region, a phenomenon that owes much to Karakol's modest altitude of 1,770m, and the moderating effect of Lake Issyk-Kul. Despite having something of a frontier feel about it – perfectly justifiable considering that Karakol was in a forbidden zone during the Soviet period – the town serves as the administrative centre for Issyk-Kul Oblast.

There is not a lot to do here; rather, it is a town to savour and absorb the atmosphere while preparing for, or recovering from, strenuous hikes in the nearby valleys. Beyond relishing the relaxed pace of the town, there is a handful of genuinely interesting sights that can be enjoyed at leisure, as well as an excellent animal market on Sundays. There are few facilities for tourists with a taste for the luxury end of the market, but for those seeking a pleasant base for hiking and adventure travel Karakol is unparalleled.

HISTORY Karakol ('black wrist' in Kyrgyz) developed as a Russian settlement in the latter part of the 19th century, having been founded as a Russian military outpost

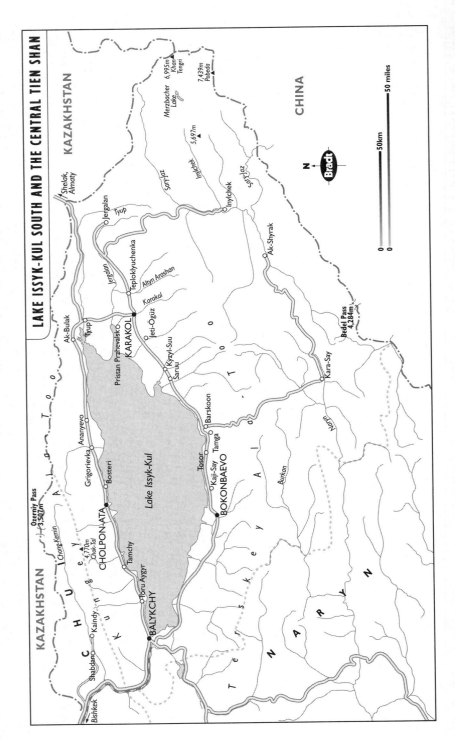

KAZAKHSTAN

KAZAKHSTAN

CHINA

6,995m
Khan
Tengri

Merzbacher
Lake

7,439m
Pobeda

5,697m

Shelek,
Almaty

Sary-Jaz

Inylchek

Jergalan

Tyup

Jergalan

Teploklyuchenka

Altyn Arashan

Karakol

Ak-Shyrak

Ak-Bulak

Tyup

KARAKOL

Pristan Przhevalsk

Jeti-Oguz

Kyzyl-Suu

Saruu

Sary-Jaz

Inylchek

Bedel Pass
4,284m

Kara-Say

Barskoon

Grigorievka

Ananyevo

Bosteri

Tosor

Kaji-Say

Tamga

BOKONBAEVO

Burkan

Lake Issyk-Kul

Naryn

Ozerniy Pass
3,507m

Chong-Kemin

4,770m
Chok-Tal

CHOLPON-ATA

Tamchy

Toru Aygyr

BALYKCHY

Kaindy

Shabdan

Bishkek

N

Bract

50km

50 miles

and administrative centre of the *uyezd* (administrative unit) in 1869. The town's population, mostly Cossacks from western Siberia, swelled considerably in the 1880s when an influx of Dungans – Chinese Muslims fleeing persecution in their home country – came to live in the town. Later influxes brought Tatars, Uyghurs, Ukrainians and more Russians to engage in agriculture and cattle-breeding. By the beginning of the 20th century the town had three breweries, seven soap factories, two saw mills, 12 flour mills, two churches, nine mosques, seven schools, a military hospital and over 1,000 houses.

The Russian explorer Nikolai Przhevalsky first came here in the 1860s and returned again in 1888 suffering from typhoid – or possibly TB – from which he died. Today there is a museum to his memory on the spot where his house once stood – 10km from the town centre, close to the lake at Pristan Przhevalsk. To honour the explorer, the town was renamed Przhevalsk by the Tsar, but under instructions from Lenin it reverted to its original name in 1921. It returned to being called Przhevalsk once more in 1939, this time at the command of Stalin, who was generally less sensitive than Lenin to local mores. This time the name stuck and the town continued to be known as Przhevalsk until Kyrgyzstan became independent of the Soviet Union in 1991.

During the Soviet period the town became home to a considerable number of scientists and military experts, as Lake Issyk-Kul and the secret submarine and torpedo-testing base at the lake's Mikhailovka inlet were just a few kilometres away. Since independence the town's population has, as elsewhere in the country, seen hard times, although the Russian population is on the whole a little less desperate to leave than it is in the rest of Kyrgyzstan.

GETTING THERE AND AROUND
Regular **buses** run to and from Bishkek's West Bus Station between early morning and mid afternoon, taking between 5 and 7 hours. Night buses also run to Bishkek and depart in the evening between 20.00–23.00. Most of these travel along the north shore via Cholpon-Ata and Balykchy. There are more limited services along the southern route to Balykchy and Bishkek via Bokonbaevo, which is a slower route to the capital. The bus fare to Bishkek is around 200som. Heading south to Kochkor or Naryn requires a change at Balykchy as there are no direct services. There are no buses to Almaty by way of the Karkara valley, although there may be occasional services that reach the Kazakhstan capital via Bishkek.

The **long-distance bus station** is at the northern end of town, a 20-minute walk or 50som taxi ride from the centre. There are also minibuses that ply between the bus station and Jakshylyk bazaar. Other limited bus services from this station run along the southern shore as far as Bokonbaevo via Tamga and Barskoon.

Minibuses leave from in front of the long-distance bus station and run along the same routes as the buses. They leave when full and are a little faster than buses, typically costing around 300som to Bishkek.

Share taxis to Cholpon-Ata, Balykchy and Bishkek leave from the same place and charge about twice the bus fare.

For most destinations along the southern shore there is the small **southern bus station** in the southwest of town, next to the municipal stadium, a 5-minute walk southwest of Jakshylyk bazaar. This has regular bus and minibus services to Kyzyl-Suu, Barskoon, Tamga and Bokonbaevo.

Local bus services to destinations like Pristan Przhevalsk and Jeti-Ögüz leave from a stand just northeast of Jakshylyk bazaar.

Taxis can be found outside Jakshylyk bazaar or at the bus stands. Trips around the town cost anything between 30–70som and whole- or half-day hire can be negotiated for excursions beyond the town limits. As always, establish a price before getting in. The old saying that, in the former Soviet Union, every car is a taxi

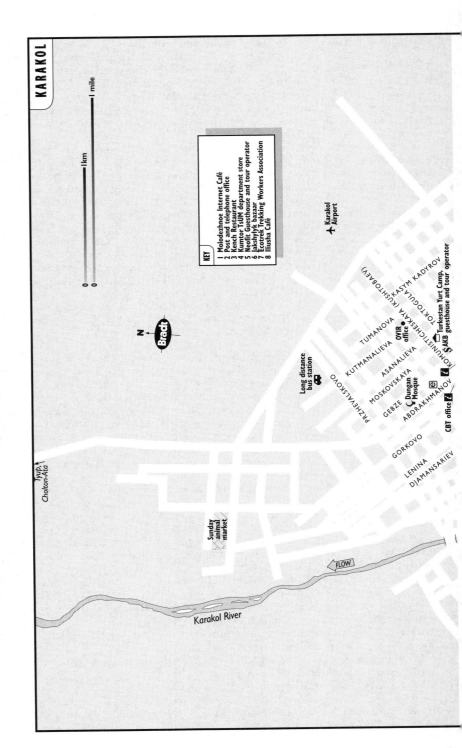

KARAKOL

KEY
1 Molodezhnoe Internet Café
2 Post and telephone office
3 Kench Restaurant
4 Kumtor TsUM department store
5 Neofit Guesthouse and tour operator
6 Jakshylyk bazaar
7 Ecotrek Trekking Workers Association
8 Illusha Café

1 km
1 mile

N
Bradt

Karakol River

FLOW

Sunday animal market

TyuP, Cholpon-Ata

Long distance bus station

PRZHEVALSKOVO

GORKOVO

LENINA
DJAMANSARIEV

ABDRAKHMANOV

GEBZE

Dungan Mosque

MOSKOVSKAYA

ASANALIEVA

KUTMANALIEVA

TUMANOVA

OVIR office

KOMUNISTICHESKAYA (KUSHTOLTOBAEV)

TOKTOGULA KASYM KADYROV

Turkestan Yurt Camp, guesthouse and tour operator

AKB

CBT office

Karakol Airport

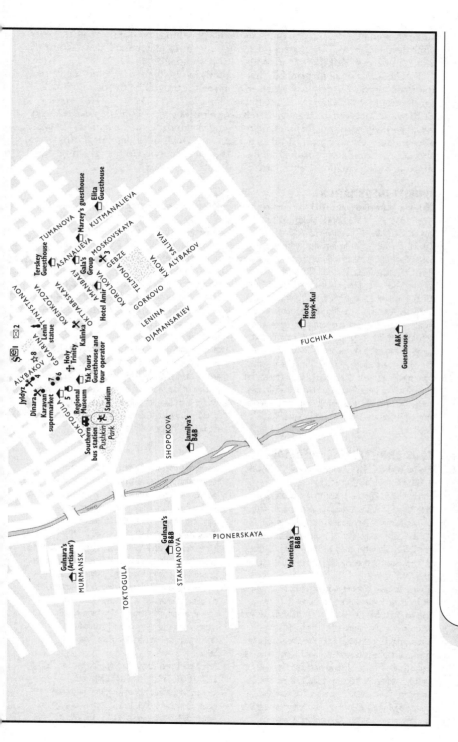

Elita
Guesthouse

Marzey's guesthouse

KUTMANALIEVA

TUMANOVA

Terskey
Guesthouse

ASANALIEVA

MOSKOVSKAYA

Gala's
Group

GEBZE

Hotel Amir

ALYBAKOV

KROVA

SALIEVA

KOROLOVA

TELMONA

OKTIABRSKAYA

KOENOZOVA

AMANBAEV

GORKOVO

TYNYSTANOV

LENINA

Lenin
statue

Kalinka

DJAMANSARIEV

GAGARINA

Hotel
Issyk-Kul

ALYBAKOV

FUCHIKA

A&K
Guesthouse

Jyldyz

Dinara

Karavan
supermarket

Holy
Trinity

Yak Tours
Guesthouse and
tour operator

Regional
Museum

Stadium

TOKTOGULA

Southern
bus station

Pushkin
Park

SHOPOKOVA

Jamilya's
B&B

Gulnara's
(Artisans')

MURMANSK

Gulnara's
B&B

STAKHANOVA

TOKTOGULA

PIONERSKAYA

Valentina's
B&B

certainly applies here, and you can basically flag anything down at the roadside, state your destination and negotiate a price. If you want to telephone a taxi, **Salam** (🖀 222 22) or **Issyk-Kul** (🖀 161) are both reliable choices.

Karakol has a small **airport** but this currently has no flights. It would appear that the main airport to serve Lake Issyk-Kul in the future will be the one ear-marked for development at Tamchy on the north shore.

Bicycle hire can be arranged at **Karakol Bikes** (🖀 269 39; e karakolbikes@ gmail.com) where mountain bikes, helmets and cycling gear can be rented. They can also organise the transport of bikes to passes for downhill rides. All profits go to support the training needs of students at the guide school. Contact them through the Tourist Information Centre or CBT.

TOURIST INFORMATION

ℹ Tourist Information Centre (TIC) Abdrakhmanov 130; 🖀 234 25, 🖀 513 56; e info@issyk-kul-info.kg. ☉ 09.00–17.00 Mon–Fri, 09.00–15.00 Sat. Karakol is privileged in having what must be the only official tourist information centre in the country (apart, of course, from what the CBT organisation has to offer). The office here, which opened in 2003 with EU development funding, has a wealth of information, brochures & listings, as well as books, postcards & maps for sale. They can give advice on trekking in the region & help organise accommodation in yurt camps & homestays. As tourism is in its infancy in the country, even here in Karakol, it helps if you have specific requests & questions to ask rather than just coming in for a general chat. Very usefully, they stock the 1:200,000 topographic maps of the region that otherwise are only available in Bishkek at GeoID.

ℹ Community Based Tourism (CBT) Abdrakhmanov 123; 🖀 550 00; m 0502 203 087; e cbtkarakol@ rambler.ru. ☉ 09.00–16.00 Mon–Fri, 10.00–14.00 Sat–Sun. Just down from the Tourist Information Centre on the other side of the road, this is another excellent source of information about the region. Often staffed by working guides at w/ends, as well as the local co-ordinator, Natalya Ovcharova. You can get a good insight into the various hiking options in the Karakol region & beyond by talking with them. CBT Karakol offers a wide variety of tours that range from a 4hr city tour by car to 6-day guided treks through the Terskey Ala-Too, from Jeti-Ögüz to Altyn Arashan. They are happy to book accommodation & offer advice on trekking without any pressure to use their own services. Naturally, they will arrange everything from guides, porters & equipment should you require it, & can arrange border permits for the Inylchek region within a week.

TOUR AND TREKKING OPERATORS

Alp-Tur Issyk-Kul 61/1 Kirpichnyi zavod; 🖀 205 48; f 501 63; e khanin@infotel.kg, e khanin2003@mail.ru. Run by a Russian called Igor Khanin, this small company mostly deals with visiting Russians. They have a tent camp in the Karakol park at the base of some excellent mountain hikes. They also offer treks to Khan Tengri basecamp & Kazakhstan, & climbing expeditions to the central Tien Shan peaks.

Ecotrek Trekking Workers Association Toktogul (corner of Lenina & Toktogul); 🖀 511 15; e karakol@rambler.ru. ☉ 08.00–17.00 daily. Located next door to the Zarina café, close to Jakshylyk bazaar, the Ecotrek Trekking Workers Association are a collective of guides, porters, cooks & horsemen who can provide a range of services to trekkers that include guiding, yurt accommodation, horse hire & transport. Their stated aims are to increase the standard of living & level of qualification of trekking workers, develop sustainable tourism & promote

ecotourism. The average cost of one of their recommended guides is US$20 per day including food, & they can organise anything from day treks in the Altyn Arashan valley to 2-week helicopter-supported expeditions to the Inylchek Glacier.

Neofit Jamansariev 166; 🖀 206 50, 🖀 257 37; f 219 02; e neofit@issyk-kul.kg, neofit.1-kul@rambler.ru; www.neofit.kg. Neofit is a Karakol company that has worked in the tourist industry since 1996 & that is able to organise trekking, cycling & mountaineering expeditions anywhere in the Issyk-Kul region & beyond. It can also arrange city tours & cultural excursions. Neofit also runs a guesthouse in the town that is popular with trekkers (see *Where to Stay*, below).

Tour Khan Tengri Kasym Kadyrov 55, Karakol; 🖀 265 59; 🖀/f 272 69; e travelkg@blk.ru; www.travelkg.narod.ru/company.htm. This Karakol-based company maintains a basecamp at At-Jailoo.

Turkestan Travel Toktogul 273; 🖀 264 89; 🖀/f 598

96; e turkestan@karakol.kg; www.karakol.kg. A highly regarded & well-established travel company based in Karakol, Turkestan have a wide range of tours & treks on offer, including treks to Merzbacher Lake, the Inylchek Glacier & Khan Tengri basecamp. They can organise climbing expeditions to Khan Tengri & Pobeda peaks, cycling tours, winter ski programmes in the Karakol valley & even helicopter flights over the Inylchek Glacier. They also share a yurt camp in the Kazakh part of the Karkara valley with the Kazakh operator Khan Tengri. Cultural tours can be arranged too, such as trips to see eagle-hunting displays or Kyrgyz musical events. Prices are not cheap but the service is certainly highly professional. Turkestan also has a yurt camp in the centre of Karakol that is open to all-comers, whether booking a service or not (see *Where to stay*, below). **Yak Tours** Gagarina 10; ℄ 569 01; e yak-tour@ infotel.kg. Yak tours is run by Valentin Derevanko, an ethnic Russian who in a former life worked as a motorcycle instructor in the Soviet army. Valentin also has a lifetime of trekking experience & is an institution in Karakol trekking circles. He runs a couple of standard trips in the Altyn Arashan valley, which are firmly at the cheap & cheerful end of the market, & you tend to get what you pay for. Valentin is happy to deal with impecunious hikers on a tight budget & can rent hiking equipment & provide transport to & from trail heads. As well as running the town's only backpacker hostel (see *Where to stay*, below) he also has a basic trekker's lodge in the Altyn Arashan valley, from where he runs a couple of standard treks. He can provide transport to & from the lodge in his jeep most days for around 300som. Valentin is very fond of engines & old vehicles like UAZ jeeps & Russian motorcycles, & can probably help if you are having problems with your own vehicle.

WHERE TO STAY A few years ago there were few options in town, apart from the Hotel Issyk-Kul just outside the town (see below) and the tawdry, state-run pile of the Hotel Karakol on Gebze, close to the university, which was well-known for having alcohol and prostitution problems, and which has since closed for business. To replace these lacklustre institutions are a number – perhaps two dozen – cosy CBT-organised homestays spread around the town, along with a few more options that exist outside the CBT remit.

Hotel Amir Amanbaev 78; ℄/f 51 315; m 0502 693 215; e reservation@hotelamir.kg; www.hotelamir.kg This is a colourfully painted, brand new hotel built in 2006 that has good facilities & nicely furnished rooms. Facilities include a conference room, a sun terrace & a good restaurant that serves Kyrgyz & European dishes. The location is quiet & the hotel is proving to be a popular choice for visiting tour groups. $$$

A&K Guesthouse (4 rooms) Fuchika 121; ℄ 522 88. A small, comfortable guesthouse that is used by some tour companies visiting Karakol. Facilities include a sauna & swimming pool. $$$ *with HB*.

Hotel Issyk-Kul** (11 dbls, 6 'lux' rooms) Fuchika 38; ℄ 207 10, ℄ 207 11; f 590 00. This old Soviet hotel is set in wooded grounds, 3km from the town centre to the southeast, near the hippodrome. One of the hotel's 2 blocks has been requisitioned & refurbished by the government, while the other is in private ownership. $$$ *with HB*.

Marzey's Guesthouse (4 rooms) Korolkova 86; ℄ 555 54, ℄ 555 55; e marzeysguesthouse@yahoo.com; www.geocities.com/marzeysguesthouse/default.htm. A guesthouse run by Marzey, an Iranian woman married to a Swiss, which has a lovely flower garden & is in a fairly central location. Marzey speaks English & has founded an organisation in the town called Ladybird that supports the education of local poor children. $$

Neofit (12 rooms) Jamansariev 166; ℄ 206 50, ℄ 257 30, ℄ 257 37; f 219 02; e neofit@issyk-kul.kg; www.neofit.kg. A centrally located guesthouse, run by the trekking company of the same name, that has clean, simple rooms — mostly with private toilets & TV. Sauna & restaurant. $$

Turkestan yurt camp & guesthouse (8 yurts, 5 rooms) Toktogul 273; ℄ 598 96. As well as the yurt camp that shares 6 toilets & 2 showers, this camp run by Turkestan Travel also has a small guesthouse. There are 2 yurts selling handicrafts. With internet access, car park, climbing wall, garden & a place for campfires to recreate that genuine *jailoo* ambience. Its very central location is also a bonus. Sometimes folklore concerts & *manaschi* recitals are staged here. $$ *without b/fast, whole yurt* $$$ *(maximum number 5), bed in a shared yurt without bedding* $ (they claim to distribute guests between empty yurts before asking them to share). *Camping is also possible*, $.

Yak Tours Guesthouse (10 rooms) Gagarina 10; ℄ 569 01; e yak-tour@infotel.kg. This place, run by

6

Valentin Derevanko & his wife, is the closest thing that Karakol has to a backpacker's hostel. There are various colourful & eccentrically decorated rooms of different sizes scattered throughout the house & comfort is partly determined by how many people are staying there – in a crush, some 'rooms' are just separated by curtains. The rooms at the top of the house are said to be nice but a bit spooky. There is just 1 bathroom for the use of guests. The food here is claimed to be the best in town, which is perhaps an exaggeration, but it is certainly good. Tents can be pitched in the garden. $, with meals $$.

CBT homestays There are many of these in town and a full list can be provided by either the CBT office or the TIC. The ones listed below are all known to be excellent, but this should not preclude using others not listed. Standards are generally very high, and all come recommended, although location may be a factor in deciding which to choose as some homestays are a considerable distance from the centre (all $–$$).

🏠 **Elita Guesthouse** Kutmanaliev 56; ☎ 501 50
🏠 **Jamilya's B&B** (2 dbls & 1 sgl) Shopokova 34b; ☎ 430 19. A popular homestay about 20mins walk from the centre; close to the river.
🏠 **Gala's Group** Moskovskaya 77; ☎ 511 55; m 0502 653 224; e galas_group@yahoo.com
🏠 **Gulnara's** Murmansk 114; ☎ 501 71, ☎ 202 91; e Kork-karakol@mail.ru. Gulnara's is also sometimes known as the Artisans' B&B & has just 3 very comfortable rooms, modern bathroom, plenty of interesting art on the walls & excellent cooking.
🏠 **Gulnara's B&B** Stakhanova 67; ☎ 555 44; m 0543 943 622, m 0502 433 431; e gulnara.2808@list.ru. Another 'Gulnara's', this time

at the comfortable home of Gulnara Mamyralieva, who is also an excellent cook.
🏠 **Valentina's B&B** Pionerskaya 3; ☎ 415 83; m 0502 748 003; e olga_karakol@mail.ru
🏠 **Terskey Guesthouse** Asanalieva 44; ☎ 262 68; m 0502 801 411; www.teskey.narod.ru. This is a very popular guesthouse because of its reasonably central location & also because of word-of-mouth recommendations. This place gets filled quickly in season & sometimes guests are diverted to a nearby annex. Its reputation is certainly justified, with spotless facilities, a flowery garden & a charming host family. Taalai Janybekov speaks excellent English & is a considerate host, full of good advice; his father has a car that can be hired for excursions.

✘ **WHERE TO EAT** Most of the guesthouses will provide evening meals on request, and this is often the cheapest, most convenient and tastiest option. For snacks in the daytime there are several places near Jakshylyk bazaar that produce freshly baked *samsi* to take away, and there a number of cafés in this part of the town. The bazaar itself has a good choice of fresh vegetables and fruit, especially in late summer, and a few food stalls selling Kyrgyz staples and some Dungan dishes. For Dungan food in more formal surroundings Valentin of Yak Tours can arrange a feast in a Dungan house for around US$10 per head.

✘ **Kench** Telmona, just east of junction with Gebze. ⏱ 11.00–01.00. In the southeast part of town near Victory Park & not too far from the Terskey & Marzey guesthouses, this is considered to be one of the best restaurants in town. Indoor dining room & covered outdoor patio with fluorescent lights, English menu with a wide range of beef, chicken & continental dishes. The service is efficient & the food reasonable. $$$
✘ **Kalinka** Abdrakhmanov/Koenkozova; ☎ 277 77. Good food served in a fancy Siberian-style log cabin near the university. Kalinka serves a wide variety of Russian dishes, including salads, borsch & blini. $$–$$$

✘ **Dinara** Lenina 160. Big purple arches lead into a courtyard with dining booths separated by purple curtains. Kyrgyz, Russian & a few Dungan dishes are served. $$
🍺 **Kumtor Café** Toktogul. To the right of the steps leading up into the TsUM building, this café has an outdoor pavilion in summer serving draught beer. $$
✘ **Jyldyz** Alybakov. Just around the corner from the TsUM Kumtor department store. This Kyrgyz restaurant has *shashlyk* & the usual dishes, & separate booths for diners. $$
✘ **Zarina** Toktogul. A central café-restaurant close to the bazaar with an English menu & a reasonably varied menu of Russian & continental dishes. $$

☐ **Edem** Toktogul. This is a sit-down place for tea & cake next to the Karavan supermarket & opposite the bazaar. Inexpensive, but service comes with a bit of a scowl. $
✗ Fakir Toktogul. A Kyrgyz restaurant next door to

TsUM serving the usual central Asian standards. Russian menu only. $
✗ Uyut Jakshylyk bazaar. A bright green, 2-storey building at the southeast corner of the bazaar that serves standard dishes at low prices. $

NIGHTLIFE Karakol is not known for its nightlife. By 20.00 the town's streets are unnervingly quiet, as if most people have gone to bed – most probably have. Like Bishkek, the streets are dark and poorly lit at night, with the trees blocking any light from the moon or the odd streetlamp. In fact, Karakol is actually darker than Bishkek so be careful at night as, although muggings and attacks may be uncommon, they are not unknown.

For those hedonists for whom a pot of tea and a chat at their homestay is not enough, there are the following haunts frequented by Karakol's youth.

☆ **Arizona** Abdrakhmanov (behind the University's Economics faculty). A discotheque that is popular with young locals. There is no alcohol served, so most hit the vodka on the street outside before entering.

☆ **Iliusha café** Toktogul, just opposite TsUM. Karaoke & dancing, with Turkish & Russian music, on the café's balcony.

SHOPPING **Jakshylyk bazaar** in the town centre has meat, fruit and vegetable stalls, as well as stationery, clothes and household appliances. Facing the bazaar on Toktogul is the **Karavan** supermarket, with an enormous selection of loose biscuits and other trekking staples. **Kumtor TsUM**, just north of the bazaar on Toktogul, is Karakol's main department store and stocks more or less everything that you might reasonably wish to find, like household goods, camera accessories and electrical appliances. For souvenirs and Kyrgyz handicrafts there is the art gallery at the southeast corner of the bazaar. The Tourist Information Centre has postcards and a small selection of handicrafts.

COMMUNICATIONS

Post The main **post office** is at Gebze, opposite the park (⊕ *08.00–17.00 Mon–Fri, 12.00–13.00 Sat, closed Sun*).

Telephones The **Kyrgyz Telecom** office is next door to the post office at Gebze 126. Book international calls at the counter and say how long you want. Calls cost 25som per minute to Europe. Dial the international code plus the number, then 3 when the call is answered. **IP telephony** is offered at one of the internet places on Toktogul close to the Molodezhnoe Internet Café.

Internet Internet cafés tend to come and go with great rapidity. At the time of research the following options were available.

☐ **Favorit** Tynstanov 19; ✆ 225 15
☐ **Molodezhnoe Internet Café** Toktogul 263: ✆ 510 51. Opposite the central park & just around the

corner from the TIC, this is the fastest & most popular internet café in town & there are sometimes queues. Good connection for 40som per hr.

There is another internet café on the same block that also offers IP telephone calls and another near to the Dungan mosque on Abdrakhmanov.

The **Kyrgyz Telecom** office (*Gebze 126;* ✆ *510 20*) also has slow internet access for 30som per hour.

MONEY

$ **AKB Bank** Toktogul; ☎ 537 45. Northeast of the park, this bank will change travellers' cheques for 3% commission, & cash advances on VISA or MasterCard are also possible.

There are several kiosks that will change dollars, euros (and possibly pounds sterling) along Toktogul, just south of the bank.

RED TAPE For **visa extensions** visit the office of **OVIR** (*Kyshtobaev 146a, room 114;* ⊕ *closed weekends & Mon*) where a 30-day extension should be relatively simple to arrange for a few hundred som.

Border zone permits, necessary for anywhere within 50km of the Chinese border – ie: for the Inylchek Glacier or the peaks of the Central Tien Shan – are trickier to arrange and are best done through a travel agency in advance. Locally, they may take at least a week to arrange. CBT claim that they can organise them within 7 days, whereas a company like Turkestan can probably do this more quickly, within a few days.

WHAT TO SEE AND DO Karakol is a spread-out sort of place without much of an obvious focus for a centre. The town centre, such as it is, is the area immediately around Jakshylyk bazaar and the central square south of the university that has stands of pine trees, some broken benches, a scattering of memorials and a statue of Soviet hero, Yusup Abdrakhmanov, 1901–38, who was the First Secretary of the Kyrgyz Communist Party from 1924–25. Another Soviet hero, Lenin, stands nearby at the junction of Gebze and Tynystanova.

Other than the obvious sights below, much of Karakol is pleasant enough to wander at will and enjoy the wooden Russian domestic architecture that characterises much of the town. In particular, the area along Lenina and Gorkovo, southeast of the Holy Trinity Cathedral, is a rewarding quarter to explore.

Holy Trinity Cathedral This wooden Russian Orthodox church dates back to 1895 when it was constructed to serve the spiritual needs of the new influx of Russian settlers in the town. It replaced an earlier stone structure that was destroyed in an earthquake in 1890 (this, in turn, had replaced a yurt, which had been the first place of Orthodox worship in the town).

The church, made almost entirely of wood on a stone foundation, was stripped of its five green domes during the Soviet period, when it also suffered the ignominy of being used as a dance club in the 1930s. Reconstruction began in the 1960s and it was re-consecrated as a place of worship in 1991, and again in 1997.

Today the church, under the auspices of Father Vladimir, oversees the entire Issyk-Kul Russian Orthodox diocese. The church's greatest treasure is an icon of the Virgin that came from the monastery of Svety Mys near Tyup, where the monks were savagely murdered in 1916 on the eve of the revolution. The icon is said to have wept tears and blood and repelled the bullets of rebel soldiers (see *Svety Mys*, page 151). For true Old Russian atmosphere, the best time for a visit is Sunday mornings before 10.00, when the choir will be singing and the air is redolent with incense and candle wax.

Dungan (Chinese) Mosque Like the Holy Trinity Cathedral this place of worship is also built of wood and, at first glance, this brightly painted, red, green and yellow building resembles a pagoda or a Mongolian Buddhist temple more than it does a typical Islamic building. The similarity with Buddhist structures is no accident as the Dungans who built it – ethnically Chinese but with a Buddhist past before conversion to Islam – unconsciously incorporated a great amount of Buddhist symbolism into its design, adding details like conch shells and the Buddhist wheel of life as well as representations of dragons and phoenixes that reflect the unmistakeable influence of Chinese mythology.

The mosque was built by the Dungan community in the years 1907–10, using a Chinese architect working with a team of 20 artisans. It was constructed entirely without nails. There is a low powder-blue minaret and, similar to many mosques in Xinjiang and Muslim China, there is a veranda either side of the entrance.

The mosque was closed down by the Soviet authorities in 1933 but then reopened for worship in 1943. These days the mosque no longer serves the Dungan community exclusively and is attended as much by Kyrgyz as it is by Chinese Muslims.

Regional History Museum This museum houses a collection spread throughout seven rooms that has a number of Scythian artefacts, including some large bronze pots, artefacts of traditional Kyrgyz culture such as leather *kumys* containers and musical instruments, and a display of Kyrgyz felt art and *shyrdaks*. There are also black and white photographs of old-time Karakol that detail the colonial Russian and Soviet history of the region, and a section on the petroglyphs found in the Issyk-Kul region. There is also the requisite display of stuffed indigenous wildlife (*Jamansariev 164;* ⊕ *09.00–17.00 Mon–Fri, 10.00–16.00 Sat–Sun; 40som*).

Sunday animal market This is well worth attending if you are in Karakol on a Sunday, and is a weekly event that is worth planning your trip around to some extent. The livestock market (*skotniy bazaar* in Russian) takes place at the northern edge of town each Sunday. Take a taxi or flag down a car to reach it (30som) and get there reasonably early, as it tends to start at around dawn and is all over by 10.00.

The market is a vast concentration of horse, sheep and cattle, but mostly the first two, which are traded in two separate enclosures. Pigs are sold here too, but these are kept separate from the main market animals because of their proscription by Islam. Kyrgyz come from all over the region to visit the market, and to buy, sell and socialise, sometimes travelling for days with their livestock to reach it.

Whether you're interested in the animals or not, the weekly bazaar gives a good insight into the culture and the livelihood of the people here. Scattered among stands of tightly tethered, complaining livestock are Kyrgyz who have come to examine and bargain for the goods on offer, trying out horses with a short test trot or assessing the weight of the fat on the behind of a fat-tailed sheep with their palms. This is Kygyz rural life in its unadorned form and here, as much as anywhere in the region, will you see wizened Methuselahs with straggly beards and white *kalpaks* going about their everyday business.

The market, which is remarkably calm and dignified given all the activity going on, is as much a country fair as it is a place of commerce. It is a great place to wander, take photographs and watch the morning unfold: it is also a good place to buy a horse or a sheep if you know what you are doing (take a sympathetic local along for advice).

Those who have visited the Sunday market in Kashgar, across the border in Xinjiang, may find the scale of the Karakol market a little disappointing, but there is certainly nowhere else in Kyrgyzstan where such old-style commerce can be witnessed in such a hassle-free, tourist-friendly manner.

Pushkin Park Karakol's largest park lies in the southeast sector of the town next to the stadium. It's a leafy expanse of grass and woodland that is a pleasant place to stroll or sit and read. The park has a monument of a border guard with a dog, which is dedicated to 11 border guards who were killed during a cross-border clash with illegal immigrants in 1926. The park also has a stone memorial to Red Army soldiers who died in battle against White Russians in 1919.

AROUND KARAKOL

PRZHEVALSKY MEMORIAL This memorial park and museum to the Russian explorer who gave the town its earlier name lies just outside Karakol near the village of Pristan Przhevalsk, 9km to the north on the shores of Lake Issyk-Kul. The museum stands on the same site as the house he had built for himself close to the lake. The monument and small chapel that stand here were built on the site of his grave in 1894, just six years after his death. In 1957, the Soviet authorities constructed the museum and gardens that stand here today, removing and desecrating the best part of a village graveyard to do so. Quite fittingly, this

NIKOLAI PRZHEVALSKY 1839–88

Nikolai Mikhailovich Przhevalsky was born in Smolensk, Russia in 1839 to a noble Belarusian family. He studied both in Smolensk and at the military academy in St Petersburg before spending a period as a geography teacher at the Warsaw Military School in 1864.

As well as a taste for military life, Przhevalsky also had a fascination with Asia and exploration; an interest that had been with him since childhood, inspired by contemporary European explorers like David Livingstone. His first exploratory trip to Asia was sponsored by the Russian Geographical Society in 1867, when he was sent to Irkutsk in Siberia to investigate the highlands of the Ussuri River. This expedition opened the door for four subsequent trips to inner Asia that heralded a new era in the geographical exploration of a region that until then was virtually unknown to the West.

In exploration terms, Przhevalsky's main obsession lay in reaching Lhasa, the mysterious and forbidden capital of Tibet. Between 1870 and 1873 he traversed the Gobi Desert to Peking, before exploring the Yangtze and crossing into Tibet itself. In his third expedition of 1876–77 he travelled through the region of Chinese Turkestan, rediscovering Lake Lop Nor, which had not been seen by another European since Marco Polo's visit in the 13th century. On his fourth journey in 1879–80 Przhevalsky visited China's Qaidam basin before traversing the Tien Shan range to Tibet once more. Finally, between 1883 and 1885, he crossed the Gobi once more to reach the eastern Tien Shan, before journeying back to Koko Nor and west to Lake Issyk-Kul.

Despite such extensive explorations, Przhevalsky's interests lay beyond that of mere geography, and he was as much obsessed with military and strategic matters as he was with scientific exploration. For Przhevalsky, as well as his sponsors, the explorer's responsibility was political as much as it was scientific and he relished his military role, viewing himself as a servant of the Russian state rather than as any sort of independent spirit.

While he was undoubtedly a dedicated geographer and biologist with a genuine scientific interest in the terrain he crossed, he chose his destinations primarily for the sake of military reconnaissance: the three areas that he explored most thoroughly – Chinese Turkestan, Mongolia and northern Tibet – were all strategically important to the Russian crown. This was at a time of imperial expansion, when the Great Game was being played to the full, and when Britain and Russia competed for dominance of the central Asian world that lay between their two respective empires.

Despite his military brief, Przhevalsky made many zoological discoveries during these journeys, discovering native species of horse and gazelle that were subsequently named

considerable slight to local sensibilities was carried out to commemorate a man who could hardly be described as a loyal friend of the Kyrgyz people (see box, *Nikolai Przhevalsky*, below).

The **grave** and **monument** stand at the north end of the park overlooking the waters of the Mikhailovka inlet. The park is landscaped with bright flower beds and planted with a variety of trees native to the region, like Tien Shan spruce. The monument itself, comprising 21 pieces of stone sculpted to form a precipitous mountain peak with a spread-winged eagle on top, is a popular spot for wedding parties to congregate for photo shoots. The inlet that lies beyond, of which you get teasing glimpses through the railings, is one of the few zones of modern-day Kyrgyzstan that remains firmly off-limits to visitors – it was once part of the old Soviet top-secret military zone that included the nearby villages of Mikhailovka and Lipenka. Now that the Soviet navy's torpedo-testing facility has closed down for good, it would seem that there is little that requires military secrecy here any more.

after him – Przhevalsky's horse (*Equus caballus przewalski*) and Przhevalsky's gazelle (*Procapra przewalski*) – as well as stumbling upon a wild population of Bactrian camels. He was equally industrious in his botanical work, bringing back a total of 16,000 specimens of 1,700 species to St Petersburg over the 21-year period of his five expeditions.

His fifth journey to central Asia brought about his downfall. After drinking infected water from the Chui River on a hunting trip he fell ill with typhus. Worsening in health, he elected to return to the shores of Lake Issyk-Kul to die. He passed away in a military hospital at Karakol without ever having achieved his greatest dream – to enter Lhasa. He had come close but his efforts to reach the Tibetan capital had always been thwarted, by bad weather, by hostile rumour and now by death itself.

During the Soviet period Przhevalsky was lauded as a tolerant explorer who had nothing but respect for the peoples of the region, but a closer reading suggests that this was hardly the truth of the matter. Przhevalsky may have been a brilliant geographer, naturalist and explorer but as a 'man of his time' he was sadly lacking in some of the human qualities that we take for granted in the modern age. Despite spending many years in their presence, he held a low opinion of many of the people that he travelled among, despising the indigenous people of the region – Kyrgyz, Mongolians, Chinese, Tibetans and Uyghur – as lowly beings that required the enlightenment of Russian colonialism to render them half-decent. It was his dislike and distrust of the Chinese in particular that led him to try and persuade the Russian Tsar to go to war with China, as he sincerely believed that only Russian colonisation could redeem them as a race.

It should not be forgotten that his journeys took place at a time when a belief in Social Darwinism was prevalent, and when most Europeans considered themselves to be morally and intellectually superior to other races. He was not alone in this: Pyotr Semyonov Tyan-Shansky himself, president of the Russian Geographical Society and an enthusiastic sponsor of Przhevalsky's expeditions, claimed that 'scientific material is necessary for the definitive conquest of these (inner Asian) lands for culture and civilisation'.

In his last book, *Ot Kyakhty*, Przhevalsky maintains that he had been kind to the local population at first, but that it was their unending trickery and stupidity that drove him to cruelty. Regarding this, he claims: 'only the experience of later expeditions convinced me that three things are necessary for the success of long and dangerous journeys in Central Asia – money, a gun and a whip'.

The view along the inlet just offers up a glimpse of cranes and warehouses, a boat or two, and a few wooden *dachas*.

The **museum** (🕐 *09.00–12.00, 13.00–17.00 daily; 50som*), near the park entrance in a neoclassical building topped by another sculpted eagle, has a large globe and an enormous 3D map of central Asia that shows the routes of Przhevalsky's various journeys. The accompanying displays detail the ways in which his passion for exploration was aroused, and how he managed to organise his trips to central Asia and beyond (by doing a bit of spying on the side). There are lots of his letters, photos and books, and also some excellent line drawings of the scenery and sights encountered during his explorations by his second-in-command. Labels are mostly in Russian and Kyrgyz but there are some that are in English. A curiosity of the museum, which should be pointed out to you by your guide, is the wall mural that changes perspective according to the viewer's position.

This would not be a proper museum, of course, without a few stuffed animals, and there are a few dioramas with representations of the region's birdlife that include griffon vultures and a golden eagle. There is also a rather moth-eaten specimen of the native Mongolian horse named after the explorer himself: the short-legged Przhevalsky horse.

The cost of admission includes a guided tour, which may be in Russian, English or, more likely, a combination of the two. Guides are friendly and will gladly answer questions, although they might not appreciate being diverted too much away from their rehearsed spiel. To reach the Przhevalsky museum and memorial from Karakol either take a minibus marked '**ДАЧИ**' (*dachi*) from the bus stand near the central bazaar or negotiate a taxi. A taxi there and back, with an hour or so of waiting time, should cost between 250–300som.

KARAKOL VALLEY This stunning valley lies immediately south of Karakol along the river of the same name that passes through the town. The valley has a ski base that is visited by local and Russian skiers in winter, while in summer it is a popular area for trekkers and campers. There are no villages anywhere along the valley, nor any facilities for tourism other than a summer tent camp, but this makes it all the more desirable as an ideal location for independent campers who bring all they need with them.

The Karakol valley has been awarded national park status so there is an entrance fee (250som) to pay at the entrance gate. Near here, a track leads up to the left along the course of the Kashka-Suu tributary to reach the ski base. The dirt road continues along the river to reach a wooden bridge across the river, where the track continues along the valley with the river to the left. The steep slopes here are covered with stands of spruce and the distinctively pyramid-shaped Tien Shan pine, while the grassy fringe beside the track is carpeted with herbs and wild flowers.

After a gradual climb along the valley for 8–9km from the first bridge, a path leads east through woodland across the river towards Ala-Köl Lake, while the Karakol valley itself continues south for a few more kilometres, before dividing into the valleys of the Köl-Tör and On-Tör rivers that run down from the high glaciers of the Terskey Ala-Too.

A tent camp run by the Alp-Tur Issyk-Kul trekking company (see *Tour and trekking operators*, page 162), with basic washing and cooking facilities, stands close to the confluence. Park permits are usually checked here. Just beyond here, a trekking route leads west towards the Teleti Pass and descends along the Teleti River to the valley of Jeti-Ögüz.

Getting there There is no public transport to the Karakol valley. To reach it from Karakol, there is the option of a taxi to the park entrance (150–200som); a more

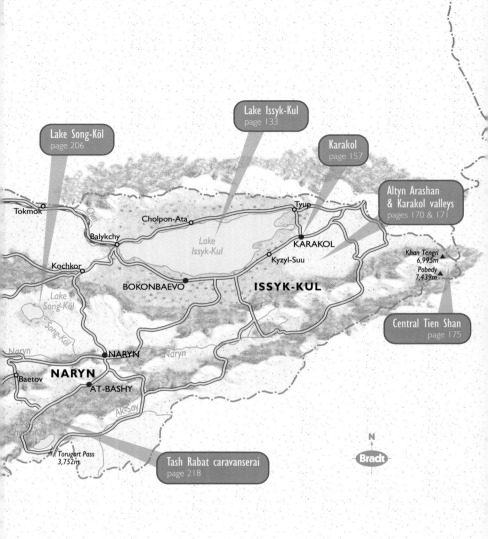

Lake Song-Köl
page 206

Lake Issyk-Kul
page 133

Karakol
page 157

Altyn Arashan
& Karakol valleys
pages 170 & 171

Tokmok

Chun

Cholpon-Ata

Tyup

Balykchy

Lake
Issyk-Kul

KARAKOL

Kochkor

Kyzyl-Suu

Khan Tengri
6,995m

Lake
Song-Köl

BOKONBAEVO

ISSYK-KUL

Pobedy
7,439m

Song-Köl

Central Tien Shan
page 175

Naryn

NARYN

Naryn

Baetov

NARYN

AT-BASHY

AkSay

Chon-Kul

Torugart Pass
3,752m

Tash Rabat caravanserai
page 218

N

Bradt

CHINA

0   100km
0   100 miles

KEY
Capital   ■
Town   ●
Village   ○
Mountain peak   ▲
Road   ——
Railway   ════

Kyrgyzstan
Don't
miss...

Staying in a
***jailoo* yurt,**
Lake Song-Köl
(LM) page 206

Hiking in the
mountains south
of Karakol
(LM) page 173

Silk Road treasures
Tash Rabat caravanserai
(LM) page 218

Arslanbob region
(LM) page 233

Karakol Sunday animal market
(LM) page 167

top **Valley and River Narvyn**
(CH) page 199

above **Valley near Lake Song-Köl**
(CH) page 206

left **Sheep grazing in front of the Pamir Alay range**
(CH) page 265

above **Red sandstone cliffs at Jeti-Ögüz** (CH) page 172

below **Kichi-Naryn River at Eki-Naryn** (LM) page 215

robust vehicle will be able to take you as far as the wooden bridge – a good place to begin a trek.

Where to stay Apart from wild camping, the only possibility is the Alp-Tur Issyk-Kul tent camp mentioned above.

ALTYN ARASHAN VALLEY

Running parallel to the Karakol valley to the east, but separated from it by the ranges of Kara-Beltek, Aylanysh and the high 4,000m-plus peaks of the Terim-Tör, is the Altyn Arashan (Golden Spa) valley. Of all the valleys that lie close to Karakol, this is probably the most popular overall, and with good reason. Even by Kyrgyzstan's high standards, the valley is extraordinarily lovely, with silver threads of streams trickling down to join the Arashan River, lush meadows sparkling with wild flowers, and smooth green slopes cloaked by dense stands of conifer higher up.

Heading up the valley, the view is dominated is by a picture-perfect view of the snow-topped 4,260m Palatka ('Tent') peak that lies far to the south beyond the Altyn Arashan hot springs that give the valley its name. Bears are said to inhabit the area, although there does not seem to be any record of attacks on humans in the region. The area includes the Arashan State Reserve, a botanical research preserve.

The valley begins close to the village of Teploklyuchenka, to the east of Karakol town. Just south of the village the road splits, veering left to reach the spartan Ak-Suu sanatorium and continuing straight on for the Altyn Arashan springs along a steep, and extremely rough, 12km track through pine woodland close to the Arashan River. The road is only suitable for a really tough 4×4 vehicle and is such a slow, uncomfortable drive that walking may be the longer but more appealing option.

Along the road up to the hot spring complex are a number of hidden cold and hot springs, and there is a small cave 500m downstream from the Yak Tours guesthouse that has hot sulphurous water piped from a nearby spring. The hot springs 'complex' at the end of the track is fairly rudimentary, but a wonderful place for a hot bath after trekking, or as a place to stay and use as a base for hikes further up the valley. Day treks may be made to nearby 3,800m peaks – around 7 hours' round trip from the hot springs complex.

Getting there Valentin of Yak Tours in Karakol makes regular trips in a decommissioned Russian army 6×6 between Karakol and his valley guesthouse that lies just short of the hot springs. He charges 200som one way but will only make the trip when there are enough passengers to make it worthwhile. Yak Tours also offer a US$25 package that includes transport, meals and lodging, and a guided day trek. Several **buses** run each day from Karakol's local bus stand to Ak-Suu. From here it is possible to hike up the valley. To save time, a Karakol **taxi** will drive to the beginning of the dirt road up to Altyn Arashan, just south of Teploklyuchenka village, for around 200som. From here it is a 5-hour walk that climbs 1,000m uphill to the hot springs complex.

Where to stay The **Kolkhoz Hostel**, which has concrete hot pools where you can bathe (100som), has dorm beds, a kitchen and dining room, and outside toilets. It is also possible to camp outside and use the facilities here. There is a very basic shop that sells a few essentials like biscuits and beer (*dormitory* $).

The **Yak Tours** guesthouse is a rather run-down wooden cabin a little further down the valley with its own hot spring ($, *or* $$ *with 3 meals*).

Camping is possible almost anywhere, with the best sites further south up the valley beyond the hot springs.

FROM KARAKOL TO JETI-ÖGÜZ Halfway between Jeti-Ögüz and Karakol, just off the main road, is the village of **Yrdyk**, which has a large Dungan population and a mosque, medical centre and a number of houses all built in typical Dungan style. The central mosque is a replacement of an earlier one that dates from 1916.

Close to Jeti-Ögüz village at the start of the valley, on the main road itself, is the smaller neighbouring village of **Jele Dëbë**. This is the home of the much-lauded Tenti Djamanakov, the 'eagle man' who has a trained hunting eagle and who will, for a suitable fee, stage a hunting demonstration. Arrangements can be made through the Tourist Information Centre in Karakol, and some tour companies also organise demonstrations. Another eagle hunter who may also be visited lives in Bokonbaevo further west (see box, *Eagle Hunting in Kyrgyzstan*, page 188).

JETI-ÖGÜZ Southwest of Karakol town, parallel to the Karakol valley, the valley of Jeti-Ögüz begins at the village of the same name and climbs south along the Jeti-Ögüz River past a well-developed health resort towards the Terskey Ala-Too range. The valley gets its name from a rock formation called Jeti-Ögüz (Seven Bulls) that lies a few kilometres south of the village on the main road. The rocks in question form a ridge of distinct red sandstone bluffs, which number seven or possibly eight depending how you count them. The rocks, remarkable though they are, do not resemble bulls in any discernible way, but Kyrgyz folklore provides the legend to explain this appellation.

The legend tells of a Kyrgyz khan who had stolen the wife of another khan who sought revenge for the deed. A wise man reluctantly offered council and suggested that the aggrieved khan should seek out and kill his stolen wife so that the khan might own a dead wife rather a living one. A scheme was hatched that enabled him to sit next to his stolen wife at a funeral feast, and as the last of seven bulls were being slaughtered he stabbed his wife and killed her. Her heart gushed blood down into the valley below, taking the carcasses of the seven sacrificial bulls with it to become the seven large red rocks that can be seen today. Another legend tells of seven rampaging wild bulls that were turned to stone by the gods in order to protect the local population.

Just before the ridge of Jeti-Ögüz stands another large red rock that also comes with legends attached. This is the fractured mass of Razbitoye Serdtse – **Broken Heart** – which resembles a heart that has splintered down the middle. The legend tells of a rich but cruel khan who spotted a beautiful girl while out hunting. Although he already had many wives the khan insisted on marrying the girl, who came from a poor family. The girl was already engaged to be married and when she heard of the khan's intentions she fled from the area with her lover. The couple were caught by the khan's servants, and the girl was taken by force while her betrothed was killed immediately. The death of her lover made her so distraught that she died on the way to the khan's residence, leaving the mark of her broken heart on the landscape. This is the 'cruel khan' variant of the legend; a similar version exists in which it was the quarrelling of two competing suitors that broke her heart.

Just south of the rocks is the **Jeti-Ögüz sanatorium** built in 1932. This was the setting for the historic meeting between Boris Yeltsin and Kyrgyzstan's first president Askar Akaev in 1991, after the abortive Moscow coup. The concrete complex has seen better days, but it is an option in summer for those who want to stay in the valley but do not wish to camp or stay in yurts. A good overview of this part of the valley can be had by walking a little way up the dirt road that leads off from the café opposite the sanatorium entrance. From here, there are excellent views over the Seven Bulls and the Broken Heart formations, and glimpses of the small canyon that lies to the east.

Continuing south along the valley for another 6km or so, and crossing the river a couple of times over rustic tree-trunk bridges, leads through a narrow canyon to an area where the valley suddenly widens out at a *jailoo*. This is the **Valley of Flowers**, which is known as Tsvetov Dolina in Russian and Kök-Jayik in Kyrgyz. The name is highly appropriate, and the best time to witness the bounty of its meadows is in early summer when edelweiss, crocuses, tulips and poppies all put on a colourful show. The valley is equally famous for its edible wild mushrooms, which are harvested in summer for the Chinese and Kazakhstan markets. Ecotour has a yurt camp in the *jailoo* here, as does another company called Saidahmat a little further south. There are also said to be petroglyphs in the area.

Getting there Buses and minibuses from Karakol's central bus stand (20som) pass by the village of Jeti-Ögüz on the main road. From the main road it is a 13km walk up to the sanatorium. It is relatively easy to flag down a vehicle on this stretch, paying 25som or so for a ride. Occasional direct buses run between Karakol and the sanatorium. A taxi from Karakol to the sanatorium should cost around 300–350som, plus another 100–150som to Tsvetov Dolina and the yurt camps.

Where to stay and eat The Soviet-era **Jeti-Ögüz sanatorium** consists of a number of fairly basic hotel buildings along with a hot pool, a treatment centre and restaurant (*summer only; FB $$ pp*).

There are a couple of restaurants and shops outside the grounds of the sanatorium. The **Kök-Jayik café** opposite the entrance has the usual Kyrgyz menu and a few seats outside (*$*).

A little further down the valley, along the roadside at the base of the Jeti-Ögüz and Broken Heart rocks, are a number of summer **food yurts** dishing up *shorpo* and *shashlyk*.

Yurt camps A stay in any of the yurt camps in the Valley of Flowers is best pre-arranged through the Karakol Tourist Information Centre (✆ *234 25*) rather than just turning up. Two companies that have yurt camps here are the Bishkek-based tour operator **Ecotour** (*www.ecotour.kg*) and a little further on, 7km from the sanatorium, is the family-run **Saidhamat** yurt camp, with slightly more upmarket facilities. Saidhamat can arrange guided walks to local attractions like the Jeti-Ögüz waterfall, and can provide horses on demand (*$$$, inc 3 meals*).

TREKKING SOUTH OF KARAKOL

Although the possibilities are almost infinite the most popular routes tend to be those listed below. All of these can be done without support by anyone who is reasonably experienced and fit enough to both hike and carry the tent, food and equipment that will be needed. Alternatively a trek can be arranged using the services of a local tour agency or through CBT.

The **trekking season** is fairly short, from the end of June until early October, and the majority trek between late July and early September; August is the peak month. Beyond this season, nights are very cold and snow is possible. Bad weather can, of course, occur at any time and rainstorms are something that should be prepared for.

A useful map for the region that shows trekking routes (available from the Tourist Information Centre in Karakol or GeoID in Bishkek), is the 1:100,000 *South-East Issyk-Kul Lake Coast* map published by Goskartografia. The 1:100,000 topological map of the area from GeoID is also invaluable.

Details on **reaching the trailheads** are given in the individual entries for each valley above. If starting in Kyzyl-Suu (Pokrovka) there are plenty of minibuses passing on the main road to and from Karakol.

KARAKOL VALLEY TO ALTYN ARASHAN AND AK-SUU This route takes a minimum of 3 days and 2 nights, although an extra day would be a bonus. The trek begins in the Karakol valley at either the park entrance or at the wooden bridge a few kilometres further upstream.

The route follows the Karakol River upstream for 3 hours or so, gently climbing all the time. Here, the river is crossed by a footbridge and the route climbs steeply to the east, along the course of the Kurgak-Tör stream flowing down from Ala-Köl Lake. After about a three-hour climb from the Karakol River through woodland and juniper scrub and over rock-fall, the Sirota campsite is reached, which is where most trekkers spend their first night. The campsite, which is in a rocky patch of pine woodland and has a very rudimentary log cabin shelter, tends to be rather cramped in the peak season, and there is generally quite a lot of litter lying about. There is an alternative place to camp beneath a waterfall 1–1½ hours further on – a beautifully scenic spot – although there is only room for about three small tents here and late in the day you take the risk of it already being occupied.

From the Sirota campsite, the path climbs up over rocks to beyond the tree-line and a small rocky plateau by a waterfall, mentioned above, is reached. From here, fantastic views back along the valley to the west may be had. The route continues to the left of the waterfall until eventually a plateau with rocky outcrops is reached, from where there are dramatic views over the brilliant blue-green waters of Lake Ala-Köl that lies immediately below.

Some hikers descend to the lake to camp for the night; the alternative – or imperative, if you are doing the trek in just 3 days – is to continue east above the lake before striking northeast up to the high ridge that is the 3,860m Ala-Köl Pass. From the top of the pass, you can enjoy views over the lake to the Takyr-Tör Glacier glistening to the southeast and the meandering stream snaking across the floodplain beneath it.

From the pass the path descends steeply down a difficult scree-slope to a wide open meadow, and then follows the course of the Köl Dike stream on its northern side. The landscape here is notably different from the other side of the pass and the Karakol valley before it. Whereas the Karakol valley might have been the Canadian Rockies or the Alps, the landscape here, with open, undulating meadows, massive walls of scree and jagged peaks to the south, seems to uncannily resemble parts of the Scottish Highlands.

Unless the option of an overnight pitch next to Lake Ala-Köl has been chosen, an overnight camp is usually made somewhere in this vicinity. A good spot to camp is in the pine woodland that lies close to the stream's southern side, having first descended through meadows from a *jailoo* that has horses and a wooden shelter. From here it is only 1½ hours down to the Arashan valley and the Altyn Arashan *kolkhoz* (collective farm), where a hot bath may be enjoyed. It is possible to spend the night here, camping next to the *kolkhoz* or a little further up the valley. From Altyn Arashan it is an easy descent of about three hours along the valley to Ak-Suu, following a dirt track that is murder to drive on but a pleasure to walk along. Transport can be pre-arranged for a pick-up at the bridge at Ak-Suu, or you could continue on a little further to the village of Teploklyuchenka, from where there is public transport to Karakol.

JETI-ÖGÜZ TO ALTYN ARASHAN This trek extends the itinerary above by adding on a leg between Jeti-Ögüz and the Karakol valley. Beginning at the Jeti-Ögüz sanatorium the route continues south along the valley through the Valley of Flowers (Tsvetov Dolina), which is a good place to camp. About 5km further on the gorge of the Teleti River leads off to the east. The route follows the river as far as a small confluence a couple of hours' upstream. The valley bottom here is another suitable place to erect a tent for the night.

From here, the route climbs sharply to the northeast towards the 3,759m Teleti Pass, from where it descends to join the Karakol valley, a 5–6 hour trek in all. Reaching the Karakol valley, the river is followed north for two hours as far as the footbridge, where the route to the Ala-Köl Pass alongside the Kurgak-Tör, detailed above, is followed. Following this route would take a bare minimum of 5 days and 4 nights.

KYZYL-SUU TO ALTYN ARASHAN This is as mentioned above but also incorporates a trek up the Kyzyl-Suu valley, west of Jeti-Ögüz, lengthening the trek by two more days, or three if the trek is started in Kyzyl-Suu village (also known by its Russian name, Pokrovka). There is a Russian man in the village, Oleg Vassilievich (\ *0396 217 25*), who can provide transport along the Chong Kyzyl-Suu valley and homestay accommodation (*150som per bed; b/fast 50som; dinner 100som*). Oleg can also arrange transport to the **Juukuchak valley** to the west, which has hot springs, or the **Juuku valley** west of that, which follows the course of one of the old Silk Routes south, over the 3,633m Juukuchak Pass to the 4,284m Bedel Pass into China. Apparently it has bones lying around that date from Silk Road times, as well as hot springs and Buddhist rock paintings. It is likely that at least some of the bones date to the Urkun incident of 1916 when many Kyrgyz attempted to flee over the mountains to China (see page 9).

Beginning at the Kyzyl-Suu sanatorium 20km up the valley from the village of the same name, the route follows the Chong Kyzyl-Suu River southeast until an old meteorological station is reached where the river splits in two. There is a rustic hot spring pool along the way, 4km short of the weather station. The route follows the course of the left-hand river, the Kara-Batak, which is followed until a suitable camping area is reached. A little further down the valley, a steep path climbs to the east alongside a stream and up to the 3,800m Archa-Tör Pass. From the pass the route descends along the Asan-Tukum gorge to reach the Jeti-Ögüz valley after a total of about six hours' hiking from the campsite. At the Jeti-Ögüz valley, the route heads north and downstream for a few hours before reaching the track along the Teleti gorge and up to the Teleti Pass and the route outlined above.

THE CENTRAL TIEN SHAN
ЦЕНТРАЛЬНЫЙ ТЯАНЬ ШАНЬ

The corner of the Kyrgyz Republic that wedges itself between Kazakh and Chinese territory to the east of Karakol is indisputably the country's wildest and least accessible region. It is here in this region that superlatives abound: the highest mountains, the coldest temperatures, the longest glaciers, the grizzliest mountaineers and the strangest natural phenomena. This is a region of ice, snow and unexplored peaks – too high and inhospitable even for most hardy Kyrgyz nomads. It is home to Kyrgyzstan's highest peak (the second highest in the former USSR), the world's fourth longest glacier, an amazing disappearing lake and, if you believe in that sort of thing, the remote location for the crash landing of a giant UFO.

Unlike the valleys closer to Karakol this is no place for gentle mountain hikes and is really only for committed, experienced mountaineers and those who avail themselves of the support services of guides and porters. Whatever the degree of tactical support enlisted, fitness and stamina are essential. Visiting the area requires a considerable commitment of time, energy and money, but those returning from time spent trekking in the region invariably insist that it is well worth it.

GEOGRAPHY The Central Tien Shan (sometimes spelt Tian Shan) forms the pinnacle of the Tien Shan mountain range, a name that translates from Chinese as 'celestial mountains' and which seems highly appropriate. This citadel of high, snow-ravaged mountain peaks is known collectively as Muztag, the 'Ice Mountain', and it is this range of twisted valleys and towering peaks connected by rivers of ice that is home to Kyrgyzstan's highest mountain, **Pik Pobedy** (Victory Peak). At 7,439m, it is a fraction lower than the CIS's highest, Peak Ismoil Somoni (formerly Communism Peak) in Tajikistan that stands at 7,495m.

The bulky peak of Pik Pobedy stands like an enormous rock sentinel watching over the Kyrgyz–China border, but it is the slightly lower guardian of the Kazakh-Kyrgyz border, **Khan Tengri** (7,010m), which is the greater beauty by far. Khan Tengri is a perfect pyramidal icon of a peak that is known locally as Kan-Too (Blood Mountain) thanks to the roseate glow its marble upper reaches emit at sunset, almost as if the light comes from within. Khan Tengri, which translates as either 'Lord of the Spirits' or 'Ruler of the Skies', is a slightly controversial member of the 7,000m-plus club, as its geological height is measured as 6,995m and it is only its glacial cap that elevates it to 7,010m. Nevertheless, Khan Tengri has been accepted as one of the former USSR's five peaks above 7,000m, and in Soviet times mountaineers who climbed this along with the remaining four peaks were eligible for the state's Snow Leopard Award. Of the five peaks – two in the Kyrgyz Tien Shan, three in the Tajik Pamirs – Pik Pobedy was considered to be the most difficult by far, followed by Khan Tengri.

Pik Pobedy is now officially known as Jengish Chokosu, a Kyrgyz translation of the mountain's Russian name that was given to it at the end of World War II. Rather than a single peak, Pik Pobedy is a massif with several summits along its ridge but only the main summit rises above the 7,000m mark. It is also the most northerly 7,000m rock peak in the world if Khan Tengri, just 16km northeast, is excluded from the equation because of its icy summit.

It is also one of the most deadly, with a very high death toll for climbers. The standard approach to the summit involves a 4km traverse along the mountain's west ridge at an altitude above 7,000m, where many climbers become trapped by storms. The route via the north face is even more treacherous.

Lying beneath both mountains is the 62km-long, 3.5km-wide **South Inylchek Glacier**, which is considered to be the fourth longest glacier in the world. The glacier, together with its northern arm, which wraps around the ridge of Khan Tengri like an icy tuning fork, locks up a vast volume of water that is released as melt-water to supply the Inylchek River and the Sary-Jaz that flows southwards into China's Tarim valley.

The glacier covers a total area of 583km² and the ice in places is as much as 540m thick. Located close to where the glacier's northern arm, the **North Inylchek Glacier**, joins its southern partner, a remarkable blue, iceberg-filled lake called **Lake Merzbacher** forms every summer as the glaciers melt. Every year, usually some time in mid-August, the lake bursts its ice banks and water and icebergs dramatically explode from the lake, draining it to suddenly swell the waters of the Inylchek River below.

HISTORY The Chinese were the first to explore this foreboding mountain zone, but it was not until the middle of the 19th century that European explorers penetrated the region. The Russian Pyotr Semyonov Tyan-Shansky was the first, for which he was given his honorary epithet 'Tyan-Shansky' by the Tsar.

This unique lake 3,500m above sea level was first discovered by the German mountaineer and geographer Gottfried Merzbacher in 1902. Whilst on an expedition for the Russian Geographical Association that was attempting to reach Khan Tengri peak by way of the South Inylchek Glacier, Merzbacher observed the unique phenomenon of a glacial lake that lost all of its water in the space of just three days.

Making another journey to the same region the following year he was able to observe that the lake had fully replenished its waters and that the filling and rapid draining were actually part of an annual cycle. How this process takes place is unclear. The lake first starts to appear when an ice dam blocks the gorge and melt-water starts to accumulate from the glacier. There is a higher basin 400m above the lower one and it is icebergs that have plunged down from this that combine to form the ice dam. The lower lake grows to around 3.5km in length and 1.2km wide until a point is reached, usually in mid August, when the lake's waters have risen to such a point that the ice dam is lifted and the accumulated water suddenly breaks free underneath the floating ice.

This is one theory; another suggests that the pressure of the water causes the ice wall to deform, opening cracks that allow the water to escape. A third theory links the drainage of the lake with a canyon in the South Inylchek Glacier, which when it fills with water and subsequently drains away, it is suggested, creates a suction effect that draws the water away from the glacial lake. Whatever the true science of the matter, the rapid drainage causes floods in the valleys of the Inylchek and Sary-Jaz rivers for about a week afterwards. The lake is then left completely empty until it starts to fill the next spring, repeating the annual cycle.

Although the emptying of the lake might appear to be a unique occurrence, there are a handful of similar events that take place elsewhere in the world – in Iceland, Greenland and Switzerland – but it is at Kyrgyzstan's Merzbacher Lake that the phenomenon is so regular and reliable. The timing of the August event is not written in stone, however – in 2003, it took place in July.

In 1857, Semyonov Tyan-Shansky followed the course of the Inylchek River upstream to discover the glacier. His pioneering journey was succeeded in the 1870s by expeditions by the geographer and biologist Nikolai Przhevalsky and then, just after the turn of the 20th century, by the German geographer, Gottfried Merzbacher. Merzbacher failed in his attempt to climb Khan Tengri but he did succeed in discovering a highly unusual lake that would become named after him, in addition to proving that Khan Tengri did not lie on the main watershed of the Tien Shan, as had been previously thought.

The area was completely closed to outsiders during the Soviet era, although some climbers from within the Soviet Union were able to come here with permission from the military authorities to experience the ultimate mountaineering challenge that the USSR had to offer. Khan Tengri was first climbed from the south in 1931 by a Ukrainian team, and from the north for the first time in 1964. Pik Pobedy-Jengish Chokusu was not climbed officially until 1956, although alternative accounts claim that the peak had previously been climbed in 1939, when the climbers had believed the peak to be less than 7,000m.

TREKKING IN THE CENTRAL TIEN SHAN The only viable time for non-winter alpinists is high summer – July to August. Border permits will be needed for any sort of visit (see *Red tape*, page 179) and should be organised well in advance. Mountaineering permits are necessary for all climbing expeditions.

Several tour companies arrange expeditions to the area for both trekkers and climbers and all of these operate basecamps in the Inylchek valley. The usual overland route into the region is via the depressed and almost deserted tin-mining town of **Inylchek**. Until the 1990s, Inylchek was a small town of around 5,000 citizens that worked in the mines and factories of the town. Now less than 20 families remain, determinedly staying on by adapting to a far more rural mode of life.

Consequently Inylchek is rather like a ghost town: an eerie sort of place with empty streets and abandoned *khrushchevki* apartment blocks. Beyond Inylchek, a dirt road continues to **Maida Adyr**, a 5-hour drive from Karakol, from where it is a 4–6 day trek to the basecamps. Maida Adyr itself is little more than a helicopter landing pad, a tent camp that provides basic food and accommodation needs, and a clutch of the ubiquitous recycled freight wagons that are seen all over the country. There is another, rather nicer, basecamp run by Tour Khan Tengri at **Ak-Jailoo** further up the valley, which has both yurts and wooden huts to stay in, in addition to space for tents (*a bed in a hut costs about US$30, in a yurt US$18, in a tent $9, 3 meals US$20*).

Helicopters are used to provide fast and expensive transport in the region, linking Maida Adyr with the basecamps, and spectacular pleasure flights over the glaciers can also be arranged. The helicopters are chartered by the tour companies but it may be possible to pay for a ride to the basecamps if they have room and you are travelling independently. They are not cheap: fares start at around US$100 per person per flight.

Trekking from Maida Adyr to the basecamps at the Inylchek Glacier takes four to six days. It is important to have some knowledge of glacier walking and an experienced guide who knows the terrain. The route follows a dirt road along the Inylchek River for 15km before arriving at a confluence with another river where there is a good campsite. From here, it is another day's hike to Chong-Tash, which is marked by a 9m-high boulder on the left bank (hence Chong-Tash, which means 'big stone'). This has a freshwater spring and is another good place to camp.

From Chong-Tash, the standard route soon reaches the glacier, which it crosses diagonally, climbing all the time. Then the right-hand moraine is followed, sometimes on the glacier itself, sometimes beside it. **Merzbacher's Glade** is reached after a long day's (8–10 hours) hike from Chong-Tash, at the point just below where the northern arm of the glacier joins the main southern one. From Merzbacher Glade, a side trip directly to the north leads to Merzbacher Lake after a few hours' ice walking. The main trek continues past several other glaciers flowing into it to reach **Red Moraine**, another camp site. Beyond Red Moraine it is another 5–7 hour glacier hike to the South Inylchek Glacier basecamps.

Another tough, and even wilder, approach is to make a 4–6 day trek from the town of **Jergalan** along the Jergalan valley and across the Sary-Jaz mountains to Chong-Tash, near the foot of the South Inylchek Glacier. It is a 2-day trek from **Maida Adyr**, or another 4 days along the glacier, to reach the basecamps. This route can be shortened by arranging 4×4 transportation in Karakol to drive as far as Echkili-Tash, from where it takes 2 or 3 days to trek to Chong-Tash.

There is no public transport into the area apart from a single daily bus to Jergalan from Karakol. It should also be possible to hire transport to go as far as Inylchek town from Karakol but a 4×4 is necessary.

Tour operators Be sure to ask all the questions that you think you need to before committing to a tour in this region, and check carefully on things like food and equipment and *exactly* what services they offer. It is also wise to check how much walking you will be expected to do each day, and what level of fitness is expected.

As well as treks to the Inylchek Glacier, Merzbacher Lake and the basecamps, some companies offer the option of an ascent of 4,832m Pik Diki, which is considered to be a 'trekking peak'; it's an 8–10 hour round-trip from the basecamp.

Several **Bishkek**-based companies offer itineraries of different lengths to the Central Tien Shan region:

Dostuck Trekking Igemberdieva 42/1, Bishkek; ☎ +996 312 545 455, ☎ 503 082, ☎ 540 237; f (+996 312) 545 455; e dostuck@saimanet.kg; www.dostuck.com.kg

ITMC Tien Shan Molodaya Gvardia 1a, Bishkek; ☎ +996 312 651 404; f (+996 312) 650 747; e itmc@elcat.kg; www.itmc.centralasia.kg

In **Karakol**, many of the tour and trekking agencies are able to offer tours and support services (see page 162).

In **Almaty**, Kazakhstan, the following specialises in expeditions to the region:

Kan Tengri Expeditions, Kasteyev 10, Almaty, Kazakhstan; ☎ +7 3272 910 200, ☎ 910 880;

f +7 3272 912 010; e kazbeg@kantengri.almaty.kz

Red tape Trekking anywhere beyond Inylchek requires a **border zone permit**. Border permits can be obtained through tour operators in Karakol, but are best arranged well in advance as they usually take several days to organise. **Climbing permits** are required for actual attempts on the peaks themselves and, similarly, these should be arranged with a local operator well in advance of your trip.

LAKE ISSYK-KUL'S SOUTHERN SHORE

The southern shore of Lake Issyk-Kul is quite markedly different from the northern shore. It lacks the Soviet-era sanatoria of the north coast and as a whole it is a poorer, drier region, with a more remote feel. There are fewer opportunities for organised bathing than on the north shore, although for the more adventurous there are plenty of options for wild camping close to the lake. There is scope for adventure away from the water too: many of the valleys that run down to the lake from the Terskey Ala-Too range to the south are rarely visited by foreign visitors and are ripe for exploration.

Heading west along the southern shore from Karakol the first places of any real significance for visitors are the twin villages of Barskoon and Tamga, but before these there are one or two places that may warrant a brief look.

Orgochor is a small Kyrgyz village just east of Kyzyl-Suu that is said to have had an internment camp for Japanese prisoners of war during World War II. The village is now home to the **Historical Museum of Jeti-Ögüz**, a museum that was set up in 1998 to document local history from a Kyrgyz (rather than Russian or Soviet) viewpoint – all labelling is in Kyrgyz only. The village is the birthplace of Sartikiev Telekmat (1799–1863) who served as ambassador to the Kokand Khanate and both China and Russia during the mid 19th century. The village has a monument to Telekmat, who was also a talented singer and orator, opposite the museum, a gift from the Kumtor mining company. On the edge of the village, just before Kyzyl-Suu, there are four Scythian *kurgani* that date from between the 6th–4th centuries BC.

The village of **Saruu**, which is reached after passing through the roadside sprawl of Kyzyl-Suu at the head of the Chong Kyzyl-Suu valley (see *Trekking South of Karakol*, page 173), also has a number of Scythian burial mounds in its vicinity that date from the 7th–6th centuries BC and measure between 20–70m in diameter and 3–8m high. There are yet more *kurgani* west of the village: 20 or so that stretch in a line along the east bank of the Juuku River.

The route up the Juuku valley is, like the Barskoon valley below, an old Silk Road route and evidence of this may be seen in Buddhist rock paintings and the bones of those who failed to make it. There is also a 19th-century mausoleum in the valley, Gumbez Balchak, 5km south of Saruu, which is built of brick and wood and is the work of artisans from Kashgar in Xinjiang.

Darkhan is the next village to the west and this has another burial mound that dates from between the 6th–4th centuries BC, which, measuring some 100m in diameter and 12m in height, is the largest *kurgan* in Kyrgyzstan.

Just before Barskoon is reached the road passes through the lakeside village of **Ak-Terek**, which has no facilities for visitors, but which is a good place to experience traditional village life that is unaltered by even the low-impact version of tourism that is characteristic of Kyrgyzstan.

BARSKOON БАРСКООН *Telephone code: 03946*

Across the river from its immediate neighbour, Tamga, and the first of the two to be reached from Karakol, this predominantly Kyrgyz village is set back a little from the main road just inland from the shoreline. Barskoon stands at the head of the Barskoon valley – an interesting diversion that is a fragment of one of the strands of the old Silk Road. There is an impressive waterfall, popular with domestic tourists, 20km along the valley road, but this same well-maintained road is also the approach to the controversial Kumtor gold mine, a Kyrgyz-Canadian venture with a less than pristine environmental record.

Barskoon village grew up around a military post while its neighbour Tamga, they approached the wreckage. An expedition was set up to investigate. A UFO group travelled for two weeks into the mountains but could not find any evidence of a crash and eventually had to leave, suffering from frostbite and exposure.

A report came to the attention of the same Russian UFO group in November 1991 that the Russian Air Force had found the crash site, but while attempting to hoist part of the wreckage from the snow a helicopter had crashed, killing all on board. As it was winter there was no opportunity to explore the crash site further until the following year. The group prepared to make a journey to the site in June 1992. This time they found the crash site, but as they approached to within 1,000m of the craft they suffered from an overwhelming sense of dread and fatigue. In addition, the group's instruments started to fail spectacularly, as if they were being affected by a powerful electro-magnetic field emanating from the wreckage. They were not able to approach closer than 800m as some of the team were experiencing radiation burns. Photographs were taken but these turned out to be hopelessly overexposed and useless, as did the video tapes they tried to record.

A third journey was planned a few months later but this was ill-fated and ended up being delayed for six years. By the time they returned the UFO was gone, as was the Russian helicopter.

Whether the name or location of Shaitan Mazar has any real bearing on the story – or is merely there for dramatic effect – is unclear. The district of Shaitan Mazar (Devil's Grave), close to the source of the Sary-Jak River, already holds some mystical intrigue for the local population as there is said to be a sacred stream here that is gifted with mysterious healing properties. Today, the name Shaitan Mazar will forever be linked with the strange, and perhaps apocryphal, incident that is claimed to have taken place on the eve of the birth of the Kyrgyz Republic. It is also the name adopted by an American heavy metal band.

across the river, developed as the location for a military hospital. Mahmud al-Kashgari, an 11th-century scholar, came from the Barskoon area, from the Silk Road settlement of Barskhan that lay somewhere near the present-day village. The scholar, who was also known as Barskhani, travelled a great deal during his lifetime: he compiled the first comparative Turkic language dictionary whilst resident in Baghdad but ended his days in Kashgar in Xinjiang where his tomb still stands.

The village is the base of the Shepherd's Way trekking company, a well-organised and knowledgeable family concern that runs horse trips in the area and can arrange visits to the workshop of a local yurt maker. If you wish to buy a yurt, and are prepared to deal with the bureaucracy of shipping the thing home, then this is a good place to do it. **The Ak Orgo yurt workshop** (*Lenin 93;* ✆ *967 54;* e @ *mekenbek@hotmail.kg*) manufactures yurts that sell for around US$5,000 for a full-sized model.

GETTING THERE Buses and minibuses running along the southern shore of Lake Issyk-Kul between Karakol and Balykchy will drop off and pick up at the junction on the main road. There are several buses each day to and from Barskoon from Karakol's southern bus station by the stadium; check for precise times. The fare is 60som.

TOUR OPERATORS

Shepherd's Way Trekking ✆ 961 33; e shepherd@elcat.kg; www.kyrgyztrek.com (in Bishkek, PO Box 2032; ✆ (0312) 297 406, ✆ 667 371; m

502 518 315). Shepherd's Way is a Barskoon-based family company run by brothers Ishen & Rash Obolbekov & Ishen's wife Gulmira. They specialise in

horse treks in the surrounding region, offering a total of 13 itineraries. They can also organise visits to traditional eagle hunters in the area. The Obolbekov's have a genuine interest in local culture & are enthusiastic in sharing their love of horses & the Kyrgyz landscape. They speak excellent English (they worked as English teachers back in Soviet times) & are very professional & experienced, having been in business for the past 15 years, & have many clients that return year after year. Shepherd's Way also run the summer horse treks offered by the British adventure travel operator, The Adventure Company (*www.adventurecompany.co.uk*).

WHERE TO STAY Most of the accommodation options are over the river in Tamga, although Shepherd's Way may be able to help find beds in the village.

THE BARSKOON VALLEY The road that leads up the Barskoon valley to the waterfall and Kumtor mine is reached 1km west of Barskoon village, turning left off the main road. The route up the Barskoon valley from the village was formerly one of the strands of the Silk Road that lead the way to the 4,284m Bedel Pass into China, a route that is no longer open. There are said to be human and animal bones still lining the route to the pass in places, which rather than being the ancient remains of Silk Road travellers are the bones of Kyrgyz herders and their livestock that perished from exposure during the mass exodus that followed the Urkun incident in 1916. A minimum estimate of 100,000 Kyrgyz are said to have died in their attempt to flee persecution from the Russian Tsarist forces.

The valley road, the A-364, serves as the main thoroughfare for traffic travelling to and from the Kumtor gold mine, hence its well-maintained condition (see box, *The Kumtor Gold Mine*, page 183). There is an impressive waterfall approximately 20km from Barskoon village, a favourite place for picnics where temporary summer yurts sell *shashlyk* and *kumys*. On the roadside approaching the waterfall is a bust of Soviet cosmonaut Yuri Gagarin (he holidayed at the nearby Tamga sanatorium after his pioneering spin in space in 1961) and a strange monument of a lorry mounted on a plinth.

Beyond the waterfall the road continues towards the mine and the Barskoon Pass at 3,754m amidst wild, treeless scenery. From here the road drops down slightly past a small lake to the wide Ara-Bel valley before rising again to the higher (4,021m) Söok Pass that leads down to the Naryn River and the military post of Kara-Sai. To continue east from here along the track to Ak-Shyrak, another military post and the end of the road, requires a border permit. It should be borne in mind that although this road is shown on some maps as continuing on to Inylchek, this is no longer possible as many of the bridges maintained in Soviet times are now permanently down.

Trekking from the Barskoon valley There are a number of **trekking routes** that lead off the Barskoon valley, both east and west. One recommended route follows the Burkan valley west to eventually reach the Balgart valley and Kichi-Naryn River to Naryn beyond, a spectacularly wild tract of true wilderness with the narrow valley hemmed in by snow-capped peaks on both north and south sides of the valley. Although this route is just about possible on both **mountain bikes** and **horseback**, it passes through large tracts of difficult, unpopulated terrain and to attempt it unsupported requires adequate preparation. It also requires the occasional crossing of shallow but freezing cold rivers. The Burkan valley is reached by following faint and unclear tracks that lead to the west after the big lake at about 3,600m along the main road. This track climbs gradually past some smaller lakes before passing through a ravine to reach the Burkan valley.

North of, and parallel to, the Burkan valley, leading west off the Barskoon valley before the Barskoon Pass is reached, is the valley of Kerege-Tash, which offers further possibilities leading west towards the Jyluu-Suu, Balgart and Kichi-Naryn valleys. Sometimes this route is impassable because of swollen rivers so seek local advice. Alternatively, a more circular trek could be made by turning north from the valleys of Kerege-Tash or Jyluu-Suu to return to Lake Issyk-Kul over high passes by way of the Ton, Tosor or Tamga valleys. With the right documentation, long treks east beyond Ak-Shyrak are also a possibility, even as far as the Sary-Jaz River in the Central Tien Shan massif.

A number of trekking companies offer combination 4×4, foot and horse treks in this region. They include Kyrgyz Travel, Alltournative, Ecotour and Shepherd's Way among others (see pages 49–51).

TAMGA ТАМГА *Telephone code: 03946*

Lying just west of Barskoon across the Barskoon River, Tamga is a smallish village that has a predominantly Russian character and population, in contrast with its larger, more Kyrgyz, neighbour, Barskoon. Tamga means 'seal' or 'letter' in Kyrgyz and the village takes its name from a Tibetan Buddhist-inscribed rock **Tamga Tash** that lies along the Tamga River gorge at some distance from the village. The village is a quiet, pretty place, with a sanatorium, lush orchards dripping with apricots in summer, and a few streets lined with traditional Russian wooden houses. Tamga also has the benefit of a beach and an area for camping near the lakeshore. Because it has a number of accommodation options it is a good choice for a relaxing stay-over on the southern shore.

Yuri Gagarin famously holidayed here after taking part in the world's first manned space flight in 1961. The **sanatorium** where he stayed is still open for business, although it has certainly fallen on harder times since Kyrgyz independence. It was purportedly built at the end of World War II by Japanese prisoners of war and the grounds of the complex, which incorporate pavilions, parkland walkways and gardens, as well as accommodation, cover a considerable area, stretching from its entrance near the town bazaar down to the lakeshore.

The village's **beach** beside the main road is a 15-minute walk from the centre of the village. The coarse sandy beach lies in front of a marshy tree-covered area that is home to a considerable mosquito population, so insect repellent is a good idea for those choosing to bathe in the lake here. Although this a popular place for swimming, picnicking and camping, the beach at Tosor, 6km to the west, is said to be better.

The village itself has just two principal streets: the one that leads to the coast road and the beach, past orchards and a silver statue of a grim-faced soldier with a machine gun, and the main street, Issyk-Kulskaya, that has the village's shops (mostly in recycled railway wagons), and the sanatorium and bazaar at its western end.

GETTING THERE As with Barskoon, it is possible to pick up a bus or a minibus heading along the southern shore road; the bus stop is by the beach and vehicles can be flagged down here in either direction. There are also direct buses to Tamga from Karakol's southern bus station. These terminate at Tamga's small bazaar, near the entrance to the sanatorium. These leave at approximately 2-hourly intervals during the morning and afternoon, take 2 hours and cost 60som.

WHERE TO STAY

⌂ **Tamga Guesthouse** (7 rooms) Ozyornaya 3; ✆ 953 33. This is Tamga's best, & most expensive, accommodation option. This guesthouse, identified by a hand-painted sign outside, is an attractive, 2-storey Russian house with a pleasant garden that is guarded by a friendly, if at first intimidating, Alsatian dog. The toilet & bathing facilities are shared & there is a sauna. Good views of the lake & the Terskey Ala-Too range can be had from the windows of the upstairs rooms & there is a rooftop observation deck. As the guesthouse for the Bishkek-based Kyrgyz Travel (*www.kyrgyz-travel.com*) it tends to fill quickly in season & so it is best to call ahead. The guesthouse can organise horse tours in the region & proprietor, Zhenya Nikoforov, can advise on directions to, or provide a guide to visit, Tamga Tash. **B&B** $$, f/bd $$–$$$.

⌂ **Askar & Tamara guesthouse** Issyk-Kulskaya 4. This relatively new guesthouse lies behind grey metal doors next door to the bazaar & sanatorium, close to where the bus stops. It has good food, indoor toilet facilities & hot showers. English is spoken. $

⌂ **Rosa guesthouse** (4 rooms) Issyk-Kulskaya 28; ✆ 254 49. This guesthouse is a friendly, family-run place with a toilet in the garden & a sauna but no shower. The name might change in the future but the street number will not – the guesthouse is in the house behind the green wooden railings. There is also a green sign that says 'Guesthouse'. $

⌂ The house at Issyk-Kulskaya 23, almost opposite, also advertises rooms to rent.

There is **another guesthouse** nearby on the road leading up from the beach, opposite Ozyornaya. This stands next door to a pair of attractive wooden houses and has the sign ТУРИСТСКЙИ НРИЮТ.

Camping can be had for free next to the village beach, although insects (ants, and mosquitoes after dusk) might be a problem, as might the night-time noise from the radios and karaoke machines of some fellow campers.

The village of **Tosor** just to the west also has a beach for camping, as well as a **yurt camp** run by Dostuck Trekking (*www.dostuck.com.kg*; f/bd $$$).

OTHER PRACTICALITIES There is a general store at either end of Issyk-Kulskaya, together with a few railway carriages along its length that sell vegetables and staple items. Next to the sanatorium is a small green market. The **post and telephone office** lies about halfway along Issyk-Kulskaya.

WHAT TO SEE AND DO

Tamga Tash Tamga Tash is a large stone carved with a worn Buddhist inscription that spells out the incantation *Om Mani Padme Hum* (Hail the jewel in the lotus) in Tibetan script, providing evidence of just how far the sphere of Tibetan Buddhism extended in pre-Islamic times. The stone, which dates from sometime between the 2nd–8th centuries AD, is located high above the Tamga River, about 6km from the centre of the village, and is quite difficult to find without local assistance. The stone is partially split into two, which local legend relates as being the result of a strike from the sword of Manas (see page 35). The trees close to the stone are festooned with votive rags in the same way they would be at any Muslim shrine in the region. There are said to be more Buddhist stones nearby in the gorge.

The road that reaches Tamga Tash is in poor condition and requires a 4×4. The Tamga River gorge lies just west of the village and is reached by heading west from the sanatorium along a dirt road that passes an impressive Kyrgyz graveyard standing on a ridge opposite an electricity transmission station.

The **graveyard** southwest of the village is well worth a look, and has two parts to it – one Orthodox Russian and the other Muslim Kyrgyz. As elsewhere in Kyrgyzstan, there are many graves that are surrounded by the wrought iron framework of a skeletal yurt, while others have low adobe walls and arched entrances. Most sport an engraved image of the deceased that has been etched from a photograph.

The **sanatorium** is a strange sort of place – a piece of old Soviet culture preserved in aspic. Perhaps it was livelier in Soviet times, but now it seems rather glum and joyless, and it is hard to imagine the anticlimax Yuri Gagarin must have felt being confined here for R&R after the unique and very solitary experience of being the first man in space.

There are a considerable number of both residential and administrative buildings within the complex, many of which appear to be half-abandoned and in the process of being taken over by pigeons. Amidst the leafy grounds that stretch down towards the lake are sports courts, gardens and a central fountain around which old women gather to sell apricots from buckets. There are also a few shops selling biscuits, vodka and cigarettes, and a café. Despite a fair number of apparently healthy people of all ages walking around, it is a surprisingly quiet sort of place, and the overall atmosphere is one of quiet resignation rather than excited people enjoying a holiday break.

BOKONBAEVO БОКОНБАЕВО *Telephone code: 03422*

The stretch of road heading west between Tamga and Kaji-Say has some of the most striking scenery along the lake's southern shore. Here, the bare, dry foothills come almost all the way down to the lakeshore to contrast appealingly with the high snow-topped peaks of the Terskey Ala-Too that lie beyond. Just inland from the lakeside village of Tosor is the **Skazka valley**, an impressive canyon of red sandstone cliffs and outcrops that have been weathered by the elements to create fantastic shapes that resemble castles and anthropomorphic forms – a popular port of call on many organised group trek itineraries. There are several sandy beaches too: at **Tosor**, where there is a yurt camp, and then again at the small village of **Kaji-Say**, where there is a concentration of cafés and an information centre that should be able to point you towards any local accommodation possibilities.

Kaji-Say was the scene of several archaeological digs back in Soviet times, when the remains of a caravanserai dating back to the 10th–12th centuries were discovered. From Kaji-Say the road continues to hug the shoreline as far as Ton, where there are radon mineral water springs. Here, the road turns inland to shortly arrive at Bokonbaevo, a small town just out of sight of the lake.

Bokonbaevo, which takes its name from a Kyrgyz poet, is the largest settlement along the southern shore between Karakol and Balykchy, and has a mostly Kyrgyz population of around 12,000. Formerly, it was a fairly prosperous town but, as elsewhere in the more industrial zones of the country, it has seen a considerable downturn in its fortunes since independence, and now unemployment, along with its faithful attendants, poverty and alcoholism, is prevalent. Despite its dusty, unprepossessing appearance, Bokonbaevo is not a bad place to stay over for a night. It has some comfortable places to stay and the town serves as a suitable base for hikes into the largely unexplored hinterland of peaks and valleys that lie to the south. There is also a *shyrdak*-manufacturing collective based in the town, and a visit to a traditional eagle hunter can easily be arranged through the town's CBT representatives.

GETTING THERE Bokonbaevo has four direct buses a day that link with Bishkek's West Bus Station, a 4-hour drive away; three of these originate or end in Karakol. There is also a direct bus service to Karakol with eight buses a day. Six buses run daily to Balykchy. Minibuses and share taxis also stop in the town to provide transport to Balykchy to the west and Karakol, Tamga and the lakeside villages to the east. Most buses leave in the morning or early afternoon.

TOURIST INFORMATION Community Based Tourism (*Argymak café, 2nd floor, Bolot Mambetova;* ☎ *931 66,* ☎ *(home) 913 12;* m *0502 740 277;* e *reservation@ cbtkyrgyzstan.* ⏲ *10.00–19.00 daily*) is located above the café near the bus stand. Enter by the door on the right and go up the staircase. If the door is locked then just stand around for a bit and someone should turn up to let you in and summon the CBT representative. As well as arranging **accommodation**, CBT's co-ordinator Bakyt Choitonbaev (*Salieva 30;* ☎ *91 312*) can organise **treks** in the region and set up **eagle-hunting** demonstrations with the celebrated local hunter Sagynbay Zarnayev, given a little notice. Some of the standard treks on offer range from 2 to 7 days and include visits to Skazka valley, overnight stays in yurt camps at Bel-Tam and Jaychy, visits to Shor-Köl Lake and the sacred mountain of Tash-Tar-Ata, and treks over the Ton Pass to the Jyluu-Suu valley and Tosor Pass. Single-day car excursions to Shor-Köl, a small salty lake, and to Kyzyl-Tuu village for felt-making demonstrations, can also be arranged.

 WHERE TO STAY There is the basic Hotel Rahat on Atakan but you are better off staying at one of the few local guesthouses that CBT have on their books. The two below come recommended.

⌂ **Jyldyz Asanakunova** Osmoeva 35; ☎ 914 12. $
⌂ **Musabek Baisetov** Kolkanova 34; ☎ 911 15. A

very comfortable family home a little out of the town centre with modern bathroom & excellent food. $

There are also a couple of yurt camps in the vicinity:

Altyn-Bulak yurt camp Contact: NGO El-Too, Salieva 30, Bokonbaevo; ☎ 913 12, ☎ 917 59, ☎ 919 86; m 0502 740 277; e anarchoi@elcat.kg, e adm52@bishkek.gov.kg. Located just inland from the coast halfway between Ton and Kaji-Say. $$

Bel-Tam yurt camp m 0502 705 198, m 0502 209 591; e beltam2003@mail.ru. Best contacted in advance through Karakol CBT. A camp 15km south of the town on the road that runs south from Tort-Kul village. *B&B* $, *meals 120som*.

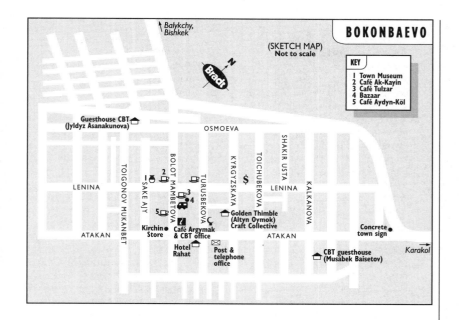

(SKETCH MAP)
Not to scale

KEY
1 Town Museum
2 Café Ak-Kayin
3 Café Tulzar
4 Bazaar
5 Café Aydyn-Köl

Balykchy, Bishkek

Guesthouse CBT (Jyldyz Asanakunova)

OSMOEVA

SHAKIR USTA

TOIGONOV MUKANBET

SAKE AJY

BOLOT MAMBETOVA

TURUSBEKOVA

KYRGYZSKAYA

TOICHUBEKOVA

KALKANOVA

LENINA

LENINA

ATAKAN

ATAKAN

Golden Thimble (Altyn Oymok) Craft Collective

Kirchin Store

Café Argymak & CBT office

Hotel Rahat

Post & telephone office

CBT guesthouse (Musabek Baisetov)

Concrete town sign

Karakol

WHERE TO EAT In addition to the homestays there are a few rudimentary cafés in the town centre like **Café Tulzar**, **Café Aydyn-Köl** and **Café Ak-Kayin**, and also the **Café Argymak** beneath the CBT office (*all* $).

SHOPPING Altyn Oymok (Golden Thimble) (*Kyrgyzskaya 73;* ⟍ *915 90*) is the outlet of a local women's craft collective set up as a community development project in 1996 to generate income for local women and to encourage innovation in *shyrdak* design. There is a range of *shyrdaks*, hats and other felt goods on sale at reasonable prices.

For everyday goods there is the unselfconsciously retro **Kirchin** store opposite the bus stand, where women sell loaves of bread next to 1950s prams and use an abacus to tot up the bill.

WHAT TO SEE AND DO There are few specific sites in the town itself, apart from a museum and a few reminders of the recent Soviet past – a Lenin bust with a hammer and sickle, and an abstract concrete war memorial. In contrast to these Soviet-era reminders, there is a recently built mosque at the corner of Atakan and Turusbekova.

The Town Museum, next to the war memorial (*Lenina;* ⊕ *09.00–16.00 Mon–Fri*) has a collection of work by local artists depicting Kyrgyz folk themes. Particularly interesting is the work of Karypbek Ryskeldiyev, a graduate of the Bishkek School of Art, who manipulates the abstract patterns on small stones to represent scenes from everyday Kyrgyz life.

AROUND BOKONBAEVO This is a fairly unexplored region of the lake's hinterland. The Terskey Ala-Too to the south form an almost an unbroken ridge of 4,000m-plus peaks, there for the taking for enterprising mountaineers, many of which remain both unclimbed and un-named.

The pickings are good for trekkers too: just southwest of the town lies the **Kongur-Olön valley**, a beautiful and surprisingly populated valley at around

Lake Issyk-Kul South and the Central Tien Shan BOKONBAEVO

6

The tradition of hunting with large birds of prey, mainly golden eagles, goes back hundreds of years in Kyrgyzstan, and probably dates back to the Mongol conquest around the 12th and 13th centuries. These days, the art is slowly dying out, and it is only practised by a handful of Kyrgyz and Kazakhs in the region.

Before the collectivisation that took place during the Soviet era the practice was an integral part of normal *jailoo* life rather than the tourist spectacle it has mostly become today. *Bürkütchü*, as the practice is known in Kyrgyz, is now mostly put on as a demonstration for tourists, but it was not so in the old days, when a whole family or even a small village might depend on the eagle hunter's skill to provide a reliable supply of animal protein and fur.

The hunters who practise *bürkütchü* are obliged to forge an intimate relationship with their birds. The birds are captured as chicks from the wild, a hazardous and, it must be said, environmentally unsound, pursuit that requires scaling precipitous cliffs and avoiding the murderous talons of an enraged and powerful parent. The training process is a highly ritualised procedure that takes three or four years. It has to be done by just one person so that the necessary bond can develop between master and eagle. The birds generally have a life expectancy of up to 40 years and so it often becomes a life-long relationship. After capture, the eaglets are hooded and placed in a cage that has a perch that sways as the hunter sings to the bird to imprint the sound of his voice. When it is almost fully fledged the trainer starts to show the bird the hides and furs of the animals it will hunt, and training continues with the eagle learning to pursue a fox fur tied to a galloping horse. Some birds fail and cannot be trained, but those that succeed repay all of their master's effort with intense loyalty: the hunter has effectively become the bird's parent.

To carry the eagle on hunting forays, a special device, a *baldak*, is fitted to the saddle to support the rider's arm. The bird hunts mostly foxes, fawns and other small animals, although they are capable of killing young wolves on occasion. A skilled combination of hunter and eagle is said to be capable of catching 50–60 foxes, a dozen badgers, a couple of lynx and a four wolves in a normal four-month hunting season that begins in late autumn. The displays staged for visitors usually take place outside of this season, and with no snow on the ground prey is harder to find, and so a semi-tame hare or rabbit is released for demonstration purposes.

Whatever the realities of Kyrgyz life over the past century, the tradition of eagle hunting is hanging on doggedly and has even been revitalised a little by the renewed interest in nomadic culture that the foreign visitors bring. *Bürkütchü* is often a hereditary calling that is passed from father to son: Sagynbay Zarnayev of Bokonbaevo, who has demonstrated the art to Boris Yeltsin no less, claims to be the sixth generation of eagle hunter in his family and he has already passed his skills on to his own son, Joldoshbek.

2,200m. This wide, 40km-long swathe of meadows, marshes and gentle slopes offers excellent, uncomplicated trekking opportunities. There is a road running the whole length of the valley from east to west. The valley's eastern end is reached by taking the road south from Bokonbaevo that loops around to the west at the valley's start. The main village at the eastern end is Temir-Kanat.

To reach the slightly lower, western end of the valley, there is a road that leads south from the main coast road at Kara-Koo to climb to the village of Dön-Talaa. The road south of here turns east towards Kongur-Olön, the village at the western end of the valley, where there are two *gumbez* (mausolea) just west of the village. There are said to have been 40 of these in the valley originally: one for each warrior that fought alongside a local leader to secure the valley in the 18th century.

A complex of ancient ruins that date from the 10th–12th centuries has been found at the valley's western end at Bar-Bulak. About 10km east of Kongur-Olön is Toguz-Bulak, the principal village of the valley's western end. A single daily bus leaves Bokonbaevo for the valley each afternoon; otherwise, a taxi can be hired for around 400–500som.

The Bishkek-based trekking company Ecotour (*www.ecotour.kg*) has a well-equipped **yurt camp** in the valley at Temir-Kanat in the east and also at Tuura-Suu, south of Bokonbaevo, just beyond the eastern limit of the valley. The yurt camps come complete with solar-heated water for washing, guided horse-hire and options for demonstrations of Kyrgyz folklore that include music and eagle-hunting.

Immediately south of Bokonbaevo, close to the village of Tuura-Suu, are the remains of an 8th-century settlement, **Khan Dëbë**. Although there is little to see other than a gateway and a 1km stretch of fortifications, a large amount of pottery has been found at the site that dates between the 8th–12th centuries. A taxi from Bokonbaevo should cost around 250som for the round trip, including waiting time.

East of Tuura-Suu, about 20km from Bokonbaevo, is the 3,847m peak of **Tash-Tar-Ata**, which is considered sacred by many locals. The top of the mountain has a small flat area where Manas is said to have lived whilst protecting the Kyrgyz from their enemies (see page 35). There is a stone pot in the ground here and it is believed that in order for young men to be strong they have to climb the mountain and drink from the vessel, asking for Manas's blessing. Surrounding the area are stone pillars known as the Forty Soldiers of Manas. The best way to reach the top is to walk up the grassy slopes on the mountain's southern side rather than approach from the north, which is densely forested. CBT Bokonbaevo can organise 1-day car and hiking excursions here.

THE SOUTHWEST SHORE

The route to Balykchy, west of Bokonbaevo, passes through a dry, scrubby, badlands' landscape that is almost like semi-desert. The road veers well away from the lake here, but those determined enough to find a way down to the shoreline will find some excellent, isolated campsites by the water. This is probably the most unspoiled and least visited sector of the lake's shoreline and an area ripe for exploration. The beautiful stretch of shoreline around the villages of Kara-Talaa and Ottuk is part of the Issyk-Kul Nature Park and an excellent region for birdwatchers. The award-winning Kyrgyz film *Beshkempir* was shot around here, in the village of Bar-Bulak near Kara-Koo.

South of the main road between the villages of Ak-Say and Kyzyl-Tuu is the **Kök-Say gorge**, where there is the Jaychy yurt camp (\ *(3947) 954 31;* m *0502 352 919;* e *yurtcamp_jaychy@rambelr.ru; B&B* $; *meals* 110som). Ecotour (*www.ecotour.kg*) have yurt camps at both **Ak-Say**, where there is the opportunity to ride camels, and **Kara-Talaa** further west, where a *shyrdak*-making workshop may be visited. There are several Scythian burial mounds in the area. Close to the lakeshore near the village of Kyzyl-Tuu is the small, very salty **Kara-Köl** Lake, where it is possible to float without sinking, rather like a miniature Dead Sea. The lake is often simply referred to as Shor-Köl – 'salty lake'. Further west at **Ottuk** village, where the road rejoins the shoreline, there is a Lenin bust with 15 flagpoles (one for each republic of the former USSR) and a yurt camp belonging to the Neman tour company.

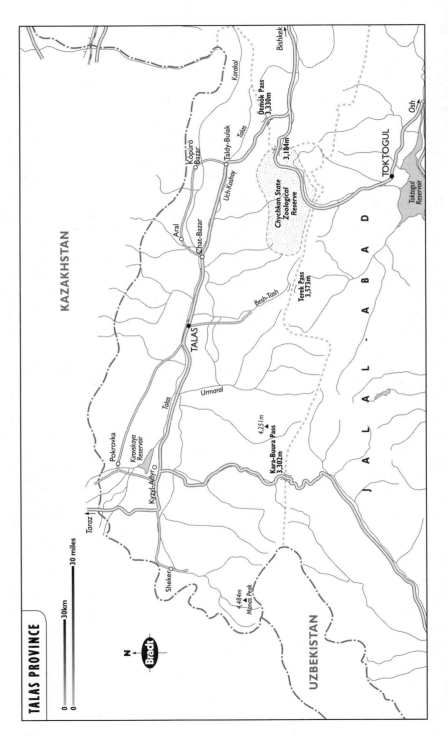

TALAS PROVINCE

0   30km

0   30 miles

N

Bradt

KAZAKHSTAN

UZBEKISTAN

Bishkek

Ötmök Pass
3,330m

3,184m

Karakol

Taldy-Bulak

Köpürö-
Bazar

Uch-Koshoy

Talas

Chychkan State
Zoological
Reserve

TOKTOGUL

Osh

Toktogul
Reservoir

Aral

Chat-Bazar

Besh-Tash

Terek Pass
3,573m

TALAS

J   A   L   A   L -   A   B   A   D

Urmaral

Talas

4,251m
Kara-Buura Pass
3,302m

Pokrovka

Kirovskaya
Reservoir

Kyzyl-Adyr

Taraz

Sheker

4,484m
Manas Peak

7

Talas Province

Talas Province (**Талас области**) in Kyrgyzstan's little-visited northwestern corner, stands apart from much of the rest of the country for reasons of geography. The main road that leads here comes not from Bishkek but from Taraz in Kazakhstan and, almost cut off from the rest of eastern and central Kyrgyzstan by the high peaks of the Ala-Too range, it is easy to imagine that the province looks as much to its giant neighbour as it does to Bishkek. In reality, this is not the case at all, and for those that take the trouble to reach here, Talas shows a face that could hardly be any more typically Kyrgyz. After all, it is here that the Manas legend has its epicentre, at the museum and *gumbez* of the Manas complex outside the provincial capital (see page 35).

Talas Province, the smallest of Kyrgyzstan's *oblasts* with an area of just 11,440km², about the same as the UK's Cumbria and Northumberland combined, and a little smaller than Connecticut in the USA, has the regional capital of Talas valley as its dead centre, midway along the valley of the same name that runs east to west. North of the valley, the Kyrgyz range defines the frontier with Kazakhstan; to the south the loftier peaks of the Talas Ala-Too separate the province from Jalal-Abad Oblast and the Chatkal valley across the 3,302m Kara-Buura Pass. Just west of here, Uzbekistan's far northern Piskom mountain range prods Talas Province with a finger of convoluted political geography. On the frontier here, at 4,484m, stands the province's highest point that, appropriately enough, is called Manas peak.

The Talas valley itself has witnessed some pivotal events in central Asian history. It was here, after all, just over the border in present-day Kazakhstan somewhere near Taraz, that the Battle of Talas River was fought against the Tang Chinese in 751; Sogdians and Turks gritted their teeth to reluctantly join forces with invading Arabs in order to defeat what they perceived to be the greater enemy, thus ending Chinese hegemony in the region and ushering in Islam, still the major faith across central Asia (see page 6). The conflict was also central to the spread of the paper-making process to the West, which hitherto had been a well-kept Chinese secret. Whatever the historical chronicles tell of earth-shaking battles in the 8th century, petroglyphs and traces of Stone Age settlements indicate that the valley has a far older pedigree.

TALAS ТАЛАС *Telephone code: 03422*

HISTORY The area around Talas has been settled for more than a thousand years, but the town did not develop until the Russians came in the mid-to-late 19th century. The town that exists today was founded in 1877 by Slavic settlers who came to farm the fertile soil of the Talas valley. A Russian Orthodox church was built in the 1920s to provide for their spiritual welfare and this remains today, along with a fair number of the town's Slavic population.

Before independence, Talas's economic links were closely connected with the larger city of Taraz (formerly Dzhambul) further west up the valley, which now belongs to Kazakhstan. When the state frontier became an international one in 1991, and Kazakhstan started to impose rigid border controls, the town was obliged to forge stronger links with Bishkek, although the only road that links Talas with the Kyrgyz capital that does not pass through Kazakhstan has to climb laboriously to 3,330m to summit the Ötmök Pass before descending to the Chui valley. Today, Talas is a quiet market town with a population of around 30,000, and is the administrative centre of Talas Oblast.

Manas, the Kyrgyz national hero and eponymous central figure of the epic cycle, is believed to have been born in the Talas valley nearby. His mausoleum lies a few kilometres outside the town to the east.

GETTING THERE Most transport from Bishkek takes the quicker, but longer, route through Kazakhstan, which heads west from Kara-Balta through Kazakh territory to Taraz at the head of the Talas valley, from where the road heads south then west to Talas town. The problem with this for non-CIS visitors is that this route requires a Kazakhstan transit visa and a double-entry Kyrgyz visa (although it is probably possible with a single-entry Kyrgyz visa, as the guards may well not stamp you out of the country, but this is taking a risk). The Kazakhstan transit visa is essential, even without placing a foot on Kazakh soil.

Without a transit visa, it is best to take a **minibus** going the more direct route over the Ötmök Pass. These leave, when full, from Bishkek's West Bus Station and are more frequent in the morning. Check on the route the driver is taking before committing yourself. The journey takes 6 hours with brief breaks, and costs 300som. The road that turns off the main Bishkek–Osh highway to lead up to the Ötmök Pass is quite rough but improves considerably after the top of the pass is reached. Because of snow on the pass they do not run in winter, and the Kazakhstan route provides the only possibility at this time of year.

Coming from Kazakhstan, there is plenty of transport from Taraz. This would be a good way to enter Kyrgyzstan (with a visa) if coming by train from Russia, as it would save the considerable amount of time taken in continuing the rail journey to Almaty or Bishkek.

The **bus station** is some way west of the town centre, a couple of kilometres out on Lenina. Both buses and minibuses arrive and depart from here, although most minibuses also drop off in the town centre opposite the bazaar, from where most local *marshrutka* services also operate. Buses, via Taraz, take around 9 hours to reach Bishkek; minibuses, 5–6 hours. Occasional local buses run west to Sheker and east to Aral and Köpürö-Bazar, although no services run south over the Kara-Buura Pass to the Chatkal valley.

Taxis for local or longer trips congregate on a corner near the bazaar.

WHERE TO STAY

CBT homestay Turdubek Aiyilchiev, 76 Kaimova; 52 919; m 0502 643 466; e cbt_talas@list.ru. Turdubek Aiyilchiev runs an excellent homestay on the edge of the town. It is quite a long way out & a little hard to find, so it may be best to get a taxi (30som) to take you there the first time. There is a yurt in the garden where meals may be taken in traditional Kyrgyz style. Turdubek's wife is a German teacher in a local school & speaks that language, although no English is spoken. As local CBT co-ordinator, Turdubek can help arrange local excursions, longer tours & onward transport. The homestay is a '3 edelweiss' establishment & so is a little more expensive than most, but the standards are high & the food excellent. *B&B* $$; *120som for dinner.*

Hotel Erlan (5 rooms) Sarygulova, near junction with Frunze. A basic but clean-enough place that has just 5 dbl rooms & a shared toilet. $

There are a few more **homestays** in the town that may be arranged through the CBT co-ordinator. English is spoken at the home of Aisuluu Madieva and Muhaya Murzahmedova, and German at the home of Kishiman Tashtekeeva.

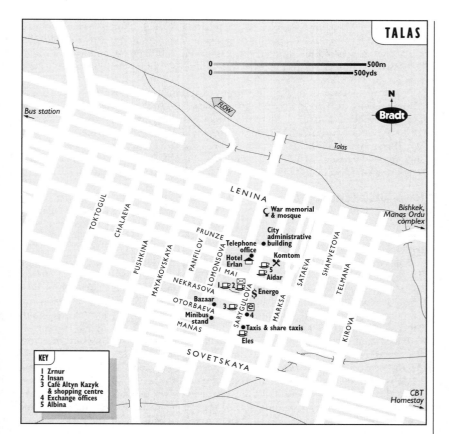

TALAS

0 _____ 500m
0 _____ 500yds

KEY
1 Zrnur
2 Insan
3 Café Altyn Kazyk
  & shopping centre
4 Exchange offices
5 Albina

✗ WHERE TO EAT

✗ **Komtom** Frunze; ✆ 52 890. This restaurant is on the 2nd floor of a building on Frunze, opposite the large Talas provincial administrative building, above a mini-market & pharmacy. It is a neat little place with a good range of mostly Russian dishes at reasonable prices. **$$–$$$**

There are several simple cafés and restaurants serving the usual staples along Sarygulova leading north from the bazaar – **Eles**, **Altyn Kazyk**, **Zrnur**, **Aidar**, **Insan** and **Albina** (all **$–$$**). There is also a large, traditional *chaikhana* on Joldoshali, parallel to and west of Sarygulova at the corner with Frunze.

PRACTICALITIES For shopping the **bazaar** has a good range of foodstuffs and household items, while just along Sarygulova is a small, modern shopping centre with its own restaurant, **Café Altyn Kazyk**. The **post office** is on Sarygulova, as is the Energo **bank**. The Kyrgyz Telecom office is further north on the corner at Frunze 202.

Money **exchange offices** may be found at the south end of Sarygulova near the bazaar, and there is an **internet café** offering IP telephony along the same stretch. The post office and telephone office can also both provide internet access.

WHAT TO SEE AND DO Talas, like almost any medium-sized town in Kyrgyzstan, sprawls in a grid pattern away from the centre, where there are the usual trappings of civilisation: a bazaar, a park or two, a few large civic buildings and a taxi rank. The Soviet-era *khrushchevki* apartment blocks are concentrated mostly in the centre too – a few blocks of grey concrete, broken paving and flapping laundry that might be Omsk, Saratov or any of the less aesthetically appealing neighbourhoods of any Russian provincial town.

A little further way from the centre in any direction lie quiet, leafy neighbourhoods of attractive Russian-style wooden houses, the legacy of the town's Slavic past. The town's **Orthodox church**, built for the Russian community in the 1920s, is worth a look. The central park behind the administrative headquarters on Frunze has a World War II **memorial obelisk**, complete with red star and hammer and sickle, which is surrounded by fencing with a Soviet-era red star motif. This sits in odd juxtaposition to the new building that stands just beyond it – a brand new **mosque**.

Manas Ordu Complex *(To reach the Manas Ordu Complex from Talas continue in the direction of Bishkek for about 10km then turn north at the junction with the eagle on a large plinth for another 4–5km. A return taxi from Talas costs around 350som with waiting time. Admission to the complex was increased from 50 to 400som for foreigners in 2007. ⊕ 09.00–20.00 daily.)*

The Manas complex of museum, parkland and mausoleum stands 15km outside Talas, just off the main road towards Bishkek at the village of Tash Aryk. Because of the Manas connection the complex is an important place for Kyrgyz, who come here as pilgrims to catch a glimpse of their nation's historic soul. Certainly, it is clear from the hushed voices and the devout, serious faces that this is as close to a religious experience as many Kyrgyz get.

For foreign visitors, a visit to the complex is an interesting outing but somehow the experience fails to satisfy completely. Perhaps it is because there is the hint of the theme park about the place: the atmosphere is quiet and reverent, the parks and gardens tranquil, but somehow the authenticity of the historical background seems to be a little doubtful. There is nothing intrinsically wrong with this: after less than two decades of having a country to call their own, many Kyrgyz are still in the process of defining themselves as a nation, so it may be that a theme park is exactly what is required.

The car park has a few stalls and yurts selling souvenirs, cold drinks and, inevitably for this bastion of all things Kyrgyz, *kumys*. Just inside the grounds of the complex is a statue of Manas on a plinth amidst well-tended flower beds. The lovingly maintained grounds and remarkable cleanliness of the complex may come as something of a culture shock after weeks travelling in the scruffier regions of central Asia – there are even waste paper bins.

The Manas gumbez The mausoleum is a few minutes' walk from the car park along well-tended pathways lined with rose bushes, trees and shrubs. There is a shaded seating area opposite the entrance where pilgrims gather as a mullah says prayers and recites from the Koran. A couple of large boulders stand nearby that some believe to be meteorites.

The *gumbez* was discovered in 1898 and has been dated to having originated in 1334, although there is some evidence of later rebuilds. The single-chambered tomb is relatively small and built of pale red bricks, with a richly decorated façade at the entrance that bears an inscription in Qufic script that repeats the Arabic word *al-mulk*, which means 'power' or 'rule'. Another, partly obliterated, inscription tells of a woman Kaniziak-Khatun, who was the daughter of a local ruler. The 16-sided dome roof is a recent addition but has been executed in a style that is thought to be appropriate to the period and building style of the original, which has not survived.

Two different stories relate the origin of the *gumbez*. The first suggests that Manas's son Semetei carried his body here and built the mausoleum for him. The other, generally more accepted, version says that it was his wife, Kanykei, and his friend and counsellor, Bakai, who built it and, in order to avoid desecration by his enemies, they put an inscription over the door that declared that it was the mausoleum of a young girl. This version corresponds better with the inscription relating to the emir's daughter, although the dates are quite wrong if we are to believe that Manas perished in the 10th century.

The archaeologists who excavated the tomb during its renovation in 1969 are said to have found the bones of a very tall man within and many insist that these were the remains of Manas himself. The exact whereabouts of Manas's remains will never be known with certainty – there are those who believe that his body lies in the Kara-Too district of Batken Province – but what is more important in the hazy territory where history and legend overlap is that a symbolic resting place be found. This is certainly that.

Manas museum The marble museum has a ground floor that is mostly dedicated to the lives of some of Kyrgyzstan's most well-known *manaschi*, with black and white photographs and text in Kyrgyz. There are also photographs showing the *gumbez* before reconstruction and some very elaborate wooden carvings of horsemen fighting and mythological scenes with dragons, snakes and eagles. There is a large dream-like mural on the wall of the staircase leading up to the second floor, the walls of which are also completely covered in murals. There are dioramas of scenes from the Manas epic and displays of the accoutrements of the Kyrgyz chivalric and nomadic tradition: saddles, leather goods, weaponry and an enormous suit of armour that is said to have been the type that Manas wore. Many of these, like the suit of armour, are quite clearly reproductions but, as elsewhere in the complex where a vague, murky territory exists between historical fact and legend, the same blurring exists here between genuine historical artefact and replica.

Above the museum is a large manmade mound that offers good views from its summit. Pathways lead up it from both the *gumbez* and the museum. The hill has a stone carved with a 13th-century Arabic inscription that relates to a fortress that used to stand nearby. A little further afield, there are also said to be 2,000-year-old **petroglyphs** in nearby Ken-Köl gorge, a few kilometres north of Tash Artyk village. A guide from the Manas complex should be able to locate them.

SOUTH OF TALAS

BESH-TASH VALLEY This beautiful valley to the southeast of Talas is home to the **Besh-Tash National Park**, which begins 13km from Talas (entrance fee of US$10) and covers 32,411ha in total. The national park was set up in 1996 and contains more than 800 plant species along with threatened brown bear, snow leopard, Turkestan lynx, eagles and falcons.

Besh-Tash means 'five stones', a name which comes from five tall standing stones that are found in the upper part of the park. As with many isolated groups of standing stones, there is a legend connected with them. This one tells of five bandits who lived in the valley and robbed everyone who travelled this way. One day they carelessly robbed a holy woman who cursed them and turned the robbers into stone.

From the entrance to the canyon, where there are hot springs, the road from Talas follows the Besh-Tash River to a height of around 3,000m in the Talas Ala-Too range, before it strikes off to the 3,573m Terek Pass. Here, there are two crystal-clear lakes, a small and a large one, the larger of which offers superb views over the surrounding mountains.

The mountain scenery here is quite spectacular and the area makes for an excellent day trip from Talas or as a base for hiking trips. There are many idyllic camping places along the valley and it may be possible to stay in yurts in summer – check with the CBT co-ordinator in Talas. With adequate provisions and experience it is also possible to trek from the lakes over the Terek Pass to Toktogul in two days.

URMARAL VALLEY Southwest of Talas, and south of the village of Leninopol, is the valley of the Urmaral River, which has many petroglyphs from the 7th to the 6th century BC, although it requires the services of a guide to locate them. Leninopol itself, on the main Talas-to-Taraz road, has several interesting Muslim mausolea from the 18th and 19th centuries, just to the east of the village. The Urmaral valley climbs up to the 3,601m Chimin-Tash Pass, which forms the boundary with Jalal-Abad Province. Close to the pass are more petroglyphs that date from the 6th to 8th centuries.

It is possible to hike, or ride, over the pass to descend to a jeep track that leads east upstream alongside the Chatkal River before striking north and climbing over the Kara-Kulja Pass to eventually reach Sary-Chelek Lake and the village of Arkyt – a tough 6–8 day trek. CBT Talas can organise guided excursions into the valley and, with adequate notice, arrange the trek to Sary-Chelek, although it is probably wiser to prearrange this with KCBTA headquarters in Bishkek.

WEST OF TALAS

The main road to Taraz in Kazakhstan passes through the small town of Kyzyl-Adyr (previously known as Kirovka) before turning north to reach the frontier. Just north of Kyzyl-Adyr is the Kirovskaya reservoir, which has a giant head of Lenin carved into the side of the dam. A ruined city, Sheldy, lies under the reservoir's waters, which for a millennium up until the 16th century was an important producer of silver goods for the whole region. When the reservoir's waters are low, particularly in the autumn, it is said to be sometimes possible to see fragments of the ruined town standing proud of the water.

There are two routes to the border from Kyzyl-Adyr but only the main route through the village of Kyzyl-Jylduz allows non-CIS passport-holders to pass through.

There is **CBT accommodation** available at the reservoir and homestay accommodation may also be available in Kyzyl-Adyr itself.

Just inside the border at Ak-Dëbë (also called Joon-Dëbë), due south of Taraz, there is the site of a settlement that existed between the 6th and 7th centuries.

SHEKER This village in the far west of Talas Oblast, snuggled up against the Kazakhstan border and within sight of the province's highest peak, Manas (4,484m), is famous for just one thing: its well-known son, Chingiz Aitmatov, Kyrgyzstan's foremost writer who was born here (see *Modern Kyrgyz literature*, page 37). The village has a small, three-room museum dedicated to the life of the novelist, which was opened in 1978 to mark his 50th birthday. The museum has a range of newspaper articles, photographs, manuscripts and books, as well as a section on his family history.

There is a **CBT co-ordinator** in Sheker, Gulipa Kazieva (*no phone, ask in the village*), who can provide food and accommodation and organise a Chingiz Aitmatov tour of the village.

The road to Bishkek heads west towards the Ötmök Pass to the village of Chat-Bazar, where another road heads off into the hills to loop through the villages of Aral and Köpürö-Bazar before rejoining the main road at the sprawling village of **Taldy-Bulak**. Close to Taldy-Bulak, but difficult to reach, is a high 3,000m plateau that has flower-decked meadows and a stone with a central hollow that is known as the 'cup of immortality', as it fills with rainwater and is said never to evaporate. Water drunk from the hollow is considered to be holy and to have magical healing properties.

ARAL Both Aral and Köpürö-Bazar lie close to the Kazakhstan border in the valley of the Talas River that nestles between the Kyrgyz Ala-Too and the slender Erchilik-Too range to the south. There are some who maintain that the Erchilik-Too mountains are where Manas's true burial place may be found, suggesting that the revered mausoleum near Talas was built just as a ruse to detract his enemies. The valley near Aral has a number of waterfalls and unusual rock formations that may be visited.

There is a **CBT project** in the village that has both houses and yurts offering accommodation. The CBT co-ordinator can also arrange treks or horseback tours to visit *jailoos* north of the valley (*Kuttubai Kargabaev, Akbai 35;* ⟍ *03459 26 137;* e *marketing@cbtkyrgyzstan.kg*).

KÖPÜRÖ-BAZAR This village lies another 30km east of Aral along the Talas valley. It stands near the mouth of a gorge and is almost entirely surrounded by mountains. Its environs are surprisingly lush and productive: there is a 12km-long expanse of birch woodland, Ak-Kain, close to the village, which is full of edible wild mushrooms in season, and the Talas River itself is heaving with trout. The area around the village is also imbued with history: there are prehistoric petroglyphs nearby at Tuyup-Tor and Kiddik-Tash; Genghis Khan is said to have rampaged through the area with his hordes (one of his wives is thought to be buried in the vicinity), and Kyrgyz tribes fought against Kalmyk invaders in the valley in the 4th century.

Köpürö-Bazar happens to be where former president Askar Akaev's wife, Mairam, hails from. Consequently the village has received more than average state funding in the past, despite what may seem like an archaic, unchanged exterior. The village has facilities for homestays and services such as guided treks and horse hire, the development of which has been supported by the British-backed Sustainable Livelihoods for Livestock Producing Communities Project (SLLPCP).

Visits to local petroglyph sites, caves, a strange local rock shaped like a skull and waterfalls may all be arranged in the village. A small mountain lake, Köl-Tör, at 3,305m, can be reached on horseback from the village. The lake is considered to be sacred by the local population and the custom is to make a pile of seven stones and make a wish, which is then supposed to come true. There is also an abandoned gold mine close to the village where you can try your hand at gold panning. The village is also the starting point for a spectacular four-day horse trek via Köl-Tör Lake and over the Korumdu Pass to the main Bishkek–Osh highway.

There are buses six times a day to Köpürö-Bazar from Talas via Aral (*CBT co-ordinator: Ormoshbek Kuramaev, Jumagulov 85;* ⟍ *03422 46 727*).

CHYCHKAN VALLEY Kyrgyzstan's main north–south trunk road between Bishkek and Osh loops through the far southeast corner of Talas Province between the 3,184m-high Ala-Bel Pass and the border of the Jalal-Abad Oblast. Much of the valley west of the pass is given over to the Chychkan State Zoological Reserve. Stalls along the stretch of the road below the pass sell birch sap and locally made honey to passing motorists; look for the signs – **МЁД** (*myod*). Other than this there is almost no habitation along the way, just open *jailoo* with occasional herders with their flocks. For those wishing to stay over in the region there is a roadside tourist complex with hotel and restaurant, Ak-Ilbirs ($$$), 30km from the pass. From here, the road follows the Chychkan river gorge, with its red sandstone walls, south to descend towards Toktogul and Jalal-Abad Province.

Brown bear

8

Naryn Province

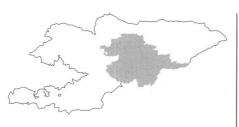

Naryn Province (**Нарын областы**), the large central province that links north and south Kyrgyzstan, is, in many ways, the most typically Kyrgyz *oblast* in the entire country. At around 45,000km² (slightly larger in area than Issyk-Kul Oblast*)*, it is the largest province in the republic. At an average of just six persons per km², the population density is the lowest in the country and the total population of the entire province is only around 270,000.

In terms of physical geography, the province is far more homogenous than Chui or Issyk-Kul, being almost entirely made up of mountainous terrain, interspersed with valleys and upland grasslands. The lowest point is at around 1,400m above sea level; the highest, almost 5,000m.

The population of the *oblast* is more uniform too, with 98% being Kyrgyz. The region is one of the poorest in the country, with a local economy that is dominated by animal herding – mostly sheep but also horses, cattle and yaks. In Soviet times, mining was well established in the province but since independence most mines have ceased production, having been pronounced uneconomical. This removal of employment that was formerly guaranteed has further contributed to the poverty of the region.

Like most of Kyrgyzstan the province is an area of high seismic activity. On 26 December 2006 the Kochkor region was hit by an earthquake that measured 5.5 on the Richter scale and damaged an estimated 5,500 buildings, including nine schools, a kindergarten and five administrative buildings; ten houses were destroyed completely. The epicentre was just 30km from Kochkor in the Terskey Ala-Too range on the borders of Issyk-Kul and Naryn provinces. Fortunately there was no loss of life.

The administrative capital of the province is Naryn, and this town is often visited by travellers *en route* to China via the Torugart Pass. The other key town in the *oblast*, certainly as far as foreign visitors are concerned, is Kochkor, a small market town that locally is best known for its potatoes, but which serves as a departure point for visits to Lake Song-Köl and other destinations in the immediate area.

KOCHKOR КОЧКОР *Telephone code: 03535*

This small market town at 1,800m above sea level in northern Naryn Province stands at the crossroads of many foreign visitors' journeys around the country. The town, which with just 14,000 inhabitants is really more of a big village, is considered to be the site of the first settlement in the valley. It was given the name Stolypin in 1909 in honour of the Russian Prime Minister who advocated colonisation of central Asia. Stolypin fell out of favour with the Bolsheviks after the October Revolution and so the town was renamed Kochkorka (Russian: **КОЧКОРКА**), its name possibly deriving from the Kyrgyz *kach kar*, which means 'go away snow' (apparently it rarely snows in Kochkor). Since independence the town has been

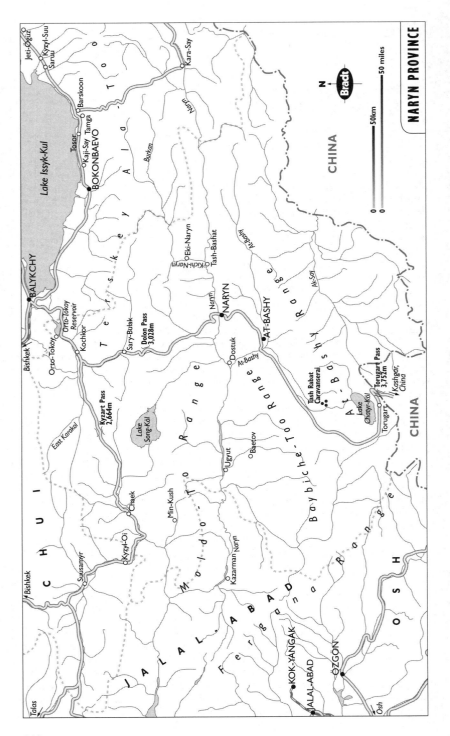

Jeti-Ögüz
Kyzyl-Suu
Saruu
Barskoon
Lake Issyk-Kul
Kaji-Say Tamga
Tosor
BOKONBAEVO
BALYKCHY
Bishkek
Orto-Tokoy Reservoir
Orto-Tokoy
Kochkor
Sary-Bulak
Dolon Pass 3,028m
Eki-Naryn
Kichi-Naryn
Tash-Bashat
NARYN
Naryn
AT-BASHY
Kara-Say
Naryn
Burkan
Ak-Bashy
Ak-Say
Dostuk
At-Bashy
Tash Rabat Caravanserai
Torugart Pass 3,752m
Kashgar, China
Torugart
Lake Chatyr-Köl
Baetov
Ugyut
Kyzart Pass 2,664m
Lake Song-Köl
East Karakol
Chaek
Min-Kush
Kyzyl-Oi
Suusamyr
Kazarman
Naryn
Bishkek
Talas
KOK-YANGAK
JALAL-ABAD
ÖZGÖN
Osh

CHINA

CHINA

OSH

C H U I

T e r s k e y A l a - T o o

M o l d o - T o o R a n g e

A t - B a s h y R a n g e

B a y b i c h e - T o o R a n g e

J A L A L - A B A D

F e r g a n a R a n g e

N

50km
50 miles

Bradt

0
0

200

better known by its Kyrgyz equivalent, Kochkor. The town used to have a more mixed population of Kyrgyz, Russians and Dungans, with even a few German families, but these days it is at least 95% Kyrgyz.

Kochkor lies in a position where the roads from Lake Issyk-Kul, Bishkek and the Suusamayr valley meet, and because of this, and in particular because of the town's convenience as a jumping-off spot for excursions to the surrounding countryside, almost all first-time visitors to Kyrgyzstan end up spending a day or two here. They could do far worse: Kochkor may be the sleepy sort of place where cattle can lie down in the road with impunity but, as far as visitors are concerned, the town has everything they need – good accommodation and food, adequate shopping facilities and a well-run information centre. Both CBT and Shepherd's Life have homestay projects here and it is by far the best place in the area to organise trips to Lake Song-Köl or yurt stays in *jailoos* to the north.

GETTING THERE Regular shared taxis (200–250som) and occasional minibuses run from Bishkek's West Bus Station to Kochkor. These, along with shared taxis to Naryn (150som) and Balykchy (60–75som), arrive and leave from outside the bazaar on the main street. Infrequent buses and minibuses running along the Jumgal valley to Chaek, Jumgal and Min-Kush leave from the same location.

TOURIST INFORMATION AND SERVICES

CBT office Pioneerskaya 22a; ↘ 22 355; m 0503 621 983; e cbt_kochkor@rambler.ru; www.cbtkochkor.com. ☉ Jun–Sep 09.00–19.00 daily. CBT Kochkor runs a very well-organised operation under the auspices of co-ordinator Myrzabek Ozubekov, which provides invaluable local advice as well offering accommodation & tour-booking services.

The office has several English-speaking staff who can advise on local destinations & the best way to arrange a trip there. The CBT office, which has a shop selling *shyrdaks* & felt goods next door, is a useful meeting point for solo travellers who want to combine with others to form groups. There is also a useful notice-board where messages may be left.

The **Shepherd's Life** co-ordinator (see below) is able to offer tours, car rental and yurt accommodation at prices slightly lower than CBT, although it is a much smaller concern with a narrower range of options available.

WHERE TO STAY CBT have a total of 17 homestays in the town, all of a good standard. Some are quite far from the centre so you should specify that you do not wish to be a long way out if this is the case. Guesthouse #12 (Asyl Kubatbekova) is probably the closest to the centre and has an indoor bathroom and washing machine. Guesthouse #10 (Kuban Karymshakov) is further from the centre but has superb food (*all B&B $; lunch or dinner 90som*).

The **Shepherd's Life** co-ordinator, Mairam Omurzakova (*Kuttuseyit uulu Shamen 111;* ↘ *21 423*) offers a choice of three homestays in town ($) as well as others in Chaek in the Suusamayr valley. There are also two very basic **hotels** in the town, one on the street north of the post office and the other just west of the museum.

WHERE TO EAT Beyond the homestays, where inevitably the best food is served, there are a few places in the centre of town near the bazaar like the Bakit café that offer basic meals or snacks. The **Café Visit** ($$) on the main street, Orozbekova, at the far western end of town away from the bazaar, probably has the most pleasant situation in town, having some outdoor tables. Near the bazaar, the **Baba-Ata** café ($$) has a handicrafts showroom upstairs. Close to the CBT office on the opposite side of the road is the **Irysky** shop and café. There are also some yurts that sell meals and *kumys* along Orozbekova between the CBT office and the bazaar.

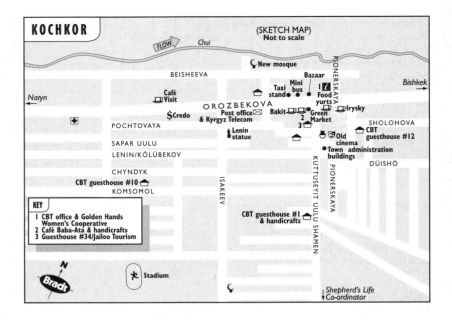

SHOPPING The green market on the corner of Kuttuseyit uulu Shamen and Orozbekova has a good range of fresh fruit and vegetables. There are plenty of small shops and stalls along the main road here where most types of standard household goods can be obtained within reason.

For *shyrdaks* and other felt handicrafts the showroom of the **Altyn Kol (Golden Hands) women's co-operative** (\ 22 534; e altyn_kol@mail.ru), right next door to the CBT office, offers an outlet for crafts manufactured by local women, with a good selection of well-made handicrafts on display. The cooperative, formed in 1996, has over 800 active female members from around the region and, like the Shepherd's Life programme, has benefited from backing by the Swiss Helvetas organisation (see page 80).

Because of the fine wool produced by sheep on nearby *jailoos*, Kochkor has gained a reputation for high quality *shyrdaks*, and this is evident in the goods on sale here. As well as *shyrdaks* there are also cushions, slippers and cuddly toys all made from high quality felt. A *shyrdak* will cost anything from US$20 upwards if bought here, depending on size and the intricacy of the design. The quality tends to be better than many of those found in souvenir shops in Bishkek or elsewhere, and the prices are generally a little lower. It is also good to know that money goes directly to the maker of the *shyrdak* rather than into the pocket of a middle man.

There are also handicrafts on sale in the showroom above the Jailoo Tourism travel agency and the Baba-Ata café, and at Jumagul Akmatova's homestay (CBT guesthouse #1) at Kuttuseyit uulu Shamen 58 (\ 22 453).

OTHER PRACTICALITIES The **Credo Bank** on Orozbekova can change dollars cash.

Telephone calls can be made from the **Kyrgyz Telecom** office, also on Orozbekova, where *very* slow **internet access** may also be had. At the time of research, this was the only place in town with internet availability; the place around the corner on Isakeev just has computer games, despite what it says on the sign outside.

WHAT TO SEE AND DO Kochkor is mainly useful as a base for arranging excursions into the hinterland and, while the town is pleasant enough, there is little specific to see here. There is a silver statue of Lenin standing on Isakeev just off the main road, and another bust of the man along Orozbekova, outside a bus depot west of the Café Visit. The same main street has curious metal cut-outs decorating its lampposts – hammer and sickles, space rockets, masonic instruments, atoms and gear wheels – that serve as reminders of the recent Soviet past. The decrepit cinema between the town park and the museum has clearly seen better days and is now boarded up and its grounds overgrown with weeds. What was once an important civic institution has no doubt since been replaced by TV screens showing pirated DVDs in anonymous back rooms around the town.

There is a brand new steel-roofed mosque near the river to the north of the post office and another one in the south of the town along Isakeev.

Regional Museum This small museum has a few rooms dedicated to showing the traditional Kyrgyz way of life, with plenty of photographs of yurts, herdsmen and windswept *jailoos*, alongside displays that illustrate the changes brought by the Soviet period – education, health and military service. There are numerous portraits of local Kyrgyz weighed down by their war medals. There are also paintings of Kyrgyz life, a large stuffed sheep, a diorama of stuffed animals and best of all, a splendid yurt that entirely fills a room. The floorboards are quite badly damaged in places and there is a general air of neglect. It is unlikely that any of the displays have changed significantly since the early 1980s (⊕ *09.00–17.00 daily except Sat, closed for lunch 12.00–13.00 approx*).

EXCURSIONS FROM KOCHKOR

SARALA-SAZ Sarala-Saz is a large *jailoo* 54km north of Kochkor that lies *en route* to the 3,573m Shamsy Pass, which leads over the Kyrgyz Ala-Too into the Chui valley. As with many similarly romantic locations in Kyrgyzstan, the country's legendary hero Manas is reputed to have frequently visited the region and played the game *ordu* here with his warriors (see page 35). The legend goes that one day, noticing that his horses were wandering away, he threw boulders in front of them to prevent their escape. The stones are said to remain there to this day as testament to his superhuman strength.

The drive up to the *jailoo* passes a number of large *kurgan* burial mounds that date from the 1st–5th centuries AD, as well as an interesting Kyrgyz cemetery just beyond the village of Shamshy. At the *jailoo* itself, which lies at around 3,300m, there is plenty of scope for walking or riding in the vicinity, with wide open vistas in all directions that have a stark, desolate beauty. With little to spoil the natural landscape other than sheep, cattle, a few yurts and the ubiquitous recycled railway carriages, this is a marvellously accessible location for an overnight stay. What is so noticeable here is the absolute quiet that permeates the place. Distant human voices and animal sounds carry so far here that it is possible to hear the movement of a crow's wings as it flies past.

With a horse and a guide it is possible to visit nearby petroglyphs or a waterfall that is half-hidden among the rocks of a small canyon and that's known locally as 'Look for me'. Upstream from the waterfall are extensive patches of wild onions, the plants that the Chinese used to think caused altitude sickness. Higher still is a permanent glacier.

Rather than hike with a specific destination in mind, it is equally pleasurable to just wander at will close to the *jailoo* and observe the Kyrgyz herders going about their everyday tasks. More adventurous spirits may wish to make a horse trek over the pass to Kalinovka and Tokmok in the Chui valley (2–3 days). A horse games festival is staged at the *jailoo* by CBT Kochkor each year in August.

Two other *jailoos* that may be visited in the Kochkor vicinity are **Korumdu**, a high *jailoo* 60km to the west in the Kyzart range, and **Tündük**, 40km northwest of the town. Both have CBT projects in place that include yurt stays and horse hire, and day tours that include horseriding can be arranged by CBT Kochkor. Another possibility is **Kapa** *jailoo*, 35km from Kochkor, from where it is possible to get a view of Lake Issyk-Kul from the peak of one of the surrounding mountains.

Getting there and accommodation CBT Kochkor can organise yurt stays at Sarala-Saz, as well as transportation there and back (there is no public transport). The road to Sarala-Saz is quite rough in places beyond Shamshy village, but it is not difficult and any robust car (ie: a Zhiguli) is perfectly capable of making the journey. Unless you arrange for the driver to return for a pick-up on another day you will need to pay for the driver's meals. CBT charge around 1300som for transport there and back, together with a night's sleepover for the driver (*Yurt accommodation, with meals $–$$*).

CHON-TUZ SALT CAVES This is actually a sanatorium, 30km from Kochkor, where, in Soviet times, caves were mined for the extraction of rock salt. The salt is still mined and is mostly used as a food supplement for farm animals. The sanatorium was formerly popular as a treatment centre for allergies and asthma as it was thought that the dry air of the salt caves was beneficial for these ailments. The sanatorium is still in use and visitors may stay whatever their state of health. There is also a *jailoo* that may be visited, a 3-hour trek above the sanatorium.

KÖL ÜKÖK Köl Ükök is a mountain lake in a gorgeous natural setting above a *jailoo* known as Tez-Tör, which lies around 17km southeast of Kochkor. Köl Ükök means 'Lake in a Chest' and some of those who visit it rate the lake's tranquillity and natural beauty above even that of Song-Köl (see page 206). In fairness, it has to be seen as a different sort of experience: Song-Köl is certainly more commercialised than Köl Ükök but at the same time it is also far bigger and better equipped to deal with visitors. In contrast to Song-Köl's wide, glimmering waters, Köl Ükök is small and jewel-like. Just like Lake Issyk-Kul, the lake has a good stock of Sevan trout in its waters, and several rivers that flow into it, but none that drain out meaning that water can only leave the lake by evaporation or seepage. The comparisons end here, however, as Köl Ükök has a maximum depth of only 17m.

From Köl Ükök it is possible to hike a couple of hours up to another spectacular glacial lake, Köl-Tör.

Getting there and accommodation Köl Ükök can be reached by way of the village of Isakeev, just 6km southeast of Kochkor, or from Kara-Suu, 7km to the east of the town. From either of these it is a 5–6-hour horse trek to the lake, or 3–4 hours to Tez-Tör *jailoo*. CBT Kochkor can organise transport, horse hire and accommodation at the standard rates.

SOUTH OF KOCHKOR The Bishkek–Naryn road leads south from Kochkor through Sary-Bulak and the turn-off for Lake Song-Köl over the 3,028m **Dolon Pass**. This is the highest point along the way and here the roadside is lined with the railway carriage dormitories of workers who maintain the road, which is kept open throughout the winter despite deep snow. In the summer months, the yurts and tents of Kyrgyz herders join the roadside carriages to sell *shorpo*, *manti* and *kumys* to passing motorists.

From the summit of the pass, the road plunges into a rocky gorge before reaching Ottuk, a small village, where the road emerges into an open valley. A little further on towards Naryn, 25km short of the provincial capital, stands a large memorial on a hillside dedicated to the Kyrgyz writer and poet Arstanbek Bunlash Uluu (1824–78), who was known to his admirers as 'The Nightingale'. His poems were banned during the Soviet period because of his calls for the preservation of Kyrgyz culture and independence of spirit, and warnings of 'dark times' to come – clearly references to the influence of early Russian colonists. The few of his works that survive today were published as an anthology in 1994.

WEST TO THE SUUSAMYR VALLEY

For the northwestern end of the Suusamyr valley, see page 129. Just after Kyzyl-Oi in Chui Oblast the road crosses into Naryn Province and leads east towards Kochkor, along the Jumgal valley via the villages of Chaek, Tügöl-Say, Kyzart, Jumgal and Uzunbulak. The eastern end of the valley beyond Kyzart is rich pasture land and there are many yurts here in summer. This road is quite decent and there are plans to upgrade it in the future.

Another more northerly route to the Suusamyr valley runs from Kochkor through the village of Komsomol to the Karakol Pass at 3,452m, then descends along the Karakol valley in Chui Province to Suusamyr village. This northern route, however, is all but deserted, having almost no villages, bad roads and very little traffic.

There are some good trekking routes to the villages of the southern route from Lake Song-Köl, which are outlined under that entry, and there is homestay accommodation available in the villages of Jumgal, Chaek, Kyzart and Doskulu through the Shepherd's Life programme.

CHAEK Chaek is the largest of the villages in this wide, arid valley. The flat landscape that surrounds the village is agricultural, with fields of vegetables and livestock, but further west towards Kyzyl-Oi the scenery becomes increasingly more dramatic with colourful rock formations and rugged cliffs.

Shepherd's Life provides **B&B accommodation** at the home of Guljan Mykyeva, the local co-ordinator, who lives near the hospital (*Moldaliev 4;* \ *03536 22 879.* $).

Other homestays that are part of the Shepherd's Life programme are run by Vera Jamantaeva, Gulzat Moldojusupova and Bural Sultankulova.

A daily **bus service** runs between Chaek and Kochkor along the valley, stopping at all the villages on the way. There is no public transport running west but a private car can be organised through Shepherd's Life.

KYZART This long, rambling village lies just a couple of kilometres off the main road that links Kochkor and Suusamyr. It is a useful start point for a trek over the mountains to Lake Song-Köl, which involves a climb of around 1,000m and a descent of around 400m. An easier option would be to do it in reverse, starting at the lake.

There is a Shepherd's Life project established in the village, which can provide **accommodation**, horses, guides and **transport** out of the valley. The co-ordinator's house can be found at the far eastern end of the village. A CBT car to Kyzart from Kochkor will cost around 1,600som, although you should be able to find a taxi that will charge less than this. There is also reputedly a 06.00 daily bus that leaves for Kochkor from the village.

Kilemche *jailoo* can be reached in a few hours on horseback from Kyzart village. The Shepherd's Life co-ordinator in the village can provide horses and organise an overnight yurt stay at the *jailoo*. From here it is possible to reach Lake Song-Köl in 5 hours by horse. Another *jailoo* in the area that also has yurts to stay in is at Chaar Archa, 10km from Kilemche.

MIN-KUSH Very much the end of the road in every sense, Min-Kush ('A Thousand Birds') lies in a valley south of Chaek surrounded by the peaks of the Moldo-Too range. Like Kazarman further to the south, it was once a prosperous mining town of 20,000, but now it has a deserted feel to it and many of its Soviet-period apartments are partially empty. Since the uranium ore mine and the felt-tip-pen factory has closed down there is hardly any work here.

Even more worryingly, there are four uranium ore waste dumps in the vicinity of the town that have stood here since the uranium mines were closed down in 1969 and that have yet to be sealed adequately. There is great concern that the threat of landslides caused by earthquakes could destabilise the dumps and cause river dams to fracture, which would result in the River Naryn (and subsequently the Syr Darya, one of the major water sources in the central Asian region) becoming heavily polluted with radioactivity. As it is, local cancer levels are already said to be high. A joint US-Russian project to clean up radioactive storage facilities in Kyrgyzstan was launched in 2003 and various inter-ministerial and international assessments of the potential hazard have been made since, although it would appear that the matter has yet to be adequately dealt with and the risk remains.

LAKE SONG-KÖL ОЗЕРО СОН-КЁЛЬ

In many ways, Lake Song-Köl (sometimes written Son-Kul) is Kyrgyzstan's poster girl. The lake is an almost archetypal destination of the wilderness variety, having all of the necessary ingredients to create a picture-perfect vignette of the Kyrgyz nomadic way of life: a wide alpine lake, nomads on horseback, yurts, lush green pasture, bare snow-capped mountains and contented herds of livestock. With the right conditions – a golden sun setting over still waters; the ring of surrounding mountains transformed into a purple velvet backdrop; unseen cattle lowing as dusk falls – it is almost too perfect to be true. Even in less than optimal circumstances – sloping rain, wind-driven sleet, an electrical storm crackling around the shore – it is still wholly exhilarating. Lake Song-Köl certainly lives up to its reputation: a heart-wrenchingly beautiful place where only the most begrudging of critics would make much of a fuss about the way that low-level tourism has crept in to mildly affect its character in recent years.

Kyrgyzstan's second-largest lake stands at 3,016m, at almost the dead centre of the country. One meaning of its name may be translated as 'The Last Lake' and this seems wholly appropriate for such a large, pristine isolated lake that can seem like it is at the end of the world. The lake is 18km wide and 29km long but only 13m deep. Altitude keeps its temperatures low, with a year-round average of around -3.5°C, a summer temperature average of about 11°C and winter freezes down to -20°C. The lake freezes over in the winter and, with over 200 days of annual snow cover, access is very difficult at this time of year. The lake comes into its own during the short summer (June–September) when the extensive *jailoos* that surround the lake are utilised for grazing by herdsmen from across Naryn Oblast. At this time of year there are a considerable number of yurts clustered in small family groups around its shores.

There are no trees at the lake, or in the surrounding hills, but in season there is an abundance of alpine flowers, most notably gentians, wild tulips and edelweiss, and herbs such as sage and chamomile. The lake is rich in waterfowl and waders, with a total of 66 species recorded that include several species of gull and duck, bald coots and the rare Indian mountain goose. Raptors are also well represented with golden eagles and various falcons present in summer. Migratory birds such as storks and cranes stop here on passage. Animals recorded in the vicinity of the lake include foxes, deer, lynx, wolves and, of course, marmots, which are plentiful in the surrounding hills. The lake was devoid of fish until 1959 when it was stocked for the first time. A two-year moratorium on fishing for some species was announced in 2004 because of depleted stocks. The lake and its immediate shoreline is part of the Karatal-Japyryk State Reserve.

The **best time to visit** Lake Song-Köl is between June and September, although the beginning and end of the season can be very cold at night – even in August it is cold at night, barely above freezing. Outside this period, there will be nowhere to stay at the lake as all of the yurts will be dismantled and the herders returned to the valleys. A visit outside the summer months is ill-advised not simply because of a lack of accommodation or cold temperatures: part of the Song-Köl experience is an appreciation of how Kyrgyz nomads live in tune with their environment and to experience the lake without people would be not to do it full justice.

GETTING THERE

By private transport There are four routes that approach the lake, more or less from the cardinal points of the compass. These vary in terms of difficulty, time taken and convenience. There is no public transport to the lake and so transport to and from it needs to be arranged, either privately, through CBT, or with a travel agency.

Probably the commonest approach is **from the east** via the village of **Sary-Bulak**, which lies 45km south on the main Kochkor to Naryn road. Sary-Bulak is little more than a truck-stop, with yurts and cafés selling food, with usually a line of Chinese lorries parked up for a meal *en route* to China via the Torugart Pass. The road climbs up from the main road through Köng-Suu village (sometimes called Tölök) and twists along the Tölök River past pasture full of sheep, cattle and horses, and higher up, yaks. This route is 85km long and takes about 1½ hours to drive. The road is quite reasonable most of the way, although the last section can be a little rough, and this route is perfectly possible in a solid Russian car like a Zhiguli. For the other routes listed below, or for driving any distance around the lake's muddy perimeter, a 4×4 such as a Niva is necessary.

Another approach that is often used if the lake is to be reached from the direction of Naryn is the route from the **southeast**, a dirt track that leads off the Kochkor–Naryn road, near the village of Kara-Ünkür south of Sary-Bulak, and follows a dramatic series of hairpin bends to reach the lake at its southeast corner. This route to the lake is 90km long from Naryn and takes about 2½ hours.

The **western** side of Lake Song-Köl may be reached from Chaek, turning off the road south at Bajzak to lead past the coal mines of Kara-Kichi, from where a track climbs up through hairpin bends to a 3,300m pass, from where it gently descends to the lake. The fourth route is from the **south**, over the Moldo Pass from the village of Kurtka (also known as Jangy-Talap), across the Naryn River from Ak-Tal on the Naryn to Kazarman road.

Outside the summer months some of these routes will be periodically blocked by snow. It is also possible to arrange a vehicle to take you in by one route and leave by another, which is an advantage if you want to fit in a visit to the lake between Kochkor and Naryn without retracing any steps. A 2-day, 1-night return trip to the lake from Kochkor booked through CBT costs 2,250som including the driver's meals. To continue to Naryn from the lake would cost more. A CBT car from Naryn charges 2,700som.

If you are planning on hiking out of Song-Köl, say to Kyzart, be aware that a one-way trip will prove expensive because you are obliged to pay for the return journey to base. The cheapest alternative to reach the lake from Naryn is probably to take a minibus to Kurtka from the bazaar, which leaves at 13.00, takes 2 hours and costs 80som. There are also occasional shared taxis. At Kurtka, the Shepherd's Life coordinator, Sveta Jusupjanova at Yntymak 45, can organise a vehicle to the south shore of the lake for around 900som – a little bargaining is acceptable.

On foot or horseback There are two principal trekking routes to the lake. The first is from the north, starting at the village of Kyzart where there is a Shepherd's Life co-ordinator. The other main approach is from the south from the village of Kurtka, 4km north of Ak-Tal on the Naryn–Kazarman road. CBT Kochkor can help organise the Kyzart approach and CBT Naryn the Kurtka route. Other routes are possible too, with proper planning, such as a 3-day horse trek from the Chon-Tuz salt caves. For those wishing to walk around the lake – an excellent idea – allow 4 or 5 days for a leisurely circumnavigation.

ACCOMMODATION AND OTHER PRACTICALITIES There are **yurts** dotted all the way around the lake, many affiliated to the CBT organisation, others to Shepherd's Life, some dedicated for the use of particular tour companies, and some belonging to families of no affiliation who will, none the less, also take in paying guests. You can, of course, **camp** almost anywhere, but bring all the food you need, warm clothes and some means of water purification.

Most of the CBT and Shepherd's Life yurts are located to the south, southeast and east of the lake. There are also some (Shepherd's Life and others) in the northwest, close to the track over the mountains that leads to Kyzart. The biggest group of all is on the east side close to the lagoon, where the road from Kochkor terminates. This is where most visitors arrive at the lake and the yurt 'village' here is where the bulk of group-tour cultural activities, like folk music recitals, tend to take place.

As well as accommodation, hot meals can be organised if you are starting or ending a walk around the lake, although you may have to wait an hour or two for it to be cooked if it is an *ad hoc* request. The strip of land that divides the lagoon from the lake is a pleasant place for a stroll whilst waiting. Horses may be hired here too, and it is perhaps a good idea to rent horses and ride some distance north or south for a little more tranquillity away from the yurt 'village'. Having said that, even here the commercialisation is at a very low level, all things considered.

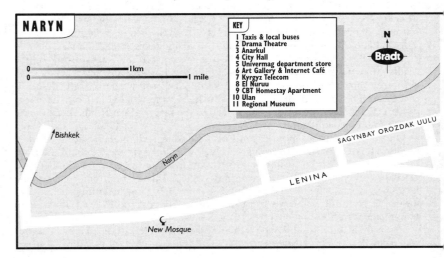

NARYN

KEY
1 Taxis & local buses
2 Drama Theatre
3 Anarkul
4 City Hall
5 Univermag department store
6 Art Gallery & Internet Café
7 Kyrgyz Telecom
8 El Nuruu
9 CBT Homestay Apartment
10 Ulan
11 Regional Museum

N

Bradt

0 ——————— 1 km
0 ——————— 1 mile

Bishkek

Naryn

SAGYNBAY OROZDAK UULU

LENINA

New Mosque

A 3-hour hike north of here along the shore (less on horseback) brings you to an area on the northeastern shore where there is a shallow river outlet and low hills that almost come down to the lake. There are a few CBT yurts here as well as others, across the river, which are used by the NoviNomad tour company. This is a wonderful spot for an overnight stay. Others recommend the western shore – it is all marvellous really.

Standard CBT rates apply for B&B, although private yurts may charge a little less. Yurt accommodation is around 350som per person with meals; horse hire is 70som per hour or 350som per day. If a horse guide is required it is also necessary to pay for him and his horse. There are absolutely no shops at Song-Köl, although some yurts may sell *kumys* and other dairy products.

NARYN НАРЫН *Telephone code: 03522*

Naryn is rarely cited as one of Kyrgyzstan's 'must see' attractions and, although there are few who can be bothered to write about the town, it still tends to get a bad press. Certainly, it is not the most attractive of places, and there is little to see in the town, but given the harsh reality that most visitors need to stop for at least a night here on their way to the Torugart Pass, Tash Rabat or elsewhere, it seems disingenuous to run it down, as it really could be far worse. Naryn may be a rough, tough sprawl that lacks much genuine charm, but it is an interesting place in a warts-and-all sort of way, and probably more typical of post-independence Kyrgyzstan than either Bishkek or Karakol. It also has an efficiently-run local CBT group and some reasonable places to stay and eat.

Naryn started life as a Russian garrison in 1868, and there is still an army base in the town today, but it was in the post-World War II period that most of the current town was constructed, and this is characterised by the large number of *khrushchevki* apartment blocks found throughout the town.

In 1920 the town was the scene of a battle between Bolshevik soldiers and White Russian forces led by *kulaks* from Tokmok and Naryn, who succeeded in killing the local party chairman, Orozbekov, and capturing the communist commander. The counter-revolutionaries were later defeated at battles at the Shamshy and Dolon passes.

Since 1927, the town has served as the provincial administrative centre for Naryn Oblast and has a population of around 45,000. The town is host to one of three

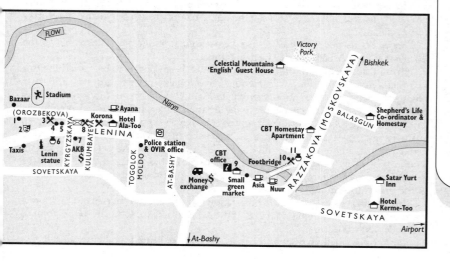

campuses of the University of Central Asia, an international university that was founded in 2000 by the governments of Kazakhstan, Kyrgyzstan and Tajikistan with backing from the Aga Khan.

The town is long and thin, following the course of the Naryn River for several kilometres east to west. Sandstone cliffs fringe the town just beyond the river to the north, while south of the town a wide flat plain gives way to arid pale mountains. The town's linear form is one possible etymology for its name, which may come from the Chinese for 'narrow'.

Another potential derivation is from the Mongolian word for 'sunny', which is not without irony: the town is undoubtedly sunny in summer – and also hot and dusty – but the winter climate here, at an altitude of 2,040m above sea level, is extremely harsh, with temperatures that plunge on occasion to as low as –40°C. Such an unforgiving climate, coupled with the relative poverty of the place, may well have some bearing on the tough character of the town's inhabitants. Naryn's population, which is almost entirely Kyrgyz, has something of a reputation for confrontation and drunkenness, although in fairness this does not seem to be any worse than elsewhere in the country.

GETTING THERE There are several direct **minibuses** daily from Bishkek's West Bus Station that run in the mornings and take at least 6 hours to reach Naryn by way of Tokmok and the Chui valley, and Kochkor and the Dolon Pass. Most minibuses bypass Balykchy and take a shortcut via the Orto-Tokoy reservoir. A similar number leave in the reverse direction from Naryn's **main bus station** on Lenina, mostly in the morning. The cost is in the order of 150–200som.

The main bus station also has regular but infrequent **buses** to Kazarman via Baetov. The Kazarman bus runs on Tuesday and Friday at 08.00, taking 7 hours and costing 200som. If there are not enough tickets sold for the bus, a minibus is used to replace the service. Buses for At-Bashy leave three times daily in the afternoons and take 1 hour, costing 25som. There is also a daily bus to the villages of Kara-Suu, Kara-Bulun and Kyzyl-Tuu (35som) that lie beyond At-Bashy on the road to Torugart. A daily bus for Baetov along the Naryn valley west leaves at 08.00, costing 80som, and several buses leave for Tash-Bashat on the road to Eki-Naryn between 08.00–16.00 (25som). To Eki-Naryn itself, there is a bus three times a week that leaves on Monday, Wednesday and Friday mornings (35som).

The **central bazaar** also has a small bus station that has daily departures in very crowded buses to villages west along the Kazarman road such as Dostuk and Kurtka (Jangy-Talap).

Foreigners are not permitted to use the occasional public buses that run over the Torugart Pass to Artysh and Kashgar in China.

Hiring a **taxi** in Naryn can pose a problem as there appears to be something of a taxi mafia in which no-one will negotiate a reasonable price to a destination. Any attempt at sensible negotiation with an individual driver is met by other drivers coming up to argue, effectively intimidating their colleague into not dropping the price. This is perversely counterproductive as they end up getting no fare at all. In many Kyrgyz towns it is quite possible, with a bit of legwork and bartering, to find a taxi at considerably less than the CBT price; this does not seem to be the case in Naryn. The irony is that Naryn seems to have more than its fair share of would-be taxi drivers; they congregate on Lenina opposite the bazaar, in the bazaar itself and at the main bus station.

Share taxis congregate at the bus station, poaching customers from buses that are due to leave. To Kochkor, it costs 150som per place; to At-Bashy, 60–75som; to Bishkek, 300–400som.

Naryn has a small **airport** to the east of the town, but it is currently closed.

Most of Naryn lies within reasonable walking distance, but consider taking a taxi for longer distances (30–50som, but haggle) or take one of the rickety trolleybuses that ply up and down Lenina.

TOURIST INFORMATION CBT Naryn (*Apartment 33, Lenina 8;* ↘ *50 865,* ↘ *50 895;* f *50 865;* m *0502 689 262;* e *naryn_tourism@rambler.ru, kubat-tour@mail.ru*), in the very capable hands of co-ordinator Kubat Abdyldaev, has an information office where homestay accommodation can be booked and advice given on travel in the region. The office staff are very knowledgeable about the region and are very helpful whether you take their tours or not. Private transport can be booked using their pool of drivers at the standard rate. As it is hard to get a good deal from local taxi drivers in Naryn, this is not a bad option. Standard 2-day tours may be arranged to At-Bashy, Tash Rabat and Lake Chatyr-Köl, along with various local tours to places such as the deer nursery at Iiri-Suu.

They can also organise longer horseback tours from Ak-Tam, west of Naryn, to Lake Song-Köl or Lake Issyk-Kul. Horseback tours with **Shepherd's Life** to Lake Song-Köl from Kurtka village to the south, or Kyzart to the north, may also be arranged here. The office also has a good store of maps, brochures and guidebooks, and a computer room with four terminals that have internet access.

WHERE TO STAY
Homestays

CBT apartment 33, Lenina 8; ↘ 50 865, ↘ 50 895; f 50 865; m 0502 689 262; e naryn_tourism@rambler.ru, kubat-tour@mail.ru. Naryn's Community Based Tourism network has a total of 8 homestays around the town, most of which are in Soviet-era apts. A particularly convenient homestay is the one just around the corner from the CBT office at apt 2, Lenina 8, which is run by Jeenkan Jumaly Kyzy & her helpful daughter Parizat. The owners live upstairs (↘ 23 963) & will bring meals down to the apt on a tray. Another very friendly place is at apt 6, Razzakova

(formerly Moskovskaya) 18, near The English Guest House, which is the home of Aisalkyn Karasartova, who speaks German & is a fine cook. Standard rates apply at all CBT homestays. *B&B* $; *dinner 90som.*

Shepherd's Life Balasgun 14, junction with Zavodska; ↘ 41 457, ↘ 50 865 (office shared with CBT); e shepherdslife@rambler.ru. The Shepherd's Life co-ordinator, Marima Amankulova, has rooms in her house in a quiet, village-like district at the eastern edge of the town on the opposite side of the road from The English Guest House. *B&B* $, *dinner 90som.*

Hotels

Celestial Mountains Guest House (11 rooms) Razzakova 42; ↘/f 50 412; www.celestial.com.kg. Also known & advertised as The English Guest House, this small hotel, tucked away from the town centre in a quiet neighbourhood next to a park, is the most comfortable place to stay in Naryn. The guesthouse has helpful, English-speaking staff & facilities that include hot showers, emergency generator, internet access, video room with library & a menu that has both national & Western dishes. Prices include evening meal & b/fast. *Rooms* $$$, *yurt accommodation* $$ pp.

Hotel Ala-Too (100 rooms) Lenina; ↘ 21 872.

The Ala-Too is a large central hotel that has seen few changes since the break-up of the Soviet Union. The cheaper rooms are quite poor but the 'lux' rooms are perfectly reasonable & it is worth paying the extra if you stay here. The café-restaurant outside appears to have been turned into a disco. *Standard room* $, *lux* $$.

Hotel Kerme-Too (9 rooms) Airport road; ↘ 22 621. This hotel, which has been privatised in recent years but not yet fully renovated, is located 3km east of the centre on the very edge of the city in a pleasant leafy cul-de-sac. Bathrooms are communal & there is no restaurant. $

Yurt camps

Satar Yurt Inn (7–10 yurts) Airport road; ↘ 50 322. Situated at the eastern edge of town close to the Hotel Kerme-Too, this is a yurt camp popular

with tour groups. Facilities include hot showers, yurt bar & canteen, heating in autumn. *B&B* $$–$$$ pp, dinner US$4.

🏠 **Salkyn-Tör Yurt Camp** (3–4 yurts) This small yurt camp is 12km from the town on the airport road at Salkyn-Tör gorge. It has a yurt canteen & heating in autumn. B&B $$–$$$, dinner US$4.

✗ WHERE TO EAT

Homestays aside, Naryn has a handful of surprisingly pleasant places to eat, in addition to places around the bazaar that dish out the standard Kyrgyz fare. The bazaar has a wide range of Kyrgyz dairy products and a good selection of fruit in season.

✗ **Korona** Kulumbaeva/Lenina. ⏰ until 23.00. This is a new, purpose-built restaurant & is probably the smartest place in town. Korona has a cavernous interior almost like a hotel lobby, with a high roof & discrete sunken lighting. The menu (in Russian) has a wide range of Russian, Chinese & Kyrgyz dishes at prices little more than anywhere else in town. The waitresses are helpful & the restaurant has a pleasant relaxed atmosphere, although it can get a bit noisy when people take to the dance floor. Popular with middle-class Kyrgyz who come with their friends to eat, drink & dance. $$$

✗ **Anarkul** Sagynbay Orozdak Uulu. Near the junction with Kyrgyzskaya, this large, multi-roomed restaurant is popular with locals at lunchtime & gets very busy with policemen & officials from the Hakimyat. It has a well-stocked bar with a variety of beers & that Kyrgyzstan rarity, an English-language menu. Be aware that not everything listed will be available. $$

✗ **Ayana** Sagynbay Orozdak Uulu. Near the Kyrgyz Bank behind the Hotel Ala-Too, this is a pleasant, airy restaurant with standard Kyrgyz & Russian dishes & — quite surprisingly — an English-language menu. $$

✗ **El Nuruu** Kulumbaeva; ☎ 50 623. A cosy little place with a well-stocked bar located in a side street near the Hotel Ala-Too. $$

✗ **Ulan** Razzakova. This restaurant is just north of the bridge at the eastern end of town near the museum. It has indoor seating as well as an outdoor area of dining cubicles that afford good views over the Naryn River & apt blocks of the town. The Russian-language menu lists mostly Russian dishes. The blue-bottle-studded fly papers that sometimes decorate the tables can be a little off-putting. $$

✗ **Asia** Lenina (near the food stalls before the bridge); 📱 0502 887 388. A local café that serves standard Kyrgyz dishes & has an outdoor seating area. Next door is the Nuur café, which is similar. $

SHOPPING The **central bazaar** has a wide range of foodstuffs and everyday items that are central to livestock rearing. There are more fruit and vegetable stalls at the eastern end of Lenina before the bridge. The Univermag **department store** stands on the corner of Lenina and Kyrgyzskaya and there a couple of **pharmacies** on Kyrgyzskaya nearby.

OTHER PRACTICALITIES Cash (dollars only) can be changed on the first floor of the **AKB Bank** on Kulumbaeva, south of Lenina. Another useful place for changing dollars is the two-storey white house just west of the CBT office on the other side of the road before the bus station. This is a drapery wholesaler but they will change cash (large denomination, crisp new dollar bills only) at a good rate if you knock on the front door. It is also probably possible to change money in the bazaar. At the time of research there were no ATM cash dispensers in the town, or banks that would change travellers' cheques.

The town's large **post and telephone office** is on the corner of Lenina and Kyrgyzskaya. International telephone calls may be made from here for about 130som for 5 minutes to Europe. A much cheaper but less dependable option is to make an IP telephone connection to Europe for just 6som per minute. One place to do this is at the internet café with the 'BIG WELCOME' sign above the door on Lenina, just before, and on the opposite side to, the police station. There is a good **internet** connection here too, but you may have to fight your way through the schoolboys that come here to play shoot-'em-up games. There is another internet café downstairs at the art gallery in the main square, and the CBT office also has reliable internet access.

The **OVIR** office, where visas may be extended, is at the Ministry of Foreign Affairs office on Togolok Moldo.

WHAT TO SEE AND DO Naryn is a long sprawling town with few opportunities for sightseeing. The centre of the town revolves around the main square that faces the municipal administrative building, the Hakimyat, where there is a tall, modern statue of a Kyrgyz couple holding an eagle aloft, which is meant to represent Kyrgyz youth. This area was redeveloped in 1999 and the **statue of Lenin** that used to stand here has been moved a couple of blocks west to the leafier surroundings of a park.

The square is also home to a new, purpose-built **art gallery**, which is worth a visit (*entrance 50som*). The gallery has the work of several Kyrgyz artists on display, like Torobekov Kojogulov, who paints scenes from Kyrgyz life and semi-abstract landscapes and still-lifes. There are also some evocative charcoal drawings, attractive ceramics with Saimaluu-Tash petroglyph designs and, naturally, a plushly decorated yurt. The main building of the recently established University of Central Asia stands opposite the art gallery. A little further west stands the Naryn Drama Theatre, with a small plaza in front of it that serves as a location for meeting friends and eating ice creams in summer. The central bazaar lies immediately north of this.

At the far eastern end of the town, close to The English Guest House and the regional museum, is **Victory Park**, a pleasant, wooded park that has a Soviet tank as its centrepiece, which faces a line of seven arches that frame the arid mountains beyond. The park is pretty-much deserted most of the time, but on summer nights it is sometimes used as the venue for drunken outdoor discotheques.

Regional Museum The museum is located just across the bridge over the Naryn River, at the eastern end of town close to The English Guest House. The different rooms here include ethnological displays on the Kyrgyz nomadic way of life, a dissected yurt, traditional costumes, which include some interesting headgear, a room devoted to the life of local revolutionary hero Jukeev Tubaldy Pudovkin, and the obligatory display of stuffed animals. There is also artwork by local artists and a few of the excellent *shyrdaks* for which the province is famous.

New Mosque The new mosque at the western end of town, a couple of kilometres from the centre, is both a dazzling and incongruous sight: a rare splash of colour – blue, turquoise, white – against the khaki-brown hills that form its backdrop. The mosque was built with the help of Saudi money in 1993 and has a number of different architectural elements in its design that combine together in a post-modernist sort of way. There is, without doubt, a definite Arabian element in its design, and the irregular, patterned frieze that frames the doorway resembles a Kyrgyz traditional *shyrdak* pattern to some extent. In contrast, the wooden cupola that tops the pepper-pot minaret seems to be at odds with the rest of the building, and devalues the integrity of the design with its *Arabian Nights* appearance.

EAST OF NARYN

The Naryn River passing through the regional capital leads east past the airport to Salkyn-Tör, an attractive canyon that is popular as a picnic spot for Naryn's citizens, and that has a yurt camp for visitors (see *Naryn accommodation*, page 211). The area is partially protected as being part of the Salkyn-Tör State Park, which covers a considerable area along the Naryn River immediately to the east of Naryn. The road continues east to reach the quiet village of Tash-Bashat. East of here, further along the Naryn River and close to the border with Issyk-Kul Oblast, lies the Naryn State Reserve, one of Kyrgyzstan's six state reserves, which was established in 1983 to preserve coniferous forest and alpine meadows.

The 200m-wide swastika that can be clearly seen in a fir plantation on a hillside near the small village of Tash-Bashat in Naryn Province is an enigma that is clouded by legend and conflicting memories. The so-called Eki-Naryn swastika is actually a reverse, left-handed swastika, with the top and bottom arms incomplete. Nevertheless, it is still an unmistakeable symbol, with all the chilling resonances that are normally associated with it.

The swastika is said to be at least 60 years old, and common legend tells of stranded German prisoners of war, forced into forestry after the end of World War II, planting rows of seedlings in this shape. This legend is probably not the exact truth. There are others who say that the plantation was planted in the 1940s by Kyrgyz labourers from a local collective farm that was managed by a German Nazi sympathiser who, like many ethnic Germans in the Soviet Union, had been exiled to central Asia by Stalin during the war. Another theory suggests that the trees were planted just after Stalin's death in 1953 under the supervision of a female German forester. Another, unlikely, suggestion is that the trees were planted in the late 1930s at the time that Stalin and Hitler were signing a peace pact together, as a symbol of Soviet-German friendship.

Whatever the exact truth, it is unlikely that German prison gangs ever worked in the area. There were labour camps near Bishkek and Osh, and some prisoners had been forced to dig uranium mines at Mailuu-Suu, but no-one in the area remembers Germans being used as labourers, although there do seem to be several recollections of a German woman supervising the planting of the plantation using local Kyrgyz labour.

There are those of the New-Age persuasion that decry the Nazi connotations entirely, saying that as a reverse swastika it is actually a representation of the sacred symbol frequently used in the Hindu and Buddhist religions, even suggesting that the name Eki-Naryn is a distortion of *Eki Narayan*, 'One God'. However, such a theory does not really correspond with the certainty that the trees were planted in the mid 20th century.

Tash-Bashat (formerly Kalinin) is famous for one thing and one thing only: close to the village on a hillside in the Naryn-Too range is an area of forest that has clearly been planted in the shape of a swastika, a tangible reminder of the horrors of Nazism in World War II (see box, *The Swastika Forest of Naryn Province*, above). The forest can be best seen from the roadside just north of the river-crossing, on the road that leads past the village's small mosque.

A very rough unmade road leads east from Tash-Bashat's village mosque up and over a steep hill to reach the **Iiri-Suu deer nursery**. The road really needs a 4×4 to be on the safe side, although I managed to reach it in a Volkswagen Golf with a feisty driver – an object lesson as to what Kyrgyz drivers will put their cars through for a fistful of som. The deer nursery, which covers 50ha, was established in 2002 for the protection of orphaned, sick and injured maral deer that are often poached in the surrounding region for their antlers, which are then sold in China. Once recovered, the deer are released back into the wild.

The reserve, which has up to 250 deer, consists of a fenced-off portion of a gorge, as well as small enclosures where younger deer are kept. While the cause is no doubt praiseworthy, a visit to the nursery is rather like a trip to a zoo at feeding time, although it makes for an enjoyable experience for children.

Returning to Tash-Bashat, the road continues north along the east bank of the Kichi-Naryn River to the village of Eki-Naryn, crossing a bridge just before the village.

EKI-NARYN The village of Eki-Naryn ('Two Naryns', ie: the confluence of the two rivers) is spread out on a flat area above the gorge of the Kichi-Naryn River, just beyond the point where the river divides into the Naryn and its equally impressive tributary the Kichi-Naryn. The road crosses the Naryn River to follow the east bank of the Kichi-Naryn for a short distance to reach the village.

Eki-Naryn is a pretty village and its setting, even by Kyrgyzstan's high standards, is glorious, with red sandstone cliffs along the river and the high peaks of the Jetim and Naryn-Too ranges looming to the north and south. The valley is so gorgeous here that it begs to be followed north and east deep into the Terskey Ala-Too. It is certainly possible to cycle, hike or ride the route that leads along the Kichi-Naryn and Burkan or Jyluu-Suu valleys to Lake Issyk-Kul over the Tosor Pass, although this would require total independence in terms of food and shelter, and would make more sense done in the opposite direction.

Returning to Naryn, rather than retracing previous steps, a 4×4 could continue northeast from Eki-Naryn along the valley to reach the tiny village of Oryook-Tam. From there it could then leave the river to loop north along the Kara-Saz stream, before heading west along a track that climbs over a couple of passes to follow the Kara-Kujur River back to the main Kochkor–Naryn road at Sary-Bulak.

There is plenty of scope for wild camping close to the village. Public buses from Naryn run three times a week on Monday, Wednesday and Friday mornings. More conveniently, a taxi costs 900som return trip including a 2-hour wait.

NARYN TO THE TORUGART PASS

The road south to China from Naryn caused some consternation when its presence was first discovered by the British in the early 20th century. This was in the latter days of the Great Game era, when British and Russian diplomats in the region kept a close eye on each others' activities, wary that their colonial competitors might gain the upper hand. In 1905, the British Consul to Kashgar, Sir George McCartney, made the unsettling discovery that the Russians had constructed a road from At-Bashy near the Russian garrison at Naryn to the Torugart Pass on the Chinese border, a road which extended a little way into China itself. The main concern at the time was the possibility of the Russians annexing China's Xinjiang Province by means of the new road.

As it transpired, the foremost motive was actually that of international trade. The Chinese side of the road that led to Kashgar was completed in the following year by means of a Russian loan to the Chinese government, which was to be repaid by imposing a toll to use the road. The Russians soon ended up having the monopoly of trade along the route, which displeased the Chinese to the extent that they raised the toll so high that the road soon fell into disuse.

The route from Naryn leads over the 2,484m Kyzyl-Bel Pass to cross a valley to bypass the small town of At-Bashy, which lies just south of the highway, 40km from Naryn. The Chinese frontier is still another 150km away, but this is the last sizeable place before the border other than a handful of villages such as Kara-Suu, Kara-Bulung, Kyzyl-Too and Kazibek. A few kilometres beyond At-Bashy are the ruins of the citadel of Koshoy Korgon, near the village of Kara-Suu.

From Kara-Suu, the highway continues straight as an arrow along the dead flat valley of the Kara-Suu River, which is squeezed between the parallel ranges of the snow-capped At-Bashy mountains to the south and the slightly lower Jaman-Too to the north. It is a largely deserted landscape, apart from occasional herders with their flocks of sheep and a couple of evocatively eroded Kyrgyz cemeteries near the roadside.

Naturally, much of the light traffic heading this way is involved in tourism of one sort or another, ferrying travellers to Tash Rabat and the Chinese border. The remaining vehicles along this road are either large Chinese lorries delivering cheap manufactured goods to Kyrgyz markets, or battered Kyrgyz trucks loaded high with scrap metal and fleeces heading for the Torugart Pass. This obvious two-way commerce brings alive the government statistics that suggest that Kyrgyzstan's foreign trade is largely dependent on animal skins and the recycling of ferrous metals. There is a stretch of road just west of At-Bashy where the road widens dramatically and improves in quality. This section was constructed as an emergency military air strip in the event of a Chinese invasion years ago; it was never used. After about 3km or so, this unnervingly wide section – a veritable motorway – suddenly reverts to its former width.

Just before Ak-Beit, where a dirt road from Chaek joins the highway, there is a turn-off south to the remarkable caravanserai of Tash Rabat, a worthy destination in its own right, whether or not the crossing to China is on the agenda, and a fairly essential side-trip for those heading for Torugart. Beyond Ak-Beit the road twists south to climb up over the 3,282m pass before reaching the Korgon-Tash outer checkpoint 4km further on, which marks the beginning of the border zone. The road worsens from this point on, turning from tarmac to loose gravel.

Leaving the checkpoint, the road skirts the western fringe of the At-Bashy range to climb up to the 3,574m Tüz-Bel Pass. From here it leads east above the southern shore of **Lake Chatyr-Köl**, a high alpine lake with a marshy shoreline that lies at the far western end of the **Ak-Say valley**, a high, wide plateau where large herds of yak graze in summer and hunters from At-Bashy come to catch marmots. This is a wonderful area for fully independent hiking and camping but it requires a border permit because of the proximity of China.

Lake Chatyr-Köl, which at 3,530m is the highest of Kyrgyzstan's larger lakes, is protected as part of the Chatyr-Köl Zoological Preserve, one of the three protected areas of the Karatal-Japyrak State Reserve that also includes Lake Song-Köl. The lake has no fish but it attracts some rare migratory birds to breed here, most notably bar-headed goose (*Anser indicus*), the world's highest flying bird, as well as birds on passage such as cranes. Because of the wet, boggy ground that surrounds the lake it can be difficult to get very close to the shoreline.

Continuing to climb above the lake's southern shore, and passing some roadside railway carriages that serve as basic dormitory hotels, the Kyrgyzstan customs and immigration post is finally reached 50km beyond the outer checkpoint. From here it is another 5km to the first Chinese checkpoint (the main Chinese customs and immigration post is well into Chinese territory, another 70km further on) and then a further 2km to the summit of Torugart Pass. Up until 2002 there was a Chinese archway that marked the border but this has since been removed.

AT-BASHY At-Bashy is an attractive small town set in a highly dramatic landscape 40km from Naryn, a few kilometres south of the main Naryn–Torugart Pass highway. With the near-5,000m peaks of the At-Bashy range looming large to the south and a large evocative Kyrgyz cemetery standing on a ridge above the town, At-Bashy's location is quite spectacular, and the town is a good choice for an overnight stay *en route* to the Chinese border, or as a base for day excursions to Koshoy Korgon and Tash Rabat.

The town is a thoroughly provincial sort of place and, as the last settlement of any size before the Chinese frontier, it does have a certain edge-of-the-world feel about it. As the administrative headquarters of the At-Bashy *rayon*, which extends along the valley, it has all the basic ingredients you might expect – a few civic buildings, a park, a small bazaar and odd fragments here and there of a Soviet past.

The town developed on the foundations of a much older settlement that dates from between the 8th–14th centuries, of which no trace remains today. Formerly there were a number of collective farms in the vicinity, but these were abandoned along with communism, and the town is a markedly poorer place today, with high unemployment.

The town's main street stretches east to west, with the bus station at the far eastern end by an equestrian statue, and some concrete yurts selling booze. Close to this stands a very traditional *chaikhana* and a new mosque. Walking west towards the centre is an enclosure where the weekly animal market is held, and a large government building with busts of prominent Kyrgyz leaders in its grounds. The centre, such as it is, is marked by an abandoned cinema and the Kyrgyz telecom building; a sign here points north towards the Shepherd's Life guesthouse.

Immediately west of here is a dusty park with a war memorial and gold-painted busts, the Ak Bank and the bazaar. The road that leads north from the Shepherd's Life sign, Aity Suleymanov, is home to the post office and the combined Ak-Say store, café and *gostinitsa*. To reach the Shepherd's Life homestay, walk down here for four blocks and then turn left at the second sign; the homestay is at the end of this road, a large rambling house that is taller than those surrounding it.

Getting there There are three buses a day between Naryn and At-Bashy (25som), an occasional *marshrutka* (50som) and share taxis for 75som. A taxi taken privately will cost 300som. There are also share taxis and minibuses to Bishkek. There is no public transport to Tash Rabat, but a taxi there and back with waiting time should cost 1,500som. Buses and minibuses leave from the bus station, although minibuses will also pick up at the bazaar if they are not already full. Most taxis congregate outside the bazaar, although there may be one or two at the bus station.

Where to stay

Shepherd's Life homestay Arpa 25; \ 03534 21 944. Homestay accommodation may be found at the comfortable home of Shepherd's Life co-ordinator Tursan Akaeva, who has a large house in the northwest of the town, just below the cemetery on the ridge. The house, which has an outside toilet in the garden, is unusually large, with an upstairs sleeping area decorated with *shyrdaks*. The atmosphere is slightly shambolic, with a constant stream of local visitors coming & going. The redoubtable Tursan can also organise local taxis & arrange transportation to Tash Rabat or Koshoy Korgon & arrange visits to local *shyrdak*-makers. B&B $, meals 120som.

Ak-Say hotel Aity Suleymanov 29. This combined shop, café & *gostinitsa* has a few basic rooms. $

Where to eat

Kadirzhan café \ 03534 22 517. This new-looking café almost opposite the bazaar is probably the best place in town. The fancy wooden entrance has what looks like a carved Chinese symbol at the front. The food is, in fact, Russian, with staples like *pelmeni* at low prices. $$

There are more cafés along the main street towards the bus station. The bazaar has a reasonable range of fruit, vegetables and dairy produce; there is a good *nan* bakery on the main street just to the west of the bazaar.

Other practicalities The **post office** is on Aity Suleymanov, north of the crossroads by the park. Kyrgyz Telecom is just south of here. There is *very* slow internet access in the telecom building.

What to see and do At-Bashy's splendour is its location and the landscape that surrounds it. Apart from remnants of the Soviet era that survive on the main street – a park with a war memorial, a Lenin bust, a police building that still has red stars decorating the wall – the town's most impressive sight is the large Kyrgyz **cemetery** that stands on a ridge just north of the town. There are actually two separate graveyards with a tiny Christian cemetery standing in between the two. The views over the town, valley and the At-Bashy range here are superb in the late afternoon or early evening. Another worthwhile walk is down to the At-Bashy River just south of the town.

KOSHOY KORGON Located about 15km from At-Bashy, Korgon is a ruined citadel at the edge of Kara-Suu village that dates from between the 10th and 12th centuries. The structure may well be Karakhanid in origin, although there is also a legend that it was built by Manas as a mausoleum for his fiend Kolshoy who fell in battle, which gives rise to its name: 'Koshoy's burial place'.

All that is left today is a large section of 2–3m high crumbling clay walls that delineate the extent of the original building; it is an impressive site nevertheless. Archaeological work was carried out on the site in 2004 and there is talk of a tourist centre being set up in the future.

The citadel is reached by turning left after Kara-Suu's mosque and war memorial and then continuing to the end of the road, where the ruins are found in a field to the right.

A taxi from At-Bashy will cost around 300som for the round trip.

TASH RABAT Tash Rabat is probably Kyrgyzstan's most remarkable monument; indeed, it is one of the most interesting sites in the entire central Asian region and its presence is in complete contradiction to the popular tenet that Kyrgyzstan is all about landscapes rather than historical sights. Tash Rabat is a Silk Road monument *par excellence*: a small but perfectly formed 15th-century caravanserai that sheltered an array of merchants and travellers along one of the wilder stretches of the Silk Road. Its location is even more remarkable: tucked away from sight, half-buried in a hillside, up a valley at 3,530m above sea level.

The building is entirely stone-built, half-sunken into the hillside from which it emerges almost organically like a rocky outcrop. It is a broad rectangle in shape, measuring 36m long but looking smaller from the outside because some of its internal structure lies beneath the hillside. The front entrance leads into a central hall that is surrounded by a network of small rooms, about 30 in all, which were used as bedrooms, prison cells, pantries and prayer rooms. A dome stands above the central hallway and this still bears faint traces of plaster and decorative paintwork. Facing the entrance just beyond the dome is the khan's seat, where the local ruler would have sat, and behind this is a small room that would have probably served as a gaol, as there are two deep, covered holes, one of which has been subsequently filled in, in which prisoners may have been confined. There is also a well for supplying water. Local rumour suggests that there was also a tunnel leading from the building through the hillside to a lookout post on the other side of the hill. It is probable that the building served many purposes: as a place of rest and Muslim worship, and as protection from both bandit attacks and the sometimes atrocious weather of the region.

The site may have been originally used as a monastery by Nestorian Christians, or even possibly by Buddhists, who lived in the region before the 13th-century Mongol invasions took place, and well before Islam came to the region. There is some archaeological evidence to suggest that the building may have been occupied as early as the 10th century, which would support this theory. Whatever the true historical facts, there is no denying the atmosphere of the place, which seems to be imbued with ghosts of the past and authentically redolent of the old Silk Road. The cold, dank atmosphere inside the building and the altitude-rarefied air both help cement this impression.

The Soviet restoration that took place in 1984 was carried out in an uncharacteristically sensitive way and, apart from some mortar added to cement the stones together, has done little to damage the integrity of the structure, the only gripe being the need to position the car park directly in front of the entrance, thus blighting photo opportunities from this direction.

Part of Tash Rabat's timeless appeal is thanks to its location in a high, velvet-green valley far away from anything that vaguely resembles civilisation. Another element of its wow factor owes much to the journey taken to reach the site. Tash Rabat lies 125km from Naryn and 90km short of the border at Torugart. After turning off the main road to the border just after the stretch of aircraft runway, it is another 15km along a small but very beautiful valley, the Kara-Kojon gorge, before the caravanserai is reached. There is an entrance fee of 50som to pay to go inside the caravanserai. The caretaker lives directly opposite and will probably find you first if you arrive by taxi.

Getting there Many tour companies have Tash Rabat firmly on their itineraries, either as a destination in itself or as an appendage to a trip to China via Torugart. CBT Naryn can organise transport and yurt accommodation for those wishing to make an overnight or longer trip here from Naryn. Individual travellers can organise taxis from either Naryn or At-Bashy, which should cost in the order of 1,500som return from At-Bashy or 2,000som from Naryn.

Where to stay There is a fair choice of yurts to stay in if you wish to overnight, either close to the monument or a couple of kilometres back down the valley. **Shepherd's Life** have a few yurts here (with signs outside to that effect so there is no confusion) that charge the usual going rate (*B&B* $, *meals 90som*). The **caretaker** has a few yurts opposite the entrance, which are a little cheaper than Shepherd's Life yurts, and there are some private yurts a little further down the valley that offer accommodation and meals to travellers.

The **Yurt Inn**, owned by the same company that also has yurt camps in Naryn and nearby Salkyn-Tör, have a small yurt camp near the monument that is a little more luxurious, with a tent lavatory and yurt-canteen (*B&B* $$, *dinner 200som*).

All of the above tend to be open in the tourist season only, which here is late May to September. Although yurts usually provide adequate bedding, be aware that it is very cold at night here. Toilet and washing facilities are either rudimentary or non-existent. Do not use the stream for toilet duties of any sort as, understandably, this upsets the locals who use its waters for drinking and cooking.

Hikes from Tash Rabat Tash Rabat makes a good base for hikes or horse rides in the vicinity. Horses may be hired from the Tash Rabat caretaker who charges around 70som per hour and who can provide a guide for 900som per day if required. A horse will certainly make it easier on your legs, although perhaps not on other parts of your anatomy.

One classic hike or ride from Tash Rabat is the ascent to the ridge of the At-Bashy range that overlooks Chatyr-Köl Lake, a tough 4–5 hour climb or 7–8 hour round trip. The ridge is at almost 4,000m and so offers wonderful views over the lake and the wide Ak-Say valley. Naturally, the altitude makes for hard work, and the weather can be very changeable too, with snow or sleet a possibility at any time of year. The route begins by following the river upstream on the opposite bank to the caravanserai. There will probably be several yurts along this stretch, and herds of yaks in addition to sheep, cattle and horses. After a couple of hours, a gorge on the right leads to up to the 3,968m Tash Rabat Pass, a steep, heart-thumping climb. It is possible to descend to Lake Chatyr-Köl in a couple of hours or less from the ridge, although, technically at least, it requires a border permit, as does any further trekking along the Ak-Say valley. CBT Naryn organise a 2-day horse trek that follows this route, staying in a yurt on the south side of the lake and visiting a nearby cave before returning to Tash Rabat on the second day.

The route over the 3,752m Torugart Pass is one of just two roads into China from Kyrgyzstan, the other being the route via Irkeshtam further south in Osh Province. While Chinese trucks regularly trundle along the route (and damage the roads with their 80 tonne loads according to many Kyrgyz) it is a different matter for foreign visitors, for whom the crossing here is more problematic.

Crossing into China via the Torugart Pass is made difficult by a combination of paperwork, random decision-making and official intransigence. This is not to say it cannot be done – it can – but it is prudent to be aware that there are a lot of factors that may go wrong, and sometimes they do. Having said all of this, the general trend appears to be one of matters easing slightly of late: long delays and turnings-back are less frequent than they were a few years ago and, with the correct paperwork and a fair wind, you should be able to arrive in Kashgar the same day as leaving Tash Rabat or Naryn. What is indisputable is the need for a degree of flexibility as well as patience and a certain spirit of adventure, but if you did not possess these last two qualities then you probably would not be in Kyrgyzstan in the first place.

The first thing to understand about the Torugart border is that it is what is known as a 'second grade' border – in other words, one through which non-nationals are not normally admitted. To allow foreigners to overcome this limitation, special regulations are in place that require those in transit to be met by a Chinese travel representative at the frontier to transport then into China itself. It is also imperative that travellers have in their possession the documentation to prove that this transfer will definitely take place.

To take your own vehicle involves far more headaches than suggested here and will take at least 2 months to organise with a Chinese agency. Similarly, it is very hard to get permission to cycle across the border. Most cyclists heading for China take the Irkeshtam route from Osh, which is far more straightforward.

PLANNING A CROSSING To cross the Torugart Pass requires a certain degree of pre-arrangement. It is best organised in advance in Bishkek, with a travel company who will make all the necessary arrangements once a firm date has been established. Because it is fairly expensive, currently around US$250–300 per vehicle from Bishkek to the Torugart Pass (half this from Naryn), most independent travellers either try to find other travellers to join them for the journey, or allow an agency to assemble a group for them. Groups usually consist of four travellers, although some agencies will only allow three because they say that they need room in the car for spare fuel and tyres.

Because an exact entry date needs to be arranged, an organised Torugart passage will slightly restrict the way you spend the rest of your time in Kyrgyzstan, as it is vital that you show up on the prescribed date. Choosing a date on which to cross is an important consideration, particularly the day of the week that is selected. Many travellers, wishing to arrive in Kashgar in time for the Sunday market, choose to travel on a Friday. The problem with this is that if anything goes wrong with the crossing on the Friday then there will be a delay of another 3 days, as the border is firmly closed on weekends (it can be firmly closed at other times too, but more of this later). Because of this, a mid-week crossing is probably a safer bet.

Another very important consideration is to avoid **public holidays** on either the Kyrgyz or Chinese side, as anything that vaguely resembles a holiday will result in one or both of the customs posts shutting up shop. In theory, the border is supposed to be open all year round, but because of holidays it is likely to be closed on the following dates: 1 January (New Year's Day), 7 January (Orthodox Christmas) and 29–31 January; 1–4 February and 23 February (Army Day); 8 March (International

Women's Day), 21 March (Nooruz) and 24 March (Anniversary of the March 2004 revolution); 1 May (Labour Day), 5 May (Constitution Day) and 9 May (Victory Day) – it is best to avoid the first 10 days of May altogether; 1 August and 31 August (Kyrgyz Independence Day); 1 October and 7 October (again, best to avoid the first 10 days of October altogether); and 7 November (Anniversary of the October Revolution).

Also be aware that those holidays that fall on weekends are normally taken on a Monday or Friday instead. China has holidays on 29 January–4 February, 1–7 May, 1 June, 1 July, 1–2 August, 12 September and 1–7 October. There are also the moveable holidays like Chinese New Year, Orozo Ait (Day of Sacrifice) and Kurman Ait (feast at the end of Ramadan). As well as holidays and weekends, bad weather and deep snow can close the pass at any time, even in July or August. Political events may also take their toll: the border was closed in October 2001 for a period as a result of the political situation in Afghanistan.

The **precise timing** of the crossing, as in the hour of the day, is also crucial as the two customs posts operate on different time zones, with Chinese time being 2 hours (3 in winter, October–March) later than Kyrgyz time. This is *official* Chinese time, or Beijing time – much of far western China operates on unofficial Xinjiang time, 2 hours earlier, but the customs post observes the Beijing convention. Because of this, and because of the slow bureaucratic proceedings at customs and the distances to be covered, it is important to arrive at the Kyrgyz post as early as possible – it opens at 09.30 and closes at 17.00; the Chinese post is open, in theory at least, between 10.00–17.00 (Beijing time). Both posts observe a 2-hour lunch break when very little is likely to happen. It is 100km from the border to the Chinese immigration post and there are bound to be delays so start early!

As well as **documentation** proving that onward Chinese transport has been arranged, a **Chinese visa** will also be required. This is not available at the border. Chinese visas can be obtained in Bishkek, but they are better applied for well in advance in your country of origin, as the Bishkek Embassy will probably insist on an invitation from a Xinjiang travel company, which entails more expense and hassle and takes at least a week – in your own country you can simply apply by post. On the application form do not mention Torugart, Xinjiang, Tibet or any overtly politically sensitive areas; just write Beijing, Shanghai, Xian and other obvious non-controversial destinations in eastern China – these will not be mentioned on the visa that is subsequently issued. Once again, this involves some advance planning as you will need to know the date on which you plan to enter China from Torugart.

Normally, Chinese visas are issued for a period of 1 month, so as long as the visa has become valid by the time the Torugart is crossed there will be no problem. **Border permits** are *not* required providing that the Torugart Pass is approached directly from Naryn (allowing a side trip to Tash Rabat).

TOUR OPERATORS There are a considerable number of tour agencies in Bishkek that will happily arrange the Torugart border crossing for you, either all the way from Bishkek to Kashgar, or just from Naryn. Itineraries may be tailored to individual tastes and many standard tours include a night at Tash Rabat, and possibly a trekking excursion from there, before the pass is traversed.

The agencies will liaise with a Kashgar-based company to arrange the onward transport from the pass, although this portion of the cost is usually paid directly to the Chinese driver in US dollars. The agency should give you written confirmation of the agreed price for this just in case of dispute. On agreeing a fee with an agency, check for any hidden extras: the quoted price should include everything – fuel, the food and accommodation for the driver, as well as that for the clients; the exit tax levied on the vehicle leaving Kyrgyzstan should also be accounted for. Also check the type of vehicle that the agency is providing as, early or late in the season when there may be snow on the ground, a 4×4 is definitely preferred. The driver himself should be experienced with the crossing, not just with the roads leading to the Torugart Pass, but also with the various procedures involved at customs.

Of the **Bishkek travel agencies**, the following companies all have considerable experience of arranging a Torugart crossing: Ak-Sai Travel, Celestial Mountains, Edelweiss, Fantastic Asia, ITMC Tien Shan, Kyrgyz Concept and Novi Nomad (see *Kyrgyz Tour Agencies*, pages 49–51). In summer 2007, the going rate was between US$120–150 for a car from Naryn to the border, and US$55 per person for a minibus from the border to Kashgar.

TRAVELLING INDEPENDENTLY It is also possible to make your own way to the Torugart Pass and book onward transport on the Chinese side directly with a Kashgar agency such as Caravan Café (*Steve Larson, Seman Lu 120, Kashgar, Xinjiang Province, PRC 844000, China;* ✆ *86 998 298 1864;* f *86 998 284 2196;* e *info2@caravancafe.com; www.caravan.cafe.com*) or John's Information Café (✆ *86 998 298 1864;* e *johncafe@hotmail.com*). They would need to send you all the necessary documentation by fax.

Crossing the border this way requires finding a taxi in Naryn to drive to the border post at the designated time to meet the Chinese vehicle, which will not be easy to synchronise. The driver will also need a foreign ministry permit stamped into his passport to travel through no-man's-land and proceed to the border post. Otherwise, you will have to be dropped off at the customs post to hitch the final 7km through no-man's-land to the border, as you are not allowed to walk.

BORDER FORMALITIES At the Kyrgyz post the confirmation of the onward Chinese transportation is shown and the Kyrgyz guards will await radio confirmation that the Chinese transport has arrived. After confirmation, which may take hours if the vehicle is delayed (likely), Kyrgyz immigration will collect customs forms, perhaps inspect your baggage and thoroughly go over the vehicle. Customs being cleared, you drive on 7km to the border zone where the Chinese driver will be waiting. This is still sometimes referred to as the 'arch', although the Chinese arch that formerly stood here to welcome visitors to China was removed in 2002 for reasons unknown. The Chinese customs post, where luggage is x-rayed and possibly searched, is a few kilometres further on. From here it is 100km along sandstone canyons to the Chinese immigration post, where immigration forms are completed and passports stamped. It is a further 60km to Kashgar.

If, for whatever reason, you cannot get through there are basic places to stay at the pass just before the Kyrgyz post. The most likely problem, other than closure for an unanticipated holiday, is that your Chinese transport has been delayed for some reason. This is rarely the fault of the travel company themselves but usually down to over-zealous customs officials creating problems just to relieve their own boredom. Long, cold waits at the top of the pass are, sadly, all too common.

NARYN TO KAZARMAN

West of Naryn the Naryn River leads upstream along a wide valley between the Moldo-Too range that lies immediately south of Lake Song-Köl and the Jaman-Too (Bad Mountains) range that hem in the northern side of the At-Bashy valley. It is a landscape of arid badlands and occasional dusty, scattered settlements. The direct road to Kazarman, and subsequently Jalal-Abad, splits into two at the village of Ak-Tal, with the route via Kök-Jar being the shortest in distance. Most traffic takes the longer southern route via Baetov, which has considerably better road conditions.

Both of these routes are fairly rough, but they do offer a rugged and reasonably direct option to the very long alternative route via Bishkek. A small bus runs twice weekly between Naryn and Kazarman and there are other daily services that run as far as Baetov (see *Getting there* for *Naryn*, page 210).

Heading west, the first village of note is **Dostuk**, where the At-Bashy flows into the larger River Naryn through a narrow gorge that is dammed and has a hydroelectricity station. The road skirts south of the river for another 60km to reach **Ak-Tal**, a small village that offers potential access to the southern shore of Lake Song-Köl along a rugged, 4×4-only track over the Moldo Pass. Ak-Tal is the birthplace of the famous Kyrgyz poet and *manaschi* Togolok Moldo (1860–1942), who has a street in Bishkek named after him and who also puts in an appearance on the 20som banknote.

The nearby village of **Kurtka** (confusingly also sometimes called Jangy-Talap and marked on maps as such), just north of the Naryn River, has homestay accommodation. The Shepherd's Life co-ordinator here (*Sveta Jusupjanova at Yntymak 45*) can organise vehicles or horses north to Lake Song-Köl or transport west to Kazarman. Close to the village is the 13th-century mausoleum of Taylik Baatyr. There is a daily afternoon bus to Kurtka from Naryn's bazaar.

Just west of Ak-Tal, the main Kazarman road plunges south towards **Baetov**, the largest town in the region, which is served by a daily bus service from Naryn, and which has homestay accommodation with the Shepherd's Life programme. Another road crosses the river and leads west along the north bank of the Naryn River to the village of Kök-Jar, from where it climbs up a steep, switchback road to the 2,839m pass that marks the beginning of Jalal-Abad Province.

From Baetov, a rough 4×4 road leads south along the Terek valley to link with the At-Bashy valley and the Torugart Pass, via a 3,268m pass and the tiny settlement of Orto Syrt. Leaving Baetov to the west, the main road to Kazarman deteriorates a little, twisting around to follow the course of the Alabuga River to the southwest, crossing the river just before reaching the village of Kosh-Döbö. From here, it swings north, away from the river, and soon leaves Naryn Oblast to enter Jalal-Abad Province over the Ak-Moinok Pass. The lacklustre mining town of Kazarman lies another 30km or so to the north (see page 230).

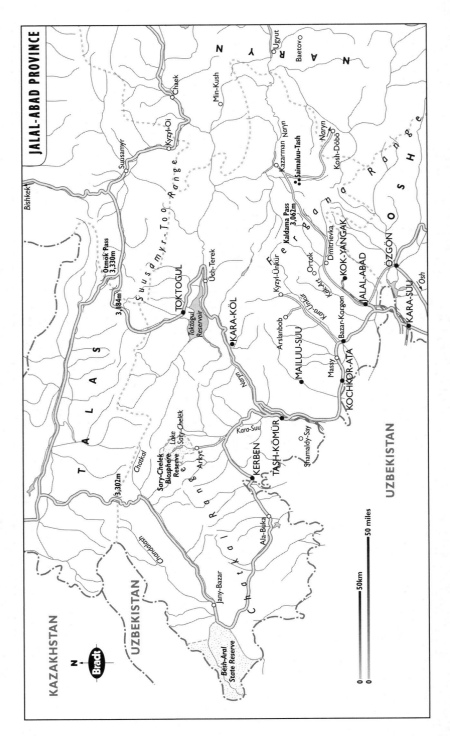

KAZAKHSTAN

N

UZBEKISTAN

UZBEKISTAN

T A L A S

S u u s a m y r - T o o R a n g e

F e r g a n a R a n g e

O S H

Range

Bishkek

Ötmök Pass
3,330m

3,184m

Suusamyr

Kyzyl-Oi

Chaek

Min-Kush

Ugyut

Baetovo

N A R Y N

Naryn

Kazarman

Kaldama Pass
3,062m

Kosh-Döbö

Saimaluu-Tash

Üch-Terek

TOKTOGUL

Toktogul
Reservoir

KARA-KÖL

Kyzyl-Ünkür

Kara-Ünkür

Arslanbob

MAILUU-SUU

Massy

KOCHKOR-ATA

Ortok

Kök-Art

Dmitrievka

KOK-YANGAK

JALAL-ABAD

Bazar-Korgon

ÖZGÖN

KARA-SUU

Osh

3,302m

Chatkal

Sary-Chelek
Biosphere
Reserve

Lake
Saty-Chelek

Arkyt

C h a t k a l R a n g e

Chandalash

Jany-Bazar

Ala-Buka

Kara-Suu

Shamaldy-Say

KERBEN

TASH-KÖMÜR

Bésh-Aral
State Reserve

Naryn

UZBEKISTAN

Bradt

N

0   50km
0   50 miles

9

Jalal-Abad Province

Kyrgyzstan's west-central province, Jalal-Abad, with its capital of the same name, is one of the most varied in the country in geographical terms. It has several mountain ranges, lakes and vast areas of broad-leaved woodland, and in the south, where the province lies on the northern fringe of the Fergana Valley, arable farming is extensive. The province covers 33,700km² in total and with a population of a little less than a million it has a population density of 29 per km² overall, slightly above the national average and about the same as West Virginia in the USA.

Its economy is based on agriculture, in which cotton, maize, wheat and tobacco are all important products, and the mining of minerals, coal and metals; oil and natural gas are also important resources, as is water, with the Toktogul hydro-electricity station producing the lion's share of the country's power supply, as well as providing neighbouring countries with electricity. The climate is generally warm and dry in summer with temperatures peaking above 40°C on occasion. Rainfall is fairly low but adequate, at about 450mm per year.

Jalal-Abad Province has some of the most intriguing and beautiful destinations for visitors in the entire country: the marvellous gallery of 4,000-year-old petroglyphs high on a mountain top at Saimaluu-Tash; the jewel-like alpine lake of Sary-Chelek surrounded by forests of wild fruit trees; and the remarkable walnut forests around the entirely Uzbek town of Arslanbob. In the extreme southwest corner of the *oblast* in the inaccessible Chatkal valley is the Besh-Aral State Reserve. The provincial capital of Jalal-Abad has a largely Uzbek character and makes for a pleasant stopover *en route* to Osh.

JALAL-ABAD ДЖАЛАЛ-АБАД Telephone code: 03722

Jalal-Abad (sometimes spelt Dzhalal-Abad, Jalalabad or Jalalabat), the province's capital and Kyrgyzstan's third largest city, lies at the southeast corner of the *oblast*, very close to the border with Uzbekistan in the foothills of the Babash-Ata mountain range. The city's proximity to the Fergana Valley is reflected in its mixed population, of which about two-thirds of a total of 75,000 are Uzbek. A branch of the Silk Road used to pass this way to trade with the settlements of the Fergana Valley, and although little evidence of this remains today, Jalal-Abad still has something of a timeless feel, in spite of its modernity.

The city, which takes its name from a 13th-century warrior, Jalal ad-Din, has a bright, relaxed feel that is different from the towns of the north. The streets are wide and well-shaded with trees, and many of the houses are typically Uzbek, hidden away behind walls and tall metal gates with rooms that face inwards onto a communal family area with the inevitable grapevine. The city's spirit of gentle liveliness is partly due to its youth: there are several universities based in the town and students throng the cafés around the centre.

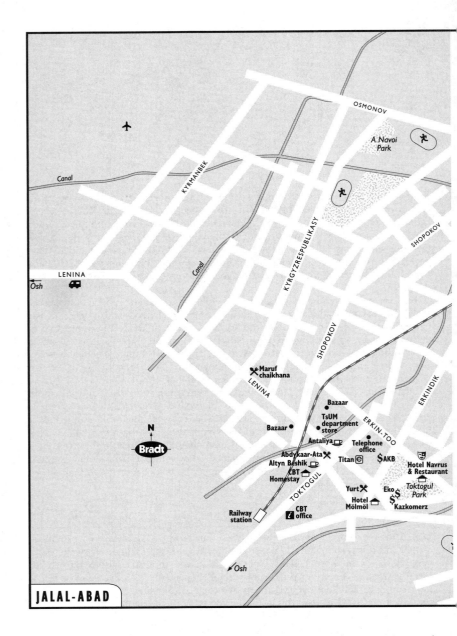

JALAL-ABAD

Russians first came to Jalal-Abad in the late 19th century when a garrison and military hospital were established here. In 1916 it was connected by railway through the Fergana Valley to Tashkent and Moscow, a conduit to transport the vast amounts of cotton that the region produced to European Russia. Later, they developed the town as a health spa, as Jalal-Abad became well-known for the various mineral springs found in its vicinity. In the Soviet period several sanatoria were developed to offer mineral water treatment programmes and warm-weather holiday opportunities

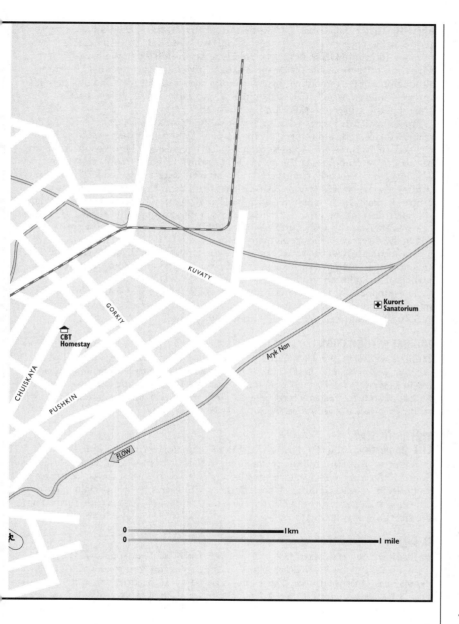

for the proletariat. The mineral water business is still going strong and the sanatorium just outside the city continues to receive its share of visitors, although nothing like the old days.

Visitors arriving in Jalal-Abad in July or August will immediately notice how much hotter it is than most places in the north of the country. This is partly because of its comparatively low altitude, but also a consequence of its proximity to the cauldron-like microclimate of the Fergana Valley.

GETTING THERE Jalal-Abad's **long-distance bus station** lies 3km west of the centre at the edge of the town. It is a long walk but can be easily reached by a number 10 minibus, which leave regularly leave from outside the bazaar (5som). There is a large timetable inside the *avtovozkal* that gives the scheduled bus times, although it is best to confirm times at the ticket kiosk outside. The bus station's spacious interior is given over to billiards and table tennis, but tickets may be bought at the grilles outside or on the bus itself.

Buses leave three times a day for Tash-Kömür, twice a day for Toktogul along the main Bishkek road, and thrice daily for Kerben (130som), further west towards the Chatkal valley. Buses for Bazar-Korgon also leave regularly, where a connection can be made to Arslanbob. **Minibuses** to Osh (75som), Özgön (35som) and Kara-Suu (75som) leave regularly from here, as do **shared taxis** to the same destinations (Osh, 150som). Shared taxis to Bishkek leave from the side of the bazaar in the town centre. It may also be possible to find a shared 4×4 for Kazarman in the bazaar, although this can be arranged with a day's notice through the local CBT (see below). Transport to Osh skirts around Uzbekistan by way of Özgön rather than taking the direct road shown on most maps.

The **train station** has very limited services, although, in theory at least, there is an occasional train to Bishkek that goes via a very circuitous route through Uzbekistan, Tajikistan and Kazakhstan.

The **airport** (➦ *51 3010*) is northwest of the centre and can be reached by minibus numbers 1 and 5 from the bazaar. There are daily flights to Bishkek (1,500–2,000som) that take about 1 hour's flying time.

TOURIST INFORMATION

🛈 CBT 3, Toktogul 20; ➦ 21 962; m 0502 376 602; e cbt_ja@rambler.ru. ☉ 09.00–17.00 Mon–Fri (at w/ends ➦ 25 643; m 0502 376 602, m 0502 284 164). This particularly helpful office will gladly arrange local homestay accommodation here & in Ortok, in addition to organising tours to Arslanbob & horse treks to Saimaluu-Tash. The co-ordinator, Ruhsora Abdulaeva, speaks good English, as does her sister who runs the guesthouse in their Uzbek family home.

🏠 WHERE TO STAY

CBT homestays The CBT office is able to offer homestay accommodation at a dozen or so places around the town, either in flats or in traditional Uzbek houses. Some of these are some way from the centre. The homestay of the co-ordinator's sister, Rukiya, in a traditional Uzbek home at Chuiskaya 33, is especially pleasant. The closest homestay to the centre is one on Toktogul ($–$$), a little further up the street towards Lenina.

Hotels

🏠 **Hotel Navrus** (30 rooms) Toktogul Park; ➦ 20 370. New in Dec 2005, this modern business hotel is very well appointed with smart wooden floors, marble fittings & long balconies overlooking the park. The entrance is around the back of the building. Friendly staff & satellite TV in most rooms. *Sgl $$, dbl $$$$, lux apt $$$$–$$$$$.*

🏠 **Hotel Mölmöl** (50rooms) Lenina; ➦ 55 059. This is the city's solitary Soviet period hotel & it is not too bad if you arrive late at night, as at least it is very central. The rooms are worn, the beds squeak & taps drip but it is clean & perfectly adequate. The small snack bar on the 1st floor where they dish up *blinis* for b/fast is a living museum of 1970s Russian kitsch. *Sgl $, dbl $$.*

There is also a basic *gostinitsa* next door to the Maruf *chaikhana*, west of the bazaar.

✕ WHERE TO EAT

There are numerous *chaikhanas* around the bazaar and some more upmarket places along the north side of Toktogul Park. Those given below are just a selection. The bazaar has excellent fresh bread and local specialities like walnut jam and excellent honey. There is also plenty of delicious fruit and nuts in season, like peaches, apricots, melons, grapes, walnuts and pistachios.

✗ **Navrus** Toktogul Park. Part of the new complex with the hotel overlooking the park; probably the smartest restaurant in town judging by the impressive cars parked in front of it. Russian, Uzbek & international dishes. $$$$

✗ **Abdykaar-Ata** Lenina, near junction with Toktogul. A good range of standard Uzbek dishes in a slightly upmarket *chaikhana* that has an outdoor terrace facing on to the street. $$

🍺 **Altyn Beshik** Toktogul. A little café-bar on Toktogul just up from the CBT office. $

✗ **Antaliya** Lenina. Just back from Lenina near the main square, almost opposite the Abdykaar-Ata, this is an outdoor café in an enclosed garden that has beer & good *laghman*. $

✗ **Manuf** Lenina, junction with Kyrgyz Republikasy. West of the bazaar, this is a traditional Uzbek *chaikhana* with outdoor seating on raised *takhta* platforms. Uzbek staples like green tea, *plov* & *shashlyk* are served. $

✗ **Yurt restaurant** Lenina, junction with Erkindik. Not actually called this, but there is a kitchen yurt that serves a number of tables under the trees here at this no-name establishment. A rather limited selection of dishes is available, but it is a nice location at night. $

OTHER PRACTICALITIES The **post and telephone office** is on Toktogul north of Lenina, at the junction with Erkin-Too. The Aigul department store on Lenina next to the bazaar has a reasonable range of consumer goods. There are several **banks** along Lenina, particularly near the park and the Hotel Mölmöl – Halk Bank, Eko Bank, Kazkomerz Bank – the last of which has a functioning ATM cash dispenser. Internet access may be had at **Titan** on Lenina, on the opposite side from the university. There is another place next door to the Antaliya café that also has cheap **IP telephone** connections and there is another IP telephone place near the top of Toktogul.

WHAT TO SEE AND DO Jalal-Abad has a pleasant atmosphere and a good bazaar but no specific sights to seek out. The central square has a gilded statue of Lenin who, unusually, is in a seated pose. The 'Kurort' sanatorium, 3km out of town, is worth a visit, if only for the view it offers over the surrounding countryside. There is a café close to the entrance of the sanatorium, Ikram-Ajy, where the panoramic view may be admired.

KAZARMAN TO JALAL-ABAD

This is the toughest part of the difficult but spectacular route taken by travellers who wish to reach Jalal-Abad from Naryn to the east without backtracking through Bishkek. Naryn to Kazarman is covered in *Chapter 8*, page 222. This stretch, an uncomfortable, 160km-long rollercoaster ride up and over the Fergana range, is considerably tougher. Unlike the major north–south trunk roads that go from Bishkek to Osh and from Bishkek to Naryn, this road is not maintained in the winter months and it is usually only open between April and October. In some years it may be closed as late as May and as early as September because of heavy snow fall.

As a destination in its own right, Kazarman has little to hold even the most enthusiastic of travellers, but the village serves as a necessary base for a visit to one of Kyrgyzstan's most intriguing and inaccessible sights – the petroglyph galleries at Saimaluu-Tash. Public transport between Kazarman and Jalal-Abad is very rare: there is little habitation along the route and consequently little demand. It is also a demanding road that is only really suitable for robust vehicles like 4×4s, although there is reputed to be an occasional minibus; most ordinary taxis usually refuse to travel this route because of the quality of the road surface. Some improvement work was carried out on the road in 2003 but it remains a difficult drive.

9

Leaving Kazarman, the road is slow but serviceable at first as it twists west through the village of Aral and past the turn-off for Saimaluu-Tash. It starts to deteriorate further after about 25km, as it climbs up to over 3,000m to top the Kaldama Pass in the Fergana range. From the top of the pass there are superb views of the valley south towards Jalal-Abad and the switchback gravel-surfaced road snaking down to the Urut-Bashi River. Descending the pass, the sudden change of scenery is abrupt and almost shocking as the vast green expanse of the Fergana Valley edges into view for the first time.

Eventually, after descending to flatter terrain, the fertility of the valley becomes a reality: the fields are full of tall sunflowers and maize in summer and in late August and early September the road itself is used for drying vast heaps of sunflower heads. There is a tangible feeling that another world has suddenly been entered, not just physically but culturally too, as the figures along the roadside are no longer the Kyrgyz herders predominant on the far side of the pass but, instead, farming Uzbeks busying themselves with their crops. A line has been crossed and this is Kyrgyzstan's south: an almost alien world for many northern Kyrgyz highlanders, but perhaps less of a culture shock to those visitors familiar with the lowland farming areas of southern Europe.

Just after the sprawling village of Dmitrievka, there is a road barrier checkpoint where luggage may undergo a peremptory examination. Hopefully this no longer happens, but beware of a crooked official here who tries to levy a 600som 'transit fee' on Western travellers. The 'fee' is pure imagination, or rather, exploitation. Stand your ground, refuse to pay and they will soon let you proceed.

From Dmitrievka it is a further 40km to Jalal-Abad through fertile farmland along a relatively good road. Just to the north of Dmitrievka, in a large area of walnut and fruit-tree forest similar to that found in the Arslanbob region, is the village of Ortok, which has a few CBT homestays and is a good centre for day hikes into the surrounding hills.

KAZARMAN КАЗАРМАН *Telephone code: 03738*

This poor, dust-blown settlement in northern Jalal-Abad Province has something of a sinister reputation as a tough mining town down on its luck. Kazarman is situated just to the north of the Makmal opencast gold mine – indeed this is part of its *raison d'être* – but the mine no longer provides the employment opportunities that it used to, and consequently the town suffers with the familiar problems that accompany high unemployment in this part of the world – alcoholism and poverty. To add insult to injury, the climate is uncompromisingly harsh here: Kazarman is relatively low in altitude at just 1,230m above sea level but, like Naryn, it suffers from a climate that is extreme, with hot dry summers and extremely cold winters.

Certainly, it is an unprepossessing place, with a scabrous central square that has the Dom Kulturi with the CBT office and a couple of shops, a poorly stocked bazaar and absolutely nothing to see. The town – or more accurately, village – is extremely isolated, even for Kyrgyzstan, and is virtually cut-off during the winter months when the roads south to Jalal-Abad and east to Naryn are closed by snowfall. There is a small airport but currently no flights. Even in summer, Kazarman is not a cheerful place and so it is hard to imagine just how dispiriting the village must be during the long, and very cold, winter months; it is hardly any wonder that many locals turn to vodka for escape. The good news is that there is an efficiently run CBT operation at work here that can facilitate onward transport to Jalal-Abad or Naryn and help organise treks to the unforgettable petroglyphs at Saimaluu-Tash.

TOURIST INFORMATION AND TOURS

CBT Dom Kulturi (upstairs), Jeenalieva; 41 755. There is likely to be no-one here but someone will phone the co-ordinator at her nearby home, or you can go there yourself — it is just 2 blocks from the central square at Bekten 36. The co-ordinator, Bujumal Arykmoldoeva (41 253; e

reservation@cbtkyrgyzstan.kg) can organise horse trips to Saimaluu-Tash from 1–3 days' duration, as well as day excursions by car & foot to *jailoos* in the nearby Kargalyk mountain range & visits to Kalmyk burial sites & salt & silver mines. Bujumal can also arrange transport for the trip to Jalal-Abad.

WHERE TO STAY
CBT homestays The English-speaking CBT co-ordinator, Bujumal Aryk-moldoeva, offers accommodation in her own large house at Bekten 36 (*41 253*), just two blocks from the central square. There are half-a-dozen other CBT options in the village that include Baktygul Chorobaeva at Kadyrkulova 35, south of the centre (*21 916*), who speaks English and has three rooms in her house, and also the homes of Ariet Bolotakunov and Nazgul Idrisova. (*All* $).

There are no restaurants to speak of in the village, other than a couple of fly-blown places near the bazaar; it is better to eat at the homestays.

GETTING THERE The **bus** service to Naryn runs twice a week, leaving Kazarman on Wednesday and Saturday mornings at 08.00. From Naryn, the bus runs on Tuesday and Friday mornings. The journey time is 7–8 hours and tickets cost 200som.

There is no regular transport for the 5-hour drive to Jalal-Abad, although there may be the occasional minibus from the village's small bus station. Some taxis may agree to make the journey but a 4×4 is a better bet. For a 4×4 booked through the CBT, the cost is in the order of 600som per seat.

SAIMALUU-TASH САЙМАЛУУ-ТАШ

The name means 'embroidered' or 'patterned stones' in Kyrgyz and this is not a bad description for this, the most remote and certainly the most spectacular collection of petroglyphs in the country. Here, high on a lonely alpine plateau, are an estimated 11,000 petroglyphs scattered over the slopes of two glacial moraines that have been named by archaeologists, not very imaginatively, as Saimaluu-Tash One and Saimaluu-Tash Two. The larger of the two, Saimaluu-Tash One, measures 3km in length.

The petroglyphs, which are etched onto shiny basaltic stone, date from at least as early as 2000BC in the Bronze Age, and may well be even older. They most probably represent votive offerings that were brought to this sacred site from the valleys below. The site itself has undoubtedly long been considered to be sacred and it is believed that the small pond that lies in the middle of the lower gallery was frequented by shamans.

The Bronze Age tradition of marking this sacred spot with rock drawings was continued by subsequent settlers in the region and one of the most fascinating things about the site is not just the sheer extent of the galleries, or the large number of petroglyphs, but the millennia-long continuity of the site as a place of spiritual activity. The earlier Bronze Age etchings are succeeded by those of the Iron Age from around 800BC onwards, and the tradition continued until medieval times when Scythian and Turkic settlers added their own quota.

This continuity of use has afforded the site sacred credentials that are still respected by modern-day Kyrgyz, who recognise Saimaluu-Tash as having spiritual power and healing qualities. Unfortunately, there are a few modern-day visitors who have clearly wanted to make their own artistic mark too, but thankfully 21st-century graffiti is not very common.

The designs on the stones are various but they tend to fall into categories. The majority are representations of animals like horses, wolves, lions and, most commonly, ibex. Many more depict hunting scenes in which deer with larger-than-life antlers are stalked by men with bows and spears. Some have scenes that show ploughing and ritual dancing, and many more have solar imagery and wavy patterns that perhaps depict the course of rivers. There are even some highly erotic stones that portray the procreative act.

The intent driving this artwork is as meaningful as its content. The petroglyphs are less the stone pages of a prehistoric sketchbook than they are individual acts of sympathetic magic in which the artist, in physically representing his desire – a successful hunt, a good water supply, sunshine for crops – has invoked the gods to help him: on top of a mountain at 3,200m is not a bad place to summon the spirits.

The site was rediscovered in 1902 by Russians doing mapping work for a road they were building between their garrisons at Jalal-Abad and Naryn – the present-day road through Kazarman. Whilst working on the road, one of the cartographers, Nikolai Khludov, started to pay attention to the stories told by local shepherds that concerned 'painted stones' in the nearby mountains. Khludov decided to organise a small expedition to investigate the site. Although his preliminary findings were reported to the Archaeological Society in Tashkent, who, in turn, organised an expedition, the site was soon forgotten and there was no more academic interest in it until 1950. In that year Saimaluu-Tash was revisited and excavated, and the petroglyphs dated and numbered. Currently the site is under sporadic investigation by the Institute of Archaeology in Bishkek.

VISITING SAIMALUU-TASH Getting to the 'Stonehenge of central Asia', as Saimaluu-Tash is sometimes playfully referred to, is not at all easy. In the first place, it normally requires reaching Kazarman, the village that is used as the base for visits to the petroglyph site, itself a rather isolated and not altogether agreeable place. From Kazarman, it is possible to travel some of the way by 4×4, but the rest has to be done on foot or on horseback. This is best organised with the local Kazarman CBT co-ordinator, or in advance with the CBT office in Bishkek or Jalal-Abad.

The site lies at 3,200m on top of a mountain and, although it is not technically difficult, the climb up to the petroglyphs is long and slow and requires a certain amount of stamina. A guide is certainly necessary. There are a few variations on the route to the site, depending on how much time is available.

A very long 1-day, or better, overnight, trip to the site can be made from Kazarman. This route entails heading down the Jalal-Abad road for 20km just beyond the village of Aral, where a left turn takes you along a much worse road to the pretty village of Atay, from where the going gets ridiculously difficult. The track from here, which is basically a rough bed of boulders, eventually leads to a small *jailoo* where there are a few tents, horses and beehives. Horses are rented here to make the journey up to the site: a 1,000m ascent along a small glacier to the mountain-top moraine where the petroglyphs are. Before the glacier is reached, the path leads through meadows above a boulder-strewn river – a gorgeously lush landscape that is at odds with the arid badlands seen closer to Kazarman.

It is possible, with an early start, to get up to Saimaluu-Tash and back along the same route in the same day, returning to Kazarman to sleep, but an overnight stay at the top means a much less rushed approach, and you will have time the following morning to make a thorough examination of the site. Petroglyphs or not, it is an idyllic setting and the ascent is worth the effort for the views alone. Those staying overnight at the petroglyph site often return by a different and longer route via the village of Chet-Bulak on the Kazarman to Makmal road. Timing is very important; the site is really only accessible during a narrow window that lasts from early August to very early September. Late in the season, locals may not be willing to rent horses as they worry about them plunging through the melting ice of the glacier (although they do not seem too bothered about hapless tourists doing the same thing!). If this is the case, the site must be approached on foot. On foot to the site from the *jailoo* it is approximately 3½ hours up and 2½ hours down. The slippery surface of the glacier is not much fun in trainers.

Another route that takes a full 4 days to do it justice is from the village of Kalmak-Kyrchyn in the Kök-Art valley, which is reached from Dmitrievka on the Jalal-Abad to Kazarman road. The route from Kalmak-Kyrchyn leads along a very rough track 20km to a honey farm where horses and guides are organised. The trek from here takes a whole day to the site. The logistics of this route can be organised through CBT Jalal-Abad with a little advance notice.

At the time of research the derring-do team at CBT Arslanbob (see page 235) were looking at developing a horse trek all the way from Arslanbob to Saimaluu-Tash. This would be a spectacular, if long and tiring, approach to the site, which would take at least a week.

ORTOK ОРТОК

This village is usually overlooked in favour of other destinations like Arslanbob, but it has much to offer as a quiet base for day hikes and exploring the local area. Like Arslanbob (see below), it lies in the midst of a large area of relict walnut forest about 60km northeast of Jalal-Abad. The forest, which virtually surrounds the village, is rich with a variety of fruit trees in addition to walnut, and there are *jailoos* that can be hiked to above the village, and a system of caves 6km away in a cliff face. Horses may be hired in the village for day treks. A 3-day trek from Arslanbob terminates here, and this could equally be done in reverse with prior arrangement through CBT Jalal-Abad.

There are already a handful of CBT homestays (⑤) in the village that can be booked in advance through CBT Jalal-Abad or simply by just turning up. Zaripa Tashtanbekova, Burma Tabaldieva and Uriat Bayalieva all have guesthouses here. One bus a day leaves from Jalal-Abad bus station to reach Ortok and Kara-Alma, 10km to the east, where there is another CBT homestay.

ARSLANBOB АРСЛАНБОБ *Telephone code: 03722*

Arslanbob is central to one of Kyrgyzstan's most remarkable regions – the vast relic walnut forest that stretches east and west of the village to cover a total area of 11,000ha. The large, sprawling village of Arslanbob serves as the market centre for the entire region as well as a summer resort with a gentle climate.

Arslanbob is actually far more than this though: unusually for Kyrgyzstan, the village itself is a highly attractive place with a population that is almost entirely Uzbek, and with gorgeous mountain scenery, friendly locals and a pioneering local CBT group, it is hard to beat as a base for hikes in the hills that surround the village or as a start or end point for more energetic treks deep into the mountains.

The village, which is sometimes referred to as Arstanbap, its Uzbek name, is named after an 11th-century hero known as Arslanbob-Ata (or Arstanbap-Ata), whom legend suggests may have been an Arab, as his name can be interpreted as deriving from *aslan* (lion) and *bab* (gate) in that language, the suffix – *ata* meaning 'father of' in various Turkic languages, so Arslanbob-Ata means 'father of the lion gate'. Another explanation of the name may be due to the tradition in the Fergana Valley at that time of adding –bob to someone's name if they were a traveller and explorer.

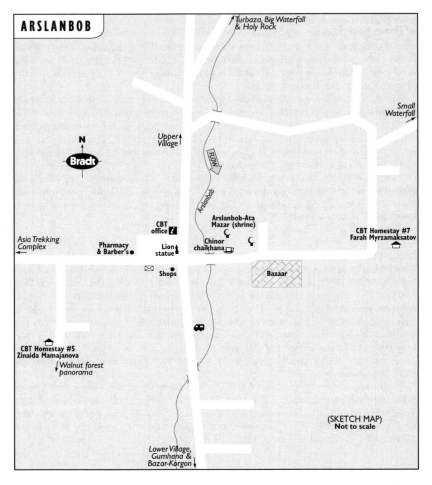

ARSLANBOB

Turbaza, Big Waterfall & Holy Rock

Small Waterfall

N

Bradt

Upper Village

FLOW

Arslanbob

Asia Trekking Complex

Pharmacy & Barber's

CBT office

Lion statue

Shops

Arslanbob-Ata Mazar (shrine)

Chinor chaikhana

Bazaar

CBT Homestay #7 Farah Myrzamaksatov

CBT Homestay #5 Zinaida Mamajanova

Walnut forest panorama

(SKETCH MAP)
Not to scale

Lower Village, Gumhana & Bazar-Korgon

Arslanbob's actual name was Salman Abdul Rahman, a scientist and military leader who is credited with planting the vast walnut forest that is central to the region's economy. Legend tells of an honest, hardworking man who had been given the task by the Prophet Mohammed of finding a paradise on earth. He eventually came across a beautiful valley with a swift-flowing mountain river flowing through it but no trees. Reporting this to the Prophet, he was issued with a bag of walnuts and Arslanbob climbed to the top of a mountain and cast the seed in every direction to create a shady garden, which he tended until he died. The name of Babash-Ata, the mountain peak that dominates the village to the north, reflects this, meaning 'father of the garden'.

Beautiful as this legend is, it does not quite match the millennia-long presence of vast walnut forests in the region. Walnuts are known in Russian as *gretchki* or 'Greek nuts' because they were said to have been sent back to Greece from Alexander the Great's campaign to central Asia; whether or not this is true, the forests certainly pre-date the 11th century. The walnuts of the area have always been highly prized and were one of the goods transported west along the Silk Road when it was in its prime.

Arslanbob lies about 70km north of Jalal-Abad and is reached by way of the town of Bazar-Korgon at the lower end of the Kara-Ünkür valley. The village, which sits at the head of a valley on the lower slopes of the 4,427m-high Babash-Ata mountain, has a mean altitude of around 1,600m above sea level, although it spreads so far up and down the valley from its centre that upper parts of the village are several hundred metres higher than this, and the lower parts several hundred less.

By Kyrgyzstan standards, Arslanbob is considered to be a conservative place due to its isolation, its predominantly Uzbek population and its religious associations – there are several sites in the vicinity of the village that are considered holy by local Muslims. In recent times, there have been accusations of the village being a recruiting ground for the outlawed Hizb-ut Tahrir, an Islamist group that advocates a single Islamic caliphate for the region, but the atmosphere of the village is extremely friendly and relaxed as long as visitors adopt reasonably modest dress. Many of the older men – the *aksakals* of the village – wear traditional Uzbek clothing and most women sport headscarves, but this cultural conservatism is tempered by traditional Islamic hospitality, which welcomes visitors with a warm smile.

Because of their long association with this mountainous region many of the Uzbek inhabitants of Arslanbob see themselves as a little different from their brothers in the lower reaches of the Fergana Valley. There is a popular belief that they have an input of Kazakh blood in the mix, as one of Arslanbob's grandfathers is said to have married a Kazakh woman. The woman's father, Sultan Bulak, gave his name to the local spring that he lived near. Many say that the Uzbeks here look far more Kazakh than those in the nearby lowlands of the Fergana Valley. All of the villagers claim to be descended from Arslanbob, their common ancestor, and say that those living in Arslanbob today represent the 26th, 27th and 28th generations.

What is without doubt is that they are all immensely proud of their village and its distinct traditions. The village's founder, Arslanbob-Ata, did well when he was sent off to find an earthly paradise by the Prophet; looking at Arslanbob, it would seem that his mission was entirely successful.

TOURIST INFORMATION

CBT ❭ 0312 443 331, ❭ 540 069; m 0503 342 476; e arslanbob_2003@rambler.ru. Arslanbob's CBT team, under the leadership of co-ordinator Hayat Tarikov, & his assistant, Lachin Sader, is one of the most dynamic & forward-looking in the country. Not only are they very knowledgeable about the local area & able to offer a wide range of tours centred on the village, they are constantly developing new routes & looking for new attractions for visitors. The CBT team are based in an upstairs room overlooking the central square, where they keep an eagle eye on comings & goings in the village. If you're arriving on the bus from Bazar-Korgon, the chances are that they will find you before you find them.

WHERE TO STAY

CBT homestays CBT have a total of 15 excellent places to stay around the village. As Arslanbob is so spread out, the homestays tend to be widely scattered too, but usually a longer walk into the centre is rewarded by a better view of the valley, especially if the property is in the upper reaches of the village. There are three more guesthouses in Gumhana village, which is 5km south of Arslanbob centre.

All of the homestays are good, but especially recommended are guesthouse #3, which is the homestay of Ibrahim Karimjanov, a German teacher in the village, which lies 2km from the centre; guesthouse #7, that of Faruh Myrzamaksutov, which has a wonderful dining area with a panoramic view; and guesthouse #5, that of Zinaida Mamajanova at Aral 13, close to the centre, which has superb food, a kind family and a wonderful array of animals snuffling around the farmyard at night. (*Homestay accommodation is at the standard rate: B&B $; dinner 90som.*)

Hotels

🏠 **Asia Trekking Complex** ☎ 52 584 (Asia Trekking in Jalal-Abad). This modern (Aug 2001), relatively luxurious, tourist complex, owned by Jalal-Abad's Asia Trekking company, is set in its own grounds to the west of the village. It was formerly a children's camp, but has since been bought up & redeveloped by the Jalal-Abad company. Most of the guests are the company's own trekking clients, but it is also open to outsiders. The complex has a sauna, a swimming pool & an outdoor dining area with good views. *Dbls* $$$.

Turbaza The *turbaza* was built in 1971 and used to be very busy in Soviet times during the summer moths when more than 10,000 visitors came each season. Now it is much quieter and a little run-down, catering mostly for domestic visitors who come for short stays or weekends. Accommodation is in wooden cabins set around the 15ha site at the top of the village. Some rooms have hot water and en-suite toilets but most do not. There is a swimming pool and also a disco that tends to shatter the village's atmosphere of peace and tranquillity when it is in operation ($).

✕ **WHERE TO EAT** There are no proper restaurants in the village, but this not a hardship as most homestays serve up huge, delicious meals with plenty of fresh produce. The shady **Chinor chaikhana** in front of the mosque is where local *aksakals* hang out, and it is a restful place to watch the world go by over a pot of tea. It is closed during the month of Ramadan.

GETTING THERE Arslanbob is usually reached from Jalal-Abad by way of a change in Bazar-Korgon.

A regular minibus from Jalal-Abad to Bazar-Korgon (which may continue to Massy) takes 45 minutes and costs 20som. There may be a shared taxi running the same route for roughly twice the price. From Bazar-Korgon bus station there is a small bus to Arslanbob that leaves hourly through the day, taking 2 hours and costing 35som. The 20-seater bus can get *very* full (I counted 48 at one point) so be prepared for someone to sit on your lap. Some minibuses also run directly to and from Jalal-Abad.

In Arslanbob, they stop by the lion statue in the main square. The bus station is a little further down the steep road that leads into the village. To reach Kyzyl-Ünkür, the main village in the next valley to the east, from Arslanbob requires changing buses at the village of Oogon-Talaa, where the road to Arslanbob joins the Kara-Ünkür valley; however, the buses that pass here are likely to be very full.

PRACTICALITIES The post and telephone office is on the main square with the lion statue. There are a few shops here that sell basic staples, a pharmacy and a barber's shop. The small bazaar is across the footbridge over the stream just beyond the mosque. There is a *Univermag* department store behind the *chaikhana* and in front of Arslanbob's shrine. At the time of writing there was no public internet access available in the village.

WHAT TO SEE AND DO

Arslanbob-Ata shrine The *mazar* or shrine of the village's founder is right in the centre of the village close to the *chaikhana* with the large plane tree. The shrine is said to have been around since the 16th century, although the building that stands today was erected in the 20th century. It is entered through a garden and colourful gatehouse behind the *Univermag* store.

The shrine is a small white, brick-built building with a walnut-wood door frame and rams' horns above the entrance. There are tables close to the mausoleum where visitors can sit and eat, and many pilgrims come to share food here and soak up *baraka*, the spiritual blessings of the shrine. The new mosque next door, with its elegantly carved ceiling, is also worth a look.

Small waterfall This is easily reached at the northeast of the village. This 25m-high waterfall is a popular spot with visitors and locals alike and this is borne out by the scraps of material tied to the trees and bushes that stand near it. Even some branches that hang over the waterfall itself have had ribbons tied to them, which must have been a highly hazardous activity for the person tying it. There are steps from the road leading down to the base of the waterfall, where there are a couple of prayer caves. One of these, known as 'The Cave of the 40 Angels', used to be frequented by a holy woman who visitors would come to petition.

To reach the waterfall, walk past the mosque and bazaar and turn left uphill. At the second road to the right, turn right (there is a faded sign on the wall pointing the way). At a junction of four roads, take the lowest one, which continues uphill past a couple of kiosks. The waterfall is now in sight and reached through a turnstile, which leads past benches and caves to the waterfall.

Large waterfall This much larger, 80m-high, waterfall is a 3–4 hour round trip from the centre of the village. It is a relatively easy walk apart from the last part, which can be tricky underfoot. Do not be tempted to try and climb up behind the waterfall – going up is easier than coming down and you may well end up stuck in a highly precarious position. As with the small waterfall, votive rags have been tied close to the site. As the votive rags attest, the waterfall is attributed with spiritual and magical powers and a visit is supposed to boost fertility.

The large waterfall lies in a cliff face due north of the village. To reach it, walk directly north from the main square along the main road that lies west of the stream. Continue steeply uphill until there is a fork in the road with a blue hut in the middle; take the right, not quite so good, road past the *turbaza*. This eventually reaches a junction at the very northern limit of the village. The left-hand fork leads across boulder-strewn open land, meadows and *jailoos* uphill to the holy rock (see below); take the right-hand fork, which leads along the course of a stream to eventually reach trees with votive rags tied to them. Cross the stream here and continue towards the waterfall, which should have come into sight by now.

Holy rock A visit to this sacred site requires a considerable investment of effort as it lies high above the village on the slopes of Babash-Ata at 2,900m (see *Trekking from Arslanbob*, page 238). This large, almost cube-shaped rock is closely linked to the legend of Arslanbob-Ata. He is said to have been killed here whilst praying, betrayed by his wife who informed his enemies of his whereabouts. His bloodstains, footprints and handprints are believed by many to be still visible on the rock. Incongruously perhaps, there is a metal step-ladder lodged in place behind the rock to enable pilgrims to climb up on top of it.

Ibn Abbas shrine This *mazar* is said to be little more than a ruinous hut in the woods and is hard to find as it lies deep in the walnut forest. If you wish to check it out for yourself then get a guide, or at least precise instructions on how to reach it, from the CBT office.

Walnut forest panorama One easy walk from the village centre, which is particularly delightful in the late afternoon, is to take the narrow road that leads south of the main square just to the west of the post office. This descends past a house to a wooden bridge over a stream and then climbs up along a steep path through walnut woodland to reach an area of red cliffs. From here, there is a panoramic view over the village, valley and walnut forest to the east. Continuing to the top of the path, a small plateau is reached that is filled with carefully tended potato and sunflower fields.

Approaching dusk, the path is quite busy with locals, mostly small parties of women and girls, on their way back to their homes in the village from the fields above it. This is a charming spot to soak up the tranquil atmosphere of the valley and enjoy the play of light on the silvery trunks of the walnut trees as the sun lowers in the sky.

TREKKING AND TOURS FROM ARSLANBOB The village is an excellent base for many treks on foot or horseback into the surrounding countryside. CBT have many standard tours and can advise on routes and logistics or devise bespoke tours. They run a number of short tours close to the village that take in the cultural highlights and organise sunset and sunrise tours that take in panoramic views of the valley at these times of day.

One-day treks to the **large waterfall** and/or the holy rock described above are easily organised with or without a guide. On foot, the round-trip to the waterfall takes 3–4 hours while the **holy rock** is further and higher and takes 3½–4 hours to reach from the centre. To reach the holy rock it is necessary to follow the road north out of the village past the *turbaza,* turning left at the junction, where the right road leads to the large waterfall. Follow this track, cross the stream, then take a right fork along a stone-lined lane. When this joins a 4×4 track bear left and continue until you reach a small path that forks off to the right to cross a *jailoo*. The holy rock should be just visible on the ridge just below the skyline; look for a large rock that looks a little like a flat-roofed hut from a distance. From here it is cross country to reach the rock.

After a while, it will start to look deceptively close, but it is not and even when you think that you are almost upon it, it is still a lot further. It is by no means a difficult climb but it does demand stamina, as the rock stands at around 2,900m, a 1,300m ascent from the village centre. The effect of altitude may be felt in the latter part of the approach. Coming down is easier of course, and with enough time and energy it is feasible to loop around via the large waterfall on the return trip.

Longer treks may be organised through the walnut forest to the east of Arslanbob to reach the village of **Kyzyl-Ünkür** by way of Gumhana, Jaradar and the tiny hamlet of Darshan deep in the forest; the last section passes impressive red rock formations before descending to Kyzyl-Ünkür. This is a total distance of about 25km and can be done in a day. Transport can be pre-arranged with CBT to return to Arslanbob. CBT have a longer 2-day horseback variant of this that loops up to Kosh-Terek, north of Kyzyl-Ünkür, in addition to a 2-day horseback loop, camping in tents overnight, that takes in the large waterfall. There is a *turbaza* in Kyzyl-Ünkür.

The village of **Üch-Terek** on the shores of **Toktogul reservoir** may be reached on a 4-day, 3-night horseback tour via Kyzyl-Ünkür village, the Kara-Ünkür and Ken-Köl valleys and Shaldyrak Pass and the Kara-Suu valley and the Kargysh Pass. The last stretch is done on foot. From Üch-Terek it is possible to continue to Jalal-Abad or Bishkek by minibus or taxi.

Probably the most classic trek from Arslanbob is a 4-day hike and/or horseback loop to a group of four **holy lakes**, high in the mountains north of the village, which takes in *jailoos*, mountain passes and the holy rock, and is tough but highly rewarding. CBT say that this can be done in just 3 days but by all accounts this is very demanding and only for the super fit. There are a variety of routes to reach the lakes, most of which require going over passes of at least 3,500m. There is a track that leads from the village by which it is said to be possible to reach the lakes in 8 hours on horseback. The lakes, which collectively are called **Köl Mazar**, and which are usually marked as Köl Kupan or Köl Kulan on maps, are a pilgrimage destination for Muslims from Mailuu-Suu (which has partial road access) who come here between June and early September to slaughter a sheep and have a local preacher say prayers for them.

Other trekking and horseriding possibilities include a 3-day hike or horse trek to **Ortok**, where there is a CBT homestay programme. Longer tours to Toktogul, Sary-Chelek and Saimaluu-Tash are currently under development, as are programmes for winter visitors to the valley that involve snow-shoe trekking or skiing.

WALNUT TIME IN ARSLANBOB

Arslanbob is at the centre of the world's largest expanse of relict walnut forest. The forest, which grows at altitudes between 1,500 and 2,000m on the south-facing slopes of the Fergana range, has a high diversity of trees and shrubs that includes major species like walnut (*Juglans regia*) and various fruit-bearing species in their wild form such as apple (*Malus siversiana*), pear (*Pyrus korshinsky*) and plum (*Prunus sogdiana*).

During the walnut season, which begins in late September and lasts for about a month, most families in Arslanbob and other villages of the valley are involved in the gathering of the harvest. Walnuts are central to the village's economy; the majority of families in the valley depend on the harvest of the woods for at least part of their income, which is usually supplemented by the renting of an arable plot for growing crops like potatoes and sunflowers.

Families generally rent a territory for nut- and fruit-collecting and wood-cutting, for which they pay a percentage to the forestry authority in Arslanbob, the *leshoz*. Five-year contracts are issued for each territory and these come with special responsibilities, such as the planting of new trees and maintenance of old stock. If the conditions of the contract are seen to have been respected then the contract can then be extended for a further 10 years. It is up to the *leshoz* and its locally appointed representatives to police the forest activities and ensure there is no illegal felling or nut smuggling going on in season.

For the outside visitor, the walnut harvest is a good time to visit as it is a particularly beautiful season with cool, bright days, clear skies and turning leaves. There is also an up-beat atmosphere about the village as nut-gathering is an essentially social activity that is carried out mostly by family and friendship groups, particularly women and children. Foreign visitors to Arslanbob at this time of year will inevitably find their pockets bulging every time they go for a stroll, as they will be plied with nuts by local collectors delighted to show off their bounty by making a small gift to the visitors they come across. It would be ungracious to refuse.

Walnuts are highly prized and with good reason: they have undeniable health benefits and are a good source of oil, protein, anti-oxidants and omega-3 fatty acids. They have even been used as currency from time to time: Alexander the Great is said to have brought sacks of walnuts back from central Asia, but had to give them up *en route* as payment to the Greek boatmen who transported his troops. The custom may have passed down into modern times: there is an Iranian film *Blackboards*, in which impoverished Kurdish tribesmen pay itinerant teachers in walnuts, the only thing they have that is of value to both parties. Travelling to Arslanbob on the bus from Bazar-Korgon, I saw a number of village schoolgirls doing much the same sort of thing as they paid the bus driver... with walnuts.

Jalal-Abad Province ARSLANBOB

9

The main road west of Jalal-Abad goes through an agricultural landscape of maize, sunflowers and cotton to pass Bazar-Korgon and the turn-off for Arslanbob, before reaching Massy and the town of **Kochkor-Ata**, close to the border with Uzbekistan.

During the Soviet period Kochkor-Ata was famous for its oil wells, but these have since been bought out by Chinese business interests. Apart from a new bazaar building and football stadium there is little to distinguish the town and nothing of interest for visitors. Continuing west towards Shamaldy-Say and the main route to Toktogul and Bishkek, a turn-off is passed that leads north to Kök-Tash and Mailuu-Suu.

Mailuu-Suu has in recent years become a watchword for environmental pollution, having a large number of unstable uranium dumps close to the town. In Soviet times the town was an important uranium mining and processing centre, but since independence most of the population of 20,000 have not only been left without work, but also find themselves trapped by poverty in a highly polluted environment.

Due to the large number of unstable uranium tailing pits in the vicinity of the town, radiation levels are high and cancer rates in the town are more than twice the national average. In the period 1946–68 the plant in the town produced and processed more than 10,000 tonnes of uranium in total, some of which was used to make the Soviet Union's first atomic bomb. What is left today is nearly 2 million m³ of radioactive waste that poses an enormous threat not just to the local region but also to the whole basin of the Fergana Valley.

Landslides in 2002 and 2005 caused great alarm because of the possible consequences of large quantities of uranium waste infiltrating the regional water supply. In 2004, the World Bank and the Kyrgyz government signed a US$11.7 million deal aimed at reducing the risk of pollution, but experts insist that a truly effective clean-up operation would cost far more – hundreds of millions of dollars – to be completely effective. In 2006, Mailuu-Suu was listed as one of the ten most polluted sites in the world according to a study carried out by the Blacksmith Institute, a New York-based organisation that supports pollution-related environmental projects.

Older maps show the road west from Jalal-Abad to Shamaldy-Say and beyond weaving between Uzbek and Kyrgyz territories. This used to be the case, but in recent years border formalities have resulted in new stretches of road being built to allow the problematic Uzbek border to be skirted. At Shamaldy-Say, where there is a bus station just outside the town, which many long-distance services stop to eat at, the main Bishkek road veers north to **Tash-Kömür**, a long, thin town that hugs the lower Naryn River for several kilometres on the west bank opposite the highway. Coming from the broad, agricultural plain of the Fergana Valley, the landscape around the town has an almost claustrophobic feel to it; the river, road and railway are tightly enclosed by deeply folded sandstone hills. It is an industrial – or perhaps, post-industrial – landscape where the lines of pylons, slag heaps and deserted factories speak loudly of the unsightly demand for energy.

TASH-KÖMÜR This rambling thread of a town has two aspects, neither particularly alluring. Along the main Bishkek–Osh highway stand a line of makeshift kiosks intent on capturing the attention of passing vehicles. Taxis throng this stretch too, which effectively serves as a roadside service station.

Across the river lies the main part of town with its shoddy bazaar, blocks of flats and bus station. This part of town gives the impression of somewhere small and provincial, but seen from the main road it becomes clear that Tash-Kömür is an altogether larger place: a Soviet-era coal town whose industry since independence has sadly gone the way of most of the rest of Kyrgyzstan's mining heritage. The small bus station has buses to Jalal-Abad at 06.40, 07.20 and 12.20 and Osh at 05.40, as well as services to Kerben (Caravan) at 10.00 and 14.30, and Kara-Jygach for connections to Arkyt and Sary-Chelek at 10.00 and 13.30. There is a basic *gostinitsa* next to the bus station that might do if you get stuck here, and a public toilet block between the bus station and the non-functioning railway station that is seriously worth avoiding. Shared taxis to Bishkek, Osh and Kara-Köl leave from the main road across the river near the bridge; a taxi from the bus station will take you to the correct spot.

KARA-KÖL From Tash-Kömür the lower Naryn River squeezes through a narrow gorge with red and purple sandstone cliffs towering above the road. The river here is a series of five dammed lakes – the Nizhnenarynskiy *kaskad* (Lower Naryn Cascade) – that have been constructed along the Naryn River for the production of hydro-electricity. Kara-Köl, the next town reached, heading north, is effectively a dormitory town for workers at the hydro-electricity station. The uppermost dam at Kara-Köl, which is not visible from the main road here, was completed in 1976 after 14 years of construction, an impressive feat of engineering.

Hydro-electricity is a considerable money-spinner for Kyrgyzstan as the electrical power produced here is exported right across the central Asian region. It is not without controversy though, as there have been arguments with the Uzbekistan government over the Kyrgyz control of water, which the neighbouring country requires in large quantities to irrigate its cotton fields in the Fergana Valley. In reflection of its role as an important source of income, the dam appears on the reverse of the 100som note.

Buses and **minibuses** stop at the roadside outside the town for regular connections north to Toktogul (80som) and south to Bazar-Korgon (140som) and Jalal-Abad (160som).

TOKTOGUL This medum-sized town gives its name to the reservoir that lies just to the south. From Kara-Köl, the main Bishkek road sweeps in a wide arc around the eastern end of the large manmade lake, following the southern shore closely to just beyond the village of Üch-Terek, before it doubles back west to reach Toktogul. North of Toktogul, the main road to Bishkek climbs steadily, following the Chychkan River to enter Talas Province and the Chychkan State Zoological Reserve, on the way to the 3,184m Ala-Bel Pass and Chui Province.

Toktogul is a quiet, reasonably attractive provincial town that is not a bad place to break the journey between Bishkek and the south. The town gets its name from the well-known *akyn* (bard) Toktogul Satylganov (1864–1933) who was born here in what was then known as Kushchusu. Toktogul's image appears on the front of the Kyrgyz 100som banknote. The reservoir that lies immediately south of the town was created in 1974 when the Toktogul Dam was completed, displacing 26 communities that now lie beneath the reservoir's waters.

There is a friendly **guesthouse** in the town, run by Ilyatbue Saratova (*Nabereshnaya/Akimkan 86*; ℡ *03747 21 464*; $), which lies immediately behind the grounds of the hospital at the western edge of the town. Ilyatbue speaks French, as does her young son, and her daughter Mirgul speaks good English. The guesthouse is a short taxi ride or a 15-minute walk from the taxi and minibus park. From the taxi park, head along Lenin towards the town centre then take the first right. Walk down this road for 10 minutes to reach a hospital that has a couple of pharmacies in front of it; walk straight on through the gate and hospital grounds to reach a tall wall that has gap knocked into it. Go through the gap and number 86 is almost directly across the street.

The main street, Lenin, has another couple of places to stay: the new Hotel Ak-Jibek on the left ($$), with its own smart café, and a Soviet-era *gostinitsa* ($) a little further along on the right. This is probably where the British travel writer Colin Thubron stayed when he describes spending the night in a workers' hostel in the town in his book *Shadow of the Silk Road*.

The Kyrgyz Telecom building is on the right a little further into town and beyond this, a 15-minute walk east from the taxi park, is the town's bazaar, the Ay-Tulan restaurant and a large leafy park opposite. A pleasant walk is to go through the park, past the war memorial to reach a sports field with a broken Ferris wheel. From here there is an excellent panoramic view of the reservoir and the mountains beyond contrasted with the flat, green agricultural area in front of the water.

From the *avtobeket* (taxi and minibus station) at the western end of town, share taxis and minibuses leave for Tash-Kömür and points south. Share taxis leave from here for Bishkek (350som) and buses leave from in front of the bazaar at the eastern end of Lenin.

WESTERN JALAL-ABAD PROVINCE

The road that leads west from Shaymaldy-Say, hugging the border with Uzbekistan, leads eventually to the small town of Kerben. The road is quite obviously truncated in parts, the old route now curtailed by having to cross Uzbek territory, and in places makeshift road barriers block once-busy side roads to prevent illicit traffic between the two countries. The small town of **Kerben** (or Caravan, its Russian name) sits on top of one of the most northerly meanders of the Uzbek Fergana Valley. It's a crossroads town that sits midway between Jalal-Abad and the lonely Chatkal valley to the west. For visitors, the town also serves as a jumping off point for visits to Lake Sary-Chelek to the north. West of Kerben the road twists around the Uzbek frontier on a circuitous, sometimes pot-holed road to reach Ala-Buka and the nearby mausoleum of Safet Bulan, before continuing to reach the southern reaches of the Chatkal valley beyond

KERBEN (CARAVAN) КЕРБЕН (*Telephone code: 03742*) Arriving in Kerben from Jalal-Abad to the east, it is immediately apparent that the pace of life here makes even relaxed Jalal-Abad seem frenetic in comparison. This calm façade seems at odds with the recent tragedy in the town in which six protestors were shot by panicking policemen at an anti-government rally in 2002, one of the key events that gave momentum to the downfall of the previous Akaev government and the so-called Tulip Revolution (see page 15). There is a monument that commemorates this tragedy at the roadside on the Sary-Chelek road.

Set in pretty agricultural landscape with lovely views of the mountains to the north, Kerben's day-to-day activity, such as it is, revolves around the crossroads of Frunze and Karl Marx, the town's two principal streets. The crossroads has a cinema, a yurt restaurant, a covered market and a park all gathered around it. Just south of the crossroads on Frunze is a large stone head of Lenin, and beyond this lies the Kyrgyz Telecom building and a hospital.

Walking west along Karl Marx past the TsUM building, there is a small bazaar on the right just before the local bus station. Continuing in this direction over the river and past a petrol station, a larger bus station is reached opposite a newly built mosque.

Immediately to the east of the central crossroads is a steep rocky mound that offers excellent views from the top. If you end up staying the night then it is highly likely that you will end up climbing this, as Kerben has few real distractions other than some good *chaikhanas*. The town receives few overseas visitors and so the presence of a foreigner may arouse a little more curiosity than usual, but nevertheless it is a relaxed and friendly place.

Getting there There are two bus stations: the **large bus station** at the western end of Karl Marx, which has regular services to Kara-Jygach (for Sary-Chelek) and Tash-Kömür (for Bishkek); Jalal-Abad (4–5 hours) three times a day in the mornings (07.20, 08.40 and 11.00); and four buses a day to Ala-Buka at 08.30, 11.00, 13.30 and 15.30. The **small bus station** has crowded snub-nose buses going to local destinations, including Arkyt at 16.00 and Kyzyl-Köl at 16.30.

There are **flights** to and from Bishkek twice a week (three times in summer) that take about an hour.

Information A CBT group is currently being set up in the town but until this happens information may be had at the home of Dilbar Sulaimankulova (Russian only). It is hoped that the CBT group here, once in operation, will be used as the CBT base for Sary-Chelek visits, as the CBT set-up in Kyzyl-Köl has no telephone.

 Where to stay

 Homestay of Dilbar Sulaimankulova Jany-Turmush 5; ☎ 22 577. Dilbar lives in a house with a large, shady garden on the northern outskirts of the town. To reach Dilbar's homestay walk north along Frunze from the crossroads, pass the bus stop & continue past a large building with a container outside that

sometimes opens as a café. After another 5mins a small road leads left over a little footbridge towards a small shop with a blue door, go left here & follow the road left around the corner on reaching a larger building. The house is then the 2nd blue gate on the left. *B&B* $; *meals 90som.*

If this is full you could try the **Gostinitsa Jyldyz** ($) just north of the crossroads on Frunze. The old **Intourist Hotel**, on Karl Marx opposite TsUM, appeared to be closed on inspection but it may have rooms if you can find someone in charge.

✗ **Where to eat** There is good home-cooked food at the homestay above. Otherwise there are a few *chaikhanas* and simple restaurants in the town (*all* $). The **Ak-Kaiyn café** between the small bus station and the bazaar is good for staples, as is the **Chaikhana Sary-Chelek** on the corner of Karl Marx and Lenina nearby. The shady and very traditional Uzbek-run **Amanbay-Ata** *chaikhana* at the crossroads next to TsUM has really good *shashlyk* and is probably the best for atmosphere, coupled with very low prices. There are more cafés along Frunze heading north from the crossroads.

AROUND KERBEN
Padysha-Ata State Reserve North of the village of Kashka-Suu, 15km north of Kerben, a road follows the river gorge lined with birch groves to reach the village of Kara-Bashat where there is the 18th–19th century mausoleum of Padysha-Ata, a pilgrimage site for Muslims from the Fergana Valley region. The Padysha-Ata State Reserve was established in the region in 2003 and covers 305km² of the lower Chatkal ridge. The reserve office is in Kerben at the Selhoztehnika building (*Umetaliev,* ☎ *22 547;* e *padyshaata_gz@mail.ru*). There is a local CBT programme that offers homestay accommodation and tours of the reserve; the co-ordinator is Arstanbek Kaletov.

Lake Sary-Chelek is one of Kyrgyzstan's true gems – a major draw that is a little difficult to reach but, as all visitors seem to attest, well worth the effort. Sary-Chelek (literally 'Yellow Bucket') is a fairly small, alpine lake set amidst conifer and relict fruit and nut forest at an altitude of 1,873m. The lake is just one part of the Sary-Chelek Biosphere Reserve that protects more than a 1,000 species of plants, 160 birds and 34 mammals that include rarities like bear, lynx and snow leopard.

Sary-Chelek is relatively small: just 7.5km long and 1,500m wide at its broadest point, with a maximum depth of 234m. The lake is fed by the Sary-Chelek River, in addition to numerous other streams and underground sources, and its outflow flows into the Kara-Suu. The hollow that the lake sits in was probably created by earthquake activity hundreds of years ago, although the precise geomorphology of its formation is unclear. The name 'yellow bucket', although hardly romantic, is perfectly apt, as in early autumn the turning leaves of the forest that surrounds the lake positively glow with golden-yellow light that contrasts sharply with the deep blue-green of the water.

Lake Sary-Chelek does not stand alone, as there are other, smaller lakes within the reserve to the southeast, but without doubt it is Sary-Chelek that is the jewel in the crown. Its glorious alpine location among forest and rocky crags is as impressive as the lake itself, and the steep slopes that surround the lake support dense forests of pine, fir and juniper. At slightly lower elevations there are tangled stands of nut and wild fruit trees that include walnut, pistachio, apple and pear. Although they are not strictly supposed to, many locals come to gather the fruits of the forest in this part of the reserve.

GETTING THERE Unless you're planning on hiking over the mountains from the north (which *is* possible), the only routes leading to Sary-Chelek come from the south, either by way of the village of **Arkyt**, which is on the edge of the reserve and serves as its administrative headquarters, or from the Kara-Suu valley in the buffer zone. The only driveable road to the lake leads from Arkyt, 16km from the lake.

Both Arkyt and Kyzyl-Köl village in the Kara-Suu valley are connected to Kerben and Kara-Jygach by a daily **bus** service. From Kerben, a bus leaves daily from the small bus station for Arkyt at 16.00 and for Kyzyl-Köl at 16.30 (2–2½ hours). Both buses go via Kara-Jygach, which can be reached by bus from Tash-Kömür by two buses a day that leave at 10.00 and 13.30 (3 hours). Returning from Arkyt there is a morning bus at 07.30 that goes to Kerben via Kara-Jygach (1 hour, 25som). The morning bus from Kyzyl-Köl to Kerben leaves at 07.00. There is a bus from Kara-Jygach to Tash-Kömür at 08.30 (it will wait for the Arkyt bus to arrive) and at 13.00. This takes 2½ hours and costs 55som. There are also share taxis to Tash-Kömür and to Bishkek. On the way to Tash-Kömür, look out for strangely eroded rock formations in the valley. A bus from Tash-Kömür to Jalal-Abad leaves at 12.20 (3½ hours, 90som) and so there is time to make a connection to get back to Jalal-Abad by mid-afternoon.

Coming from either Bishkek or Jalal-Abad, the most direct route is by way of Tash-Kömür and Kara-Jygach, where it is possible to pick up the daily bus coming from Kerben as it passes through to Arkyt or Kyzyl-Köl in the late afternoon. This is quite a long, uncomfortable journey to do in a single day, and a better bet from Jalal-Abad might be to spend a night in Kerben *en route*, making it an even longer route but at least a more leisurely one. A faster but more expensive alternative to all of this is to hire a **taxi** from Tash-Kömür to Arkyt.

Once in Arkyt, a vehicle may be hired to reach the lake the following day. From Arkyt it should be possible to go to Sary-Chelek and back and have a few hours' walking there for around 800som. Walking to the lake from Arkyt will take at least 3 hours, mainly uphill, along the road, although the views are splendid and ever-changing along the way. Even driving, it is worthwhile stopping a couple of times to enjoy the view down over Arkyt and the valley.

TREKKING TO SARY-CHELEK Kyzyl-Köl, the most northerly of the string of villages along the Kara-Suu River, is more distant and has no direct road to Lake Sary-Chelek, so it makes sense to come here only if you plan to trek to the lake or wish to go for hikes in the equally attractive buffer zone. The CBT co-ordinator in the village can organise an overnight trek to the lake via Kara-Suu Lake and the Kemerty Pass. There are also 4- and 5-day combined horseback and trekking circular routes that can be made from Kyzyl-Köl, which take in Sary-Chelek, Kara-Suu Lake and various passes.

The CBT co-ordinator in Kyzyl-Köl, Bazarkul Jooshbaev (m *0503 319 814, or through Dilbar Sulaimankulova in Kerben:* ↘ *03742 22 577*), lives at the north end of the village. He can arrange accommodation in Kyzyl-Köl or other villages of the Kara-Suu valley, and provide horses and guides for treks to the lake or elsewhere.

Other **cross-country trekking options** offered by CBT include a 7-day horseback and trekking tour over the Talas range, which begins or ends in Kyzyl-Köl. As this requires some degree of pre-planning it is best organised in advance through the KCBTA office in Bishkek. This could be done independently with the right equipment and mountain experience. It begins near Leninopol west of Talas, and heads due south to the 3,601m Chimtash Pass before following a valley east over a low pass to the 3,161m Kara-Kulja Pass, before skirting a couple of the minor lakes to reach Lake Sary-Chelek and then finally either Arkyt or Kyzyl-Köl.

Another possibility is trekking east from the north of the Chatkal valley along the Aflatun valley and over the Ashu-Tör Pass, a tough 5-day hike.

Several Bishkek companies offer trekking and horseback itineraries to Sary-Chelek and it is worthwhile comparing what is on offer by visiting their offices in Bishkek before heading south. Similarly, the Geo-ID map shop in the capital may also have 1:200,000 maps that show some of the routes.

DAY HIKES AT SARY-CHELEK A day trip to the lake is all too brief but it is possible to make a short circular hike close to the lake that passes some of the smaller lakes in the reserve and gives a good flavour of the various landscapes contained by the park.

Starting at the car park by the lake, head right from the keeper's house to follow a track that leads gently uphill to the east past some beehives in a meadow. Climb to the top for a great view of the lake then return to the track that skirts around the back of the hill and descends slightly to a meadow, before climbing again, passing some dead trees on the left to follow a ridge above an eastern inlet of the lake. The path goes gently uphill through meadows that have large, scattered boulders and then continues towards an enormous scree slope and corrie on the other side of the valley and descends almost to the valley floor.

Follow this until, just beneath the scree slope, the path, which is quite well-defined at this point, veers to the right (south) and downhill. The path descends to a meadow and then leads north again across meadows and around a spur, and then east following a ridge. After approximately 2 hours' walking a small lake (Iyri-Köl) comes into view and the path leads along its shore to the left. At the end there is an orchard and a 4×4 track. Follow this to the right to reach a much smaller lake that is more like a pond.

At the southern end of this lake there is a small path that climbs off right from the main track. Climb this up to a steep wooded ridge then continue along the path on the east side of the ridge, which rises and falls with superb mountain views, before descending more steeply through hay meadows. Lake Sary-Chelek suddenly comes into view again and then, shortly afterwards, another lake by the road to Arkyt (Kula-Köl) is viewed. The path stays high above the lake before eventually descending to a small *jailoo* and honey farm. The path continues above the north side of the lake before descending to the road by a bridge just to the south of the starting point. The entire walk should take between 3½–4 hours in total.

ARKYT АРКИТ

Arkyt is a very pretty mountain village that follows the course of the river for some distance upstream. The central part of the village has a bus stop, a post office, and the *zapovednik* or park administration headquarters (↘ *03742 22 284*), with a museum next door that has stuffed animals, examples of local flora and a topographical model of the reserve. Next door is a government guesthouse. A little further downhill is a shop that has a rudimentary café that could probably prepare food if given some notice. There is another shop in the northern part of the village. These both just have basic supplies like biscuits and fizzy drinks, but nothing fancy like mineral water. The bus terminus is in the northern part of the village close to the radio tower. To leave the village to the north and enter the park through the upper barrier beyond the radio tower there is an entrance fee of 400som to pay per person per day.

 WHERE TO STAY There are several homestays scattered around the village. In the south of the village is the homestay of **Gulnara Khadirova**. There are a couple more in the centre, at the homes of **Sultan Chukotaev** and **Respek Urmanaliev**. Respek's homestay (\$, *with evening meal*) is a rambling farmstead reached by crossing the footbridge just north of the *zapovednik* and following the dirt road as it curves uphill to the right. His house is at the top of the hill on the right-hand side. Respek also has a car and will ferry you to the lake for a negotiated fee, and may also offer to fire up the sauna for you.

The north of the village towards the radio tower has another guesthouse that is signed from the street. There is a clean but austere **government guesthouse** next to the park administration building.

There is also a *turbaza* south of Arkyt, at the village of Jylgyn, that has basic wooden chalets to rent (\$) and a converted *dacha* at the lake itself that offers rooms (\$–\$\$) that should be pre-booked at the park administration headquarters. Camping at the lake requires permission, again from the *zapovednik*.

WEST TO THE CHATKAL VALLEY

ALA-BUKA This small town, 50km west of Kerben, is the gateway to the 12th-century **mausoleum of Safed Bulan**, 8km away. Four buses a day run to and from Kerben to Ala-Buka, and a daily bus leaves the town for Jany-Bazar in the southern Chatkal valley.

Mausoleum of Safed Bulan and Shah Fasil
The shrine stands on the outskirts of the village of the same name. The brick-built mausoleum is said to have been built in the 12th century and still has considerable potency as an important Sufi pilgrimage site in the region. Many Uzbeks from Uzbekistan's Fergana Valley come here, as well as their kinsmen from Kyrgyzstan. Visitors should respect this and dress and behave appropriately.

The *mazar* contains the graves of two revered individuals: Safet Bulan, a pious local woman, and Shah Fasil, a warrior and descendant of the Prophet Mohammed.

Shah Fasil is reputed to have first brought Islam to central Asia, while Safed Bulan was responsible for burying the heads of thousands of decapitated prisoners captured in battle.

Legend tells that a grandson of the Prophet Mohammed came with an army to the region in order to convert the local populace to Islam. When the Arab army was at prayer the locals attacked the proselytising soldiers, taking 2,700 prisoners whom they proceeded to behead. A woman travelling with the army searched in vain through the carnage for the head of her lover and, although she did not find him, she proceeded to carry out the gruesome task of washing and burying all of the heads of the fallen, before staying on at the village to look after the graves of the fallen. In gratitude for this pious act of purification, she was given the honorary title *safed*, 'white', and the village was named after her.

Another, altogether more ethnocentric, version of the legend suggests that Safed Bulan had originally been a black woman and that Allah turned her skin white as a reward for her deed. A mausoleum was erected to her when she died and in later years her grave was joined by that of Shah Fasil, who came to the area to avenge the massacre of his father, Mohammed ben Jarir, who had been Safed Bulan's lover. The legend is supported to some extent by archaeological evidence, which suggests that a large battle took place near here.

The mausoleum complex consists of several vaults, a mosque and a large holy stone within a courtyard. Shah Fasil's tomb, although stark externally, has a tall central cupola set in an octagonal base and a lavishly decorated interior that has fine decorative panels, ornaments and complex Farsi calligraphy depicting verses from the Qu'ran covering every centimetre. Opposite Shah Fasil's mausoleum stands the tomb of Safed Bulan, next to the room that is said to contain the skulls she washed. Pilgrims come from far and wide to parade clockwise around the graves, the standard procedure at any Sufi site. Only women may enter the tomb of Safed Bulan.

CHATKAL VALLEY This highly inaccessible valley in the far west of Jalal-Abad Province is where the road from Jalal-Abad turns to the northeast towards Talas Province. The colder, northern part of the valley climbs up to the 3,302m Kara-Buura Pass to descend along the Kara-Buura river into Talas Oblast. There is little contact between the two provinces along this route as the pass becomes impassable during the winter months due to snowfall, and there is no public transport that connects the Chatkal valley with Talas at any time of year. Even the southern part of the valley is difficult to reach and, with many more easily accessible destinations to tempt visitors, it is no surprise that very few visitors to Kyrgyzstan make it this far; those that do tend to come for rugged outdoor activities such as rafting expeditions or trekking. The whole region is, as they say, ripe for exploration.

That the valley has long been settled is evidenced by archaeological finds that date back to the Neolithic period. Metal ores were extracted here in the Bronze Age and bronze vessels have been found in burial mounds from this region that date from the 1st and 2nd millennia BC. It appears that the livestock breeding that still characterises the economy of the region today has been important since the Iron Age and that later, between the 4th–12th centuries AD, the valley was fairly densely populated by a mixture of settled farmers and nomadic herdsmen.

Trade used to be important too and Silk Road commerce along the valley transported silver from Talas and walnuts from Arslanbob to destinations south and west. As with almost everywhere else in the central Asian region, Genghis Khan's violent forays into the region disrupted settled life severely and this, coupled with feudal warring, heralded a sharp decline from the 12th century onwards.

The most important centre in the valley today is the small market town of **Jany-Bazar**, which has limited public transport reaching it from further east in

Jalal-Abad Province. Jany-Bazar serves as a centre for visiting the Besh-Aral State Reserve and also has the 18th-century Idris Paygambar mausoleum on a hill nearby, which was built for an Arab mystic who came to the region. The brick mausolea were constructed between the 18th and 19th centuries. There is a guesthouse for pilgrims in the town that has rooms to rent, and it should be possible to find homestay accommodation in the town. A daily bus runs between Ala-Buka and Jany-Bazar, leaving both destinations in the morning.

With adequate preparation it is possible to trek to Sary-Chelek or the village of Kyzyl-Köl from the northern part of the Chatkal valley, crossing high passes and taking 5 days. Coming in the reverse direction this can be organised with the CBT co-ordinator in Kyzyl-Köl.

BESH-ARAL STATE RESERVE This reserve of 63,200ha, established in 1979, is the main draw for most visitors to the Chatkal valley. It covers part of the lower reaches of the Chatkal valley next to the Uzbekistan border and consists of coniferous and deciduous forest, alpine meadows and steppe. It was created to specifically protect the habitat of certain endemic species found only in the Western Tien Shan, like Menzbier's marmot, endemic species of tulips, and other flora that are listed in Kyrgyzstan's Red Book. Snow leopards, Tien Shan bear and Turkestan lynx are all present, as are raptors such as lammergeyers and eagles. Most of the reserve can only be reached on horseback, although a car is able to provide limited access. There is an entrance charge of the equivalent of US$10 for foreign, non-CIS visitors and this should be paid at the administration office in Jany-Bazar on the main street near the park (↘ *03759 21 222*, ↘ *21 271*, ↘ *31 266*) where transport, horses and compulsory guides may also be arranged.

Wolf

10

Southern Kyrgyzstan

Kyrgyzstan's most southerly region consists of two provinces, **Osh** (Ош областы) and **Batken** (Баткен областы), which make up the southern arm of the country that extends westwards south of Uzbekistan's Fergana Valley. The southern border with Tajikistan is demarcated by the high ridges of the Turkestan and Alay mountains, the most northern range of the Pamirs, while to the east is China's Xinjiang Province and the Great Game market town of Kashgar (Kashi), accessible from Kyrgyzstan across the border at Irkeshtam. The Batken region used to be part of Osh Province but was awarded provincial status in 1999 to become an *oblast* in its own right.

Osh Province has an area of 29,200km² with a population of around 1,300,000 and a population density of 44.5 per km², the highest in the country apart from Bishkek; neighbouring Batken is almost 17,000km² in area with a total population of just 400,000, which is less than 24 people per km². Together the two provinces make up just under a quarter of Kyrgyzstan's total land area. The vast majority of Kyrgyzstan's Uzbek minority live in Osh Province, where they are the majority ethnic group in many areas.

OSH ОШ *Telephone code: 03222*

Although you would not know from looking at it, Osh is Kyrgyzstan's oldest city. As Kyrgyzstan's second largest city, with a mixed population of around 250,000, it is considered to be the capital of the south and has served as the administrative centre of the *oblast* since 1939. It is a lively city that despite its smaller size can seem busier than Bishkek. It has the largest mosque in the country and one of the largest and most crowded markets in all of central Asia. Central to the city is the steep outcrop of Solomon's Throne, which is an important Muslim pilgrimage site as well as a popular place for locals and visitors alike to enjoy the view over the city. The city has a strong Uzbek presence and in many ways looks westwards towards the Uzbek Fergana Valley rather than north to the capital Bishkek. The Uzbekistan border is just a few kilometres from the city, a 10-minute *marshrutka* ride away. However, international wrangling between Kyrgyzstan and its immediate neighbour has meant that from time to time border crossings are not always as straightforward as they might be.

HISTORY The city of Osh, which claims to be 3,000 years old and 'older than Rome', is certainly one of the oldest permanently inhabited settlements in the central Asian region. Although 3,000 years of history may be an exaggeration, the settlement dates back at least to the 5th century BC. It was known as early as the 8th century AD as an important centre for silk production and as a trade centre at a crossroads on the Silk Road. Legend states that Alexander the Great visited the city on his way to India, but there again most legends make some sort of claim for the Macedonian warrior king. King Solomon is also said to have visited and slept on top of the hill that still bears his name – Taht-i-Suleiman (Suleiman Mountain or

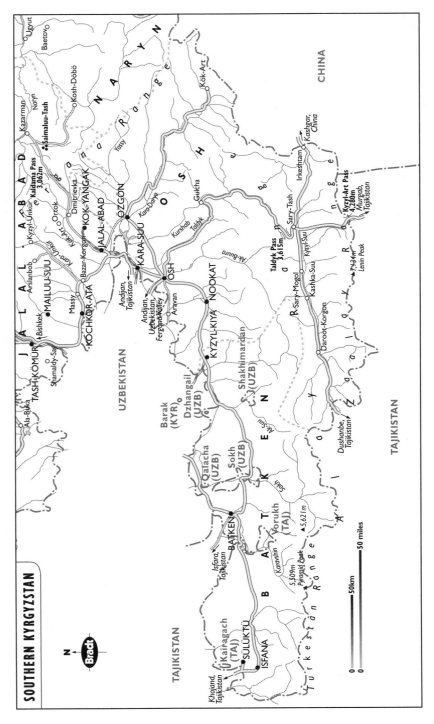

SOUTHERN KYRGYZSTAN

N

CHINA

UZBEKISTAN

TAJIKISTAN

Ugyut

Baetov

Kosh-Döbö

Kök-Art

Kashgar, China

Kazarman

Naryn

Saimaluu-Tash

N A R Y N

R a n g e

Yassy

Inkeshttam

Kök-Tu

Kyzyl-Ünkür

Kaldama Pass 3,062m

Dmitrievka

Ortok

KOK-YANGAK

ÖZGÖN

Kara-Darya

Sary-Tash

Kyzyl-Art Pass 4,280m

Murgab, Tajikistan

Kara-Ünkür

Bazar-Korgon

JALAL-ABAD

Gulcha

A L A I

Arslanbob

MAILUU-SUU

KARA-SUU

Kurshab

Taldyk

Kyzyl-Suu

Lenin Peak 7,134m

Bishkek

Massy

KOCHKOR-ATA

Andijan, Tajikistan

OSH

Ak-Buura

Taldyk Pass 3,615m

Sary-Mogol

Kashka-Suu

Ala-Buka

TASH-KÖMÜR

Stamaldy-Say

Andijan, Uzbekistan, Fergana Valley

Aravan

KYZYL-KIYA

NOOKAT

Daroot-Korgon

Shakhimardan (UZB)

Dushanbe, Tajikistan

Barak (KYR)

Dzhangail (UZB)

Ak-Suu

Qalacha (UZB)

Sokh (UZB)

Sokh

Vorukh (TAJ)

BATKEN

Karavshin

Pyramid Peak 5,621m

5,509m

Khojand, Tajikistan

Kairagach (TAJ)

SULÜKTÜ

ISFANA

Isfara, Tajikistan

T u r k e s t a n   R a n g e

0   50km
0   50 miles

A L A I

O S H

A L A Y

B A T K E N

Kosh-Döbö

Bradt

250

Solomon's Throne). What is more certain is that the founder of the Indian Mughul Dynasty and descendant of Tamerlane, Zahiruddin Muhammad Babur, who was born nearby just across the Uzbekistan border in Andijan, came to Osh to visit Solomon's Throne before venturing on to India. Of Osh, he wrote in his memoir, the *Baburnama*:

> There are many sayings about the excellence of Osh. On the southeastern side of the Osh fortress is a well-proportioned mountain called Bara-Koh, where, on its summit, Sultan Mahmud Khan built a pavilion. Farther down, on a spur of the same mountain, I had a porticoed pavilion built in 902 [AD1496–97].

Babur is credited with having built the mosque on top of Solomon's Throne, which even today is still referred to as Babur's House.

The Solomon connection led over the years for Taht-i-Suleiman to become a holy place for central Asian Muslims, and it is even believed that the Prophet Mohammed prayed here. Between the 10th–12th centuries it was the third of the great cities of the Fergana Valley, but in the 13th century the Mongols came and did their level best to destroy the place. Slowly Osh recovered and rebuilt itself over the next few centuries and the city went on to become part of the Kokand Khanate in 1762.

Russians first came to Osh in 1876 during the height of the Great Game era between Tsarist Russia and Britain, when Russian forces overpowered the khanates that hitherto had controlled the city. Following the October Revolution in 1917 the Soviets made their mark on the city and some of this legacy remains today, including a large statue of Lenin in one of the city parks. In the post-independence period the city became a byword for the inter-ethnic conflict that erupted in 1990 between Uzbek and Kyrgyz factions, although the worst of this took place at the town of Özgön, 50km to the northeast. Happily, there appear to be no outward signs of such ethnic tension today and most of the city's inhabitants rub shoulders well enough, despite frequent dissatisfaction with the Kyrgyz-dominated Bishkek government.

GETTING THERE

By air There are up to three flights a day to and from Bishkek with Kyrgyzstan Airlines and Altyn Air. The flight takes just 1 hour and, on a clear day, is a wonderful way to get a bird's eye view of the country's rugged topography. Flights cost between 1,800–2,000som one-way and are sometimes discounted to less than this.

The airport is 8km north of the city. *Marshrutki* numbers 2 and 7A run between the airport and the city centre and charge 6som, otherwise a taxi charges 130–160som.

By bus and minibus Osh has a couple of bus stations, as well as separate taxi and minibus stands.

The **Old Bus Station** tucked away next to the bazaar and the river on Alisher Navoi has frequent services in small buses and minibuses to destinations like Özgön (35som), Jalal-Abad (70som), Aravan (15som) and Kara-Suu (15som), plus occasional buses to various destinations in the Alay valley and a daily service to Kyzyl-Kiya and Batken (via the Uzbek enclaves).

The **New Bus Station** is inconveniently located 6km north of the city and has services north and west to Tash-Kömür, Toktogul and Kerben, although nothing to Bishkek as large buses are no longer allowed through the tunnel at the Töö-Ashuu Pass. Buses to Kashgar in China (US$55) also leave from here on Wednesday and Sunday evenings. The 7A minibus runs between the bus station and the bazaar and Kyrgyzstana in the city centre, and 7 and 13 between the new and old bus stations. On **Alisher Navoi**, over the road from the Hotel Alay, is another bus and taxi stand where transport to Aravan and Nookat can be arranged. A shared taxi to Aravan costs 25som.

Taxis to Batken leave early morning from the car park by the GUM department store near the Hotel Alay (400som per seat or 1,600som per car via the Uzbek enclaves; 2,000–2,500som to go around them).

By taxi The big taxi stand on Alisher Navoi next to Kelechek bazaar has share taxis to Bishkek (900–1,400som), Jalal-Abad (150som) and Özgön (70som). This is also the place to look for a taxi to the Alay valley south of Osh, although it might be difficult to find other passengers to share with.

Crossing into Uzbekistan The Dostlyk border with Uzbekistan is very close. Kyrgyz taxis are not allowed to cross the border so a taxi (60som) or minibus (5som) number 7, 16, 36 or 37 or 38 should be taken to the border post from the centre of Osh. Apart from sporadic periods when there is marked international tension between the two countries, crossing on foot is usually straightforward and after customs another taxi can be taken onwards to Andijan.

GETTING AROUND *Marshrutki* run up and down the main thoroughfares of Kurmanjan Datka, Lenina and Kyrgyzstana between the south of the city and Jayma bazaar. Minibus numbers 2 and 7A serve the airport and the city centre. Minibus 7A runs between the New Bus Station and the city centre, and minibus numbers 7 and 13 operate between the new and old bus stations. The flat fare is 5som.

Taxis, mostly Daewoo Ticos assembled just across the border in Andijan, charge 40–60som for a journey within the city centre. A taxi to the airport should be 130–160 som, although drivers will probably quote more on first asking.

TOURIST INFORMATION The Osh CBT office (*Kelechek Plaza, Alisher Navoi;* m *0502 574 940;* e *osh_cbt.mail.ru*), on the second floor of a furniture shop overlooking Kelechek Plaza near the bazaar, can organise transport, arrange homestay accommodation in the city and advise on local sites of interest. The office has a shop attached with a reasonable range of souvenirs on sale.

TOUR OPERATORS

Daniyar Abdurahmanov Osh Guesthouse, apartment 8, flat 48 Kyrgyzstana; m 0502 372 311; e daniyar1@mail.ru. Daniyar, who works through both the Osh Guesthouse & the Taj Mahal Hotel, speaks good English & is able to arrange transport to China via Irkeshtam, or to Murgab in Tajikistan.

Chyngyz Myrbek Ametov ☏ 33 605; e oshchyngyz@hotmail.ru. A local teacher who speaks fluent English & good French & who can also offer translation services as well as that of a guide.

Kyrgyz Nur Lenina 277/8; ☏ 25 565, ☏ 23 042; e kyrgyznur@rambler.ru; www.kyrgyznur.narod.ru. This small, young company offers a variety of tours & services in southern Kyrgyzstan that include ecotourism, trekking, horse tours, cultural tours & mountaineering. Trekking & mountaineering programmes to the Alay region cost between US$25–50 per day. It also offers a variety of treks along the Pamir Alay ridges & in the western Tien Shan, plus 4–6-day treks

to Irkeshtam & Torugart Pass.

Kyrgyz Tur Kyrgyzstana; ☏ 24 791, ☏ 74 702; m 0502 538 972. One of several travel agents on Kyrgyzstana, near the junction with Alisher Navoi, that can book air tickets for flights to Bishkek.

Garant International Travel Corporation Kyrgyzstana 17/2; ☏/f 56 447. Air tickets to Bishkek & general travel services.

Munduz-Tourist Sovetskaya 1; ☏ 26 614. Offer a range of travel services including air tickets & local tours.

Sputnik Kyrgyzstana 30/4; ☏ 25 339, ☏ 29 724; f 25 339; e manzura.d@mail.ru; www.sputnuk.in.kg. Also branches at the airport (☏ 94 082; e airport_osh@mail.ru), at Lenina 314 (☏ 55 490, ☏ 77 310; f 74 310; e booking_1@mail.ru) & Kurmanjan Datka 287 (☏ 57 946, ☏ 22 211; e booking_3@mail.ru). Sputnik can book domestic & international flights.

Airport,
New bus station

Jalal-Abad

KARASUYSKAYA

Osh
Guesthouse   Ala-Too
Turkestan
Jayma
Bazaar   1
Money   2
Changers   Dell
New   Gulnara
Mosque   Ilkhom

ZAINA BETINOVA

0 ———————— 500m
0 ———————— 500yds

Travel
agents
Nurbek   Hotel   Jeep
Istanbul Kristall stand
Buses, taxis Kara   Kelechek
to Aravan   Alma   ALISHER NAVOI   Bazaar
Hotel Alay   CBT
Hotel Sara   3   Share   taxis
Taxis to   Old bus station office
Rabat Abdul Batken   Telephone office
Khan Mosque
Historical   Solomon's   Babur's House   Yak-40
Cultural   Throne   (Dom Babura)   Greenwood
Museum   Silk Road
Muslim   Museum   Bakai
Cemetery
GAPAR AYTIEV
Aravan   Hotel
Sanabar
Gurman

KYRGYZSTANA

Sary-Tash

GAGARIN

ABDYKADYROV

Ak-Buura
FLOW

MOMINOVA

N

Bradt

TES
Guesthouse
Hotel
Osh   Stadium
BAYALINOVA
Demir
LENINA   Drama Theatre
AKB
LOMONOSOV
Lenin
Statue
City Administration
Building
NOOKATSKAYA   Orthodox Church
Huadalay
ALIEV   KURMANJAN DATKA   OVIR office
SOVETSKAYA   GOLUBEV

FRUNZE
Rich Men
MICHURIN   CBT
Guesthouse #1
CHAPAEV

SUYUMBAEV

KEY
1 Demir Kyrgyz Bank
2 Taj Mahal Hotel
3 Kurmanjan Datka Statue

WHERE TO STAY
Hotels

Barak-Ata guesthouse (8 rooms) Ibraimova 22/1.
A small, modern guesthouse to the south of the city
centre with satellite TV, sauna, swimming pool &
small business centre. $$$–$$$$

Kristall (20 rooms) Navoi 50a; 20 447, 73
896; f 73 894. Kristall is a new hotel near the
bazaar that has a dual-pricing policy in which

foreigners pay double. The cheapest rooms share a
bathroom. Friendly but rather inexperienced staff.
Conference hall, 2 dining halls, casino.
$$$–$$$$$, suites $$$$$.

Batyrov's guesthouse (4 rooms) Suyunbaeva 1. A
clean, modern place in the southeast part of the city.
Only one room has en-suite facilities. $$$

🛏 **Jetigen** Jim 1/1 (5 rooms); 📞 39 910. Near Jayma bazaar on the ground floor of a high-rise; all rooms come with AC, cable TV & bath. Conference hall, sauna, business centre. $$$

🛏 **Osh** (62 rooms) Bayalinova 1; 📞 75 614; f 56 326. This former state-owned Intourist hotel in a side street between Lenina & Kurmanjan Datka was fully renovated in 2006, but a triple pricing system makes it poor value for foreign visitors. There is a large casino next door. *Sgl or dbl without TV* $$$; *dbl, lux, apt* $$$$; *lux supreme* $$$$$.

🛏 **TES guesthouse** (5 rooms) Say-Boyu 5; 📞 21 548; f 56 385; m 0502 345 546; e afc-osh@mail.kg. A small, tidy guesthouse just south of the centre, near the stadium & Delfin swimming pool. Kitchen & laundry service available. Conference room for 30, outdoor patio, living room with satellite TV, internet access, European b/fast. The guesthouse is popular with NGO workers so book well ahead. $$$

🛏 **Taj Mahal** (10 rooms) Zaina Betinova 13; 📞 39 652. A modern, pleasant hotel close to the bazaar, which tends to fill quickly. The lobby is reached by entering through the glass doors by the ATM machine next to the Demir Bank & going up to the 1st floor. The Taj Mahal also has an unnamed annex further down Zaina Betinova opposite the entrance to Jayma bazaar, which has slightly cheaper rooms. Dbls only. $$–$$$.

🛏 **Alay** Kurmanjan Datka 230; 📞 57 729. An old, cavernous Soviet-era hotel at the junction of Kurmanjan Datka & Alisher Navoi that was partly refurbished fairly recently. There's no sign over the door, but the lobby is through the last door on the street. Anonymous spartan rooms but pleasant enough, with shared bathrooms apart from the 'deluxe' suites. *Good value for sgl rooms* ($), *which unusually are half the price of dbls* $$, *deluxe suite* $$$.

🛏 **Sanabar** (4 rooms) Gapar Aytiev 9a; 📞 25 437. A small, relatively new hotel at the junction of Kurmanjan Datka & Gapar Aytiev, just south of the silver dome souvenir shop at the base of Solomon's Throne. Plain rooms with bathroom but no b/fast served. $$

🛏 **Sara** (15 rooms) Kurmanjan Datka 278a; 📞 22 559, 📞 22 998, 📞 56 998; f 59 129; e adil.kazakbaev@usa.net; http://hotel-sara.8m.com. A small hotel, just around the corner from the Hotel Alay, with clean, simple rooms, some with en-suite bathrooms. $–$$, *semi-lux* $$, *lux* $$$.

🛏 **Nurbek** Jayma Bazaar. This basic *gostinitsa* in the bazaar is probably the cheapest place to stay in Osh – 100som per bed in twin rooms. Take the steps leading down into the bazaar from just across the river on Alisher Navoi; the hotel is in a yard, 100m further on to the left. $

Homestays

🛏 **CBT** Kelechek Plaza, Alisher Navoi; m 0502 574 940; e osh_cbt.mail.ru. The CBT office can arrange homestay accommodation at a number of locations around the city, mostly in flats. CBT homestay accommodation in Osh is generally a little more expensive than elsewhere in the country – around 500som for B&B.

🛏 **Guesthouse #1**, the home of Dinara Abdyrakhmanova, at Kurmanjan Datka 58 near the Rich Men café in the south of the city, is quiet & comfortable & has room for 12 guests. $$

🛏 **Imidjan Makhmadov's homestay** Bokonbaeva 51; 📞 51 318. A comfortable homestay in a traditionally carved home in the suburbs of the city. $$

🛏 **Osh Guesthouse** Kyrgyzstana, apartment 8, flat 48; 📞 30 629; m 0502 883 093, m 0502 372 311; e oshguesthouse@hotbox.ru; www.oshguesthouse.hotbox.ru. Not so much a guesthouse, more of a crash pad, but cheap, centrally located & understandably popular with backpackers. This is a good meeting place for those wishing to join with others to share transportation. A 4-bed dormitory & 1 dbl room with shared bathroom; also, a common room with cable TV & internet access. Friendly, English-speaking staff, although the place is usually overcrowded & none too clean. Daniyar, who is based here, can help with transport to China & Tajikistan & help organise shared taxis to Bishkek & Tashkent. To find the guesthouse, which is just a Soviet-period flat, walk north on Kyrgyzstana from Zaina Betinova & the mosque; go past several restaurants & then turn left down an alley by some kiosks (one of which has the guesthouse signed on its wall) opposite the Suleyman-Too restaurant. Veer right to reach the middle of 3 apt buildings (the white one); the flat is on the top floor. Arriving by taxi, ask for '*Aeropag*', which is the large shop on Kyrgyzstana that has the apartment block behind it. $

✖ **WHERE TO EAT** There is a large concentration of traditional Uzbek restaurants along Kyrgyzstana close to the mosque and the bazaar – Ala-Too, Turkestan, Ilkhom, Gulnara and Jibek Jolu. These all serve excellent *shashlyk* and green tea and have brightly lit terraces that are pleasant places to sit outside on a warm night (all $).

A vast range of bread and takeaway food like *manti* is sold from stalls near the entrance to Jayma bazaar along Zaina Betinova. The bazaar itself has every type of food imaginable and even hard-to-find items like ham and yak meat.

✕ **Rich Men café** Kurmanjan Datka 60; ☎ 24 303. Quite a long way south of the city centre, with an indoor dining area & outside courtyard, this is one of the choicest places to eat in the city. The English-language menu lists a good range of dishes at reasonable prices that include a wide range of cold appetisers & salads, many beef, chicken & fish dishes, & a decent selection of Georgian & Romanian wines. Also 'farinaceous foods', ie: pasta dishes. There is usually live music after 19.00 (25som cover charge). $$$

✕ **Greenwood** Lenina, between the park entrance & post office. ☺ Closed Sundays. Set back from the road behind some trees, this is a pleasant café-bar that serves reasonable pizzas, salads & beer. The music is loud inside but there is also a quieter outdoor dining area. Medium sized pizzas 100som. $$–$$$

✕ **Gurman** Lenina/Abdykadrov; ☎ 29 122. A courtyard café-bar with outdoor seating, bar & barbeque, south of the post office. $$

✕ **Huadalay** Lenina. A good Chinese restaurant in the same block as OVIR in the south of the city opposite the park. Look for the big red gate. Good for vegetarians with options like tofu dishes & sweet &

sour vegetables; also pork & meat dishes. English menu. $$

⛄ **Istanbul café & pastanesi** Navoi 22. As its name suggests, a café & patisserie that serves sticky Turkish pastries & cakes as well as light meals. This would be a good place for b/fast if it opened a bit earlier (rather than around 10.00) & the service was a little more enthusiastic – a Turkish b/fast of eggs, cheese, salad, jam, olives, tea & bread costs just 50som. $$

✕ **Kara Alma** Alisher Navoi/Kurmnajan Datka. This is a large café opposite the Hotel Alay in an outdoor courtyard shaded by plane trees. There is a variety of seating options: tables & chairs outside, Uzbek raised-seating platforms, & an indoor dining area. The large kitchen area faces onto the courtyard. Pleasant, courteous staff offer efficient service; good roast chicken. $–$$

✕ **Gulnara** Kyrgyzstana. Opposite Ilkhom café, just down from the mosque, this is probably one of the better restaurants along this stretch. Excellent beef *shashlyk* & decent salads. $

✕ **Ilkhom** Kyrgyzstana 28; ☎ 24 942. Among the competition along this stretch this place comes recommended. $

SHOPPING **Jayma bazaar** is one of the oldest and busiest markets in central Asia and sells every type of item imaginable, from fruit and vegetables to cutlery, metal goods, musical instruments, baby cribs, traditional clothing and silk. There are a few souvenir stores around the entrance to the bazaar from the steps of Alisha Navoi by the river. This is a good place to buy a cheap but good quality Kyrgyz *kalpak* for less than a 100som. The silver dome souvenir shop at the bottom of the walkway up to Solomon's Throne has a small selection of souvenir items, as does the CBT office at Kelechek Plaza. Prices are generally lower than Bishkek but there is less variety.

Osh Market is a well-stocked **supermarket** set back from the road on Gapar Aytiev, close to the junction with Kurmanjan Datka.

OTHER PRACTICALITIES

Health For urgent matters, the **Municipal Hospital** is on Kyrgyzstana, opposite the junction with Zaina Betova and the new mosque. The **Polyclinic health centre** on Abdykadyrov is another option.

Money There are several **banks** around the city. The **AKB Bank** on Kurmanjan Datka will change travellers' cheques for a fixed commission and can organise money transfers through Western Union. **The Bakai Bank** at the junction of Kurmanjan Datka and Gapar Aytiev will give cash advances on most credit cards. Most useful, though, is the branch of **Demir Kyrgyz Bank** next to the Taj Mahal hotel on Zaina Betinova, which has an **ATM machine** that will give both US dollars and Kyrgyz som. The bank has another branch on Kurmanjan Datka just north of the AKB Bank.

Jayma Bazaar has a whole row of money exchange stalls just inside the entrance where Zaina Betinova starts to curve round. These buy and sell Tajik, Uzbek and Chinese money in addition to the usual currencies. If leaving Kyrgyzstan, it may be a good idea to get a little foreign currency in advance, particularly for Tajikistan along the Pamir Highway, as there are no money-changing facilities until Murgab is reached. All of the exchange stalls seem to offer the same rates.

Communications The main **post office** is on Lenina in front of the park. **Kyrgyz Telecom** is also on Lenina, further north and close to the equestrian statue of Kurmanjan Datka, the feisty female leader known as the 'Queen of the South' who was instrumental in persuading local Kyrgyz to accept Russian control of the region. There are several places along Alisher Navoi that offer inexpensive international IP telephone calls.

Internet cafés come and go in the city but at the time of writing a good one with a fast connection was reached by going up the outdoor flight of steps at Kelechek Plaza on Alisher Navoi, just west of the CBT office. Another good internet café is **Dell** (↘ *24 380*), on Kyrgyzstana opposite the new mosque, which has flat-screen monitors and a reasonably fast connection.

Red tape For visa extensions and registration, the City Administration Building and the OVIR office are at the southern end of Lenina, opposite the park and close to the Osh Hotel.

WHAT TO SEE AND DO Today, there is little evidence of Babur's residency, or of the city's 3,000-year-old-heritage. While the city is an instantly likeable and friendly place there are no 'must see' sights, although the ageless Jayma bazaar and the hill of Solomon's Throne are both well worth a visit. Before the Russians arrived and developed Bishkek as the regional capital, Osh was the largest urban centre in the territory of present-day Kyrgyzstan. With *chaikhanas*, busy mosques, Uzbeks in skullcaps and a bustling bazaar, Osh still feels more authentically central Asian than the upstart capital.

Jayma Bazaar The bazaar stretches north from Alisher Navoi, divided by the Ak-Buura River, which has a number of traditional *chaikhanas* along its west bank, dishing up *chai* and *laghman* in a relaxed convivial atmosphere. It is a vibrant, crowded place with a constant stream of shoppers weaving their way through it, dodging out of the path of men pushing loaded carts who urge 'Bosh! Bosh!' as they inch their way through the crowd. Most of the people working here are Uzbeks, but Kyrgyz and Tajiks are also highly visible too, set apart by their distinctive headgear.

As with any true bazaar, the goods on sale are demarcated in clearly defined zones: moneychangers, dried fruit, *lepyoshka* (flat loaves), meat, gold jewellery and so on. The bazaar is open every day, but Sunday is generally the busiest day and Monday the quietest.

Near the bazaar is the Shaid Tepa mosque, the largest mosque in the country, which was originally constructed in wood between 1908–10, but which served as stables and blacksmiths during the Soviet period. It reopened in 1943 and in recent years has been renovated with Saudi backing.

Solomon's Throne Solomon's Throne or *Taht-i-Suleiman* is the city's focal point: an arid rocky outcrop that arises abruptly from the city centre above a large Muslim graveyard. The hill is topped by **Dom Babura** (Babur's House), a small shrine that identifies the place where, at the end of the 15th century, the teenage Zahiruddin Muhammad Babur built a shelter for his spiritual retreat from the world while he pondered his future. The original shelter was destroyed in 1853 by an earthquake and its replacement in the 1960s by an explosion. The 'house' today is a small, 1990s steel-roofed structure.

To reach the summit take the path from the silver-domed souvenir shop near the base on Kurmanjan Datka. There is a small entrance fee (3som) to be paid at the gate at the base of the footpath, and from here the path switchbacks up the slope along numerous steps to the summit, a 20-minute walk. Babur's House is an important pilgrimage site for Uzbeks and many come here to pray or have prayers said for them by the resident holy man. More mundanely, the rocks around Babur's House make an excellent vantage point for enjoying the sunset and it is especially busy with people, mostly families and young couples, in the late afternoon and at dusk.

Just behind the shrine is a smooth, sloping slab of rock where the custom is to slide down foot-first; there is usually a queue of local families lining up to do just this. Sliding down the rock is said to confer considerable health benefits and many believe that it also helps with fertility problems, a belief linked to the fact that the hill itself is said to resemble a pregnant woman.

Continuing west along the path from the summit, the **Historical Cultural Museum** (⊕ *09.00–17.00 Wed–Sun, closed 12.00–13.00; 60som*) is reached, housed in a cave with a rather unfortunate sheet-metal frontage. This has a modest collection of the usual Soviet-period museum accoutrements: pottery fragments, miscellaneous rocks, stuffed animals, photographs of local shamans and, of course, a yurt.

Silk Road Museum This purpose-built museum at the base of Solomon's Throne, opened in 2001 to celebrate the Osh 3,000th anniversary event (see page 249), has a number of archaeological, geological and ethnographic displays that include weapons, pottery and drinking vessels. There are also displays on the Kyrgyz migration from Siberia, the Kokand Khanate, petroglyphs from Saimaluu-Tash, traditional handicrafts like felt and leather goods, and displays detailing the *manaschi* tradition of story-telling. A 1953 map shows the territories of the different Kyrgyz tribes and clans. The interpretive material is in Kyrgyz and Russian only (⊕ *09.00–18.00, closed 12.00–13.00; 60som*).

Rabat Abdul Khan Mosque This small mosque near the start of the footpath up to Solomon's Throne is the city's oldest mosque, and dates from the 16–17th century, although the present-day building is mostly a 1980s rebuild. This is a busy, working mosque that may not admit female visitors; ask politely first. Obviously, modest dress is required of both sexes and shoes must be removed before entering.

Other sites Two contrasting historical figures look out over the city from their respective stone plinths – Vladimir Ilyich Lenin and Kurmanjan Datka. Lenin's lofty statue is found in the park south of the stadium along the street that still bears his name. Close to the park, in wooded grounds on the other side of Lenina, is a small Russian Orthodox church. The equestrian statue of Kurmanjan Datka (1811–1907), 'The Queen of the South', at the junction of Alisher Navoi and Lenina, represents an altogether different sort of hero: a female Kyrgyz ruler who helped to liberate the Fergana Valley from the Kokand Khanate in the 19th century and, although at first she opposed it, she eventually persuaded her people to accept Russian rule (see page 256).

The smaller park closer to the city centre behind the post office has a grounded Aeroflot Yak-40 for those curious about Soviet aviation.

KARA-SUU This mostly Uzbek town, 23km northeast of Osh, sits squarely on the Kyrgyzstan–Uzbekistan border with its counterpart, Qorasuv, across the river on the Uzbek side. The close proximity of the border is the reason why the town's enormous Turutali market, which takes place here twice a week on Saturdays and Tuesdays, has developed to become such a major trade centre.

In Soviet days, Kara-Suu/Qorasuv was a single settlement known as Ilyichovsk that spread across both sides of the river, but with the coming of independence for both Kyrgyzstan and Uzbekistan the town's Uzbek population found themselves politically divided for the first time. Despite the newly introduced frontier, a brisk trade continued between the two sides until 1999, when the Uzbek authorities destroyed the bridge across the Kara-Suu River that linked the two closely related communities. The bridge had been a lifeline for many from the Uzbekistan side of the border, who came to Kyrgyzstan to buy cheap Chinese goods and trade fruit and vegetables from the fertile farmland of the Fergana Valley. Despite the best attempts of the Uzbek authorities to curtail it, cross-border trade continued by means of improvised ropeways that brought both goods and people across the river, but this was a hazardous pursuit and each year up to 50 traders died by falling into the fast-flowing river. As well as the danger of crossing the river, corrupt Uzbek border guards would also demand bribes to allow the traders to pass. Despite these considerable obstacles, trade continued as best it could.

In 2005, riots broke out in Qorasuv following the massacre by Islam Karimov's troops in nearby Andijan in which an estimated 500 protestors were killed. Locals attacked government officials, stoned police cars and burned buildings, and within hours of the insurrection the destroyed bridge had been hastily replaced with a number of improvised footbridges. An estimated 6,000 Uzbek refugees streamed across the Kyrgyz border at Kara-Suu to safety before it was sealed by Kyrgyz troops.

The grey market trade at Kara-Suu increased markedly following the Andijan tragedy because of all the improvised bridges that had been built. As a result, many more Uzbeks were able to make a scant living carrying goods back into Uzbekistan. Following the resurgence of the Kara-Suu market, several illegal crossings were set up elsewhere in the area to facilitate cross-border trade. One example of this was at the Uzbekistan village of Suratash, where locals pooled their resources to build an access road and concrete barrier, and collected 100 Uzbek som in 'transit tax' from everyone wishing to cross to the minibuses and taxis that were waiting on the Kyrgyz side to whisk shoppers directly to Kara-Suu market.

The market is an enormous money-spinner for the regional economy, although the 'grey' wealth generated at Kara-Suu certainly comes at a price – in the past 2 years, two directors of the market have been murdered by unknown assassins. There have also been protests at the increasing number of Chinese Uyghur traders setting up shop at the market and some of these have been beaten up, accused of undercutting the prices of the Uzbek traders. In addition to the trade in Chinese goods, which is largely electronic equipment and clothes that sell at a much lower price in Kyrgyzstan than they do in Uzbekistan, there is also said to be an illicit trade in raw cotton surreptitiously filched from the collective farms of Uzbekistan's Fergana Valley.

The market itself covers an area of around 15ha and, like Dordoi Bazaar in Bishkek, goods are stored in and sold from shipping containers that are piled two-high. It is said that there are around 1,500 containers in total and that overall the market trade employs anything up to 15,000 people.

Kara-Suu market is nothing like the traditional bazaars in Osh or Kashgar and is unlikely to have anything that a typical foreign visitor may wish to buy unless they are on the lookout for a flat screen television set or a DVD player. Notwithstanding this, it is an impressive place to visit just for its sheer size and spectacle, and makes for an easy half-day trip from Osh. The main road in front of the market is lined with busy *chaikhanas* and is an unending traffic jam of honking taxis and vans massively overloaded with bolts of cloth, computers and DVD players precariously balanced on roof-racks. Facing the market on the other side of the road is a huge hangar that seems to be entirely devoted to the sale of lurid Chinese socks.

Getting there Regular, very crowded, minibuses (15som) leave from Osh's Old Bus Station and drop off in front of the market. Shared Daewoo Tico taxis run the same route and charge just 20som per seat.

ARAVAN The small Uzbek town of Aravan lies 25km southwest of Osh, nuzzled against the Uzbekistan border. Just outside the town is a holy site that pays tribute to the syncretic tradition that suffuses central Asian Islam with earlier pagan beliefs.

The Celestial Horses of Aravan The Celestial Horses of Aravan, as they are known, are petroglyphs that have had an important role in regional folklore and that have become a pilgrimage site for Muslims in the Fergana Valley.

The rock carvings, which can be seen with a little patience on a south-facing cliff-face just outside Aravan, are thought to date from the 1st century BC. The horses etched into the rockface are thought to represent the legendary, blood-sweating 'Celestial' or 'Heavenly' Horses of Fergana that were so admired by the Chinese of the Han Dynasty at the time, especially by Wu-Ti, the dynasty's ruthless emperor. The site was excavated twice in the 20th century and evidence has been found of animal sacrifices at the cliff-base below the carvings. Today, there is a small Sufi shrine at the site and a shelter for pilgrims.

Visiting the site The carvings and the nearby spring are considered sacred to local Muslims and it should be remembered that this is an important religious site rather than just one of archaeological interest to tourists. It goes without saying that one should dress accordingly and behave in an appropriately decorous manner.

The cliff-face is reached by going through a green gate on the main road near the hospital on the outskirts of the town. The gate has a sign above it that says: *Dul-Dul at Ziyarit Zhai*, which refers to the Sufi shrine found within. A path leads down next to a Russian Orthodox and Soviet cemetery on the left and then crosses a stream to come to the base of a cliff where there is a pilgrims' shelter on the left and the small shrine of a Sufi sheikh on the right. The petroglyphs are rather hard to see, high on the cliff above, and slightly to the left of, the shrine; they're about three-quarters of the way up, just above the top branches of a willow tree. Binoculars would be a great help, although they're not essential.

Sadly, there is also much modern-day graffiti around the base of the cliff, testament to the popular belief that making one's own mark at a sacred site such as this will bring its own spiritual benefit. Hornets, too, seem common here in late summer.

From Osh, regular shared taxis for Aravan (25som) leave from the bus stand on Alisher Navoi, just west of the junction with Kurmanjan Datka. The road to Aravan follows the Uzbekistan border so closely that recently erected Uzbek watchtowers and barbed wire can be seen at the roadside. Approaching Aravan, ask to get off at the hospital ('*balneetsa*'); the green gateway is just before the right turn to the hospital and a garage on the left-hand side of the road. Minibuses also run from the Old Bus Station (15som).

Chil-Ustun The Chil-Ustun cave system is close to Aravan in the limestone hills above the Ak-Buura and Aravan river basin. The cave system takes its name from the Tajik for 'forty columns', a reference to the stalactites found in the cave network. The entrance to the Chil-Ustun system is about 4km from Aravan, high on the southern slope of a 1,460m-high mountain of the same name. The 380m-long main cave has three big chambers that are connected by narrow corridors, the largest of which is 100m long, 50m wide and 20m high. Numerous stalactites hang from the roof of the cave and the walls bear inscriptions in a variety of languages that are said to include Sanskrit. Other caves nearby include Sasyk-Unkur (140m deep), Suvli-Kamar (120m), Chil-Mayram (130m) and Teshik-Tash (180m).

Another canyon, in the Tuya-Muyun region 20km south of the Chil-Ustun cave system, has the deepest cave in the entire country, the 240m-deep Fersman Cave. None of these caves are set up for tourist visits in any way at all, and all require torches, ropes and a knowledgeable local guide to locate them; enquire at tour operators in Osh like Kyrgyz Nur, or at the Osh CBT office.

ÖZGÖN ӨЗГӨН *Telephone code: 03233*

HISTORY The town of Özgön (also spelled Ozgon or Uzgen; Russian: УЗГЕН) lies 55km northeast of Osh on a cliff-top above the wide plain of the Kara-Darya River. These days the town is visited mostly for its well-preserved 12th-century Karakhanid monuments and for its interesting Uzbek-dominated bazaar, but it also has an unfortunate recent past that most would prefer to forget.

In the summer of 1990, the town momentarily became famous for the inter-ethnic fighting that broke out between the town's Kyrgyz and Uzbek communities over issues concerning land tenure. The violence was thankfully short-lived, but the sudden eruption of blood-letting resulted in hundreds tragically losing their lives, an event that still leaves a shadow over the town today. Conservative estimates say that around 300 lost their lives on both sides of the ethnic divide; others claim that it may have been as many as 1,000. Both Kyrgyz and Uzbeks alike criticise the Soviet authorities at the time, who seemingly just stood by as the violence unfolded. These days there is no tangible evidence of the event, nor any perceptible sign of tension, but with such a comparatively recent event fresh in the memory of most of the town's citizens, it does the beg the question as to exactly what lurks behind the mask of Özgön's apparently calm exterior.

Özgön is a town with at least two thousand years of history. It is mentioned by Chinese chroniclers in the 2nd century BC and there are even the usual claims that Alexander passed this way and camped in the vicinity of the present-day town. Özgön went on to became an important Silk Road centre, with an economy based on trade and coin production, and later, during the period of Karakhanid rule, it was further developed as one of the capitals of the Karakhanid State that became known as Mavarannahr. The Karakhanid heyday was during the 11th and 12th centuries, and as the khanate fell into decline in the 13th century following the raids of Genghis Khan, so did Mavarannahr.

Today the town is mostly an agricultural centre with sunflowers, tobacco and especially rice all being important crops. Özgön has a university, a brewery and a distinctive bazaar that is very Uzbek in character.

GETTING THERE Regular buses, minibuses and share taxis run between Özgön and Jalal-Abad to the northwest and Osh to the southwest. A minibus from Osh's Old Bus Station costs 35som. The bus station is on Manas, a 5-minute walk from the bazaar. There are also fairly regular minibus and shared taxi services to Bishkek.

WHERE TO STAY AND EAT Özgön is best visited as a half-day trip from Osh or Jalal-Abad, and there is no real need to stay over, which is just as well as the only *gostinitsa* in town, on the corner of Manas and Gagarin, is fairly primitive. There are plenty of basic *shashlyk* and *laghman* places in the bazaar for a meal, as well as slightly more formal restaurants along Manas between the bazaar and the Karakhanid mausoleum complex like **Café Shirin**, just west of the bazaar entrance, and **Café Islam** (*both* $). The large, cool dining hall almost directly opposite the bazaar entrance is also quite reasonable for Uzbek staples.

WHAT TO SEE AND DO
Karakhanid mausoleum complex This complex of buildings is reached by turning left out of the market and following the main road Manas for 10 minutes to come to a park with a silver statue of Lenin. The site is a little further on and can be seen from the Lenin statue.

The complex consists of three adjoining 12th-century mausolea and an 11th-century minaret. The stubby, pepper-pot shaped **minaret** dates from the mid 11th century and although it has been thoroughly reconstructed it is considerably shorter than was originally intended, as its upper 7m plunged earthwards during an earthquake in the 17th century. The 20m minaret that remains is of bands of fine honey-coloured brickwork and carved terracotta. The cupola was built in 1923–24 to top the truncated structure. Ruins of a medieval *madrasa* have been found nearby (*entrance to the minaret is 10som, or 20som with a guide; cameras 20som*).

The three **mausolea** all date from the 11th or 12th centuries and two of them are very finely detailed. The most northerly one was built in 1152–53 for Jalal ad-Din al-Huseyn, and is a fine surviving example of early Islamic art. The portico is decorated with delicate terracotta ornamentation and there are inscriptions on the arch in Naskhi script, together with Kufic script above the entrance. The slightly taller, central mausoleum is older, dating from the 11th century, and was probably built for Nasr Ibn Ali, the founder of the Karakhanid Dynasty, who died in 1012–13. This is the most reconstructed of the trio and consequently the least elaborate in terms of detail. The southern mausoleum was built a little later than its northern counterpart, which it superficially resembles, between 1186–87 for an unknown recipient. This has an even more lavishly decorated entrance than the northern mausoleum and has intertwined floral motifs, inscriptions and terracotta ornamentation.

If the complex already seems strangely familiar it is because the three mausolea adorn the reverse side of the Kyrgyz 50som note. There are good views of the Kara-Darya River valley from the complex, and even better ones from the top of the minaret.

AROUND ÖZGÖN
Ak-Terek About 43km northeast of Özgön, the village of Ak-Terek, on the banks of the Jassy River, has a whole range of possibilities for trekking and horseriding in the region, with mineral springs, a nearby gorge filled with walnut trees, and the Kara-Shoo National Park just 40km away beyond the village. CBT Osh organise a 4-day tour for experienced horseriders that begins with sightseeing in Özgön before continuing to Ak-Terek, from where a horse trek is made east along the Jassy River through a gorge and several villages before climbing up to the Besh-Terek, Kara-Döbö and Baibiche *jailoos*. This continues the following day to Kypchylma gorge and another *jailoo* camp. From here, the Kara-Shoro National Park is reached on the third day of riding from Ak-Terek.

There is homestay accommodation in Ak-Terek at the homes of Gukush Arstanova, Sharapat Datkabava and others. This could be booked in advance from Osh or, alternatively, on arrival in the village. There are daily buses to and from Özgön.

The M-41 highway south from Osh leads to the remote village of Sary-Tash, which is a crossroads of sorts, with the road to Kashgar leading east to the Chinese border at Irkeshtam and the road south struggling over the immense barrier of the Pamir Alay range into Tajikistan's Gorno-Badakhshan Autonomous Region.

The road to Sary-Tash is spectacular, and one of the most beautiful drives in the country. Leaving Osh, the highway climbs slowly out of the fertile plain to follow the Taldyk River on the way to the 2,408m Chyrchyk Pass, before descending down to **Gulcha** at the confluence of two rivers. CBT have recently established a homestay network in the village, so there is scope to spend a night here if necessary. The CBT co-ordinator in Gulcha is Talant Toksonbaev.

From Gulcha, the highway follows the Alay valley south through rugged mountains and red sandstone cliffs above the snaking river. Just before the village of Sary-Tash is reached, a roadside sign enthusiastically bids you a 'Harry Journey' as you start to think about leaving Kyrgyzstan for pastures new.

SARY-TASH Spending a night in this rather unprepossessing village is a necessary evil for independent travellers who wish to travel to China or Tajikistan under their own steam. Whatever its other limitations might be, it cannot be denied that, with the high, snow-spattered ridge of the Pamir Alay looming to the south, Sary-Tash (Yellow Stone) is set in a natural setting that is quite beautiful. However, at 3,173m above sea level, it can get very cold at night

The village has a shop and basic café and there is supposed to be a guesthouse just north of the town on the road from Osh, in addition to rooms at the café by the crossroads (200som). Just asking around will no doubt unleash a few offers of homestay accommodation. The cost will be negotiable, of course, but 250–300som is a fair price for bed, breakfast and evening meal.

Getting there For individual travellers who have come from Osh and intend to continue to China or Tajikistan, hitch-hiking out of here is said to be very difficult, particularly south to Murgab in Tajikistan, as very little traffic uses this road. Transport to Irkeshtam is marginally better, but it is still possible to get stuck here for hours. Most of the passing vehicles heading for Irkeshtam are big, slow Kyrgyz trucks taking scrap metal into China.

To reach Sary-Tash from Osh there is a daily bus that leaves at around 08.00 in the morning and takes most of the day. A taxi costs 1,200–1,500som or 300–400som in a shared taxi, although the latter can be hard to find. Start early.

SARY-MOGOL The Sary-Tash 'crossroads' leads north to Osh, east to China and south to Tajikistan. A little way along the Tajikistan branch, another road leads west along the Alay valley to the village of Sary-Mogol. At 3,100m above sea level, Sary-Mogol sits in the shadow of Pik Lenina (Peak Lenin), a gigantic, 7,134m wall of rock, ice and snow that demarcates the Kyrgyz-Tajik border 20km south of the village. Peak Lenin is purported to be one of the easiest of the world's 7,000m peaks to climb and most of the foreign visitors who come to Sary-Mogol tend to have some sort of business with the mountain.

With no jobs, a harsh winter climate and poor conditions for agriculture, life is immensely tough here, and most of the adult male population have left to seek work elsewhere. However, tourism of a non-mountaineering kind has definite potential here too, and a CBT network was established in the village in 2007. The CBT co-ordinator is Umar Tashbekov, who can arrange transport and accommodation in the village, as well as yurt stays near Peak Lenin basecamp.

West of Sary-Mogol, the road along the valley continues to Daroot-Korgon and the Tajik border. At the time of writing this route into Tajikistan was closed to foreigners (see page 57).

Getting there A daily bus (160som) runs between Osh and Sary-Mogol in the morning from the Old Bus Station. Any buses running between Osh and Daroot-Korgon also pass through the village. The CBT co-ordinator can arrange transport to Achik-Tash basecamp from the village.

PEAK LENIN Now officially known by its non-Soviet name of Koh-i-Garmo (Warm Mountain), this mountain is still referred to as *Lenina* by most locals and climbers alike. At 7,134m, Peak Lenin is the third-highest mountain in the CIS, and has a reputation for being a relatively easy climb. This is not to make light of it, as climbing Peak Lenin is hardly a stroll in the park, and many climbers have died attempting to reach the summit. Despite being considered relatively straightforward for a 7,000m+ mountain, Peak Lenin is by no means a trekking peak and a successful ascent requires all the essential equipment of ice axes, crampons etc and, most importantly, a great deal of mountaineering experience. The greatest dangers are avalanches and suddenly changing weather. In 1974 an eight-woman team perished on the mountain in a storm, and in 1991 an icefall trapped 44 climbers, leaving only one survivor.

Peak Lenin is essentially a broad-based pyramid with a northern face that is far steeper and more difficult than its other slopes. Attempts on the peak are invariably made from the southern, Kyrgyzstan side, although there are many variants of the approach, with 16 different routes to the summit. In keeping with its reputation as a relatively easy 'walk up' summit, Peak Lenin is one of the world's most frequently climbed peaks above 7,000m.

ACHIK-TASH Achik-Tash at 3,600m is the main basecamp for climbing Peak Lenin, but it can be visited in its own right for lower-level trekking. Nearby is Lukovaya Polyana (Wild Onion Meadow), which is a relatively easy hike from the basecamp. The Bishkek-based IMC Pamir trekking company (*www.imcpamir.netfirms.com*) maintain a basecamp at Achik-Tash that has accommodation in wooden huts, in addition to tents. The same company organises a 24-day expedition to the peak from Osh that builds in plenty of time for acclimatisation. Several other Bishkek companies such as ITMC Tien Shan and Top Asia also operate basecamps here in the summer months (see *Kyrgyz Tour Agencies*, pages 49–51). Staying here independently requires total self-sufficiency, so stock up on fuel, food and other supplies in Osh before setting off. Because of altitude and an unpredictable climate, the trekking season here is naturally a fairly short one – from mid-July to early September.

THE IRKESHTAM CROSSING TO CHINA

From Sary-Tash onwards the quality of the road declines appreciably and even in a 4×4 it can take 3–4 hours to reach the border from Sary-Tash, and much longer in one of the scrap-iron trucks that lumber up and down this road. Leaving the village behind, the road slowly climbs up from the Alay valley over a 3,536m pass, before winding downhill to the river basin that has the dreary hamlet of Irkeshtam and the Chinese border beyond. In snow, the road is reduced to a single track, which means that if a truck breaks down – highly likely – then all other transport is forced to wait behind. The Kyrgyz checkpoint is reached at the bottom of the road from the pass. There is a rugged no man's land of around 10km between the borders and, for those travelling independently, it is necessary to hitch across this in whatever transport is available.

It must be said that the border guards on the Kyrgyz side are not the best ambassadors for their profession and, coming from China especially, they may try to extract bribes from travellers or insist that there is a fine to pay for not having a 'health certificate'. Obviously, they have the upper hand in this sort of situation but, as with everything else, bargain.

Close to the Kyrgyz border post is a trucker's café and basic *gostinitsa* but, given the drunken and confrontational atmosphere of the place, it is really not recommended. A little better are some of the trailers further down where a cheap bed for the night is also a possibility. Better still is not to stay here at all, but for those travelling independently that requires good timing and a certain element of luck.

On the other side of no man's land, Chinese customs is altogether more organised than back at the Kyrgyz post and the officials here are normally polite but thorough. Luggage has to be taken to a hut for examination. Kyrgyz luggage is normally more rigorously searched than that belonging to travellers, although great interest is often taken in Western reading material like guide books. Maps are sometimes confiscated, so it is best to hide these.

From here, it is another 4km to the second Chinese post, which has a large immigration building. Luggage has to be taken inside to be x-rayed, immigration forms completed and passports stamped. Taxi drivers usually hang around outside to offer onward rides to Kashgar, but they tend to drive a hard bargain. From Chinese immigration it is about 3 hours to Kashgar from here, and the road is excellent in comparison to the Kyrgyz side of the border.

As with the crossing at the Torugart Pass, problems can arise because of unforeseen circumstances: power cuts that result in Chinese computers not working; broken-down vehicles impeding progress; extra-long lunch hours and unexpected holidays that mean that one or both sides of the border have closed for the day.

Good timing is crucial because of the different time zones that each side operates by. The Chinese authorities observe Beijing time, which is 2 hours ahead of Kyrgyz time. The Chinese post is supposedly open from 09.00–11.00, 12.00–14.00 and 16.00–18.00, and closed for lunch between 14.00–16.00 (12.00–14.00 Kyrgyz time). The Kyrgyz border opens at 08.30 and it is usually possible to cross between 09.00 and 12.00 travelling in the direction of China. Arriving even minutes after midday can mean having to spend the night at the border, although conflicting reports tell of travellers having passed through as late as 14.30. Going through all the border posts can take anything between 4–6 hours. Coming from China, it is possible to cross into Kyrgyzstan between 11.00–18.00 (Beijing time) apart from during the lunch break period between 14.00–16.00.

The Irkeshtam crossing is technically open all year round, although there is the potential for it to be closed by heavy snowfall from time to time. It is closed on Kyrgyz and Chinese public holidays (see *Torugart Pass*, pages 220–1) and at weekends.

Considering the problems that can occur with both the Torugart and Irkeshtam crossings into China, the question remains: given a free choice, which is the better of the two? Until recently, there was no choice in the matter as Irkeshtam was closed to foreign travellers until 2002. Unlike Torugart, Irkeshtam needs no special permit or prior arrangement of transport to meet travellers on the other side of the border, and this could be seen as a distinct advantage, as it allows for more flexibility of plans. There is no simple answer but common wisdom seems to dictate that if you have sufficient money but a tight schedule, it may be best to travel to China via the Torugart Pass; with plenty of time at your disposal but less money, take your chances with Irkeshtam.

GETTING THERE Buses running from Osh to Kashgar (US$55) take around 24 hours and leave on Wednesday and Sunday nights from Osh's New Bus Station. It is possible to book a seat the day before for 100som, paying the US$55 on the day of departure. This is a Chinese sleeper bus with bunks, and locals will compete for the lower bunks, although the upper ones are fine. The bus is supposed to leave at 20.00 but will more likely depart between 22.00–22.30 to arrive at the border around 08.00. Bribes may be collected from passengers at some stage in the proceedings, but generally locals have a much rougher time of it than Western travellers. Border proceedings will take up to 6 hours in total. To speed things up, it is possible to take a taxi from the Chinese side into Kashgar, which will shave a couple of hours off the total journey time.

Coming the other way, buses from Kashgar leave on Mondays and Tuesdays and cost US$50. There have been incidents in which Kashgar bus station staff have refused to sell bus tickets to foreigners; if this happens a local travel agent can be employed to purchase them.

The main problem with travelling on the bus is that, coming either way, it passes through the best of the scenery in the hours of darkness. A way round this is to travel the stretch between Osh and Sary-Tash in daylight by bus or taxi, stay the night in Sary-Tash, then, early the next morning, hitch a lift to Irkeshtam, cross the border then take a taxi from the Chinese side. This is, of course, fraught with uncertainty, but it is certainly more adventurous and may or may not prove to be fun. The real limiting factor is reaching the Irkeshtam border in time to get through (12.00 Kyrgyz time). Traffic from Sary-Tash is sporadic and the trucks are quite slow so, in doing this, it is essential to be prepared for an unplanned overnight stay at the Irkeshtam border.

For some idea of prices: taxis from Osh to Sary-Tash are around 1,200–1,500som (300–400som per seat in shared taxis); a lift in a truck to Irkeshtam is 100–200som. Jeeps to Irkeshtam from Osh (from the jeep stand on Alisher Navoi) cost between US$100–150. Taxis from the Chinese border to Kashgar are US$10–15 per person. Trucks across no man's land probably will not charge anything.

THE ROAD SOUTH TO TAJIKISTAN

Just outside Sary-Tash village is a lonely police checkpoint next to a collection of radar domes. From here, the road makes a beeline south towards what appears to be the impenetrable barrier of the magnificent Pamir Alay. The road climbs gently at first and then steeply along a very rough, rocky road up to the 4,280m Kyzyl-Art Pass and the Kyrgyz customs post. The air is gaspingly thin here: a reminder that this is the highest road in Kyrgyzstan, and this is not far off its highest point.

The Tajik post is reached shortly after: a couple of chilly metal caravans where passport details are laboriously written into ledgers by the dim light of a paraffin lamp. Even in summer, it is freezing cold at night here and it feels rather like the edge of the charted world – it almost is. Few travellers visit Tajikistan and even fewer have the necessary paperwork that allows them to enter the Gorno-Badakshan autonomous region and take the Pamir Highway south. To do so is neither cheap nor easy to organise, but it is undeniably one of the last truly adventurous road trips that can be made in the 21st century. It feels like a privilege, and it is. Entering Gorno-Badakshan along the Pamir Highway from the Kyzyl-Art Pass, even southern Kyrgyzstan can start to seem a little touristy.

For a number of reasons, mostly to do with the high altitude terrain and a very sparse population, there is virtually no public transport along this route, and to enter Tajikistan requires both a Tajik visa and a GBAO permit, which both need to be pre-arranged well in advance. The best option is to arrange transport in Osh to go at least as far as Murgab, from where ACTED, a sort of CBT equivalent for Tajikistan, can help organise onward travel to Khorog, either by way of the direct route through the Pamirs or by the spectacular Wakhan corridor along the northern border with Afghanistan.

Interestingly, despite a change of country, virtually all of the population between the Kyrgyz border and Murgab are ethnic Kyrgyz rather than Tajik.

GETTING TO TAJIKISTAN Transport for the 2-day trip to Murgab can be organised in Osh, providing that a Tajik visa and a GBAO permit have been obtained in advance. A robust vehicle is required for the journey – a 4×4 Niva or an ex-army UAZ – and sufficient fuel must be carried, as there will be virtually nothing available until Murgab. Transport can be arranged by asking around at the jeep park, although most drivers tend to quote wholly unrealistic prices for the journey and many of them do not have experience of the route.

Overall, it is easier to make use of an agent like Daniyar Abdurahmanov (m *0502 372 311;* e *daniyar1@mail.ru*), who owns the Osh Guesthouse and who also operates through the Taj Mahal Hotel, and has plenty of experience of arranging transport along this route. He can usually arrange a vehicle and driver within 24 hours. A typical price is US$150 for the vehicle, plus an extra US$15 for the driver to sleep over at Karakol, the first village in Tajikistan before Murgab is reached. This is well worth doing, as Karakol is a stark but interesting ethnic Kyrgyz village high in the Pamirs by a beautiful blue lake. To travel all the way to Murgab from Osh would make for a very long day and the landscape *en route* is so good that you really do not want to rush it. Daniyar can also help put a group together if you are travelling alone. Excess Kyrgyz som should be exchanged for Tajik somani in Jayma bazaar before leaving Osh.

BATKEN PROVINCE БАТКЕН ОБЛАСТЫ

Batken Oblast was created in 1999 from the three most westerly *rayons*, or regions, of what was then part of Osh Province: Batken, Chong-Alay and Kadamjay. This came as a result of more direct and visible governing in the region following an unstable period in which there had been frequent incursions by militants from the Islamic Movement for Uzbekistan (IMU). A couple of well-documented kidnappings involving Japanese geologists and young American climbers put the region firmly off-limits for several years. Travel to the Batken region was advised against until quite recently, but this advice has since been relaxed by the British Foreign and Commonwealth Office (FCO), although it would be wise to check the current FCO recommendations before proceeding to travel to the region.

The north of the *oblast* occupies part of the southern Fergana Valley that extends into Uzbekistan, an area of rolling dry hills and semi-desert steppe; the province's southern boundary is defined by two stark, treeless mountain chains – the Alay, which extends east into Osh Province, and the Turkestan range, both subsidiary ranges of the Pamirs. The most remarkable feature of Batken Province's geography, however, is political rather than physical, as the *oblast* is host to no less than six island enclaves that belong to neighbouring Uzbekistan and Tajikistan.

In terms of tourist potential, the province is the least well known in all Kyrgyzstan, partly a result of its isolation and partly because travel was proscribed here until recently. Another considerable problem is the existence of the enclaves that demand visas even for swift transit and create logistical problems for those wishing to travel through the province.

Mountaineering expeditions have long favoured the province, which offers speciality mountaineering challenges like the sheer walls of 5,504m Ak-Suu peak southwest of Batken and the sharp peaks of the Turkestan range that are carved by wind and ice to resemble sharks' teeth.

Kyrgyzstan's Batken Province has several isolated foreign enclaves within its territory. These eccentric political paint splatters on Kyrgyzstan's national map first came about when Stalin created the jigsaw of interwoven borders that characterises central Asia today. The various borders were drawn up between 1924 and 1936, ostensibly based on political and economic considerations that attempted to group linguistically distinct populations together. It is all too easy to argue that the creation of such enclaves was part and parcel of Stalin's ruthless divide and rule strategy. This, no doubt, is part of the explanation, but it would seem that local politics came into the equation too, and that a certain degree of bartering of territories took place between local leaders at the time. Such territorial haggling was also probably responsible for predominantly Uzbek areas, such as that in the vicinity of Jalal-Abad, becoming attached to Kyrgyzstan rather than finding themselves belonging to what might appear to be their more obvious natural home in Uzbekistan.

Four of the Batken enclaves belong to Uzbekistan: Sokh, the largest territory at 325km², which paradoxically has a population that is almost entirely Tajik; Shakhimardan, a territory of 90km², which is mostly Uzbek; and two much smaller enclaves that are located to the north of Sokh and north of Shakhimardin, close to the Uzbek border – Qalacha and Dzhangail.

Two more enclaves belong to Tajikistan: Vorukh, a large, 130km² enclave west of the provincial capital that is linked by road to Isfara in Tajikistan, and Kairagach, another tiny settlement north of Sülüktü in the far west.

Kyrgyzstan is not alone in the region in having political enclaves. Uzbekistan's Fergana Valley also has two small enclaves of its own: Sarvak, just 14km long and 500m wide, which belongs to Tajikistan; and Barak, an isolated Kyrgyz village of just 600 that lies 13km from the Kyrgyz border stranded between the Uzbekistan towns of Margilan and Fergana. As Uzbekistan is one of only two double-landlocked territories in the world, that is completely surrounded by territories that are themselves landlocked (the other is Liechtenstein), it must follow that by a unique quirk of political geography both Sarvak (Tajikistan) and Barak (Kyrgyzstan) share the inimitable honour of being the world's only *triple-landlocked* territories.

The existence of these enclaves, which probably did not affect people's lives that much when they were first created, has serious consequences for those who live in them today. Political differences and frequent antagonism between Uzbekistan and Kyrgyzstan has made ease-of-movement between the Uzbek enclaves and the surrounding territory problematic at times, while Barak, the lone Kyrgyz exclave within Uzbekistan, faces exceptional difficulties in terms of the movement of its citizens to and from the Kyrgyz 'mainland'.

BATKEN The journey west to Batken from Osh passes through a dreamy agricultural landscape of tobacco and rice, with the stunning backdrop of the snow-capped Alay range ever-present to the south. The road is generally good apart from some of the dusty stretches skirting the Sokh enclave that are barely more than dirt tracks. Close to Batken, the road itself is used for drying and threshing rice, and piles of rice-straw line the roadside in places at harvest time. The Batken region is also well known for its apricot orchards and the *oruk* (dried apricots) they produce.

The provincial capital is a pleasant enough town and a reasonable place to spend the night *en route* to Khojand in Tajikistan. Batken was awarded city status in 2000, although the place has more of the atmosphere of a large village. Since it became capital of the recently created *oblast* a number of new government offices have been opened. In contrast to the Tajik-populated enclaves of nearby Vorukh and Sokh, Batken's population of around 12,000 is almost entirely ethnic Kyrgyz.

Getting there With an Uzbek transit visa and a double-entry Kyrgyz visa it is perfectly possible to reach Batken from Osh by the regular daily **bus** service (200som) or a **shared taxi** (400som). Without the appropriate visas, things are more problematic as the direct route goes straight through the Uzbek enclave of Sokh. Some taxi drivers insist that it is possible to pay the Uzbek border guards a small 'appreciation' so that they turn a blind eye to the foreigner in their midst; others say that the Kyrgyz guards do not bother stamping visas in and out of Kyrgyzstan and so a double-entry Kyrgyz visa is unnecessary – this is probably true but it is all rather uncertain and dependent on the guards, the mood they are in, and whether or not they like your face. It is best to seek up-to-date advice as this situation appears to change constantly.

A more reliable alternative is to take a taxi that goes *around* the Uzbek enclave on rough, dirt roads, thus avoiding the problem altogether. Naturally, this will cost more because of the greater distance travelled. At the time of writing, these dirt roads were being upgraded, and so it is possible that the 'detour' route will become more standard in the future.

Shared taxis to Batken from Osh leave from the square behind the Hotel Alay next to the equestrian statue. They tend to leave fairly early in the morning, usually around 07.00–08.00. Unfortunately, it can sometimes be difficult to find other passengers who want to take the longer route because the visa requirements do not affect locals in the same way as they do foreign travellers. If this is the case, a private taxi will cost around 2,000som, otherwise it should cost 500som per place. Be sure to ascertain that the driver is going *cherez obyezd* ('via the detour'). By this route the journey time from Osh is around 7 hours.

Batken's small airport has **flights** to and from Bishkek three times a week in summer with Altyn Air. The flight takes 1 hour 10 minutes and costs upwards of US$48.

Where to stay and eat
CBT CBT have recently established a presence in the town and should be able to provide homestay accommodation. The local co-ordinator is Sabyr Shaimardankulov.

Damira Checheeva homestay 60 Let Oktyabria 14. A recommended homestay that has good food, a pleasant garden & comfortable rooms. $
Intourist Hotel (20 rooms). South of the park & town municipal buildings, this institution has undergone few changes since independence. Shared rooms with 2–4 beds, 2 grotty shared bathrooms for the whole place, service with a scowl & blatant overcharging. Avoid if at all possible. $

The town has a few reasonable places to eat (*all* $). **Cafe-bar Asylbek** is on the main road west of the park and hospital, and there is a pleasant, shady outdoor *chaikhana* next to the entrance to the park on the same street. The **Café Minim** to the east of the municipal building is a very friendly place with good food and a pleasant atmosphere.

What to see and do Batken is leafy and pleasant but it does not really have any sights. Fans of Soviet era statuary can seek out the golden figure of Lenin in hailing-taxi pose, and the gold and red Great Patriotic War memorial in the park. There is also some more modern Kyrgyz-themed sculpture in the park, with a statue of what appears to be an angel holding a *tunduk*. This and other similar pieces in the town are the work of local sculptor Turgunbay Sadyov.

FROM BATKEN TO TAJIKISTAN Transport to Isfara in Tajikistan leaves from the west side of Batken's hospital. There are fairly regular buses and taxis (40som) making the short hop to the border from where it is another 10 minutes on to Isfara. Border formalities here seem to be astonishingly brief, the Kyrgyz post not even looking at passports and, at the Tajik post, just a cursory examination and a passport stamp is required, without even the need to get out of your taxi. From Isfara there are frequent buses onwards to Khojand, and money changers at the bus station who will change any remaining Kyrgyz som into Tajik somani.

AK-SUU AND TURKESTAN RANGE Southwest of Batken, the mountains of the Turkestan range offer superb opportunities for highly experienced and adventurous climbers. The jagged peaks here are often likened to those of the southern Patagonian Andes and are better described as rock towers than mountains. The whole of the Turkestan range provides unique challenges to climbers in search of sheer rock faces and big wall climbing.

It was in this area that Japanese geologists and American climbers were kidnapped in 1999 and 2000 by IMU militants from over the border in Tajikistan (see page 14). The area appears to be safe for the time being, although this should be verified before travel. As well as advanced climbing skills, a visit to this region requires specialist back-up, and climbing and border zone permits may be required. Contact one of the Bishkek trekking and climbing operators for further details.

Approaches to the range are usually by way of the Ak-Suu, Leilek and Karavshin valleys that lie to the south of the Vorukh enclave. These valleys also offer excellent opportunities for adventurous trekking, although engaging the services of a local guide is highly advisable.

The ultimate challenge for extreme climbers is the north face of the almost perfect pyramid of 5,509m Pik Piramidalny (Pyramid Peak), which dominates the upper Leilek valley and offers the archetypal 'big wall,' with its 2km-high sheer rock face. The highest peak in the Turkestan range is 5,621m Pik Skalistiy, which lies a little further east, due south of Vorukh.

Appendix I

LANGUAGE

Kyrgyz is the official language of state and parliament, although Russian also remains an official language for the time being. Kyrgyz is a member of the central Turkic group of languages and is similar to Kazakh. 'Standard' Kyrgyz is based upon the northern dialect found in Kyrgyzstan, which contains words from Mongolian languages as well as from Russian. Southern Kyrgyz has many words of Persian, Uzbek and Tajik origin. Modern Kyrgyz is written with a slightly modified Russian Cyrillic script: the alphabet below shows the Cyrillic alphabet, its Latin equivalent and a guide to pronunciation.

Cyrillic		Latin		Pronunciation
А	а	A	a	as in 'father' (if stressed), or 'fat' (if unstressed)
Б	б	B	b	as in 'back'
В	в	V	v	as in 'victim'
Г	г	G	g	as in 'good'
Д	д	D	d	as in 'deal'
Е	е	E	e	'ye' as in 'yen'
Ё	ё	Yo	yo	as in 'Yorkshire'
Ж	ж	Zh	zh	as in 'pleasure'
З	з	Z	z	as in 'zoo'
И	и	I	i (ee)	as in 'feet'
Й	й	Y	y	as the 'y' in 'toy'
К	к	K	k	as in 'kangaroo'
Л	л	L	l	as in 'laugh'
М	м	M	m	as in 'map'
Н	н	N	n	as in 'note'
О	о	O	o	as in 'sort'
П	п	P	p	as in 'pen'
Р	р	R	r	as in 'red'
С	с	S	s	as in 'set'
Т	т	T	t	as in 'test'
У	у	U	u	as in 'tool'
Ф	ф	F	f	as in 'father'
Х	х	Kh	kh	as in the Scottish 'loch'
Ц	ц	Ts	ts	as in 'sets'
Ч	ч	Ch	ch	as in 'chop'
Ш	ш	Sh	sh	as in 'shore'
Щ	щ	Shch	shch	as in 'fresh chives'
Ы	ы	Y	y	as in 'fill'
Ь	ь			soft sign, not pronounced on its own
Э	э	E	e	as in 'ever'

Cyrillic		Latin		Pronunciation
Ю	ю	Yu	yu	as in 'ab<u>u</u>se'
Я	я	Ya	ya	as in '<u>ya</u>m'

The following adopted Cyrillic characters are also used in Kyrgyz

Ө	ө	Ö	ö	'ur' as in 't<u>ur</u>f'
Ң	ң	Ng	ng	as in 'lo<u>ng</u>'
Ү	ү	Ü	ü	'ew' as in 'f<u>ew</u>'

The combination Dzh (ДЖ) is usually written as J in Kyrgyz.

BASIC KYRGYZ GRAMMAR
As with other Turkic languages, suffixes are added to fixed stems to indicate grammatical functions, and added to nouns to indicate gender and number. There are six cases: nominative, genitive, dative, accusative, locative and ablative. Sentence order tends to be subject, then object, then verb. As a Turkic language, there has to be vowel harmony within a word, so if a rounded vowel is contained by the stem, it must also be present in the suffix eg: *tüshündüm* – I understand; *tüshündüngüzbü?* – Do you understand?

RUSSIAN
Although most Kyrgyz delight in foreigners' attempts to use their native tongue, Russian is, in many ways, a more useful language, as it's spoken by almost everyone in Kyrgyzstan, including minorities like Uzbeks, and of course ethnic Russians. Russian is also the *lingua franca* throughout the central Asian region. Russian is a notoriously difficult language to learn, with Byzantine rules of grammar, but learning a little goes a long way, and even to just know the basics is invaluable. Bringing along a Russian dictionary and/or phrase book is highly recommended.

The vocabulary below is given in both Kyrgyz and Russian: the Russian words have been spelled phonetically and the stress underlined to help with pronunciation. In Kyrgyz, the stress usually falls on the last syllable.

WORDS AND PHRASES
Essentials

English	Kyrgyz	Russian
Good morning	*assalamu aleykum*★	d<u>o</u>bra-ye <u>oo</u>tra
Good evening	*assalamu aleykum*★	d<u>o</u>bri v<u>y</u>echyer
(★ literally: Peace be upon you; the response is *Wa aleykum assalam*)		
Good night	*tününgüz beypil bolsun*	spak<u>oy</u>ni n<u>o</u>chee
		(on going to bed)
		da sveed<u>a</u>nya
		(on leaving)
Hello	*salam*	zdr<u>a</u>svooytye
Goodbye	*kosh*	da sveed<u>a</u>nya
My name is...	*menim atiym...*	menya zav<u>oo</u>t...
What is your name?	*atëngëz kim?*	kak vas zav<u>oo</u>t?
I am from...	*men ... keldim*	ya eez...
...England/Britain	*...anglia...*	...<u>a</u>nglee-ya
...America	*...amerikadan...*	...am<u>y</u>ereeka
How are you?	*kanday siz?*	kak dyel<u>a</u>?
fine	*jakshë*	kharash<u>o</u>
not bad	*jaman emes*	nyepl<u>o</u>kha
please	*chakëruu*	pazh<u>a</u>lsta
thank you	*rakhmat*	sp<u>a</u>seeba
Excuse/Pardon me	*kechiresiz*	eezven<u>ee</u>tye/prast<u>ee</u>tye
OK	*makul*	kharash<u>o</u>

English	Kyrgyz	Russian
Yes	oba/oshandoy	da
No	jok	nyet
No problem	ech nerse emes	nyet prablyem
Sorry	kechiresiz	eezveneetye
I understand	men tüshündüm	ya paneema-yoo
I don't understand	men tüshünbödüm	ya nye paneema-yoo
Do you understand?	tüshündüngüzbü?	viy paneema-yetye?
Have a good trip!	ak jol bolsun	sh-chashleevava potee!

Questions

English	Kyrgyz	Russian
How?	kancha?	kak?
What?	kancha?	shto?
Where?	kayerde?	gdye?
Which?	kaysë?	kakoy?
When?	kachan?	kagda?
Who?	kim?	kto?
How much?	kancha turat?	skolka eta sto-eet?

Numbers

	Kyrgyz	Russian
1	bir	adeen
2	eki	dva
3	üch	tree
4	tört	chyetiyrye
5	besh	pyat
6	altë	shest
7	jeti	syem
8	segiz	vosyem
9	toghuz	dyevyat
10	on	dyesyat
11	on bir	adeenatsat
12	on eki	dvyenatsat
13	on üch	treenatsat
14	on tort	chyetiyrnatsat
15	on besh	pyatnatsat
16	on altë	shesnatsat
17	on jeti	syemnatsat
18	on segiz	vasyemnatsat
19	on toghuz	dyevyatnatsat
20	jëyërma	dvatsat
21	jëyërma bir	dvatsat adeen
30	otuz	treetsat
40	kërk	sorak
50	elüü	pyadyesyat
60	altëmësh	shesdyesyat
70	jetimish	syemdyesyat
80	seksen	vosyemdyesyat
90	tokson	dyevyanosta
100	bir jüz	sto
1,000	bir ming	tiysyacha

Time

English	Kyrgyz	Russian
What time is it?	*azër saat kancha boldu?*	*katori chas?*
it's...o'clock	*...saat*	*...chasa*
today	*bügün*	*syevodnya*
tonight	*kechinde*	*syevodnya vyechyeram*
tomorrow	*erteng*	*zaftra*
yesterday	*keche*	*fchyera*
morning	*erteng menen*	*ootra*
evening	*kech*	*vyechyer*

Days

Monday	*düshömbü*	*panyedyelneek*
Tuesday	*seyshembi*	*ftorneek*
Wednesday	*sharshembi*	*sryeda*
Thursday	*beishembi*	*chyetvyerk*
Friday	*juma*	*pyatneetsa*
Saturday	*ishembi*	*soobota*
Sunday	*jekshembe*	*vaskryesyenye*

Months

January	*yanwar*	*yanvar*
February	*fewral*	*fyevral*
March	*mart*	*mart*
April	*aprel*	*apryel*
May	*may*	*my*
June	*iyun*	*ee-yoon*
July	*iyul*	*ee-yool*
August	*awghust*	*avgoost*
September	*sentabër*	*syentyabr*
October	*öktöbür*	*aktyabr*
November	*noyabër*	*na-yabr*
December	*dekabër*	*dyekabr*

Getting around
Public Transport

I want to go to...	*men...barmakmën*	*ya khachoo pa-yekhat f...*
How much is it?	*kancha turat?*	*skolka eta sto-eet?*
Is it far?	*alësbë?*	*eta dalyeko?*
far	*ales*	*dalyeko*
ticket	*bilet*	*beelyet*
bus station	*vozkal/aptobus ayaldamasë*	*aftavakzal*
railway station	*poyuz istansiasë*	*vokzal*
airport	*ayeroport*	*a-eraport*
bus	*aptobus*	*aftoboos*
train	*poyuz*	*po-yest*
plane	*samolyot*	*samalyot*
taxi	*taksi*	*taksee*
bicycle	*welosiped*	*vyelaseepyet*
motorbike	*motorsikil*	*matatsiykl*
petrol	*benzin*	*byenzeen*
departure	*ayrëlüü*	*atpraviyenee-ye*

Directions

English	Kyrgyz	Russian
Which direction?	*kaysë baghëtta?*	*fkakom napravlyenee-ee?*
Go straight ahead	*tüz keterberingiz*	*eta pryama*
turn left	*solgo buruluu*	*pavyerneetye nalyeva*
turn right	*onggho buruluu*	*pavyerneetye naprava*
north	*tündük*	*syevyer*
south	*tüshtük*	*yook*
east	*chëghësh*	*vastok*
west	*batësh*	*zapat*
near	*jakën*	*ryadam*
far	*ales*	*dalyeko*

Signs (Russian)

Entrance	ВХОД
Exit	ВЫХОД
Open	ОТКРЫТ
Closed	ЗАКРЫТО
Toilets – men	МУЖСКОЙ
Toilets – women	ЖЕНСКИЙ
Information	СПРАВКИ
Prohibited	ЗАПРЕЩЕНО

Accommodation

English	Kyrgyz	Russian
hotel	*mëymankana*	*gasteeneetsa*
guesthouse	*konok üy*	*dom dlya pree-ye-zhikh*
apartment	*bölmö*	*kvarteera*
cheap	*arzan*	*dyeshovi*
clean	*pakiz*	*cheesti*
Do you have any rooms?	*bosh bölmö barbë?*	*oo vas yest namyera?*
I'd like…	*magha…kerek*	*ya khachoo…*
…a single room	*…jalghëz bölmö…*	*…adnyamyesni nomyer*
…a room with two beds	*…eki kishilik bölmö…*	*…dvukhmyesni nomyer*
How much is it per night?	*bir tünösö kancha bolot?*	*skolka eta stoeet fsootkee?*
I am staying for…	*men…tünöyüm*	*ya astanaveelsa*
…one night	*…bir kün*	*…na adnoo noch*
…a week	*…bir juma*	*…na nedyelyoo*
Where is the toilet?	*daaratkanasë kayerde?*	*gdye too-alyet?*
room	*bölmö*	*nomyer*
bed	*karawat*	*kravat*
toilet	*daaratkana*	*too-alyet*
bathroom	*moncho*	*va-naya*
shower	*dush*	*doosh*
I'd like to pay the bill	*men talongho pul tölöymün*	*mozhna zaplateet?*

Food

English	Kyrgyz	Russian
I am a vegetarian	*vegetaryan min*	*ya vyegeetaree-anyets (m)*
		vyegeetaree-anka (f)
I don't eat meat	*et jebeymin*	*ya nye yem myas-nova*
The bill please	*eseptesheli*	*sh-chot pazhalsta*
breakfast	*ertengmenki tamak*	*zaftrak*
lunch	*tüshkütamak*	*abyet*
dinner	*kechki tamak*	*oozhin*

Basics

English	Kyrgyz	Russian
bread	*nan*	*khlyep*
cream	*kajmak*	*sleefkee*
eggs	*jumurtka*	*yitso*
rice	*kürüch*	*rees*
meat	*et*	*myasa*
salt	*tüz*	*sol*

Drinks

English	Kyrgyz	Russian
beer	*pivo*	*peeva*
tea	*chay*	*chay*
coffee	*kofe*	*kofye*
vodka	*arak*	*votka*
yoghurt drink	*ayran*	*kefir/yogoort*
milk	*süt*	*malako*
water	*su*	*vada*

Shopping and communications

English	Kyrgyz	Russian
How much is this?	*bul kancha turat?*	*skolka sto-eet?*
I'm just looking	*men jönele karap jatam*	*ya prosta smat-ryoo*
That's expensive	*al këmbet*	*eta doraga*
Is that OK with you?	*makulbu?*	*viy nye vazrazha-yetye?*
OK	*makul*	*kharasho*
cash	*nak pul*	*naleechni-ye dyengee*
credit cards	*ötümdüü kartochka*	*kryedeetna-ya kartachka*
travellers' cheques	*sayakhat chegi*	*darozhni chyek*
receipt	*öjöt*	*kveetantsi-ya*
expensive	*këmbat*	*daragoy*
cheap	*arzan*	*dyeshovi*
bank	*bankasi*	*bank*
post office	*pochtokana*	*pochta*
stamps	*marka*	*marka*
telephone call	*el aralëk telefon*	*zvanok*

Emergency

English	Kyrgyz	Russian
Help!	*jardam beringiz!*	*pamageetye!*
Call a doctor!	*dokturdu chakërëngiz!*	*viyzaveetee vracha!*
There has been an accident	*al jerde kërsëk bolghon*	*pra-eezashol nyesh-chasni sloochee*
I am injured	*men jarat aldëm*	*menya ranyeni*
I have been robbed	*men tonodu*	*menya agrabeelee*
Go away!	*ket!*	*ookhadeetye!*
Thief!	*ooru!*	*vor!*
first aid	*tez kutkazun*	*pyerva-ya pomash-ch*
police	*milisanë*	*mileetsi-ya*
hospital	*dokturkana*	*balneetsa*
I am ill	*oorup kaldëm*	*Ya bolyen/balna (m/f)*

Health

English	Kyrgyz	Russian
diarrhoea	*ich ötkök*	*panos*
doctor	*doktur*	*vrach*
nurse	*medsestra*	*myedbrat/myetsyestra (m/f)*

275

English	Kyrgyz	Russian
pharmacy	darëkana	aptyeka
painkillers	ooru toktutuu darësë	bolye-ootalya-yoosh-chee-ye
antibiotic	antibiotic	anteebee-oteekee
antiseptic	antiseptic	anteesepteechyeska-ye sryetstva
condoms	prezervativ	pryezyervateef
contraceptive	töröttün aldën alaturghan	proteevazachatachna-ye sryetstva
I have...	men...	oo menya...
...a pain	...ooruu	...boll
...a stomach ache	...ich oorusu	...baleet zhivot
...a fever	...temperatura	...temperatoora
asthma	astma	astma
diabetes	diabet	dee-abyet
I'm allergic to...	menim...ge alergiyam bar	oo menya alergeeya na...
...antibiotics	...antibiotikter...	...anteebee-oteekee
...penicillin	...penitsilin	...pyeneetsileen

Other

black/white	kara/ak	chorni/byeli
this/that	bul/al	eta/tot
fine/wet	jakshë/nëm	kharoshi/mokri
last/next	ötkön/keler	paslyednee/slyedoosh-chee
boy/girl	bala/kyz	malcheek/dyevachka
big/small	chong/kichinekey	balshoy/malyenkee
good/bad	jakshë/jaman	kharoshi/plakhoy
hot/cold	ëssëk/suuk	garyachee/khalodni

KYRGYZ GESTURES

To show welcome	Pressing the right hand to the heart
To apologise	Touching right or both hands to chest
To beckon	Hand palm down with fingers curling and unfurling
To show shameful behaviour	Pinching or rubbing own cheek downwards
To stop a taxi	Arm out straight, palm downwards
To attract attention	Raise hand and say 'kechiresiz'

FCO TRAVEL ADVICE
know before you go
fco.gov.uk/travel

Bradt Travel Guides is a partner to the 'know before you go' campaign, masterminded by the UK Foreign and Commonwealth Office to promote the importance of finding out about a destination before you travel. By combining the up-to-date advice of the FCO with the in-depth knowledge of Bradt authors, you'll ensure that your trip will be as trouble-free as possible.

www.fco.gov.uk/travel

Appendix 2

GLOSSARY OF KYRGYZ TERMS

ak-sakal	literally 'white beard', a village elder
Ak-jol	literally 'white road', meaning *bon voyage* or have a good trip!
akyn	story-teller or bard
ala-kachuu	practice of bride-kidnapping
ala-kiyiz	unstitched felt carpet
archa	juniper
askhana	traditional cafe
at chabysh	traditional long distance horse races
ayran	yoghurt-like drink
aytish	performance competition between two *akyns*
bai	Kyrgyz clan leader
baibiche	respected female elder
batyr	khan or tribal leader
bakshi	shamans
berkutchi	eagle (or bird of prey) hunter
beshbarmak	'five fingers', a Kyrgyz dish traditionally eaten with the hands
boorsok	deep-fried pieces of dough
bosogo	yurt door frame
bozo	beer-like drink made from fermented millet
bozoy	literally 'grey house', a yurt
chabana	cowboy, herder
chaikhana	traditional tea-shop
chapan	traditional Kyrgyz padded coat
chiy	reed mat for rolling *shyrdaks*
chuchuk	horsemeat sausages
djigit	young horseback warrior
dostorkon	tablecloth spread on ground for food
eptchi shak	women's section of the yurt
er shak	men's section of the yurt
gumbez	mausoleum
jailoo	alpine meadow for summer grazing
jook	wooden chest for clothes and bedding in a yurt
kajmak	cream made on *jailoo*
kalama	flat bread
kalpak	white felt, triangular-shaped hat worn by Kyrgyz men
(or *ak-kalpak*)	
kalym	dowry or bride-price
kamcha	horse whip
kanat	yurt framework of poles

kerege	trellis wall support of yurt
kok boru	'grey wolf', another name for *ulak tartysh*
komuz	three-stringed guitar-like instrument
kookor	anchor-shaped leather *kumys* container
korut	dried cheese balls
kuirik	highly regarded tail fat of sheep
kumys	mildly alcoholic drink made from fermented mare's milk
kurak	patchwork
Kurman Ait	holiday and feast at the end of Ramadan
kyz-kumaj	'kiss the girl' horse game
manap	tribal leader
manaschi	*akyn* who recites from Manas cycle
mazar	tomb or shrine of holy man
nardi	game like backgammon
omin	ritual face-washing gesture at the end of a meal
oodarysh	horseback wrestling
ordo	game played with pieces of animal bone
Orozo Ait	holiday at the beginning of Ramadan
samagonka	homemade *arak* or vodka
shokulo	tall conical hat traditionally worn by Kyrgyz women
shyrdak	carpet made of felt pieces sown together in a pattern
temir komuz	mouth harp
tunduk	round, wooden central roof-piece of yurt
tush kiyiz	wall-hanging
tiyin enmei	game of picking up a coin from horseback
tyor	the best place in a yurt reserved for honoured guests
ulak tartysh	horseback polo played with a headless goat
upai	game like marbles, played with sheep's knee bones

Appendix 3

FURTHER INFORMATION

BOOKS Although relatively few books concentrate on Kyrgyzstan specifically, there are many that include the country as part of the central Asian region.

History and politics

Anderson, John *Kyrgyzstan: Central Asia's Island of Democracy (Post-communist States and Nations)* Routlege, 1999. A rather out-of-date study of the political development of a country in transition.

Grousset, Rene (author) and Walford, N (translator) *The Empire of the Steppes: History of Central Asia* Rutgers University Press, 1988. An authoritative account of the historical development of the region from the arrival of the Scythians to the last Mongolian emperor.

Hopkirk, Peter *The Great Game: On Secret Service in High Asia* John Murray, 2006. A fascinating account of the Great Game as played between the forces of Russia and Britain in the late 19th century. This is more of a page-turner than most historical accounts. Not relating specifically to Kyrgyzstan, but offers excellent background on the way the whole region developed in Imperial times.

Marat, Erica *The Tulip Revolution: Kyrgyzstan One Year After* The Jamestown Foundation, 2006. A quick-off-the-press account of the political machinations of 2005.

Naumkin, Vitaly *Radical Islam in Central Asia: Between Pen and Rifle* Rowman & Littlefield, 2005. A thorough study of various radical Islamic movements in the region.

Rashid, Ahmed *The Resurgence of Central Asia: Islam or Nationalism?* Zed Books, 1994. A look at the way Islam has resurged in the central Asian region in the wake of post-Soviet independence.

Roy, Olivier *The New Central Asia: Creation of Nations (Library of International Relations)* I B Tauris & Co Ltd, 2000. A good overall survey of the newly formed central Asian states and their geo-political position, although it is now rather out of date.

Soucek, Svat *A History of Inner Asia* Cambridge University Press, 2000. A full history of the entire central Asian region from the arrival of Islam until the Soviet period.

Whitfield, Susan *Life Along the Silk Road* John Murray, 2000. The history of the Silk Road as told by a series of stories from different characters who might have inhabited the region in the past.

Whitlock, Monica *Land Beyond the Oxus: The Central Asians* John Murray, 2003. A BBC journalist examines the changes taking place in central Asia in the late 1990s, mostly, but not exclusively, focusing on Tajikistan.

Wood, Frances *The Silk Road: Two Thousand Years in the Heart of Asia* University of California Press, 2004. The entire 5,000-year history of the Silk Road with plenty of photographs by explorers like Stein, Hedin and Mannerheim.

Culture

Antipina, Klavdiya (author) and Paiva, Rolando (photographer) *Kyrgyzstan* Skira, 2007. An expensive, but beautifully photographed, coffee-table book of traditional Kyrgyz costume by a Russian anthropologist and a French photographer.

Baldick, Julian *Animal and Shaman: Ancient Religions of Central Asia* I B Tauris, 2000. A survey of ancient customs and religions of central Asia from the Scythians onwards.

Clayton, Sally Pomme (author) and Herxheimer, Sophie (illustrator) *Tales Told in Tents: Stories from Central Asia* Frances Lincoln Children's Books, 2006. A nice collection of stories for children, from the central Asian region.

Harvey, Janet *Traditional Textiles of Central Asia* Thames & Hudson, 1997. A full survey of all types of textiles from the region, including felt and embroidery.

Kalter, Johannes *The Arts and Crafts of Turkestan* Thames & Hudson, 1984

Knobloch, Edgar *Monuments of Central Asia: A Guide to the Archaeology, Art and Architecture of Turkestan* I B Tauris & Co Ltd, 2001. An admirably thorough survey of central Asia's historic sites and monuments, including those of Kyrgyzstan.

Sahadeo, Jeff and Zanca, Russell (editors) *Everyday Life in Central Asia: Past and Present* Indiana University Press, 2007

Natural history

Sparks, John *Realms of the Russian Bear: A Natural History of Russia and the Central Asian Republics* Little Brown & Co, 1992. Now out of print but still worth getting hold of if you can, this is a beautifully illustrated volume on the flora and fauna of the former USSR, with a large section on the Tien Shan and Central Asia.

Van Der Ven, Joost *Looking at Birds in Kyrgyz Republic, Central Asia* Bishkek, 2002. This is a hard-to-find guide to Kyrgyzstan's birdlife in Russian and English.

Travel

Akchurin, Marat *Red Odysssey: A Journey Through the Soviet Republics* Harper Collins, 1992. A Russian's view of the republics of the central Asian region in the period just before independence. Out of print.

Bealby, Jonny *Silk Dreams, Troubled Road* Arrow Books, 2003. This is the first of several travel books to chronicle a long-distance journey by horse through the region in post-independence times.

Child, Greg *Over The Edge: The True Story of Four American Climbers' Kidnap and Escape in the Mountains of Central Asia* Villard Books, 2002. A rather dry, journalistic account of the kidnapping of young American mountaineers in the mountains of Batken Province in 2000. Controversial at the time, with implications that the much-publicised account did not contain the whole truth, the naïve and none-too-bright climbers do not evoke that much sympathy in the light of this book.

Farr, Saffia *Revolution Baby: Motherhood and Anarchy in Kyrgyzstan* Spire Publishing, 2007. This is a humorous account of ex-pat life in Kyrgyzstan leading up to and during the revolution of March 2005.

Levine, Emma *A Game of Polo with a Headless Goat* Andre Deutsch, 2003. The title says it all. This has good coverage of the *ulak tartysh* horse game in Kyrgyzstan.

Maillart, Ella *Turkestan Solo: A Journey Through Central Asia* Tauris Parke Paperbacks, 2005. A captivating account of a feisty Swiss woman's solo journey through central Asia in 1932, which included a traverse of Kyrgyzstan's Tien Shan range.

Nazaroff, Paul *Hunted Through Central Asia: On the Run from Lenin's Secret Police* Oxford, 2002. More derring-do in central Asia, as the title suggests. Rather stereotyped characters and also plenty of descriptions of the flora, fauna and geology of the region.

Paine, Sheila *The Golden Horde: From the Himalaya to the Mediterranean* Tauris Parke Paerbacks, 2006. The author visits Kyrgyzstan as part of her fascinating odyssey in search of an amulet.

Thubron, Colin *The Lost Heart of Asia* Vintage, 2004. A lyrical account of Thubron's first journey to central Asia in the early 1990s, which included some time in Kyrgyzstan. This is beautifully written prose: rich, deep and thought-provoking.

Thubron, Colin *Shadow of the Silk Road* Harper Collins, 2007. A second journey into central Asia made more than a decade later. Wonderful, expressive writing that does not patronise the reader but quietly impresses with its erudition and Old World sensitivity.

Watson, Claire Burgess *Silk Route Adventure: On Horseback in the Heart of Asia* Robert Hale, 2007. A redoubtable female banker goes on an 18-month, 6,000km horseback trek through central Asia and Mongolia.

Tolstoy, Alexandra *The Last Secrets of the Silk Road: Four Girls Follow Marco Polo Across 5,000 Miles* Profile Books, 2004. Four ex-public schoolgirls go horseriding across central Asia and squabble a lot. No sign of Marco Polo.

Whitell, Giles *Extreme Continental: Blowing Hot and Cold Through Central Asia* Orion, 1996. A highly entertaining description of a journey through the new states of central Asia in the early 1990s, just after independence from the Soviet Union.

Mountaineering and trekking

Maier, Frith *Trekking in Russia and Central Asia* Mountaineers Books, 1997. Long out of print and completely out of date in terms of political geography, this guide is still very useful to browse for a general overview of what the region has to offer for adventurous trekkers.

Literature

Aitmatov, Chingiz *Jamilia* Telegram Books, 2007. A new English edition of one of Aitmatov's best-known works.

Aitmatov, Chingiz *The Day Lasts More Than a Hundred Years* Indiana University Press, 1988. Out of print but easily available secondhand.

Aitmatov, Chingiz *The Place of the Skull* Grove Press, 1989. Out of print but available secondhand.

Rosenberg, Robert *This Is Not Civilization* Mariner Books, 2005. An American- abroad novel based upon the experiences of a young Peace Corps volunteer's stay in Kyrgyzstan.

Language

Krippes, Karl *Kyrgyz-English/English-Kyrgyz Concise Dictionary* Hippocrene Books, 2003. The only complete Kyrgyz-English dictionary available and currently out of print.

Rudelson, Justin Jon *Central Asia: Languages of the Silk Road* Lonely Planet Publications, 1998. This has brief sections on the Kyrgyz, Uzbek and Tajik languages (but not Russian).

WEBSITES Some of the tour operators listed in *Chapter 2: Practical Information* and *Chapter 3: Bishkek* also have useful websites.

www.cbtkyrgyzstan.kg	Community Based Tourism in Kyrgyzstan
http://eng.gateway.kg	Kyrgyzstan Development Gateway
www.eurasianet.org	Regional news website
www.helvetas.kg	General information on the country
www.iwpr.net	Institute for War and Peace Reporting
www.kirgistan-reisen.de	Information on Kyrgyzstan in German and English
www.kyrgyzembassy.org	Kyrgyz embassy in the USA
www.kyrgyz-embassy.org.uk	Kyrgyz embassy in the UK
www.kyrgyzstan.org	Information about Kyrgyzstan
www.silkpress.com	Website of a magazine about the central Asian region
www.timesca-europe.com	*Times of Central Asia* website

Index

Page numbers in bold indicate major entries; those in italic indicate maps.

China 3–5, 7–9, 11, 14, 18–22, 25, 46–7, 58,
   86, 124, 127–8, 134–5, 139, 153,
   167–8, 173, 175–6, 179, 182, 199, 207,
   210, 214–16, 219–22, 249, 262, 264–5
Chinese 6–8, 12, 20, 24, 33, 36, 71, 86, 121,
   123, 125, 135–6, 159, 166–7, 176, 191,
   210, 215, 221, 258–60
Chinese border 4, 8, 43, 55, 133–4, 176,
   215–16, 219–22, 249, 262–5
Chinese Turkestan 6, 8, 168 see also
   Xinjiang
Chok-Tal airport 142
Cholpon-Ata 5, 45–6, 70, 88, 134–6, 141,
   144–9, *145*, 150, 156
Chon Ak-Suu valley 149–50, 154, 156
Chong Kyzyl-Suu River 175
Chong Kyzyl-Suu valley 179
Chong-Kemin National Park 44
Chong-Kemin River 44, 127
Chong-Kemin valley 126–7, 141, 149, 154–5
Chong-Tash 178
Chong-Tash massacre 11, 37, 87, **118**
Chon-Tuz salt caves 204
Christianity 6, **24–5**, 123, 136, 218
Chui Province 40, **115–32**, *116*, 199, 205,
   241
Chui River 4, 119, 123, 127, 136, 169
Chui valley 4, 6, 8, 20–2, 24–5, 46, 72, 83,
   87, 112, 115, 120, **121–6**, 127, 129,
   150, 192, 203–4
churches 121, 124, 150, 152, 166, 191, 194,
   257
Chychkan River 241
Chychkan State Zoological Reserve 198,
   241
Chychkan valley 197–8
Chyngyshev, Tursunbek 16
Chyrchyk Pass 262
cinema 29, **37–8**, 189
CIS (Commonwealth of Independent
   States) 13, 18, 52–3, 56, 78
climate 4–5, 45, 60, 86, 134, 207, 210, 227,
   229–30, 262–3
climate change 5, 134
climbing 115, 119, 176, 262–3, 266, 269,
   281
climbing permits 179
collective farms 121, 129, 217
community based tourism see also *individual
   towns and cities* 51–2
conservation 42–4, 140

cooking stoves 64, 74
Cossacks 8, 20, 86, 111, 150, 159
crafts **31–3**, 46, 51, 181, 186–7, 189, 194,
   202, 257
cuisine see food and drink
cultural etiquette 78–9
culture **26–40**, 78–9, 257, 280
currency 65–6, 266
cycling **68**, 125, 132, 182, 215, 220
Cyrillic alphabet 10, 21–3, 270–1

dachas 119, 130, 150, 246
dairy produce 34–5, 70
Daroot-Korgon 57, 263
deer 115, 137, 207, 214
deforestation 42
disabled travellers 63–4
djigits 39–40, 146
Djumagulov, Apas 13, 16
Dmitrievka 230, 233
documentation see red tape, visas *and*
   permits
Dolon Pass 204
dress 20, 30–1, 79, 112
drinking water 59
Dungan food 34, 72
Dungan revolt 8
Dungans 8, **21**, 22, 26, 71, 86–7, 121, 150,
   159, 166–7, 172, 201

eagle hunting 51, 74, 172, 186, **188**
eagles 188, 195, 248
earthquakes 12, 42, 129, 135, 199
economic reform 17
economy 17–18
edelweiss 41, 173
education 25–6
Eki-Naryn 214–15
Eki-Naryn swastika 214
elderly 79–80, 139
electricity 65
embassies 52, 107–8, 221
emergency telephone numbers 63
enclaves and exclaves 9, 13, 22, 151, 266,
   267, 268
endangered species 42–3
entertainment 74
entry and exit stamps 53–4, 155
environmental problems 12, 42, 128, 134,
   137, 140, 183, 206, 240
Erchilik-Too range 197

Bradt Travel Guides

www.bradtguides.com

Africa

Africa Overland	£15.99
Algeria	£15.99
Benin	£14.99
Botswana: Okavango, Chobe, Northern Kalahari	£15.99
Burkina Faso	£14.99
Cape Verde Islands	£13.99
Canary Islands	£13.95
Cameroon	£13.95
Congo	£14.99
Eritrea	£15.99
Ethiopia	£15.99
Gabon, São Tomé, Príncipe	£13.95
Gambia, The	£13.99
Ghana	£15.99
Johannesburg	£6.99
Kenya	£14.95
Madagascar	£15.99
Malawi	£13.99
Mali	£13.95
Mauritius, Rodrigues & Réunion	£13.99
Mozambique	£13.99
Namibia	£15.99
Niger	£14.99
Nigeria	£15.99
Rwanda	£14.99
Seychelles	£14.99
Sudan	£13.95
Tanzania, Northern	£13.99
Tanzania	£16.99
Uganda	£15.99
Zambia	£15.95
Zanzibar	£12.99

Britain and Europe

Albania	£13.99
Armenia, Nagorno Karabagh	£14.99
Azores	£12.99
Baltic Capitals: Tallinn, Riga, Vilnius, Kaliningrad	£12.99
Belarus	£14.99
Belgrade	£6.99
Bosnia & Herzegovina	£13.99
Bratislava	£6.99
Budapest	£8.99
Bulgaria	£13.99
Cork	£6.99
Croatia	£13.99
Cyprus see North Cyprus	

Czech Republic	£13.99
Dresden	£7.99
Dubrovnik	£6.99
Estonia	£13.99
Faroe Islands	£13.95
Georgia	£14.99
Helsinki	£7.99
Hungary	£14.99
Iceland	£14.99
Kiev	£7.95
Kosovo	£14.99
Krakow	£7.99
Lapland	£13.99
Latvia	£13.99
Lille	£6.99
Lithuania	£13.99
Ljubljana	£7.99
Macedonia	£14.99
Montenegro	£13.99
North Cyprus	£12.99
Paris, Lille & Brussels	£11.95
Riga	£6.95
River Thames, In the Footsteps of the Famous	£10.95
Serbia	£14.99
Slovakia	£14.99
Slovenia	£12.99
Spitsbergen	£14.99
Switzerland: Rail, Road, Lake	£13.99
Tallinn	£6.99
Ukraine	£14.99
Vilnius	£6.99
Zagreb	£6.99

Middle East, Asia and Australasia

China: Yunnan Province	£13.99
Great Wall of China	£13.99
Iran	£14.99
Iraq	£14.95
Iraq: Then & Now	£15.99
Kyrgyzstan	£15.99
Maldives	£13.99
Mongolia	£14.95
North Korea	£13.95
Oman	£13.99
Sri Lanka	£13.99
Syria	£14.99
Tibet	£13.99
Turkmenistan	£14.99
Yemen	£14.99

The Americas and the Caribbean

Amazon, The	£14.99
Argentina	£15.99
Bolivia	£14.99
Cayman Islands	£12.95
Colombia	£15.99
Costa Rica	£13.99
Chile	£16.95
Dominica	£14.99
Falkland Islands	£13.95
Guyana	£14.99
Panama	£13.95
Peru & Bolivia: Backpacking and Trekking	£12.95
St Helena	£14.99
USA by Rail	£13.99

Wildlife

100 Animals to See Before They Die	£16.99
Antarctica: Guide to the Wildlife	£14.95
Arctic: Guide to the Wildlife	£15.99
Central & Eastern European Wildlife	£15.99
Chinese Wildlife	£16.99
East African Wildlife	£19.99
Galápagos Wildlife	£15.99
Madagascar Wildlife	£14.95
Peruvian Wildlife	£15.99
Southern African Wildlife	£18.95
Sri Lankan Wildlife	£15.99

Eccentric Guides

Eccentric America	£13.95
Eccentric Australia	£12.99
Eccentric Britain	£13.99
Eccentric California	£13.99
Eccentric Cambridge	£6.99
Eccentric Edinburgh	£5.95
Eccentric France	£12.95
Eccentric London	£13.99
Eccentric Oxford	£5.95

Others

Your Child Abroad: A Travel Health Guide	£10.95
Something Different for the Weekend	£12.99

WIN £100 CASH!

READER QUESTIONNAIRE

Send in your completed questionnaire for the chance to win £100 cash in our regular draw

All respondents may order a Bradt guide at half the UK retail price – please complete the order form overleaf.

(Entries may be posted or faxed to us, or scanned and emailed.)

We are interested in getting feedback from our readers to help us plan future Bradt guides. Please answer ALL the questions below and return the form to us in order to qualify for an entry in our regular draw.

Have you used any other Bradt guides? If so, which titles? . . . .
. . . .
What other publishers' travel guides do you use regularly? . . . .
. . . .
Where did you buy this guidebook? . . . .
What was the main purpose of your trip to Kyrgyzstan (or for what other reason did you read our guide)? eg: holiday/business/charity etc. . . . .
. . . .
What other destinations would you like to see covered by a Bradt guide?
. . . .
Would you like to receive our catalogue/newsletters?
YES / NO (If yes, please complete details on reverse)
If yes – by post or email? . . . .
Age (circle relevant category) 16–25   26–45   46–60   60+
Male/Female (delete as appropriate)
Home country . . . .
Please send us any comments about our guide to Kyrgyzstan or other Bradt Travel Guides. . . . .
. . . .
. . . .
. . . .

Bradt Travel Guides

23 High Street, Chalfont St Peter, Bucks SL9 9QE, UK
☏ +44 (0)1753 893444 f +44 (0)1753 892333
e info@bradtguides.com
www.bradtguides.com

CLAIM YOUR HALF-PRICE BRADT GUIDE!

Order Form

To order your half-price copy of a Bradt guide, and to enter our prize draw to win £100 (see overleaf), please fill in the order form below, complete the questionnaire overleaf, and send it to Bradt Travel Guides by post, fax or email.

Please send me one copy of the following guide at half the UK retail price

Title	Retail price	Half price
... .	....	....

Please send the following additional guides at full UK retail price

No	Title	Retail price	Total
...	....	....	....
...	....	....	....
...	....	....	....

Sub total ....
Post & packing ....
(£1 per book UK; £2 per book Europe; £3 per book rest of world)
Total ....

Name ....

Address..

Tel .... Email ....

☐ I enclose a cheque for £........ made payable to Bradt Travel Guides Ltd

☐ I would like to pay by credit card. Number: ....

Expiry date: ... / ...   3-digit security code (on reverse of card) .....

Issue no (debit cards only) .....

☐ Please add my name to your catalogue mailing list.

☐ I would be happy for you to use my name and comments in Bradt marketing material.

Send your order on this form, with the completed questionnaire, to:

Bradt Travel Guides KYR1
23 High Street, Chalfont St Peter, Bucks SL9 9QE
☎ +44 (0)1753 893444   f +44 (0)1753 892333
e info@bradtguides.com   www.bradtguides.com